WEALTH & POVERTY

WEALTH & POVERTY

AN ECONOMIC HISTORY OF THE TWENTIETH CENTURY

EDITED BY
SIDNEY POLLARD

ANDROMEDA

Volume editor Sue Martin
Art editor Dave Sumner
Designers Frankie Macmillan,
Tony de Saulles, Gill Mouqué
Cartographic manager Olive
Pearson
Cartographic editor Zoë Goodwin
Picture research manager Alison
Renney
Picture research Diana Phillips,
Angela Murphy
Project editor Peter Furtado
Project art editor Ayala Kingsley

 AN EQUINOX BOOK

Planned and produced by
Andromeda Oxford Ltd

Copyright © Andromeda Oxford
Ltd 1991

Published by
Andromeda Oxford Ltd
11–15 The Vineyard
Abingdon
Oxfordshire OX14 3PX

ISBN 1 871869 04 8

Printed in Singapore by CS
Graphics

ADVISORY EDITORS

Professor Carlo Cipolla
University of California, Berkeley

Professor David Landes
Harvard University

CONTRIBUTORS

Dr Gerold Ambrosius
University of Bremen

Dr P L Cottrell
University of Leicester

Professor James Foreman Peck
University of Hull

Lucy Newton
University of Leicester

CONTENTS

PREFACE

Wealth and poverty consist of more than the kind of things that can be measured by economists. People may have little money yet be rich in experience or in the number of their children; or poor in health or happiness despite vast material possessions. The present book, however, limits itself to the more restricted concept only, to the prosperity that can be described in terms of money and resources.

Economists have always been concerned with wealth, its increase and its distribution. Indeed, the first major book on economics was entitled *The Wealth of Nations*, written by the British economist Adam Smith in 1776. They are well aware that poverty exists too, though no one who looks at the history of the 20th century can fail to be impressed by the enormous increase in overall wealth and personal income achieved by humanity, in spite of the simultaneous and unprecedented rise in population.

There can be no doubt that average income per head in the advanced or industrialized countries has increased many times over since 1900, to an extent utterly unimaginable at the beginning of the century. The main cause for all this has been the advances in science and technology, which have reduced manufacturing costs, made new products available and saved both time and labor. As far as the fulfilment of the needs of the majority of the population of the industrial countries is concerned, the 20th century has been a glittering story of success. The distribution of the new riches thus created, however, has been anything but satisfactory. Even in the wealthiest countries, poverty and want have not been eliminated, or only eliminated in recent decades; but for most of the world poverty and cramped, unhealthy or dangerous conditions remain the rule. Despite the worldwide reach of Western financial institutions, business and media, the achievements of technology remain far beyond the grasp of the majority, or (as in the case of radio and television) access to them actually serves to underline to the poor how much they are lacking.

Moreover, population is growing increasingly fast and even in those wealthier countries where population is constant, the disposal of growing incomes is adding heavily to the burden of demands made on the environment. Together these facts have begun to overload the natural resources of the Earth. Pollution of the soil, the air and the water, overcrowded cities and the destruction of crucial elements in the environment such as large parts of the tropical rain forests and of the ozone layer are the direct though unintended consequence of the economic activities of businesses and governments in the 20th century.

The new problems of poverty, as well as of wealth, are as great if not greater than those confronting earlier times. But at the same time, our means of overcoming these problems have grown beyond compare since the beginning of the 20th century. The test facing the world as it approaches the year 2000 will be the responsible division of available resources among the nations of the world; whether this division is achieved will depend on the extent to which short-term economic pressures on government and companies can be resisted to allow them to protect the planet in the long term.

Sidney Pollard   Bielefeld

INTRODUCTION

This volume is intended to cover the economic history of the 20th century. Its theme cannot be fully understood without reference to events which lie strictly outside the purely economic field, such as wars or revolutions; but economic history nevertheless has a logic of its own, by which the events and development of each period can be related to the preceding period, so that we can perceive some pattern in the unfolding of the world economy.

Economic factors play a significant part in all other major historical developments and events, above all in political history. They generally lurk behind ideology or political philosophy, and even the highest ideals of patriotism or the quest for liberty are not entirely immune from them. Thus the events leading to World War I are now associated by all historians – to some degree at least – with competing economic interest groups of investors, exporters, armaments manufacturers and banks among others. Similarly the political reforms beginning in Eastern Europe in the mid-1980s had at their base the failure of the economic system to come up to expectations: above all the shortages and poor quality of simple, everyday goods can, it appears, be altered only when central control, and party control, are replaced by other forms of management. It is that economic failure which makes political reform a necessity.

Again, the power play of international diplomacy and the military threats with which it is often combined depend to a considerable extent on the economic power with which they are backed. Thus the Czar of Russia could put enormous armies in the the field in World War I, but their poor supply, for which the backwardness of the Russian economy was responsible, made them a far less efficient fighting force than the opposing German armies. Ultimately the whole Eastern Front collapsed in revolution in 1917 because the economy at home had broken down. Similarly, modern world organizations like the United Nations are dominated, numerically, by the poorer countries of the "Third World", and these can force through any decision they wish by majority vote. But these votes, backed by governments representing the majority of humanity, have little effect unless they are supported also by the industrialized nations which have the economic means to finance them or turn them into reality.

Two definitions of economics
Most readers will have a fairly clear idea as to what is meant by "economic" – what aspects of history, in other words, will be covered in this volume. Yet a precise definition is by no means easy. For many, the economic aspects of life are those which are, or can be, acquired in a market and which therefore have an actual or implied exchange value that can be expressed in money. On this basis, earning a living, investing or in other ways acquiring an income, and spending it, by individuals, families or institutions, constitute economic activity. Financial and exchange activities come under the same heading. Property relations, inheritance, taxation, and the interests and programs of groups or classes concerned with these, form another part of the subject.

An alternative definition considers that economic problems are those which occur when the resources available are inadequate to meet human needs, so that the question arises of how to allocate them. Air to breathe, though vital for life, is not under normal circumstances an economic issue because we have enough of it; but the ownership and use of land is, as soon as population reaches a certain density. More significantly, goods and services which require human labor for their creation are usually scarce in relation to demand, and questions of how to produce and allocate them are, according to this view, at the heart of economics.

An example may make this clear. If we speak of the "economics of education", it is generally understood that we are not concerned immediately with the qualities of the teaching or with its truth, with cultural values or with the psychology of teacher or pupil. What we are likely to be concerned with are the costs of teachers' salaries, school buildings or books; or the benefits of the schooling to the individuals concerned or to society as a whole, measured by their later earning capacity. If the money had not been spent on education, it might have been spent, by the state or by the taxpayers, on other things, and that is why the costs are significant; and if the pupils in later life produce more and earn more because of their schooling, it will give them or society more of the things which would otherwise be in short supply.

Both definitions, that of exchange (money) value, and of the allocation of scarce resources, capture something of the economic problem and both are implicit in the present book.

Economics is a highly technical subject and its practitioners, like other scientists, use technical terms of their own, which are not easily understood by outsiders. This book tries to avoid difficult language, but cannot altogether dispense with some complexities. Four issues, in particular, will recur, and some guidance to their understanding may be helpful at this stage. One concerns money, the second the national income, the third the distinction between market economies and centrally planned economies, and the fourth the controversy between "Keynesians" and monetarists.

The functions of money
Money, before the development of the complex modern financial world, had to serve three main functions. It provided a measure of value, so that the value of different goods could be compared with each other; it facilitated the exchange of goods, taking the place of barter; and it provided a store of value, for saving for later use. Early forms of money frequently consisted of coins or precious metals (notably gold and silver) which had an exchange value of their own as metal if melted down. By 1900, this rather clumsy way of using metal coins had given way to substitute paper, especially for large transactions, in the form of such things as bank notes, bills of exchange and checks, the last two transferring bank deposits which were themselves a quite sophisticated form of holding money. Nevertheless, there was a fixed relation of most of these forms of paper money to a certain quantity of gold, so that paper money did not vary greatly from the value of the gold it was meant to represent; and since most of the world was on a "gold standard" money of one country could easily be converted to money of another.

▶ New York's financial district c.1917.

Two changes have occurred in the 20th century. First, the world came off the gold standard, temporarily (mostly) in 1914 and permanently (with some exceptions) in the 1930s, so that the value of "money" could, and sometimes did, fluctuate widely. This made it less useful as a measure, as a medium of exchange and as a store of value. The fixed international exchange mechanism was also destroyed in the process, with serious consequences. If the currencies of countries are no longer directly related to a quantity of gold, then there is no longer any obvious way of knowing how much one is worth in terms of another – say, how many American dollars will exchange for a British pound. In principle, there will be two influences determining their exchange rate. One is what has become known as the "purchasing power parity", in other words, what each currency will buy in the market at home. The argument is that if a certain quantity of wheat, for example, can be bought for a pound in Britain, and the same quantity costs four dollars in the United States, the exchange rate will be around four dollars to the pound. If the wheat prices do not correspond to four to one – if, say, it takes only two dollars to buy the wheat costing a pound in Britain, and the exchange rate is four to one – it will obviously pay someone to buy wheat in the United States and ship it to Britain, thus turning two dollars into four (leaving transport costs out of the equation). This would happen to every commodity that was out of line, so that the trading deficit of the country with the overvalued money would drive down the value of its currency until it corresponded with its purchasing power parity. However, this mechanism does not work fully, quite apart from a certain inaccuracy because of transport costs. The reason is that not all commodities and services enter international trade; and if they do not, then, no matter how different their prices, they cannot be transferred to even out the exchanges. Thus houses may differ widely in value without being exported and imported, and the same applies to the services of teachers, civil servants, or taxi drivers. Here is one reason why, in spite of purchasing power parity, some countries, particularly poor countries, appear to be "cheaper" to the tourist than others.

At the same time, there is another influence affecting exchange rates, arising in the financial sphere itself. For when merchants, tourists and others need to make payments in another country, they normally do not acquire the foreign money directly, but get it from a financial institution, such as a bank. These institutions thus handle large amounts of money of different countries, and many of them specialize in this business, creating a financial "market". There, quite apart from the real trading surpluses and deficits, exchange rates will also be affected by other factors such as the expectations of future changes, changes in interest rates, deliberate actions of governments and central banks, and speculative moves taking all these into consideration. In the long run, exchange rates cannot move too far from purchasing power over commodities, or else the commodities would move; but this takes time, and while the tendency may go in that direction, a stream of financial decisions may keep the rate well above or below this.

The second major change that has occurred in the 20th century to upset the old and simple notions of money, is that other documents which could be sold or exchanged easily, such as certificates of government debt, could in certain circumstances also be considered as "money." Central banks and governments learned to manipulate these, as well as the quantity of "money" in circulation, its exchange rate against foreign money, and even its internal value, by price controls and blocked accounts. There thus emerged what came to be called "monetary policy" as an additional method by which a society

could control its economic environment. But in the process much of the former meaning and function of money was lost.

Calculating economic progress

In theory it should be possible to measure economic progress by adding together all the goods and services available to the population, and then seeing how that total compares with the total available in other years. In order to do this, the prices of all goods and services have to be converted into constant terms, eliminating price changes. Given a correct exchange rate, we can even compare one country with another. If the total is divided by the number of inhabitants, "national income" per head offers further interesting comparisons.

All this, however, involves complex and costly counting and census-taking, constructing price indices and meeting the so-

called index number problem, which arises because the weight of individual items in the total changes over time as well as differing between countries, and is a problem which cannot be solved satisfactorily by mathematical means. There are also problems of definition as to what constitutes "goods" and "services". The first attempts to construct such national income figures were made in the 1930s (though recent calculations have attempted to find values for much earlier periods); they became common after World War II, and by the 1960s international criteria began to be agreed, so that international comparisons have become increasingly meaningful. Only the planned economies of the Eastern bloc keep to a different system, a main difference being that they concern themselves with commodity production only, neglecting services. In consequence, their statistics include only the gross or net material product

(NMP) which omits such things as distribution, educational or health servies, administration and the like.

Within the inevitable constraints of uncertainty and inaccuracy, it has proved possible to calculate national output, as well as the total of incomes which, with certain marginal adjustments, should come to the same thing. So should the total of expenditures, though these are less commonly calculated directly. Gross national product (GNP) includes additional investment made in the year; net national product (NNP or NMP) does not. Excluding foreign transactions, we have gross or net domestic product (GDP, NDP). These quantities offer a useful shorthand for many purposes and are used widely in this volume, but they have limitations, partly because of the

▲ Immigrants to the New World in the early years of the century.

inaccuracies in the basic estimates, and in part because of the problem of comparing different bundles of goods and services over time and across frontiers.

Market economies and centrally planned economies

Among the major issues of economic policy in this century has been the opposition, in theory as well as in practical politics, between the economic order of the market economy and the economic order of the centrally planned economy, usually summarized as "capitalism" versus "socialism". Many countries have adopted a socialist economic order, namely Soviet Russia, China and the countries of Eastern Europe among others.

The modern industrialized world is a product of capitalism, or the market economy. It did not emerge as a result of deliberate decision or planning by any authority, nor of the actions of people determined to create a new economic order; on the contrary, it developed as a consequence of uncounted millions of individual decisions, each made for individual, usually short-term ends. That such numerous, wholly uncoordinated decisions should result in a highly efficient, progressive order which put all previously existing social systems in the shade, has been a puzzle to many. To its defenders, the dispersed decision making process has been a major source of the strength of capitalism, since decisions are taken by people who know what they are about, who can react quickly and who normally bear the consequences of their actions.

Yet, at no time has any country allowed the market alone to determine everything. Even the most liberal system always maintained numerous controls over economic activity, beside ensuring through a system of law and contract enforcement that the framework existed for the system to work at all. Thus public administration and military defense, taxation, subsidies or protective tariffs, laws to protect children and consumers, the definition of liability for damages and the maintenance of a legally acceptable currency are just a few of the many economic functions that have almost never been left to the "market" since the earliest days of capitalism. Other functions have been undertaken in some cases by political authorities, but in others were left to private enterprise, among them education, and the building and maintenance of roads, canals and railways.

There have always been, and are still, many differences in detail among the market economies, including those derived from differing traditions, geographical conditions, resources, political necessities and many other factors. It is thus difficult to define what true distinctive features all market economies have in common to distinguish them from the socialist ones.

Beside the disparate decision-making, and the absence of detailed central planning, the feature which has most often been taken as the key distinguishing mark of the capitalist economy is the private ownership of the means of production. These may constitute a set of ladders and brushes owned by an independent house painter, or the multibillion dollars worth of the capital equipment of the international combines in the motor manufacture or oil-refining trades. What they all have in common is that they are used to generate an income, the largest possible income (on certain conditions), to their owners. Under capitalism it is these owners or their agents who make the decisions, and their employees, the propertyless workers, take their orders from them. The system thus works indirectly: the bakery companies, for example, do not produce bread because they have an ultimate interest in bread baking: they do it because there is a profit in it.

◀ **Work on the Grand Coulee Dam, Washington, USA, 1937.**

While this system had, by the early 20th century, proved its efficiency by providing a level of economic welfare unimaginable in previous ages, it had also attracted a great deal of criticism. Among the major critiques were that it was based on greed and selfishness; that it led to an unjust distribution of incomes and economic power; that it was highly unstable, being unable to prevent fear and panic in the market and exaggerating slight disturbances into major slumps and collapses; that it encouraged the wrong decisions by ignorance of the decisions of others or, if firms got together for common planning, that it allowed them to use their monopoly power to exploit the public; and finally, that working for profit rather than for service induced suppliers to provide the cheapest, poorest quality goods and services for the highest prices they could get away with.

All of these objections, except for the first, have long been recognised also by "capitalist" countries, and the history of the social legislation of the 20th century could almost be written round the theme of how these doubts were met: examples are health and quality laws protecting consumers, fiscal and financial policies to counteract business cycles, and detailed controls over financial markets. However, there was also a widespread view that minor tinkering could never make the system acceptable, that it was objectionable in principle, and an alternative system had to be found. That system was socialism. In essence as a set of ideas it stood complete by the beginning of the 20th century. It was put into practice first by the Soviet state which arose as a result of the 1917 revolution.

Among the main principles of Lenin and his followers was the common ownership of the means of production: no one would then have an interest to exploit customers or workers. Second, central planning would ensure that social and individual needs were met in some determinable order of priority, without panics, depressions or other market disturbances. Decisions would be made, not by the capitalists, whose economic power had also allowed them to monopolize political power under capitalism, but by the new ruling class, the workers, or at least by their representatives, the leading members of the Communist party.

Soviet planning began in earnest with the first five-year plan in 1928. Having the power to set priorities, the planners put the greatest weight on creating heavy and capital goods industries, and these did emerge with astonishing rapidity in the 1930s. Consumer goods and agriculture were neglected, and the real income of the population did not reflect the enhanced capacities of steelworks and power stations. Planning covered not only production but also prices, allocation, wages, technical training, labor recruitment, the creation of new towns and many other features which in the West were left either to market forces, or to a variety of uncoordinated public agencies. Foreign trade was also part of the planned order, but it was kept small, as Stalin favored autarky (complete self-sufficiency) for Soviet Russia, not least for military and strategic reasons.

The system was taken over almost in its entirety by the Eastern European planned economies after World War II, while China, which was at first also inclined to follow the Soviet model, later added special features of her own. The years since 1928 have therefore seen the competitive coexistence of the two systems.

Their respective merits are subject of intense debate all over the globe. One key argument for capitalism is that it has led to a much higher level of income and of technical competence than the rival system. In virtually every field, with the possible exception of space exploration, the West is far in advance of the East, and its standards of living are in consequence much higher. Second, the market economy has to react to consumers' wishes, and meets them much more successfully, with service, choice, attractive shops and packaging, all of which are deficient under socialism. The drive is competitive and therefore cannot be ignored. Lastly, it is said that the Soviet-type "command economy", in which firms and managers react to commands from above, not to market signals from below, leads to a political command society, to a lack of freedom in every sphere.

A major argument for socialism is that it offers security, the right to work, and a wide range of cheap or free social services. No-one gains directly by offering worthless products, by the waste of advertising, by pandering to artificially created needs. Differences between rich and poor are smaller, and colonies, or former colonies, are not exploited, as they allegedly are by capitalist countries. Greed and ruthlessness are not rewarded, as in the West.

There are some who profess to have seen a convergence of the systems in the 1980s with capitalism becoming more controlled and "social", the planned economies permitting more free enterprise. That view, also, is controversial.

Conflicting economic theories

The most difficult of the issues affecting the economic policy of capitalist countries in recent decades has been the debate between Keynesians and monetarists. Until the 1930s at least, traditional "neoclassical" economics as well as traditional policymakers tended to assume that there was an inherent self-rectifying system in capitalist economies. Crises were well known, and the regular phenomenon of the trade cycle from boom to slump, recurring every seven to eleven years, had been recognized since the middle of the 19th century. Most crises had particular causes, such as the outbreak of a war, or the faulty or fraudulent conduct of a large bank, but they were quickly brought under control, and in any case could not be blamed on the economic system as such. As for the cycles, the very fact that they recurred meant that any divergence in one direction, such as perhaps overoptimistic investment plans, would sooner or later call forth a response in the opposite direction. What took place, in the neoclassical view, were fluctuations about a trend rather than an uncontrolled shooting off from the trend in a single direction.

These comforting assumptions came to be questioned in the Great Depression of the 1930s. Moreover, even in the "boom" years of the late 1920s, there were some countries such as Britain or Germany which did not experience the full employment which had characterized booms in the past. Two new phenomena thus called for an explanation: a persistent irremovable core of unemployed of perhaps 10 percent of the labor force; and a slump which was so severe as to put in question the survival of the capitalist system itself.

Many alternative explanations were offered. The theory which, after some years, found most widespread support was the one proposed by the British economist John Maynard Keynes in a book first published in 1936, *The General Theory of Employment, Interest and Money*. Keynes set out to prove that what economists called "equilibrium", a state from which there was no reason for the system to move, and toward which it tended to drift (unless it was disturbed from outside by noneconomic factors), could exist not only, as the classics had assumed, when resources were pretty nearly fully employed, but at almost any level of employment. It was therefore quite feasible that if no decisions were made actively to stimulate change, the advanced countries of the world might settle down to suffer permanently heavy unemployment.

The key element in Keynes's thinking was the possibility that savings and investment in an economy might not coincide. Every time a citizen saves part of his or her income, he or she removes purchasing power from the market. Something, somewhere, which has had a cost and thus generated an income, will remain unsold, and will not be replaced by the wholesaler or shopkeeper. The maker will lose the order and will eventually make someone redundant.

Fortunately for society, there are also people who spend money which they have not earned. Companies making investments often need funds beyond those they have recently accumulated themselves, and draw on their own savings or borrow the savings of others from their banks or from other lenders. If the totals of these additional investments equal the totals of savings, there will be no purchasing power lost to the economy as a whole, and all will continue to be employed at much the same rate as before. If, however, optimistic firms seek to invest more than society as a whole has saved, then (ignoring possible capital imports from abroad) the demand for goods and services will exceed supply, since this cannot be increased if all are fully employed; and if demand exceeds supply, then prices will rise. If, however, planned investments as a whole are less than savings, some purchasing power will be lost, and unemployment will be the result. Unemployed people, in turn, spend less, which will make firms less likely to wish to invest in the future, so that there will be a further shortfall of investment in the next round, and there may well set in a downward spiral of incomes and employment.

Traditional doctrine had held to the optimistic notion that this contingency could not happen – that is, that savings and investments cannot diverge for any time from each other, because there exists a mechanism to bring them together, as long as governments do not foolishly intervene in the process. This mechanism is the rate of interest, which might be called the price for credit. Thus, if potential savings exceed planned investments, savers will not be able to place their funds and the rate of interest will drop. As the price of loans drop, more firms will find borrowing attractive, until all the offered savings are disposed of, and equilibrium restored. Similarly, if planned investment exceed savings, investors will bid up the rate of interest, until more people are induced to save rather than spend, or some potential investors are put off by the high price for loans. Given a free market and no interference, savings and investment can therefore, according to this view, not diverge from each other for any length of time, and neither large-scale unemployment nor inflation should occur.

It was a key point in Keynes's thinking that the rate of interest did not perform this function, and the movements and impact of the rate of interest thus assumed a major importance in economic debate. According to him, investors made their plans according to their expectations of profit; if these were much higher than the rate of interest that they were charged, they would go ahead with their investment. Savers, however, reacted to quite different considerations. Savings depended, above all, on peoples' incomes: it was not only that the rich, having a larger income, could save more, they also tended to save a higher proportion of their higher income. The rate of savings also depended, among other things, on what he called "liquidity preference", the fact that most people prefer to have their funds easily available, and not tied up in such a way that they cannot get hold of them. Thus savers, if they are to be persuaded to lend their money, must be offered a payment, the interest, to induce them to forego their "liquidity".

▶ **The May Day Parade, Moscow, 1954.**

There was thus no preordained reason for savings and investment plans to coincide. The former, given certain stable relations such as liquidity preference, depended mainly on incomes; the latter, mainly on profit expectations. They could diverge for long periods on end. Keynes thought, in fact, that in the long run, as societies became richer, they would automatically save more, and the tendency for savings to exceed planned investments, and thus for unemployment to occur, would be strengthened.

Fortunately, if this analysis is accepted, it contains a solution to the central dilemma. Governments, and only governments, had the means to prevent the economy settling down at a potential equilibrium at the level of less than full employment. They could create credit, by spending funds which they had not raised in taxes: to employ people on public works, for example. The people thus employed would spend their wages, and create more jobs in a "virtuous spiral" by means of the employment "multiplier". Also, by lowering interest rates, a government could stimulate private investors to borrow more and thus move to an equilibrium at a higher level. It had been well known, up to then, that a government could always create jobs in the short run by printing money; but the assumption had been that the result would inevitably be inflation. On Keynes's terms, this would not be the case when there was much unemployment: instead, the extra purchasing power would set people to work. Only when the economy neared full employment would the additional credit be converted into price increases.

At the theoretical level, the attraction of this theory lay not merely in its offer of a way out, but that it should offer one while preserving the essentials of a liberal-capitalist system. For Keynes remained convinced of the merits of free enterprise and of the superiority of market steering of economic decisions in detail. Only the overall level of incomes and employment needed to be controlled, thus avoiding the danger of the complete loss of liberty implied in a system of centralized planning.

At the practical level, it took some years for deliberate Keynesian policies to be adopted anywhere, though it might be argued that certain successful measures of the New Deal in the United States after 1933, in Sweden at the same time, and even the "cheap money" policy in Britain, had shown that the Keynesian remedies worked. After World War II, several countries, including the United States, Britain and West Germany, officially accepted the duty of governments to seek to maintain full employment, a novel obligation derived from Keynesian thinking, and until the early 1970s, most governments seemed to act within an implicit Keynesian policy framework. As the world maintained a remarkable degree of full employment and rapid economic growth, expression of the overconfident belief that at least the economically advanced part of humanity had learned to avoid crisis and stagnation became widespread.

The failure of Keynesianism
"Stagflation" – the simultaneous occurrence of economic stagnation, including much unemployment, and inflation – in the 1970s showed that the optimism had been misplaced and that Keynesian assumptions needed revision, since they had held that the co-existence of unemployment and inflation was impossible. In consequence, views critical of Keynesianism came to the fore. The most influential among these were the views of the American economist Milton Friedman and the monetarists.

Friedman's ideas had been developed in Chicago as early as the 1950s. They had predicted precisely the phenomenon of

stagflation – the Achilles heel of Keynesian assumptions. Friedman had fastened on one important facet ignored by Keynes, namely that people learn from their experience and develop what monetarists came to call "rational expectations" – expectations built on the lessons of the past. In particular, Keynes had been prescribing for the conditions of the 1930s – a period marked by deflation, falling world prices and heavy unemployment. Price rises were not an issue. But a population experiencing a constantly high demand for labor and an upward movement of prices, as happened in the postwar decades, will not hesitate to ask for wage rises ahead of price rises, in anticipation of further rises, and employers will be confident in being able to pass these rises on to their customers in turn. Inflation thus feeds on itself and will accelerate if the lack of a pool of unemployed labor competing for jobs does not serve to temper wage demands. Conversely, unemployment would necessarily weaken the power of wage earners to push up wages and, under given conditions in every country, there would be a relation setting the rate of unemployment for any given rate of inflation – the "natural rate of unemployment".

In the monetarist view, as much as in the Keynesian, governments have an important role to play. For the inflationary spiral can continue only for as long as it can be fed by an expanding supply of "money", and the money supply is ultimately under the control of the government. Thus the money supply assumes a key function among monetarists, analogous to the interest rate for Keynesians. What is comprised under the term "money" is, as noted above, not always clear, and monetarists have developed various definitions; at one extreme the definition includes only cash, whereas at the other it includes all sorts of saleable securities. The quantities of these forms of money have become major instruments of policy. In particular, if the quantity of money supply is restricted by government action, employers will not be able to pay the wage increases demanded, and if the power of the trade unions is such that they enforce them nevertheless, they will price themselves out of the market, causing their members' unemployment. Again, as under Keynes, the government only sets the overall limits, and it is entrepreneurs who have to fight the detailed battles.

The monetarist view is thus sharply critical of Keynesian recommendations. For it is the easy credit expansion by governments, to maintain full employment according to the Keynesian recipe, which was responsible, according to the monetarists, for the world's inflationary pressure. The more generous the credit creation, the worse the unemployment to be endured in order to reach stability again.

In the 1970s most Western governments adopted, implicitly or explicitly, monetarist notions, and these have also entered the decision-making processes of international agencies such as the World Bank and the International Monetary Fund. These matters are still in dispute, but it is clear that the monetarist solutions have not proved an unalloyed success. In particular, the notion that the money supply can be controlled, in view of the almost infinite possibilities of multiplying the "money" under government control by paper, has proved untenable.

The effects of technical progress
Economic policymaking has taken on a new importance in the latter part of the 20th century, because the technical means were not previously available to carry out decisions, at least with a modicum of information. The revolution in information and communications technology has had altogether more influence on the economic life of nations than is often realized.

The creation of a single world in this way had numerous

consequences, not all favorable. The less developed and colonial territories were developed more rapidly, but often more onesidedly. Dependence on a single crop could bring rapid collapse as well as rapid riches. In the more advanced nations, the very rapidity and efficiency of international linkages tended to thwart the attempted control over their own destiny which Keynesian theories (and other practical developments pointing in the same direction) had made possible.

In one sense, the failures of the world economy in the interwar period, and by extension the conditions which gave rise ultimately to World War II, may be seen as arising from the failure to take account of the intercommunicating world by conducting policy purely within the boundaries of traditionally sovereign states and in the light of traditional national egotism. Certainly, attempts to keep national industrial and agricultural policies, protection and currency manipulations independent of larger international trends did not help in avoiding or reducing the effects of the Great Depression.

By the same token, the international economic policies and structures that were consciously created after World War II in order to avoid the mistakes of the 1920s and 1930s, by taking into account of the world's economic interdependence, have made the world's economies safer and undoubtedly more successful. However, many problems remain. Among the most intractable is the continued economic, technical and political inability of the poorer nations to enter a path of modernization and technical progress.

Throughout this volume, technical progress is taken for granted as an underlying trend, without constant explicit reference to it. The significance of that underlying trend deserves special emphasis, as, beyond a certain point, technical progress cannot be reversed. Once achieved, it cannot be forgotten or unlearned, though there may well be outside factors, from religious prejudice to lack of means, to prevent its application in particular places. The reasons for this progress lie both in the social environment and in technology itself.

The social environment works its influence largely because of its competitive character. Individuals, enterprises and firms have to be constantly on the lookout to improve their performance by better technical methods, or, more defensively, to prevent others from getting ahead of them. Even if most people prefer a quiet life, a single innovator can spoil the calm somnolence of a whole lethargic branch of industry, and he does not even need to come from that branch of industry himself but may offer a competing product or service of quite a different origin or composition. Thus the search for improvement is built into the system. Even if the whole world were to become an economic cartel, it would be driven on by the urge of individuals to improve themselves and excel over their neighbors. The same drive on a competitive basis is also inherent in political units, especially states, in their search for military security or superiority, as well as for economic prowess.

This drive is reflected in turn in growing expenditure on the search itself, on research and development (R & D), which for a large proportion of the active and trained population has become their form of employment. Technical progress is thus ever less left to chance, and each age sees resources devoted to it which to previous generations would have seemed unimaginable. At the same time, the means of research and of finding answers become themselves more powerful. This is paralleled by the achievements and the research effort of pure science. There are currently more people employed in finding answers to technical and scientific problems than there have ever been in the entire history of mankind.

But a second impetus comes from technology itself. Every

innovation makes use of some knowledge, some technical means existing before, now being combined in new ways. Much that was thought of in the past, but was then impossible, now becomes possible as new methods of calculation, new materials, new sources of energy remove earlier obstacles. This also grows in an exponential way. Part of the cause of an ever-expanding technology is technology itself.

Within the economic sphere, technology means new commodities and services, or old ones available more cheaply in terms of human effort. What in one generation is considered a luxury to the few, becomes accessible to all in the next. As elementary needs are met, at least in the more advanced economies, as people no longer die of starvation or of diseases associated with it, as they no longer freeze in winter or are

stifled in airless hovels in summer, they can begin to meet needs which have hitherto been disregarded. Societies too, countries and cities, can afford to construct the infrastructure of roads, parks, schools and power supplies, all of which have changed the material life of humanity faster in this century than ever before.

Progress in the real sense has not been universal, nor has it been without its cost, and the cost, coupled with the still un-checked growth of the world's population, may yet overwhelm us. Technology, if abused or used wrongly, will be harmful in-stead of beneficial. But so far, driven by its own impetus, and the impetus provided for it by outside forces, it has carried economies upward without, and at times in spite of, the decision of governments, of civil servants, of entrepreneurs

and managers. Moreover, it has allowed them to cover up their mistakes and to assert claims for the success of their economic policies, when the advances really belong to the irreversible upward drive of technology.

An economic history, therefore, with all its internal logic and impetus, cannot in the end stand alone. It depends on political and even military events, on demographic changes and social development, and on technical change, among other things. History, the human destiny, remains indivisible. But some-where near the central motor that drives humanity forward there will be found the needs, the ideas and the solutions that are encompassed in our economic history.

▲ A steel factory in modern China.

19

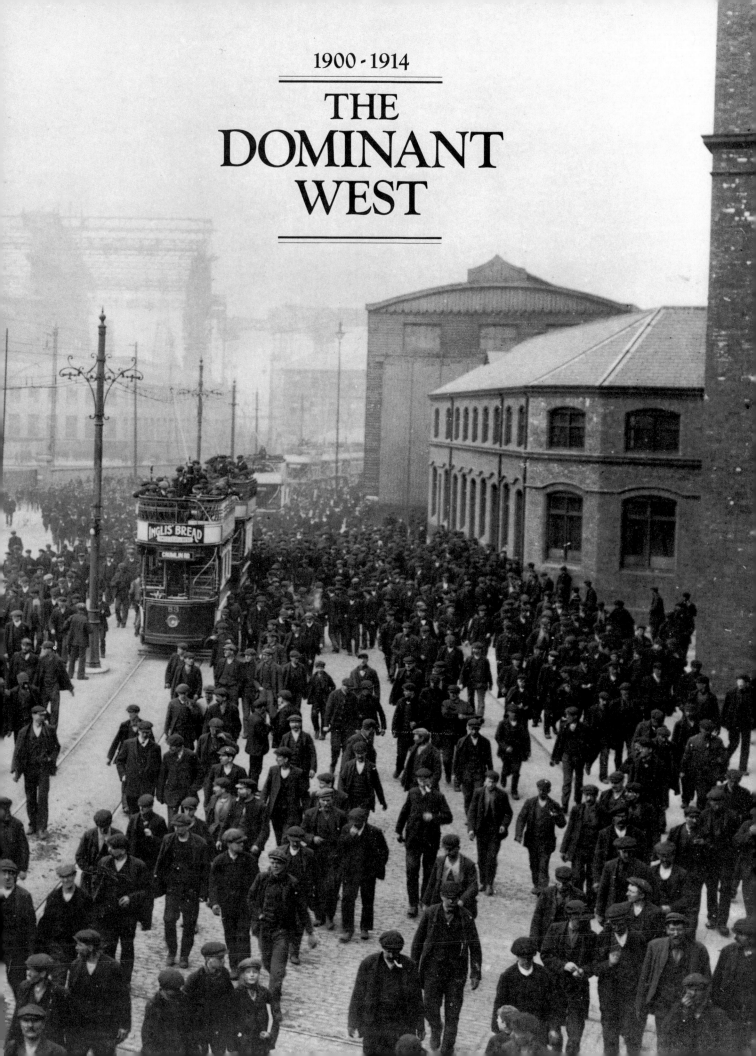

1900 · 1914

THE
DOMINANT
WEST

Time Chart

	1900	1901	1902	1903	1904	1905	1906
Industry	• Sep: Strike of 150,000 miners in the USA • 26 Oct: Belgium adopts old age pensions • American Federation of Labor (AFL) formed from 216 trade unions (USA)	• J.P. Morgan founds the United States Steel Corporation	• German steel company Krupp buys the Germania–Werft shipyard in Kiel (Ger)	• 3 Jan: Report of the Irish Land conference suggests revision of rental payments • Henry Ford founds the Ford Automobile Company (USA) • J.P. Morgan founds the International Mercantile and Marine Company shipping trust in New York (USA) • Foundation of the Telefunken wireless telegraphy company (Ger)	• C. Duisberg merges the chemical plants Bayer, Agfa and Badische Anilin to form I.G. Farben (Ger) • Foundation of the Daimler automobile plant near Stuttgart (Ger) • Foundation of the Rolls Royce automobile company (UK)	• Foundation of the International Agricultural Institute in Rome (It)	• Foundation of the Mercedes automobile company in Berlin (Ger) • Katanga Mining Union founded in the Belgian Congo
Technology	• 2 Jul: First trial flight of rigid airship *Star*, designed by F. Graf Zeppelin • First escalator demonstrated at the world exhibition in Paris	• 13 Dec: Marconi send the first radio telegram across the Atlantic Ocean • K.C. Gillette applies for a patent for his exchangeable razor blade shaver (USA)	• Aswan dam built by B. Baker is completed (Egy) • R.A. Fesseden develops the wireless telephone (USA) • A. Korn invents photo-telegraphy (Ger)	• 17 Dec: First controlled powered flight by the Wright brothers (USA) • L. and A. Lumière develop the first viable color photography (Fr) • Industrial artificial silk developed (USA)	• 4 May: Beginning of the construction of the Panama Canal • Invention of the electron valve by J.A. Fleming (UK) • Completion of the Trans-Siberian railroad (Russ)	• J.W. Rubel and C. Hermann develop offset printing • Fouche and Picard invent oxyacetylene welding (Fr) • Introduction of compressed air hammers in coal mining (Ger)	• L. Baekeland founds the synthetic resin industry (Bel) • A. Fisher constructs the first washing machine with a horizontal cylinder (USA)
Finance	• Mar: Gold dollar become the official currency of the USA • Establishment of the Hokkaido Takushoko Ginko, bank for financing the development of Hokkaido (Jap)	• J.P. Morgan merges the Carnegie Steel Corporation and the Federal Steel Corporation to the US Steel Corporation (USA) • Establishment of the Banco Hispano Americano and Banco de Vizcaya (Sp)	• Establishment of the Industrybank (Jap) • Establishment of the Banco Español de Credito (Sp)	• Mar: Fixing of a constant gold-silver parity (USA) • Jul: An international monetary conference in Berlin demands a constant currency parity between countries of the gold and the silver blocs • Bankers Trust Company established in New York	• Establishment of the Banque de l'Union Parisienne (Fr) • Establishment of the Bank of Italy by Giannini in San Francisco (USA) • Establishment of the Bank of the Ministry of Finance (China)	• Loan agreed for Russia on the condition that Russia supports France at the Morocco conference in Algeciras (Fr) • Manufacturers Trust Company established in New York (USA)	
Economic Policy	• Feb: Beginning of severe strikes in Vienna, Brussels and Bohemia	• Feb: Strike against the tax policy of the Catalonian government (Sp) • Jul: Beginning of a steelworkers strike in the USA • Dec: Demonstrations and riots by unemployed workers in Budapest (Aust-Hung)	• Jan: Establishment of the first Labor Office • Feb: Reduction of miners' working hours to nine per day • Apr: Consultations regarding the merging of all cartels and syndicates into a single economic association (Ger) • Oct: Strike of two-thirds of French miners	• Mar: Legislation for the regulation of childrens' labor enforced (Ger) • May: British Colonial minister J. Chamberlain begins campaigning for an imperial tariff association (UK) • Nov: Strike of Spanish miners, demanding their wages be paid weekly	• Jun: Establishment of the German Employers Association • Aug: End of disruption in the petrol industry at Boryslaw. Demand met for a reduction of working hours (Aust-Hung)	• Jan: Strike of miners in the Ruhr and in Belgium, demanding a reduction of working hours (Ger/Bel) • Mar: Introduction of the eight-hour day for miners under 18 (UK) • Aug: Severe strikes and disruption in Russia and Poland • Sep: Trade Union Congress demands the introduction of an eight-hour day and free trade (UK)	• Mar: Beginning of a severe strike movement in Germany • May: US government prohibits any further expansion of the Rockefeller Oil Trust by passing the Sherman Act
International		• Sep: Congress of the International Association for the legal protection of workers agrees on a package of workers' legislation for all countries • Foundation of the International Trade Union in Amsterdam	• Jan: Germany obtains a licence from Turkey to build a railway from Konia to Baghdad • Mar: Agreement between UK and Persia regarding the construction of a telegraph line • May: International Congress of Miners demands nationalization of all mines • 28 Jun: USA buys rights off French Panama Company	• Feb: Trade agreement between UK and Persia • Nov: Canada decides on a further increase of taxes on German imports • Dec: New trade agreement between Italy and Austria	• Jan: Trade agreement between the USA and China • Aug: International Congress of Miners demands the introduction of a fixed minimum wage • Germany signs commercial treaties with Belgium, Russia, Switzerland, Serbia and Austria-Hungary	• May: Meeting of the International Conference for the Protection of Laborers discusses night work for women	• Jul: Tariff war between Austria and Serbia • Night-work by women internationally forbidden
Misc.	• Boxer Rebellion in China suppressed	• Coronation of Edward VII on the death of Victoria (UK)	• 31 May: End of the Boer War	• 3 Nov: Panama made independent of Colombia	• Beginning of the Russo-Japanese war	• Oct: First revolution in Russia	• Foundation of the Labour party (UK)

22

1907	1908	1909	1910	1911	1912	1913	1914
J.P. Morgan organizes a fund by order of the US treasury to support destitute companies during the economic crisis (USA) • Shell Oil Trust founded (UK) • Ball bearing plant founded in Göteborg (Swe)	• General Motors Company founded in Detroit (USA) • Ford develops assembly line for the mass production of the Model T (USA) • Zeppelin airship company established (Ger)	• Ford specializes its car production on the Model T (USA) • German Gelsenkirchener Bergwerks AG begins steel production in Luxembourg	• Rotary hoe first used • Establishment of the Rockefeller Foundation for the promotion of science (USA)	• Standard Oil Trust dissolved on the basis of antitrust legislation • Poor harvest in Russia. Famine in many parts of the country	• May: The world's largest ship, *Imperator*, launched (Ger) • Dec: 245 miners killed by an explosion in a coal mine in Hokkaido (Jap)	• I. Kreuger founds his match plant (Swe) • BASF builds an ammonia plant in Oppau (Ger)	• Jan: Introduction of minimum wages and profit-sharing at Ford (USA)
Chemotherapy introduced by P. Ehrlich as a treatment for infectious diseases (Ger) • Lumière brothers invent color-scanner plate to improve color photography (Fr)	• Invention of the gyro-compass by H. Anschütz-Kaempfe • A. Wilm invents the alloy Duralmin (Ger)	• 24 Feb: First color moving picture shown in Brighton (UK) • 25 Jul: L. Blériot flies across English Channel in 27 minutes (Fr)	• G. Claude invents the fluorescent light tube (Fr) • B. Ljundström constructs the high-pressure steam turbine (Nor)	• E. Rutherford develops the theory of the atomic nucleus structure (UK)	• Krupp patents acid resistant chrome-nickel steel (Ger) • V. Kaplan begins development of a turbine for the exploitation of small waterfalls (Aust-Hung)	• 14 Aug: Opening of world's longest water pipe in Los Angeles (USA) • F. Bergius develops coal high pressure hydrogenation (Ger)	• Feb: Opening of the Tanganyika Railway from Dar es Salaam to Lake Tanganyika • Aug: Opening of the Panama Canal (USA)
• 21 Oct: Financial crisis in the USA, with the collapse of 31 national banks and 12 state banks • Swiss National Bank established as the central bank of Switzerland • Establishment of the Bank of the Ministry of Transport (China)	• The gold standard comes into force (Ger) • Establishment of the first savings banks in the USA • Appointment of the National Currency Commission to devise a new banking system (USA)	• Jun: Reichsbank notes become legal tender (Ger)	• Note-issuing monopoly for the Swiss National Bank • Merger of the Guarantee Trust Company, the Morton Trust Company and the Fifth Avenue Trust Company to form the First Bank (USA) • Establishment of the first industrial banks (USA)	• 9 Sep: Collapse at the Berlin stock exchange due to the Morocco crisis and German colonial policy • Nov: Circulation of bank notes fixed to 6.3 billion francs until 1925 (Fr) • Establishment of the Australian central bank	• J.P. Morgan acquires the majority share in the Guarantee Trust Company and in the Bankers Trust Company (USA) • Establishment of the Swiss Bank by the merger of two provincial banks • Sumitomo Bank and Yasuda Bank become stock companies (Jap)	• Dec: Twelve Federal Reserve Banks and one Federal Reserve Board established (USA) • Establishment of the National Credit Bank (Fr) • Establishment of the Bank of China	• Jul: Run on many central banks in Europe. Decrease in the gold reserves of the Bank of England from £38.6 to £28 billion • Aug: Closing of the stock exchanges and the suspension of the convertibility of many currencies with the outbreak of World War I
• Jan: Establishment of a colonial action committee, urging an intensive colonial policy • May: French sailors in Marseille proclaim a general strike for better working conditions	• Mar: Meeting of employers in Berlin agrees on collective wage agreements (Ger)	• Aug: Severe strike movement in Sweden • Dec: Complaint by the Standard Oil Company at the Supreme Court against the demanded suspension of its trust and against the anti-cartel legislation (USA)	• Jan: English miners strike for an eight-hour day (UK) • Apr: Measures taken by the Russian government for the economic development of Siberia, including the construction of a railway from Moscow to Irkutsk • Aug/Sep: Dockers strike in Germany and in the UK for higher wages • Oct: Strike of French railwaymen	• Jan: Miners' strikes in the Belgian coal district • Aug: Beginning of strikes by English railwaymen (UK)	• Mar: Miners' strike in the Ruhr ends in failure (Ger) • Apr: Gold miners' strike in Siberia suppressed by the army (Russ) • Apr: Law on minimum wages for miners put into force (UK)	• Aug: USA declare an economic boycott against Mexico	• May: Trade unions of miners, transport workers and railwaymen found a common committee for collective bargaining (UK) • Aug: All parties in the Reichstag agree on a large war credit for the government (Ger)
• Jun: Agreement between Japan and France on trading in China • Jul: Agreement between Japan and Russia on trading China • Aug: China opens seven towns in Manchuria for international trade	• Feb: International navigation conference in London establishes passenger fares • Sep: International Conference for the Protection of Labor demands prohibition of night work for children	• May: Mutual consultations of German and English workers • Jul: Agreement between USA and Germany on the use of patents	• Feb: Agreement on the construction and management of the St Gotthard railway between Germany, Italy and Switzerland • Jul: Commercial treaty between Austria-Hungary and Serbia	• Japanese commercial treaties with the UK (3 Apr), France and Germany (28 Jun) • Dec: Agreement between the UK, Russia and France prohibiting the capture of seals			• Anglo-German and Franco-German agreement on the management of railways in the Ottoman Empire
• Formation of the Triple Entente of Russia, France and the UK	• Austria-Hungary annexes Bosnia-Herzegovina		• Japan annexes Korea • 1 Jul: Union of South Africa becomes a Dominion	• Chinese revolution initiated by the Young Chinese Movement	• Italy occupies the Dodecanese Islands (Turk) • First Balkan war. Turks virtually expelled from Europe	• Second Balkan war. Bulgaria cedes territory to Serbia, Greece and Romania	• 28 Jun: Assassination of Franz Ferdinand in Sarajevo (Serbia) initiates crisis leading in August to the outbreak of World War I

Datafile

The economic growth of industrial and industrializing countries accelerated from 1890 so much that the 25 years before World War I have been called a second industrial revolution. Among the causes for this, emphasis has been laid upon new technologies such as electricity and mass production which created new products like the motor car. But this period also witnessed the final maturity of long-established manufacturing techniques. Further, industrialization took root in an increasing number of countries, spreading out from its original cores in northwestern Europe and New England. Mass markets grew rapidly, particularly in the established industrial countries – Britain, the United States and Germany.

Imported capital

- Norway
- Sweden
- Denmark

Capital (percent) — 1890s, 1900s, 1910–1914

◀ Industrialization in Scandinavia generated a demand for capital which initially could not be met from local sources. Foreign capital therefore played a vital role over a short period in the emerging industrial economies of Sweden, Norway and Denmark in the 1890s and 1900s. This overseas capital introduced the electrochemical industry to Norway and was responsible for the development of iron ore mining in northern Sweden.

Food consumption 1910–14

- Pure alcohol (litres)
- Eggs/cheese
- Fruit
- Fats
- Meat
- Potatoes
- Cereals

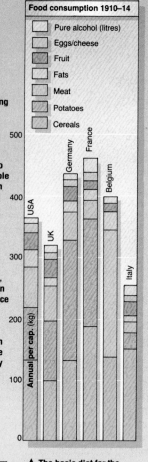

Annual per cap. (kg)

◀ Until the 1870s Britain had been the dominant industrial economy and France the other major industrial power. However, from the 1880s this position changed with the emergence of the United States as the world's biggest center of manufacturing, and the rapid growth of the German economy. The arrival of the United States and Germany as world economic powers further displaced France. Also, the beginnings of industrialization in Russia resulted in yet another alteration within the world economic environment.

Domestic investment in Europe

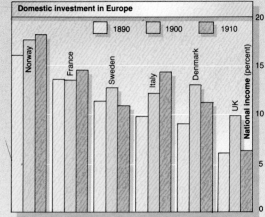

1890 · 1900 · 1910

National income (percent)

World manufacturing

7% · 5% · 17% · 30% · 19% · 22%

1900

- USA
- Germany
- UK
- France
- Russia
- Others

▲ Although data sources for investment before 1914 vary in quality and approach, it seems clear that newly industrializing regions and countries such as Scandinavia and Italy were characterized by relatively high levels of national income devoted to investment, as was France. By contrast, Britain's rate of investment was low.

▼▼ During the 1890s and 1900s Europeans formed a declining proportion of American immigrants, falling from over three-quarters of the total in 1890 to just over half by 1910. Britain and Scandinavia continued to be important, but to this "old" migration was added a "new" from Southern and Eastern Europe, especially Italy and Russia.

Economic growth 1890–1913

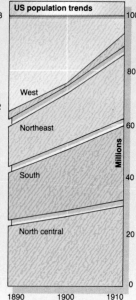

Annual percentage (per capita)

Russia, Scandinavia, Italy, Germany, France, Netherlands, UK, Austria-Hungary

US population trends

West, Northeast, South, North central

Millions

1890 · 1900 · 1910

▲ The basic diet for the mass of the population consisted of starch, which was eaten in the form of grains or potatoes. In richer countries there was greater variety, provided by meats, fats and fruits. There were also substantial national variations, partly the result of differing geography, local availability and varying tastes.

◀ Between 1890 and 1910 the total population of the United States increased by 42 percent. By 1910 the population was almost equally divided between the North Central region, the South and the Northeast, the latter two regions having faster rates of population growth. Population was increasing most rapidly in the West.

Population growth in Europe

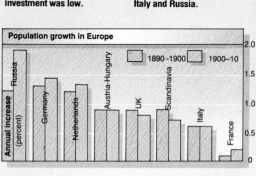

Annual increase (percent)

1890–1900 · 1900–10

Russia, Germany, Netherlands, Austria-Hungary, UK, Scandinavia, Italy, France

Migration from Europe

1890 · 1900

Population (percent)

Italy, UK, Scandinavia, Austria-Hungary, Germany, Netherlands, Russia, France

▲ The European economy as a whole was growing at an average rate of 1.5 percent per year at the turn of the century. Most of the newly industrializing countries, such as Italy, were expanding rapidly from a low initial base, whereas generally the larger established industrial nations were growing more slowly.

▶ Industrialization led to a decline in the proportion of the labor force engaged in agriculture, forestry and fishing. This shift of labor into manufacturing and service industries is a clear marker of economic growth. In Britain that process was substantially complete by 1900 but in Eastern and Southern Europe it was just beginning.

Agricultural labor 1900

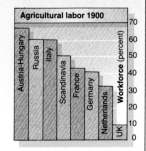

Workforce (percent)

Austria-Hungary, Russia, Italy, Scandinavia, France, Germany, Netherlands, UK

INDUSTRIAL AND URBAN GROWTH

Centers of growth

The migration of labor

Technological developments

The new mass market

The retailing revolution

Urban growth and urban transport

International economic rivalry

By the beginning of the 20th century there were two main geographical centers of industrialization in the world – northwest Europe and the northeastern United States. Within these areas modern economic growth was already well established, whereas in other regions such as Scandinavia, northern Italy, Russia and the northern central states of the United States, industrialization was just beginning to get under way. This geographical dispersion of the process of modernization coincided with an overall acceleration in the rate of material advance experienced by most industrial economies from the 1890s. The concepts and techniques that are now used for measuring economic growth, involving national income calculations, did not become current until the interwar period, but when using a modern measure such as Gross National Product (GNP) per capita at constant prices, it would appear that economic growth was taking place in Europe at a rate of around 1.5 percent per annum between the late 1880s and 1913. Such rates of growth are, however, only estimates, or even "guesstimates", since, unlike similar figures for later in the century, they are based upon a very wide range of contemporary data of varying qualities.

▼ The modern canning industry developed from the 1870s, but the mechanization of the preparation of fruits and vegetables only began at the turn of the century. Consequently the food processing and packing industries continued to employ substantial numbers of low-paid unskilled workers, often women and children, to prepare produce, in this instance, beans.

The post-1890 period of renewed growth involved, as in earlier years, regional variations within Europe. Faster growth of both that group of countries which had experienced industrialization relatively later, such as Germany, and those countries and regions where industrialization was just beginning, such as Russia, Scandinavia and Italy, contrasted with countries that could be labeled as "early industrializers", such as Belgium, Switzerland and the United Kingdom, which grew at less than the European average. The United Kingdom continued to be the richest European country, but the richest by far of all the advanced industrial economies was the United States, which in 1913 had a real GNP per capita five times greater than the European average and 25 percent higher than that of the United Kingdom. This divergence was of long standing, having been apparent from the second quarter of the 19th century. The American rate of economic growth between 1890 and 1913, the period of resumption of faster growth, appears to have been around 1.8 percent per annum, greater than that of the major European industrial economies but not so rapid as in the newly industrializing countries like Scandinavia or Russia.

▼ Between 1880 and 1920, more than 23 million immigrants settled in the United States. This flow of people across the Atlantic from Europe in crowded ships was marked by considerable year-to-year fluctuations, with peaks in 1892, 1907 and 1914. These peaks coincided with periods of prosperity in America; the migrants were drawn by employment opportunities. Such attractions were made known in Europe through advertisements, coupled with offers of financial assistance, placed by American railroad and steamship companies together with managers of mills and factories.

Population growth and migration

Economic growth amongst the advanced industrial countries during the 25 years or so before 1914 was the product of many factors. It was assisted by population growth, a result of birth rates exceeding death rates. Birth rates had fallen in northwestern Europe from the mid-1870s but this new demographic trend did not become established amongst the populations of Eastern Europe until after 1900. A decline in infant mortality was largely responsible for the fall in the death rate and was most pronounced by 1913 in Scandinavia and Western Europe. In contrast, infant mortality rates remained high in Eastern Europe, with rates of over 200 per thousand continuing during the first decade of the 20th century in Russia and Austria-Hungary.

Unlike the rest of Europe, France had had, since the 1860s, an extremely low rate of population increase, which transformed it from one of the most densely settled countries in 1800 to one of the least by the eve of World War I. Moreover, the low birth rate gave France an aging population in advance of other European countries, which had substantial effects before 1914 both on the size of the French labor force and on French consumption patterns.

Rates of natural increase were modified by international migration. It has been estimated that between 1850 and 1914 more than forty million people left the Old World for the New, equivalent to 10 percent of Europe's population. By the 1900s, the movement of Europeans to the western hemisphere was largely a flow from the Mediter-

▲ From the 1880s
immigrants to America came
increasingly from Southern
and Eastern Europe. By
the late 1890s this "new"
immigration made up more
than half of the transatlantic
flow and in 1910 over
three-quarters of it. Within the
"new" migration, Italians, like
this mother with her children,
predominated; nearly two
million Italians moved to the
United States between 1898
and 1907, in response to
population pressure at home.
However, Italians were so
poor that they could only
afford to migrate either
during periods of domestic
prosperity, such as the 1880s,
or with financial assistance
from those who had already
made the arduous journey to
America.

▶ Between 1880 and 1920 a
third of the Jews of Eastern
Europe migrated, 90 percent
to the United States. Over one
and a half million Jews
arrived in America between
1900 and 1914, with a peak of
152,000 in 1906. They went
partly in reaction to population
pressure, and partly to avoid
persecution in Russia. Most
were young and skilled, and
often whole families moved,
the father travelling first.
Russian Jews settled
particularly in New York,
Chicago and Philadelphia.
New York's Lower East Side
had 540,000 Jewish migrants,
the crowded tenements
containing workshops,
basement synagogues,
saloons and cafés.

ranean region and the Balkans, which acted as a
safety valve to the population problem that
bedeviled the peasant-based societies in these
areas. As a result, the high rate of natural increase
in Italy, at 16.4 per thousand, was transformed
into a relatively slow rate of population growth of
0.65 percent per annum during the opening
decade of the 20th century.

Generally migration, whether within an
economy or international, involved movement
from the countryside to the town. The agricultural
labor force was a reserve army upon which urban
manufacturing and service industries could draw
as they expanded. Consequently the size of an
economy's agricultural labor force represented a
potential for economic growth as well as a
measure of the extent of industrialization. The
relative size of the agricultural labor force fell after
1890 in industrial and industrializing countries
in Europe, principally as a result of two
developments – national economic growth and
international migration. These processes had
gone farthest in the case of Britain, the first industrial nation, and consequently, the British
economy was faced with a labor problem in the
1900s, since nearly all the gains in productivity
arising from the movement of the labor force out
of agriculture into industry had already accrued.
In most other European countries this transfer of
labor had still to take place in a major way. While
this did represent a potential for future growth, it
also meant that their manufacturing industries
were faced with domestic markets of low consumption power, so that, as in the case of
Sweden, their industries had to depend to some
extent on export markets.

Labor, as a factor of production, was important
not just in terms of numbers and its location
within an economy, but also with regard to its
quality – its skills and education. Increasingly

from 1890 workers in manufacturing were semi-
skilled or unskilled machine minders, rather than
industrial artisans owning their own tools and
both jealous and proud of their skills. At the same
time, as science and applied technology came
more to the fore in the closing decades of the 19th
century, an educated workforce became more
necessary.

By the 1900s primary education was becoming
commonplace in Europe. Secondary education
was still an innovation and was available to
relatively small numbers, but Germany was establishing a lead. All countries had tertiary education systems and in many there were specific institutes designed to advance industrial technology. Many of the latter had their roots in the
early part of the 19th century when they had been
established with state support as a means to
emulate Britain's industrial progress. Britain,
however, continued to be a laggard in this matter
and there remained within many branches of
British manufacturing industry a continuing emphasis on hand skills and empiricism, which had
served well initially, but by the 1900s was becoming increasingly outmoded.

In the United States, population was growing
rapidly immediately before 1914, at rates comparable to the highest in Europe, those of Russia.
As in Europe, birth and death rates were falling,
the former from the 1840s. However, whereas
most European countries were losing population
as a result of international migration, the United
States was a major migrant receiver. Generally international migrants were young, so that the
median age of the American population in 1890
was 22, and still only 24 in 1910. The continuing
influx of foreign labor contributed to the expansion of the economy. During the 25 years before
1914, there was an overall decline in the number
of migrants from Europe and, within this total,
there was a fall in the flow from northwestern

▼ By 1914 Germany had the largest electrical manufacturing industry in Europe. One of the biggest German firms was the Allgemeine Electricitäts-Gesellschaft of Emil Rathenau, whose Berlin workshops in the 1900s produced very large three-phase motors and transformers. Electricity was increasingly generated in this way to provide fixed motor power. Electrical power could now be directly applied to tools, so dispensing with inefficient power transmission mechanisms.

Europe, but a rise in the numbers coming from Russia and Italy. There was also internal migration from rural settlements to towns and the proportion of the labor force employed directly in agriculture declined from over 42 percent in 1890 to under 32 percent by 1910. As in Europe, the American labor force was now increasingly educated, at least to a primary level; in 1900 over three-quarters of the 5–17 age group were at school.

The growth of investment
Modern economic growth involved increased investment in producer goods. It also increasingly meant investment in more specific assets such as machinery and plant that produced only a limited range of products, was therefore more risky. Because different measures have to be used for

national income, it is particularly difficult to make precise comparisons between countries. However, while levels of investment had always varied over time, by 1900 the differing national fluctuations of what became known as the "trade cycle" were coming broadly into line as a result of economic integration brought about by the development of the world economy. Accordingly, by 1900 industrial countries were experiencing a common pattern of booms and slumps, not only in trade but also in investment.

In all the European countries for which reliable figures are available, the growth of investment was faster than the rate of population growth. The only exception was the United Kingdom in the 1900s, a reflection of British investment overseas rather than at home, and of the slowing down of the rate of British domestic economic growth dur-

Energy and Power

The further development and wider geographical diffusion of industrialization led to a rapidly growing use of energy. It has been estimated that world production of commercial sources of energy increased by nearly a thousand percent between 1860 and 1913. This growth in the generation and use of energy went hand in hand with the replacement of animate sources of power by inanimate sources. In the United States, for instance, animals had provided over three-quarters of such power in 1849, but by 1923 their share had fallen to barely three percent of an overall capacity, which had increased from 10 to 684 million horsepower, much of it concentrated in manufacturing, mines and quarries, railroads and shipping.

The main source of energy was coal; in 1913 coal was responsible, directly and indirectly, for nearly ninety percent of the world's energy output, with oil, gas and water providing the balance. World coal production increased from 132 million tonnes in 1860 to 314 million tonnes in 1880, and to 701 million tonnes by 1900. The United States was by far the biggest producer, followed by the United Kingdom and Germany, and to a lesser extent France and Belgium. Coal was used in metal smelting and refining and in steam generation, the latter particularly in coal-rich economies such as Britain and Germany. From the 1880s electricity gradually became important, generated from steam turbines or falling water. In America the amount of electricity used rose from four percent of all power in 1899 to nearly forty percent by 1914. In 1912 the output of electricity from central generating stations in the United States totaled 17,600 million kW hours. Britain produced only 2500 million kW hours from public supply power stations. Hydroelectricity grew in suitable countries; in 1910 Canada had a total water-power capacity of 0.73 million kW hours and Switzerland had one of 0.604 million kW hours.

▶ Electrical generation still began with raising steam.

ing the Edwardian period. Actually, in nearly all European countries the rate of domestic investment fell somewhat after 1900, but the British experience was nonetheless significantly different, though it is difficult to assess the extent to which the relatively low level of national income employed in domestic investment was a significant factor in the retardation of British economic growth from the 1890s.

As with labor, there were international flows of finance – savings – by which capital formation in receiving countries could be financed. Britain, France and Germany were the major exporters of capital, British savings being largely directed to countries outside Europe. The main European countries to draw upon such savings were those countries where industrialization was just beginning – Russia, Scandinavia and Italy (though in the case of Italy such international borrowings were exceeded by remittances sent home by migrants overseas). By 1914, Sweden too had become a capital exporter. The United States was a net capital importer, but these inflows merely augmented an already high internal rate of saving. Domestic investment grew at 3.5 percent a year between 1890 and 1910, though it slackened during the ensuing decade. In these terms American economic growth was similar in nature to German – the momentum of an earlier industrialization being sustained by continuing high investment – and consequently both countries stood apart from the United Kingdom where growth was faltering after 1890 and domestic investment was low, especially after 1900.

Technological change

Beyond increasing quantities of labor and capital, there were other processes that were important for economic growth. One was increasing returns to scale, both as individual producing units grew larger, and therefore more economical to run, and as production became more specialized. Another was improved efficiency in the allocation of resources, as with the transfer of labor from low-productivity employment to high-productivity. This so-called "structural change" also encompassed the elimination of monopolies and discrimination in the markets for both finished goods and factors of production–land, labor and capital. Lastly, there was technological progress.

The resumption of growth after 1890, in the advanced economies of Europe as well as the United States, has often been called a second industrial revolution, resulting from a new stream of innovations. This involved the harnessing of electricity and organic chemistry and the development of the internal combustion engine, and witnessed the growing production of a widening range of consumer durables such as the sewing machine, the typewriter, the bicycle and the motor car. Their production in turn required other developments which were also part of this new cluster of innovations, namely, precision manufacture and assembly-line mass production. Although these had begun during the mid-19th century, they were dependent for their fuller development upon the availability of mass-produced steel from the 1880s and special steel alloys from the 1890s, as well as on standardization gauges, which reduced costs of manufacture primarily through dispensing with expensive "fitting" by hand. At the same time there was also a wider use of already established technologies, as was the case with steam power, especially in Britain, Germany and the United States, economies with ready access to cheap coal. In Britain, the use of steam power rose by nearly ten times between 1870 and 1907.

There were, then, two currents of technological change at work – the final working out of an old and the inception of a new. They came together in different economies at different times and in different ways, helping to generate disparate patterns of growth. Germany expanded on the basis of both old and new manufacturing techniques. In France, which had not really experienced the first industrial revolution, modern growth only began with the second, starting in the 1890s. American growth has been conceived of in terms of long phases, with one such beginning at the end of the 1880s and being sustained until 1929. Newly industrializing countries adopted old and new technologies almost simultaneously at the turn of the century, as happened with ball bearing manufacture in Sweden and the production of electrical equipment in the Hungarian half of the Dual Monarchy.

The hallmark of this second industrial revolution was a closer alliance between science and technology, and its power source came progressively to be electricity. The origins of its commercial application lay in the provision of lighting in the 1870s. In the 1880s and 1890s it was developed as a source of motor power, powering among other things the streetcar and the elevator. It offered particular advantages to those economies without sufficient sources of coal, such as France, Switzerland and Italy, but the development of hydroelectricity was often costly, requiring substantial investment in dams and long-distance

▲ The growth of railroad networks from the 1850s created a demand for standardized components, like these wagon and engine-driving wheels being made at the Krupp works, Essen, in 1900. Down the centre aisle workers are manhandling wheels on which metal tyres are being fitted by heat shrinking. On either side wheels are being trued by turning on large lathes, powered from overhead shafts via belting. For these movements an overhead crane is employed, while the whole layout of the shop allows an uninterrupted flow of work. The railroads' demands on engineering led Krupps to become a substantial enterprise as early as the 1870s, when it employed 16,000 workers; by 1912 its payroll numbered nearly 70 thousand workers, a fifth of the population of Essen. The firm also employed 13,000 in its own collieries.

▶ Handmade cans for food packing had appeared in the 1820s, but the food industry was not revolutionized until the 1880s. During the last two decades of the 19th century, machines like this one were developed to produce cans and to solder, automatically, the lid onto the body of the can. The growth of the canning industry led to substantial increases in the demand for tinplate and until the 1890s Britain was the major world supplier. In 1889 the United States took 327,000 tonnes of tinplate from the South Wales industry, 80 percent of British exports, but the United States then raised import duties sharply.

Rudge in his bicycles. Ball bearings came to be found in nearly all the new consumer durables, the production of which expanded greatly at the turn of the century, and which, like the sewing machine, were the result of whole series of technical advances since the mid-19th century.

The technical demands of precision manufacture and standardized interchangeable parts had already existed in the production of small arms, locks, clocks and agricultural machinery, but now an ever higher degree of precision was required and was justified by market demand. Precision was achieved by the employment and further development of light machine tools such as the turret lathe, which had been invented in the United States in the 1840s, and the universal milling machine, again an American invention (1861). With the availability from the 1890s of special self-hardening tool steels, these machine tools became more widely used: for instance, milling machines were employed widely in bicycle production. Automobile engines of the 1890s and 1900s set even higher requirements in terms of work across a range of complication, delicacy and precision, which could only be achieved through the substitution of grinding for cutting and scraping. In the 1890s grinding wheels came to be made with new amalgams of abrasives, in particular carborundum in 1896, and were employed in new ways, as with plunge grinding, developed by the American Charles H. Norton. This was adopted before 1914 in the United States for automotive engineering, but not in Europe, although it was used in both Britain and Germany in the building of railroad locomotives.

As well as the diffusion of new machine tools in mechanical engineering, from the 1870s this branch of industry shared an interest with the primary metal-producing industries in cost control through improved work organization and plant layout. This "scientific management" viewed labor as an animate machine, capable of being made more efficient by the reduction of wasted or redundant effort. Although this system was most highly developed in America, European

transmission networks to transfer the energy to industrial and urban centers. Nonetheless, such was the high cost of coal-based power in these economies that within a few years, the basic innovations came about through advances in hydroelectricity. The practicality of hydroelectricity, coupled with the long-distance transmission of current, was demonstrated in 1885 when electricity generated in Creil was consumed in Paris, nearly 100 kilometers (60 miles) away. Six years later hydroelectricity was transferred 179 kilometers (112 miles) from Lauffen to Frankfurt.

The manufacture of electrical equipment, for the generation and the application of energy, was dominated by the United States and Germany. In 1913 the output of their electrical manufacturing industries amounted to £73.8 million and £65 million respectively after 1900 British output expanded, reaching £30 million by 1914.

New production methods
The generation and consumption of electricity required steel and the manufacture of precision, interchangeable, machine parts. Other developments reduced wasteful friction: the ball bearing, invented in 1877 by William Brown of Birmingham, England, was used from 1886 by Daniel

◀ Germany became a powerful economic force as the center of the development of new technologies. Werner von Siemens was a founder of the electrical industry. In 1903 his firm merged with Schuckert, establishing a concern able to rival AEG.

▲ In the late 19th century precision engineering had reached the stage of being able to produce complicated devices such as the typewriter, made by German firms from 1900. But their assembly was expensive and only profitable if a mass market could be tapped. Firms turned to advertising and, in the limited German market, to manufacturing other products.

engineers were also interested. It reached its pre-1914 climax in Detroit in the new Ford factory, where production had to be streamlined to meet a high demand for the Model T car in the 1910s. The answer was found in the moving assembly line. The results were spectacular: the time taken to produce a car fell from 12 hours 8 minutes in 1913 to 1 hour 33 minutes in 1914, when throughput amounted to 1,000 vehicles a day.

The retailing revolution
The new products of the early years of the century were aimed at a mass market; their economics depended upon a high output to reduce the unit costs of their manufacture. However, despite this lowering of costs, food and housing remained the largest items in the family expenditure of lower income groups.

Wages were rising, especially in northwestern Europe and the northeast of the United States. This was a result of increased employment in manufacturing with its much higher productivity, unionization of the workforce and, in northwestern Europe, the decline in family size. Of equal importance was the fall in the cost of food in America and in Britain and Denmark, the two European countries which did not protect their domestic agriculture against imports. Food prices fell during the last quarter of the 19th century as a result of the growth in world supplies and the fall in intercontinental transport costs following the completion of national railway systems and improvements in oceanic shipping.

The importance of this decline in the cost of food as against manufactures (the prices of which

were also falling) can be gauged from expenditure patterns. The family of a British workman earning £78 a year in 1901, which was then considered to be "good weekly wages", spent 41 percent of this on food. But in Europe, where agriculture was protected, the ratio was higher. A family with an equivalent income in Belgium spent 61 percent of it on food, in Germany 57 percent and in France 56 percent. A comparable American figure is not available, but outlays on food comprised just over 25 percent of total household expenditure on consumption in the United States in 1909. Even in Britain, for all the drop in food prices, in the mid-1890s nearly one-third of the urban working classes still lived below the poverty line.

Developing transport systems linking new sources of supply led in America and Britain to the growth of chains of grocery stores owned by a single company. One of the first American multiple food store chains was the Great Atlantic

▲ Modern retailing began in the advanced economies of the West in the 1880s. Its major feature was the mass sale of standardized packaged goods, but producers also recognized the advantages of differentiating markets. Display was made easier by the availability of cheap plate glass used in windows and cabinets, and middle-class customers were served by uniformed armies of assistants. Some distributors, such as Maillards, set up chains of outlets in grand hotels, like this candy store in a hotel on Fifth Avenue, New York.

◄ The need to change distribution systems was forced by the expansion of supply. A particularly British feature was the development in industrial cities of cooperative retail stores. By the 1900s most were affiliated either to the Cooperative Wholesale Society or the Scottish Wholesale Society which, in turn, imported foodstuffs from abroad, including tea from their own plantations in Ceylon.

and Pacific Tea Company established in the mid-1850s, and an early European pioneer was the Aerated Bread Company in the London area. New major wholesalers pioneered branding, advertising and the use of a sales force, and firms such as Quaker Oats, Campbells, Heinz and Bordin developed extensive purchasing and sales networks of their own. With the spread of refrigeration in the mid-1880s, other American food processors moved into mass distribution. The fresh meat packers – Swift, Armour, Morris and Cudahy – and the brewers – Pabst, Schlitz and Anheuser Busch – were among the first in the field.

Britain was the closest to American trends, being an open wealthy market for the world supply of primary products. The "retailing revolution" in Britain came with the development of multiple shops to sell imported foodstuffs. It began with "colonial wares" such as tea, the international supply of which was expanding through plantation production. Thomas Lipton opened his first shop in Glasgow in 1872. By 1890 he had 70 shops in London alone and in 1898 the firm, with 245 shops and 3,800 agencies selling its packeted tea, was turned into a public company. Regional chains of grocery shops developed in France too, while in Belgium the firm of Delhaize Frères, established in 1871, had 565 branches by 1904.

Imported foodstuffs were not the only basis for the development of chains of multiple shops; others were developed in Britain to sell books and stationery (initially from railway station kiosks), footwear, ready-made clothing, and drugs and other pharmaceutical products. In Britain shoemaking became factory-based from the late 1880s and by the 1900s it generally involved American machinery. Clothing came to be made in factories at about the same time: the number of factories in Leeds increased during the decade after 1881 from seven to 54. Initially factories concentrated upon men's clothing; however, by the turn of the century millinery and dressmaking had come within the orbit of the factory. By 1900 there were 257 multiple retailers controlling 11,650 shops in the United Kingdom, while in America there were 60 different chains of stores.

Among other innovations, cooperative production and distribution became a feature of northern industrial Britain, while mail order business was developed in America: with efficient communications, this provided a method of reaching the dispersed communities of rural America. The business was begun in 1872 by A. Montgomery Ward in Chicago, who was followed two decades later by Sears, Roebuck & Co.

Middle-class shopping and consumption was transformed from the 1850s with the remodeling in Paris of Bon Marché in 1852 by Aristide Boucicant. He decided to sell good quality apparel at reasonable and fixed prices through shop assistants whom he paid on commission. Sales were further maximized by advertisements. Modern department stores grew up in London and New York during the 1860s. In Germany they spread after the formation of the Empire – Tietz in 1879, Karstadt in 1881 and Althoff in 1885. The most rapid expansion of the American shops – Macy's of New York, Marshall Field of Chicago, and John Wanamaker of Philadelphia and New York – was at the turn of the century. Most such establishments aimed at the bourgeois market, but the working classes got their department stores in the form of bazaars. Woolworths pioneered this genre in both America and Britain and Marks & Spencer in England. In Britain there was also the Cooperative store, with its continually expanding range of goods.

... Under the influence of the large department stores and clothing bazaars' which gradually penetrated into the small towns from the cities ... a certain strong demand for cheaper dress and ready-made novelties was carried into the circle of working-class women in the last decade before the war.

W. ZIMMERMANN

William Lever and "Sunlight" Soap

A mass market in Britain began to develop through the steady rise in money wages from the mid-1860s and the fall in the cost of foodstuffs from the mid-1870s. This provided opportunities for businessmen alert to these trends, one of whom was William Hesketh Lever. As the son of a British wholesale grocer who joined the family firm in 1867, becoming a partner in 1872, Lever was well placed both to observe and respond to new trends in consumption patterns. Initially he expanded the range of goods in which his firm dealt and widened the geographical area that it served. But he also took an interest in American retailing, especially branding, backed by advertising and other forms of more aggressive sales promotion. Lever was more than an astute salesman. In 1885, again following American trends, he moved into manufacturing, so combining volume production with mass distribution. He acquired an existing soap works, and chose the name "Sunlight" for his new product. From 1889 Lever developed Port Sunlight, near Liverpool, not just as a manufacturing enterprise, but set within its own garden village, a reflection of both Lever's flair for grand affairs and his paternalistic style of management.

▲ Lever's success was recognized when he was created a baronet in 1911. He became Baron Leverhulme in 1917.

► Employing American-style methods of sales promotion and branding, Lever transformed the market for soap, which for mass sales until the 1880s had consisted of unbranded, unwrapped soap cakes, retailed like potatoes. His forceful approach caused a hostile reaction amongst other producers.

Urbanization

The beginnings of mass markets during the quarter of a century before 1914 came about not only through the gradual rise in working-class levels of income in some economies, but also as a result of the increasing concentration of people in growing towns and cities. By 1914 there were 51 cities on the continent of Europe with populations of over 250,000, together with a further 15 in the United Kingdom and 20 in the United States. In continental Europe the populations of these substantial cities grew so fast between 1890 and 1910 that they nearly doubled in size. The American experience was generally similar, though in Britain the pace of expansion was slower, because the country was already more urbanized. Even so, there was an average expansion in Britain of one-third over the same period. The outcome of this further urban development was that by 1910, nearly 23 percent of the American population resided in cities with populations of more than a quarter of a million. In Germany the proportion was 14.6 percent and in the United Kingdom 30.9 percent.

What was remarkable, however, was the continuing increase in the size of cities which were already very large, a trait noticeable in both advanced economies and those countries which were industrializing, like Russia. Between 1890 and 1910, the most rapidly expanding cities amongst this group on the continent of Europe were primarily either German – Essen, Hamburg, Düsseldorf, Nuremberg, Frankfurt-am-Main, Stuttgart, Leipzig, Dresden, Bremen and Hanover – or Russian – Lódź, Kiev, St Petersburg, Warsaw and Moscow. The only other European city in this group was Rotterdam, the population of

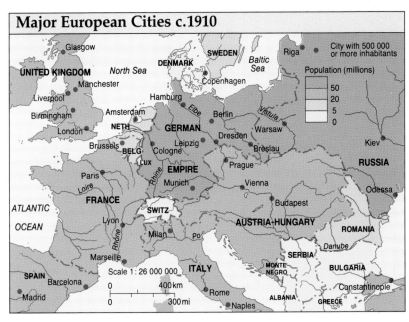

Major European Cities c.1910

which grew by 211 percent between 1890 and 1910. The forces for expansion were of varying kinds and not always the direct result of the development of manufacturing industry.

In Germany, Düsseldorf and Essen became large cities by 1910 as a result of the growth of industry – iron, steel, coal and engineering. But Frankfurt-am-Main and Leipzig were historic trading towns, long-standing sites of industrial fairs. During the 19th century Frankfurt became a modern commercial and financial center and toward the end of the century it acquired a local manufacturing base involving "new" industries such as electrical equipment manufacture.

▲ Urbanization is a good guide to the spread of industrialization. In early 20th-century Europe the population was increasingly moving to towns or cities. This was especially the case in northwestern Europe, the established industrial belt of the continent, which ran southeastwards from Glasgow to Paris, Lyons and Cologne. However, around this core of industrial cities, industrialization was spreading outwards, into Central Europe and in Mediterranean Europe.

◄ Some towns, such as Hamburg, became giant cities by the turn of the century not so much because of the growth of production, but rather as commercial service centers. Hamburg was the outlet for the products of Central Europe, in particular the industries of the middle Rhine and Bohemia, and was also the point of access for imports of raw materials from the rest of the world economy. Accordingly, manufacturing was largely restricted to supporting the activities of the port – shipbuilding and processing – and a large part of the population was involved in service trades, as merchants, bankers or clerks.

► Britain retained world dominance in shipbuilding. By 1913 the British mercantile marine had over eleven million tonnes of steam ships. With steam and sail combined, the United Kingdom accounted for a third of the world fleet in 1911; the German share was under ten percent, and the American less than three percent. During the five years before 1914 British shipyards built nearly two-thirds of the total tonnage launched.

Leipzig retained its importance as a trade fair city as well as a center of printing and publishing. In the north, Hamburg and Bremen developed processing industries and shipbuilding, while in southern Germany the further expansion of Stuttgart and Nuremberg at the turn of the century reflected the development of modern manufacturing methods in Württemberg and Bavaria.

Russian urbanization, and in particular the yet further growth of "giant" cities, was a reflection of the beginnings of industrialization. Like Lódź, St Petersburg was a cotton manufacturing center, but by 1900 it, together with the Moscow region, was also responsible for 20 percent of Russian iron and steel production. It also possessed some of the newer industries – electrical engineering, rubber, organic chemicals and the manufacture of motor cars – and by 1914 was also a major Russian financial center. Similarly, Moscow was by 1900 acquiring some of the characteristics of a mature industrial city. Important for metal refining and metal working, the city was also a center for textile production; its factory workforce increased from 67,000 to 100,000 during the 1890s.

The only "giant" British city which experienced continued rapid growth was Birmingham, which was a center for engineering and metalworking, producing by 1911 electrical products, tools, dies, munitions, bicycles and motor cars. But other cities grew too: Sheffield became a center of production of high-speed steels in the 1900s. Belfast, Hull and Newcastle thrived on shipbuilding and marine engineering – shipbuilding was the economy's most successful staple industry in international terms. Newcastle was a coal export port, while Hull's importance and continuing growth also derived from its processing industries; together with Grimsby, it grew with the development of steam trawl fishing. Bristol too expanded rapidly from a diversified economic base, with general engineering employing over ten thousand people by 1911, a port, and processing industries such as tobacco as well as brewing.

The process of the continued growth of some very large cities in the United States had characteristics in common with Germany, Russia and Britain. But it was the expansion of engineering in states like Ohio, Indiana, Illinois, Michigan and Wisconsin that led to the further growth in size of Detroit and Cleveland, as well as Chicago, and to a consequent change in their function from internal marketing centers to industrial conurbations. There were also some relatively small towns that mushroomed into very large cities by 1910, like Los Angeles, whose growth reflected the general rapid expansion of population in the American West, particularly California.

The further development of Cleveland and Detroit took place from a firm basis – they were Great Lakes ports which had expanded substantially as distributing centers following the completion of the Erie Canal in 1825. In Detroit the development of automobile manufacture sustained the city's growth. Cleveland had been a more substantial internal marketing center but, although enjoying good rail connections, the city's hinterland was essentially limited, and it remained best known as an oil processor. Chicago was

preeminent amongst the internal marketing centers of the United States. By 1880 it was the butcher, meat packer, grain distributor and lumber merchant of the United States. It also began to develop as an industrial center through the growth of a steel industry based upon the resources of the Lake Superior region, and it gained other industries which diversified its growing manufacturing base – shoe companies fleeing from organized labor in New England, German breweries, Jewish tailoring, and telephone factories which all drew in migrant labor.

New York, along with its satellite Newark, was the only eastern seaboard port city that continued to grow substantially at the turn of the century, nearly doubling in size between 1890 and 1910. The city's major function was as a port with an associated commercial and financial complex, but it also had a manufacturing function, embracing the clothing trade and tobacco processing, as well as printing, a shoe industry and glassmaking. Only Greater London was bigger in numbers.

Major North American Cities c.1910

CANADA

L Michigan
L Huron
L Ontario
Chicago
Detroit
L Erie
Boston
Cleveland
New York
Pittsburgh
Philadelphia
ATLANTIC OCEAN
St Louis
UNITED STATES OF AMERICA
Baltimore

St Lawrence
Hudson

City with 500 000 or more inhabitants
Scale 1: 24 000 000

◄ At the end of the 19th century some towns and cities along the southern shores of the Great Lakes, which had been primarily marketing centers, were transformed into sizable industrial places with the growth of engineering. This new development attracted labor from Canada, from the black population in the South, and from the Old World. In Chicago in 1890, over 40 percent of the city's population were foreign-born, and in 1915 Chicago had the third largest urban Polish community in the world.

Urban transport systems

Cities in advanced economies during the 19th century were places of dense settlement, until urban systems of mass transport were developed. The omnibus, a French innovation, catered primarily for the middle-class residential districts; it was the horse tramway which provided public transport, cheap enough for at least some sections of the working classes. This had started as isolated lines in New York and New Orleans in the 1830s and by the 1870s had spread to many European cities. However, the market for such transport systems was restricted by the technology employed, the conditions under which they operated and that problem of all commuter systems – the daily fluctuation in load.

Steam proved generally to be suitable only for suburban and rural light railways and tramways, particularly in Europe. Electrical traction was explored from 1881, and was quickly adopted in the United States. In Europe the switch to electric traction involving the Sprague system of overhead wires was less rapid. Other methods were already working – battery and conduit – and above all, there was a European esthetic objection to the overhead wire, especially along grand boulevards and in public squares. Authorities in Berlin, Birmingham, Munich, Nancy, Paris and Vienna initially refused to have the skylines of their city centers disrupted by cat's cradles of wires. However, by 1914 the electric tram with the offensive overhead wire had become commonplace in European cities. Between 1886 and 1910 the number of tram passengers in Austria-Hungary, France, Germany and Great Britain increased from 920 million to 6.7 billion. German and French towns and cities got off to a quick start, but British electrification came a decade later. Glasgow proved to be a model, the city deciding in 1894 to operate its own system and electrifying it from 1899 with Westinghouse equipment; other British municipalities followed, and the Glasgow example of municipally operated electrified tramways soon spread to the rest of Europe, France excepted.

Even with the tram, city streets remained so congested that planners considered placing the urban railway either above or below ground level. American cities, beginning with New York in 1867, built elevated lines, as later did some European cities such as Berlin and Vienna, whereas in London an underground system was developed, beginning with the opening of the Metropolitan line in 1863. The construction of London's first true "tube" underground railway, the City & South London, began in 1886. Employing electric traction, it opened in 1890. Glasgow, Budapest, Paris, Berlin and Hamburg all developed underground systems. In the United States, elevated city lines were electrified, beginning with New York in 1895, and the development of electric subways also got under way. The first New York subway was opened in 1904. At the same time, a further threat to the tram's dominance was beginning to appear. In 1903 and 1904 motor buses started to convey London passengers; carbon compounds now began to replace ammonia as the pollutant of urban streets.

◀ The electric trolley car made possible the development of suburbs, permitting towns to spread outwards, but it also connected the countryside to the cities, increasing their importance as retail and commercial centers. Above all, the trolley transformed the journey to work for the ordinary man.

▶ Traffic jams acted as a spur to the development of the underground railway network in London. This was designed initially to connect the main railway termini, but it then spread outwards and grew into a commuter network.

▼ Building the new urban transport systems initially caused disruption. However, their construction represented sizable investment which accelerated economic growth and in particular encouraged the growth of the electrical manufacturing industry.

Industrial concentration

By the 1880s, large concentrations of industrial capital had emerged, especially in Germany and the United States, and by the 1900s some large companies were wielding monopoly power over their respective industries. The growth of firm size is a complex process. Technical and financial economies that arose from higher production capacities were important. These led to production economies of scale and also allowed firms to become more specialized. There emerged clearer differentiations of internal functions, such as management structures, the conduct of marketing, the growth of internal finance and the support of research and development, where it was cheaper to undertake such activities within a firm, rather than employing outside specialists. In particular, some "new" products required closer contact with the customer; German sewing machine and bicycle producers, for example, moved into both retailing and managing their own exports. As a result of such growth, output in some industries became concentrated in the hands of fewer firms. The increasing size of enterprises went hand in hand with the gradual disappearance of family-based firms and the consequent divorce of ownership from control. Salaried managers became a new industrial caste and, in at least some German industries, measured their success through the continuing growth of their respective firms, often undertaken by acquiring other enterprises.

Industrial concentration was carried further in the United States, Germany and to some extent in Britain by the formation of cartels, trusts and holding companies in industries such as sugar, oil and iron and steel, and by a spate of mergers. Following the Wall Street crash of 1893, American companies rationalized production by concentrating manufacturing in a limited number of plants, and coupled this to national marketing and distribution networks. Britain's efforts at rationalization were not so successful.

Vertical integration – whereby companies acquired their sources of raw materials and took over the firms that bought their semi-finished wares – also took place, especially in the American metals industries and in German chemicals. By 1905, big business had come to stay in the United States and Germany, and had gained a toehold in Britain.

International economic rivalry

The growth of American and German manufacturing from the 1880s led to the displacement of Britain as the "workshop of the world". Britain's share of the world market was sharply cut back during the 1890s, and Germany became her major competitor in Europe. American competition arose from the mid-1890s, but the bulk of American exports were still made up of raw materials, and so did not affect British trade. The rise of this competition did not become a matter of national concern until German and American products entered the domestic British market.

Germany had technological superiority in organic chemicals and electrical equipment, and the global spread of German exports was coupled with the growth of a German mercantile marine, now in a position to rival British companies. Imports of American machinery and manufactures rose eightfold between 1890 and 1899. American promoters were behind the programs for the electrification of the London underground, whilst American shipping acquisitions forced the British Government to provide subsidies and finance to the Cunard Co. to construct two fast mail ships, so as to secure the continuance of the British character of the firm. The Imperial Tobacco Company held off the attack by the American Tobacco Co. on the British market in 1902. These experiences led to British concern that weakening economic power might also mean waning political power, a concern which persisted through the first decade of the century, even after the jingoism of the Boer War period had subsided.

THE MODEL T FORD AND THE MASS MARKET

The man who designed the car for everyday life was Henry Ford. The son of a farming family of Irish and Flemish origin, Ford's reputation as an automobile engineer was established by his second car, built between 1897 and 1899 with the backing of local Detroit merchants. Whereas Ford at this stage wanted to build racers, his backers were interested in commercial vehicles; Ford left and his original company was established as the Cadillac Motor Co.

Ford in 1902 turned to the development of a car to be sold to the mass market. The Ford Motor Co. was formed in June 1903, when the mass-market Model A was put on public sale at a retail price of $850. The first small car that Ford produced in any quantity, involving standardized design, was the N of 1906–07, which sold initially at $600. In 1906–07 the company moved to Highland Park, which at first occupied 24 hectares (60 acres) but eventually spread to 92 hectares (230 acres), of which 21 hectares consisted of floor space. Here, from 1 October 1908, the Model T went into production. It was a standardized utility vehicle with interchangeable parts; Ford had been responsible for the basic concept, but the detailed design had been undertaken by two company engineers – C. Harold Wills and Joseph Galamb. Depending upon specification, complete cars were first sold at prices in the range $850 to $1000, but by August 1916 these had fallen to $345 to $360. It was the company's sole product until 1927, with output expanding rapidly until the early 1920s.

By 1913 there was a Ford car dealer in every American town with population greater than 2000. The T, always a basic car, was particularly attractive to the rural communities of the American mid-West and High Plains. Its volume production, reaching 2000 a day by 1916, was only achieved by the development of the moving production line at Highland Park between 1910 and 1914. This involved bringing the work to the labor force, and at waist height to reduce redundant effort. The concept of a continually moving track was introduced in the spring of 1913, initially for the assembly of the flywheel magneto coil.

Giovanni Agnelli, one of the founders of Fiat, returned to Turin in 1912 after a VIP tour of the Highland Park factory convinced that he had seen the future: "I have just returned from America where I wanted to see for myself the danger that is threatening – competition is becoming more and more difficult every day." Fiat decided to integrate the production process on the American pattern, and by the end of World War I the immense new Lingotto factory had begun to rise on the outskirts of Turin.

▶ The Model T was the car for rural America in the 1910s. During 1916–17, they were built at a rate of about 2000 a day and, by 1921, five million had been produced. Based on a common chassis and running gear, the car could be refashioned in many ways.

▲▶ When the Model T was launched in 1908 it was cheap. However with mass production it became even cheaper and within eight years the price of the basic model had fallen by 60 percent, despite wartime inflation in the United States.

The Ford Four Cylinder, Twenty Horse Power, Five Passenger Touring Car $850.00 Fob. Detroit

Ford Motor Company
Detroit

◄ Ford constructed cars from the late 1890s and this is his first — the 1896 car — which owed much to two other Detroit automobile enthusiasts C. B. King and O. E. Barthel.

◄◄ Ford's success came from the economics of production engineering, arising from the interchangeability of parts, married with the assembly line. The latter had its origins in Chicago meat packing.

► Manufacture in volume needed a flow system of production and the "line" had many applications. Here cakes on a conveyor belt are being iced at waist height.

▲ From the 1880s "scientific management" aimed at making human labor more efficient through inducing it to behave like a machine. By the 1980s, robots, controlled by computers, were dispensing with human labor.

39

Datafile

Increasingly from the mid-19th century the advanced industrial economies came into greater and greater contact with the nonindustrial world. The temperate and tropical belts, formally colonized, provided raw materials, markets for some manufacturers, and places of settlement and investment. Until the 1880s the main contacts were with the temperate primary producers and the Orient. By 1900 the focus shifted to the tropical world, especially Africa.

UK in Latin America

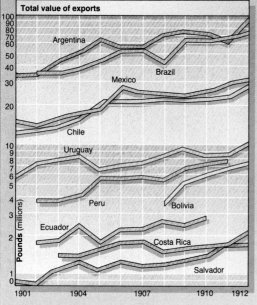

Total value of exports

▲ By 1914 a quarter of British overseas lending consisted of investments in Latin America. Before 1890 the main areas of investment had been Argentina and Brazil, but after the turn of the century British investment encompassed the whole of the continent. It principally consisted of the finance of railroad construction.

◄ During the early 20th century Latin American exports grew substantially. The most important trading economies were the large, temperate, countries of Argentina and Brazil. Argentina supplied Britain with grains and from 1901 chilled beef, whereas Mexican trade was largely directed to the United States.

► Japanese overseas trade grew steadily from the early 1890s until 1914, when it expanded rapidly as a result of the war-induced boom, and especially the lack of European competition in Asian and Pacific markets. Until 1914 Japanese exports consisted largely of semi-manufactures, with a new trade in cotton yarn developing from the late 1890s. In 1914 raw silk, silk piece-goods, cotton yarn and cotton cloth comprised over 50 percent of exports, and they were to retain this dominance until the mid-1930s.

Japanese foreign trade

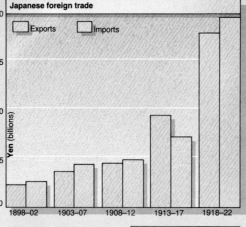

Population 1900

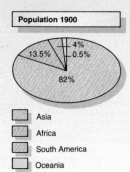

- Asia
- Africa
- South America
- Oceania

◄ Estimates of world population, and its distribution, at this period are difficult. Asia was the most populated continent of the nonindustrial world and has sizeable, crowded cities. In Africa, population may even have been declining slightly at the beginning of the 20th century.

► The pace of railroad construction in the industrial world slowed from 1900. By contrast, in the colonial world the turn of the century saw the establishment of primary routes.

Railroad systems

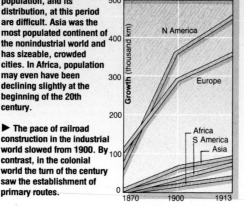

In 1913 probably about two-thirds of the world's population lived outside the industrial and industrializing economies of Europe and the United States, though it is difficult to be precise because of inadequate and unreliable information. From the 1830s there was a growing divergence in average income per head between the populations of the industrial and industrializing countries on the one hand, and that of the rest of the world on the other, and by 1913 average incomes per head in developed countries were about three and a half times higher than those prevailing in the rest of the world. But within the "underdeveloped" world itself there were equally striking contrasts in material advance. In 1913 three temperate countries of recent European settlement – Australia, Canada and New Zealand – had average incomes per head higher than the average for all developed countries; in Australia and Canada average incomes indeed approached those of the most developed of the industrial economies. At the other end of the spectrum, average incomes per head in Latin American countries such as Argentina, Chile and Uruguay were only just over half of the average of developed countries, whereas in Asia they were only barely over a quarter.

COLONIES AND PRIMARY PRODUCERS

European influences
The West and the
tropical world
Expanding transport and
trade
Formal and informal
colonization
Japanese industrial
growth

These wide and growing differences in average income were the product of many factors. One was the restricted geographical diffusion of industrialization – the main driving force behind the growth of incomes – before 1914; another was the unequal gains which arose from the trade between the industrial economies and the rest of the world. Third, and particularly with respect to the Dominions of the British Empire, were the advantages that accrued to the colonizing settlers from low ratios of population to natural resources. The increasing economic contact between the industrial economies and the rest of the world led in the latter to extensive, rather than intensive, economic development – the wider spread of commercial agriculture and the extraction of minerals. Although incomes rose as a consequence, the growth was not as rapid as that in Europe and North America.

European influences

Trade with the rest of the world, and in some cases investment and settlement, carried with them the diffusion of a European lifestyle. In certain areas, such as Latin America, there was already a foundation of European culture and social mores as a result of earlier Spanish and

▼ The temperate and tropical worlds became increasingly important to the advanced industrial economies as sources of raw materials and foodstuffs. New plantation systems were developed by Western capital and management, but frequently this involved transferring labor to work them. During the expansion of the Ceylon tea industry from the 1800s, Tamil labor from southern India was brought to the island to work the estates.

Portuguese colonization. This led to the development of large cities, usually ports, similar in architecture, layout, transport and other utility systems to Western cities such as London, Berlin, Paris and Madrid, through the influence of local middle-class groups who looked particularly to Europe for fashions and styles of living. By the 1880s European economic and social contact were also beginning to affect the tropical world and China, although European migration to these areas remained minimal.

From the 1860s the temperate lands in both the northern and southern hemispheres, together with India, were developed by European colonizers to provide the industrial economies of the world – in particular northwestern Europe – with foodstuffs and raw materials. The renewed momentum of growth of the industrial economies from the 1890s increased this demand, particularly for raw materials, and especially for basic ingredients of the new technologies of the late 19th and early 20th centuries, such as copper, rubber and bauxite. It was precisely these new economic demands which from the 1880s led to increased American and European involvement with those areas of the tropical world that would be able to supply their requirements.

Transport and trade

A growing marker of the impact of the advanced economies upon the rest of the world was the spread of the railroad, as its construction was largely initiated by American and European promoters and financed by American and European capital. Further, the track and rolling stock were usually supplied by either American or European firms, and the senior administrative staffs of the operating companies were generally American or European. In 1870 only 6.2 percent of the world's railroad lines lay outside the continents of Europe and North America. By 1900 that proportion had increased to over 18 percent and it rose to over 26 percent in 1913. Railroad construction during the years before 1914 expanded considerably in Central and South America, but the most dramatic increase was in Africa.

The volume of trade experienced by the tropical world as a whole increased threefold between 1883 and 1913. This was largely a result of increased exports from the tropics of cotton, oilseeds, cocoa, coffee, tobacco, bananas and rubber, with minerals making a contribution only after 1900. Alongside this production for export, the output of rice and other foodstuffs increased to supply the growing local labor forces involved

in commercial export agriculture. The substantial post-1880 expansion of tropical exports led to rises in net national income per head, some countries and regions in particular experiencing very rapid export-led growth. Exports from West Africa grew by a factor of 5.48 between 1883 and 1913. Comparable expansion was experienced by Thailand, Ceylon, Central Africa and Indochina.

The growing railroad systems in the non-industrial world, both temperate and tropical, frequently radiated out from ports, some new, others well established. Hong Kong had been a barren island in 1841, but in 1900 41 percent of China's foreign trade was conducted through this British colony. The Treaty of Shimonoseki (1895) allowed foreigners to invest in, and operate, factories in Chinese treaty ports and in Hong Kong. This resulted in the development of textile and flour mills, cement works, tobacco processing, vegetable oil extraction and match manufacture.

By the 1860s the major merchants of Calcutta, together with the agents and managing agents of shipping and insurance companies, jute and cotton mills, other manufacturing companies, tea plantations, and coal and other mines were almost exclusively European. Further, as was to happen in Hong Kong from the 1890s, so in

▼ Cotton had been developed in Egypt as an export crop since the 1830s. By 1913 the area devoted to cotton cultivation was twice as great as in the mid-1890s, partly due to cotton now being included in the crop rotation every two years, as opposed to every three, and partly made possible by the greater supply of water made available for irrigation by the Delta barrage and the Aswan dam. Egyptian exports of cotton rose rapidly between the early 1890s and 1913. Britain took half of the crop exported, and Egypt's other main customers were the United States, Germany, France and Russia.

▲ Laying out estates drew upon land and labor, both relatively cheap resources in the underdeveloped countries. Not all of this development was the result of Western capital, however. In Ceylon, indigenous entrepreneurs played a major role. The 1911 census counted 93,000 owners, managers and "superior staff" on estates and plantations, of which only 1,600 were expatriate Europeans.

Calcutta 30 years earlier European mercantile houses had begun to diversify their activities away from trade through acting as labor contractors for the railways, acting as agents for railway companies and insurance companies, owning ships and investing in jute mills, cotton spinning mills, tea plantations and coal mines. Where such enterprises were established by European mercantile houses as joint stock companies, they were frequently formed under British law and therefore registered in London.

As in Calcutta and Hong Kong, British mercantile houses in Brazilian ports from the 1870s spread their range of activities through investing in the development of local manufacturing capacity – textile plants, the shoe industry, and sugar and flour mills. The British-dominated Brazilian ports also became centers for the ac-

tivities of local, indigenous entrepreneurs. Coal, iron and textile machinery from Britain constituted 14 percent, 11 percent and 9.9 percent respectively of Brazilian imports during the opening years of the 20th century. There were comparable developments in the other major Latin American ports – Buenos Aires, the second port of the Americas, visited by 5137 vessels totaling 13.8 million tonnes in 1913, and Montevideo, with an international trade about half as great.

Amongst the Brazilian middle classes, especially during the mid-century, Paris was the ideal, but it was with Britain that Brazil had its greatest commercial dealings because of the dominance over the country's trade of British export-import interests. The desire of the Brazilian urban middle classes to copy European patterns of consumption required foodstuffs, furnishings and luxury goods. Urban improvement in Brazil moved in parallel with developments in Europe. Between 1862 and 1895 £2 million was invested in the sewage and water supply systems of Rio de Janeiro, and gas lighting companies were established in the late 1870s. By 1912 there were nine British-owned urban transport companies in Brazil. During the 1880s the British introduced sport. The first soccer match was played by the English in São Paulo in 1886; it was to become the national sport of most Brazilians.

Formal and informal colonization
In spite of the rise in incomes amongst the primary producers from mid-century and within the tropical world from the 1880s, critics had grounds for stressing the negative aspects of the international activities of Western societies. The opening up of the markets of the less developed world to Western manufactures led to the decline

Malayan Rubber

The demand for rubber grew substantially after 1900, mainly as a result of the development of the automobile industry in the United States. This led to the growth of a commercial plantation industry, largely in Malaya, with the result that by 1914 exports from Malaya accounted for 38 percent of world trade in rubber. The industry began in the last quarter of the 19th century, when plants germinated at Kew Gardens in England from seed collected in South America were sent to Singapore. Trial tappings may have taken place earlier, but commercial exploitation did not begin until the mid-1890s when, with the rise in rubber prices due to the growth of the bicycle trade, the crop provided as an attractive alternative to coffee.

Initially rubber in Malaya was interplanted with earlier cash crops, such as coffee and coconuts, but the area of rubber stands in the Federated Malay States increased from 140 hectares (345 acres) in 1895 to 17,573 hectares (43,425 acres) by 1905. Commercial exports from Malaya began in 1904–05, joining supplies from Ceylon drawn from trees planted in the early 1890s, and this commercial plantation supply was well received, though wild "jungle" production, largely from South America, still dominated the market. The labor force largely consisted of Indian immigrants.

The development of mass production techniques in the American automobile industry resulted in phenomenal expansion in 1909–10, when the number of plantation companies floated reached a peak of 80. Prices rose to 12s 9d per ton in April 1910. By 1913 they had fallen to 2s 9d but plantation development continued, albeit at a slower, more circumspect, pace. Malayan exports became a regular flow from 1909, rising from 3,331 tonnes to 47,457 tonnes by 1914.

▼ The need for rubber grew as the demand for bicycles and cars increased, with the output of the American automobile industry rising rapidly. The supply of rubber was enlarged by plantations in Malaya and the East Indies and from 1900 the plantation product carried a higher market price than the wild Amazonian supply.

of local handicraft industries; and Western imports acted as a brake upon the local development of modern industry. Further, the expansion of commercial agriculture in the temperate and tropical "undeveloped" world disrupted tradiional labor markets, whilst the "development" process was generally not only propelled but controlled by Western capital. Foreign mortgage companies financed the new farms and plantations, their products were processed and stored in Western warehousing and silo companies, their domestic transshipment was undertaken by foreign-controlled railroads, their export was conducted through foreign-controlled ports, financed by foreign merchant houses, banks and insurance companies and their international movement took place in foreign-owned ships.

Development, therefore, occurred under the auspices of a foreign, frequently British, import-export complex. The profits arising from it went largely overseas and although these, together with the proceeds of enhanced exports, amortised the foreign investment that had initiated them, locals, especially the growing urban masses, saw this process as a stream of "tribute" arising from the informal foreign control of their country. This was a populist feeling, often articulated by middle-class radical politicians in opposition to the ruling elites who generally dominated government and had a symbiotic relationship with foreign capital, from which they had materially benefited. Accordingly, economic development initiated by foreign capital often widened the social gulf and struck the sparks that would lead to economic nationalism.

Such "informal" Western control was a particular characteristic of American and European expansion in the temperate world, especially that of the British in southern Latin America. Western expansion in the tropics and the Far East occurred primarily from the 1880s in a political climate of the "new imperialism", which was characterized by contemporaries as showing a strong link

between political and economic power. In addition to the formal colonization of some areas there was also informal economic colonization of traditional regimes which now had much faded auras of grandeur, as in the Ottoman Empire, the Persian Empire and China. China in particular was forcibly opened up from the mid-19th century through the treaty port system (that gave Europeans trading rights through particular ports) and the use by Europeans of extraterritorial rights. The Japanese, however, though interested in Western technology, consciously decided that their country was not to be subjected to the same process of competitive Western economic and political expansion and penetration.

▲ Diamonds were discovered at Kimberley in 1870 and by 1874 it was a cosmopolitan community of 50,000 people. In the early 1870s South Africa exported £1.6 million worth of diamonds annually. Kimberley created the migrant labor system; African workers were confined to the compound to stop illicit diamond dealing and prevent desertion.

▼ Gold mining at Witwatersrand grew from 1886. The Kimberley pattern of large-scale units provided the means for mechanical extraction.

Japanese industrialization

Japan was the only country outside Europe and North America to experience industrialization before 1914. Average income in Japan probably increased from being on a par with the Asian average in 1860 to exceeding it by 60 percent in 1913. This increase, while exceptional in Asian terms, was nevertheless not sufficient to keep up with the economically developed countries. The onset of modern Japanese economic growth had come with two shocks: the country's forced opening to the West in the mid-1850s through the imposition of free trade treaties, and an internal revolution which resulted in the accession of Emperor Meiji in 1868. The Emperor's government pursued two policies – *fukoku kyohei* (a rich country and strong army) and *shokusan kogyo* (increased production). These were conducted through the deliberate import of Western technology, with the government investing in infrastructure and manufacturing industry. For political reasons the government set its face against large imports of financial capital, so the beginnings were slow, the first signs of growth appearing in the mid-1880s; but it was propelled forward by increases in agricultural productivity and the rise from the 1900s of a "hybrid" manufacturing sector based upon small-scale industry but using the electric motor.

There was no change in agricultural organization, the Japanese countryside being characterized by small family farms. Agriculture continued to produce the same major products – rice, wheat, barley and the important industrial raw material, silk. Agricultural productivity rose as a result of a shift to arable production, the increasing application of fertilizer and improved irrigation techniques. Through the Land Tax the government was able to cream off the growing agricultural surplus and redistribute it to the emerging new industries. Increased agricultural productivity also allowed the transfer of labor from the countryside to the "hybrid" and modern manufacturing industries in the towns and ports. Finally, the peasant silk industry, along with tea, was a source of export products. The modern sector of the Japanese economy consisted above all of cotton textile production, which used domestic raw material supplies until the mid-1880s, when they were replaced by cheaper Indian imports.

By 1905 finished cotton and silk textile exports were replacing the traditional agricultural crops of tea and raw silk. The domestic modern industrial sector had by then reached a sufficient size for excise duties on consumption, income and business taxes, together with the customs duties, to replace the Land Tax as the fiscal engine of growth. Japan's labor force was now an urban proletariat, some of whom had received tertiary technical education. Investment in traditional techniques of production was declining and economic growth was becoming increasingly propelled by export demand, as the low level of income restricted the home market. During the years before 1914 the foundations of Japanese heavy industry were laid through the development of iron and steel, engineering and shipbuilding behind protective tariffs.

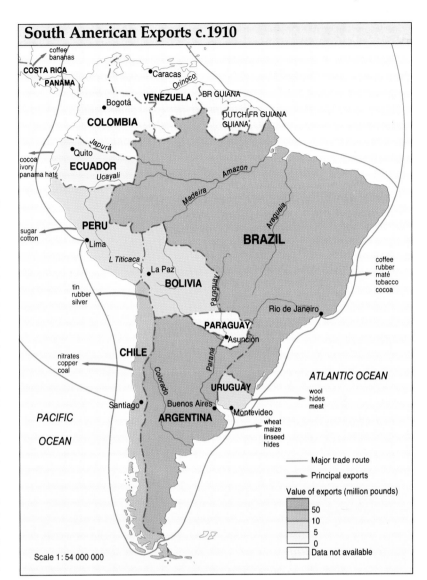

South American Exports c.1910

coffee
bananas

COSTA RICA
PANAMA

•Caracas
Orinoco

VENEZUELA   BR GUIANA

Bogotá
COLOMBIA

DUTCH FR GUIANA
GUIANA

Japurá

cocoa
ivory
panama hats

•Quito
ECUADOR

Ucayali

Amazon

Madeira

Araguaia

sugar
cotton

PERU

•Lima

BRAZIL

L Titicaca

coffee
rubber
maté
tobacco
cocoa

•La Paz

BOLIVIA

tin
rubber
silver

Paraguay

Rio de Janeiro•

PARAGUAY

•Asunción

ATLANTIC OCEAN

CHILE

Paraná

URUGUAY

wool
hides
meat

nitrates
copper
coal

Colorado

Santiago•   Buenos Aires•

•Montevideo

wheat
maize
linseed
hides

ARGENTINA

PACIFIC

OCEAN

—— Major trade route
→ Principal exports

Value of exports (million pounds)

50
10
5
0
Data not available

Scale 1 : 54 000 000

▲ Latin America increasingly became an important source of raw materials and foodstuffs during the late 19th century. Coffee exports from Brazil led the way, but from the 1880s the opening up of the Argentinean pampas led to the shipment to Europe of grain and, with refrigeration, meat in the 1890s. In contrast Chile developed as a major supplier of nitrates, for the production of fertilizers and explosives, and of copper.

◄ By 1914 Japan was a major cotton producer, exporting substantial quantities. The origins of the 1914 industry lay in private mills, beginning in the early 1880s, of which the most important was the Osaka Boseki. It developed double-shift operations, involving night work, so that the mill was in production for 22 out of 24 hours a day. The labor force was largely made up of young female workers, drawn from the countryside, housed in purpose-built dormitories and subject to quasi-military discipline.

THE SPREAD OF RAIL TRANSPORT IN AFRICA

The "scramble for Africa" during the 1880s, when the European Powers rushed to plant their flags in every corner of the continent, had largely consisted of arbitrary boundary lines drawn on frequently inadequate maps in smoke-filled conference rooms in European capitals. But from the 1890s the African interior began to be penetrated by steel rails, often from newly laid-out ports. It was often the European and American railroad builders in Africa who first surveyed the land in detail, and their subsequent activity frequently involved a close public and formal alignment of state power with private capital. Germany, through state-backed corporations, built lines in Tanganyika from 1891, in Southwest Africa from 1897, in Kamerun from 1900, and in Togo from 1904. Italian construction got underway in Eritrea from 1887 and in Libya from 1911. The French built in Dakar and Niger from 1881, in Djibouti from 1897, in Dahomey from 1900 and in the Ivory Coast from 1904. However, the most substantial builders of railroads in Africa from the 1890s were the British.

The intentions of the railroad builders, like those of the imperialists themselves, mixed economic motives with strategic, and projects were financed which brought new lines to regions that were sometimes under the control of rival imperial powers. In eastern Africa the two main centers of British construction were the Sudan and Kenya. The Sudanese system was of military origin. In East Africa a railroad was built by the British from Mombasa to Lake Victoria, starting in 1895 and completed in December 1901 with an overall length of 954 kilometers (600 miles). Railroads had been laid in South Africa since 1860 and following the Boer War they were consolidated, with the lines in the Transvaal and Orange Free State becoming Central South African Railways. At the same time and during the Boer War period, new trunk lines were built in southern Africa, largely to provide communication with Northern and Southern Rhodesia.

The mixture of political and economic motives was manifested when the British imperialist Cecil Rhodes planned the Cape-to-Cairo railroad, which reached Bulawayo in 1897 with a branch to Salisbury in 1902, thereby providing a continuous route of 3392 kilometers (2100 miles) connecting Cape Town and Beira. But instead of aiming for the Rift Valley and the Nile as originally planned its builders took the railroad to the Wankie coalfield, reached in 1903. The lure of minerals then diverted the route even further from the original plan to the copper-rich area of the southern Congo border in 1909. By 1910 it had arrived at Elizabethville in the Belgian Congo. Here it linked with the railroad that ran inland from Benguela to the Katanga copperbelt, for which the British held the mining concession. British trade with central and southern Africa between the 1880s and the period 1911–15 increased by a factor of 3.3, whereas total British trade over the same period grew by less than two times.

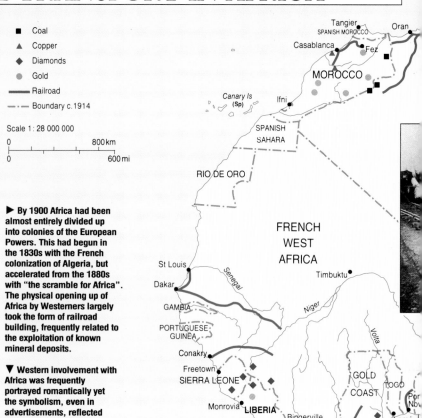

Coal ■
Copper ▲
Diamonds ◆
Gold ●
Railroad ▬
Boundary c.1914 - ‑ -

Scale 1 : 28 000 000

0   800 km
0   600 mi

▶ By 1900 Africa had been almost entirely divided up into colonies of the European Powers. This had begun in the 1830s with the French colonization of Algeria, but accelerated from the 1880s with "the scramble for Africa". The physical opening up of Africa by Westerners largely took the form of railroad building, frequently related to the exploitation of known mineral deposits.

▼ Western involvement with Africa was frequently portrayed romantically yet the symbolism, even in advertisements, reflected European concepts of dominance and superiority.

Gulf of Guinea

▼ Building tracks across a poorly explored continent posed considerable engineering difficulties, as a result of both the geology of the continent – it was a tableland – and its vegetation – the jungle. However in the tropics the local supply of hardwoods eased the construction of bridges.

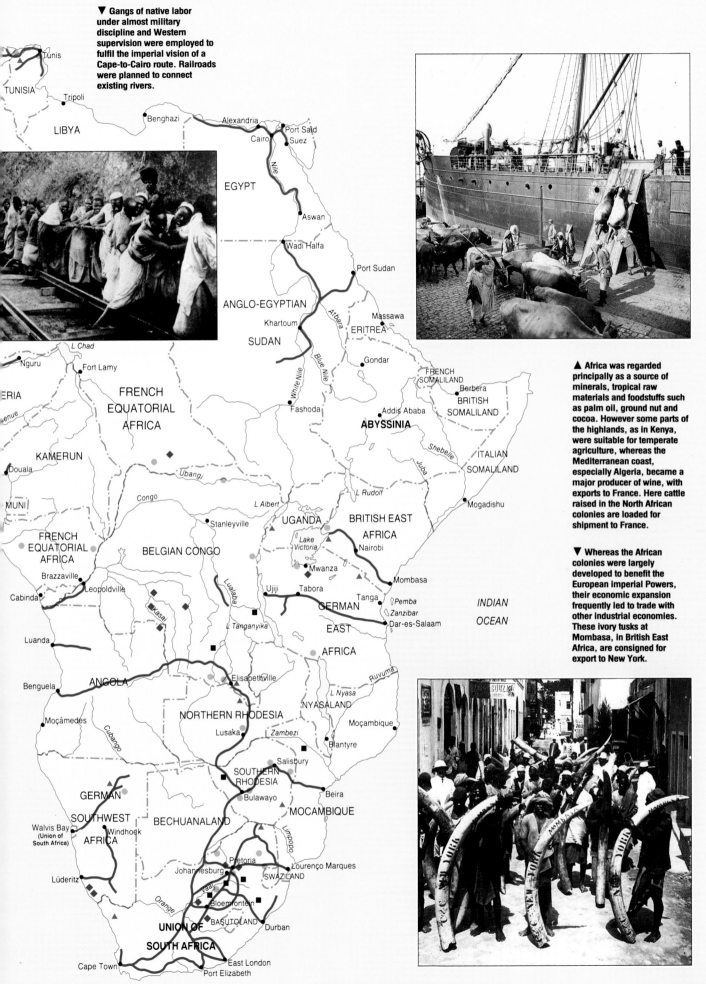

▼ Gangs of native labor under almost military discipline and Western supervision were employed to fulfil the imperial vision of a Cape-to-Cairo route. Railroads were planned to connect existing rivers.

▲ Africa was regarded principally as a source of minerals, tropical raw materials and foodstuffs such as palm oil, ground nut and cocoa. However some parts of the highlands, as in Kenya, were suitable for temperate agriculture, whereas the Mediterranean coast, especially Algeria, became a major producer of wine, with exports to France. Here cattle raised in the North African colonies are loaded for shipment to France.

▼ Whereas the African colonies were largely developed to benefit the European imperial Powers, their economic expansion frequently led to trade with other industrial economies. These ivory tusks at Mombasa, in British East Africa, are consigned for export to New York.

TUNISIA
Tunis
Tripoli
LIBYA
Benghazi
Alexandria
Port Said
Cairo
Suez
EGYPT
Nile
Aswan
Wadi Halfa
Port Sudan
ANGLO-EGYPTIAN
Khartoum
SUDAN
Atbara
Massawa
ERITREA
FRENCH SOMALILAND
Berbera
BRITISH SOMALILAND
White Nile
Blue Nile
Gondar
Fashoda
Addis Ababa
ABYSSINIA
ITALIAN SOMALILAND
Shebelle
Juba
Mogadishu
L Chad
Nguru
Fort Lamy
FRENCH EQUATORIAL AFRICA
KAMERUN
Douala
Ubangi
MUNI
Congo
L Albert
L Rudolf
Stanleyville
UGANDA
Lake Victoria
BRITISH EAST AFRICA
Nairobi
FRENCH EQUATORIAL AFRICA
Brazzaville
BELGIAN CONGO
Mwanza
Mombasa
Cabinda
Leopoldville
Lualaba
Ujiji
Tabora
Tanga
GERMAN
Pemba
Zanzibar
Kasai
L Tanganyika
Dar-es-Salaam
Luanda
EAST
INDIAN OCEAN
Benguela
ANGOLA
Elisabethville
Ruvuma
AFRICA
Moçâmedes
NORTHERN RHODESIA
L Nyasa
NYASALAND
Moçambique
Cubango
Lusaka
Zambezi
Blantyre
Salisbury
Walvis Bay (Union of South Africa)
GERMAN SOUTHWEST AFRICA
Windhoek
BECHUANALAND
SOUTHERN RHODESIA
Bulawayo
Beira
MOCAMBIQUE
Lüderitz
Pretoria
Johannesburg
Lourenço Marques
SWAZILAND
Orange
Vaal
Bloemfontein
BASUTOLAND
Durban
UNION OF SOUTH AFRICA
Cape Town
East London
Port Elizabeth
Limpopo

47

Datafile

By 1900 the world in many substantial respects had become an integrated economic community. One of the main factors responsible for this coalescence was the increasing speed of communications arising from the growth of telegraph networks, the further expansions of the system of oceanic cables and, in the advanced world, the growing use of the telephone. Distance still remained a problem, but continents were now straddled by railways and oceans crisscrossed by steamship lines. This produced a global market place, although dominated by the advanced industrial economies. Consumers in industrial cities could buy the produce of the whole world, while the advanced industrial economies were exporting manufactures to the Third World. International trade did knit the world together, but such strands of interdependence were now augmented by flows of labor and capital. However, as with visible trade, the migration of capital and labor overseas was largely a process which reinforced the economic power of the advanced economies.

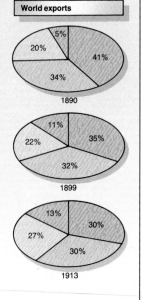

Trade beyond Europe

▲ There was sharp contrast in the trading patterns of the main European industrial economies. Both France and Germany were more dependent upon intra-European trade than Britain. Only 30 percent of British exports went to other European economies in 1913, only half as much as from France and Germany.

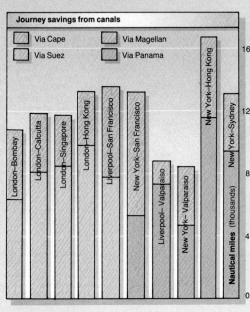

Journey savings from canals

◄ The opening of the Suez and Panama canals in 1869 and 1914 respectively had a considerable effect upon intercontinental oceanic routes, by reducing voyages that had previously involved either rounding the Cape of Good Hope or the more perilous journey around the Horn. However, the canals could only be used by steam vessels.

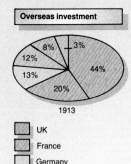

Overseas investment

◄ From the mid-1850s the British economy developed as the world's banker, supplying long-term finance, particularly for the construction of railways overseas. French and German capital exports were largely directed to the outer periphery of Europe. American finance began to be of global importance from the 1880s.

► The British share of world trade in manufacturing declined sharply during the 1890s as a result of the rapid emergence of German and American economic power.

World exports

The outstanding characteristic of economic affairs during the 19th century had been the emergence of a world economy. This was a result initially of the further development of trade, of swelling numbers of migrants, and lastly, from the 1850s, of the international migration of capital, above all from Britain to the United States, Australia and New Zealand, and Canada. These processes were eased by the fall in international transport costs and the increased speed of international communications. Until the mid-1880s the sailing ship remained the main mover of bulk cargoes. Mass-produced steel, together with major improvements in machine tool capabilities, finally tipped the balance in favor of steam from the late 1880s. High-pressure steam, when put in harness with triple-expansion engines, and nurtured by the development of a worldwide chain of coaling stations, made possible the operation of the steam tramp (cargo ship) of the last decades of the 19th century. The commercial operation of the steam tramp, nonetheless, depended upon a global communication system of intercontinental cables, through which owners and managing agents could readily give sailing orders to masters. The first Atlantic submarine cable was successfully laid in 1866.

In the growing complexity of world economic intercourse, trade and finance now moved from

ECONOMIC INTERDEPENDENCE

bilateral to multilateral relationships, whereby international balances were settled indirectly through transactions with "third" countries. Such a pattern of settlements, which became firmly established during the third quarter of the 19th century, did facilitate the further growth of international dealings, but also made the world economy more vulnerable to shocks. The growing integration of world economic activity provided the industrial and industrializing economies with new sources of food and raw materials and new markets for exports of manufactures. Areas of European temperate settlement also became important suppliers to the Old World of additional food, as well as being the new homes of increasing numbers of Europeans.

European trade

European foreign trade, excluding Russia, increased enormously between 1830 and 1914. In 1913 European trade was dominated by the three major industrial economies – Germany, France and the United Kingdom. These economies had collectively a share of two-thirds of total European exports and conducted over three-quarters of intra-European trade. Britain was less dependent upon intra-European trade as opposed to world trade than were Germany and France. From the 1870s a new pattern of trade started to develop.

▼ Exports from the tropical world grew substantially at the turn of the century. Nigeria's export trade expanded from £1.8 million in 1900 to £6.1 million by 1914, on the basis of palm products – which accounted for nearly 70 percent – tin, groundnuts and cocoa. Their development frequently involved slave or near slave labor.

An ever larger share consisted of the exchange of equivalent manufactures between the industrial economies in place of the exchange of manufactures for raw materials and foodstuffs. British imports of manufactures were nearly 19 percent by 1913. At first these largely consisted of fine textiles for the middle classes, but they were joined by organic dyestuffs and scientific instruments from Germany and motor cars, electrical machinery and iron and steel from the United States. Textiles, especially cottons, were a particular characteristic of British manufactured exports; the export trade of Germany and the United States was characterized by a greater importance of iron and steel. Although both Britain and Germany were advanced industrial economies before 1914, both also exported primary goods. Britain was a major world supplier of coal, and from 1900 Germany was an important provider of beet sugar to the rest of Europe.

French exports throughout the 19th century consisted primarily of high quality textiles – silks, cottons and woollens – for the richer markets of Europe and the United States, though Japanese competition for silks in America began in the 1890s. The French North African colonies became a significant market for French cotton cloth by 1913. French exports of other goods, such as chemicals and motor vehicles, were also growing.

▲ The Spanish–American war in 1898 led to the development of the United States as an imperialist power, reflecting expanding American economic might and wider trade. In 1903, the United States signed a treaty with the new Republic of Panama, acquiring a perpetual lease of the Panama Canal Zone, thus gaining control from Colombia. However, even after the completion of the canal in 1914 domestic railroads were more competitive than shipping for intracontinental freight haulage.

► Ceylon's railroad system had been built under the control of the colonial government from 1858. The main line from Colombo was extended from Haputale to Bandarawela, a hill station, in the mid-1890s. It had been surveyed as early as 1875, but the country to be traversed was difficult. Bandarawela was over 1200 m (4000 ft) above sea level, and involved gradients of 1 in 44 as well as the crossing of the Kahagulla ravine.

Changing markets

Europe's growing interconnection with the rest of the world as a result of trade was most evident in the changing sources of imports of raw materials and foodstuffs. For example, by 1913 only three percent of British imports of cereals came from Europe, as North America, India and Argentina were now the main suppliers. However, following the removal of colonial preferences the share of British sugar imports from the Empire fell; by 1913, Europe supplied over half. Similarly, Baltic timber gained at North America's expense, supplying over eighty percent of British wood imports by the eve of World War I. French and German imports of wool switched to Australia and Argentina by 1913. After 1869, the raw material for the French silk manufacturing industry came from China, and by 1913 Brazil was the source of two-thirds of German coffee imports, whereas North Africa supplied over half of French imports of wine.

The growth of American exports turned the American visible trade account – that concerned with tangible goods – into continual surplus from the mid-1890s. The most significant factor was the increase in the relative share of semi-finished and finished manufactures, so much so that by 1914 they constituted half of the total value of American exports. Europe remained America's most important market, but with a declining share; rising markets were Canada, Asia and Latin America. Fewer manufactured goods were now imported, and imports mainly they con-

sisted of those basic materials that were unavailable within the domestic economy for geological and climatic reasons – tropical fibers such as jute, coffee, tropical fruits and olive and coconut oils, together with rubber, nickel and tin.

European overseas investment

There was substantial migration from Europe overseas, especially to the United States, but later to southern Latin America, particularly Argentina. And to the increasing flow of goods and migrants, there was added from the mid-1850s exports of finance capital from some of the advanced economies. London was the premier financial center of the world economy, but New York's international importance was growing substantially, although it did not yet rival the older centers of Paris or Berlin.

Until the 1880s overseas investment had largely consisted of loans to governments, together with finance for railroad construction: over 40 percent of overseas securities bought by British investors between 1865 and 1914 were destined to finance railroad companies abroad. British overseas investment in this period was largely concentrated on the temperate regions of recent settlement – the United States, southern Latin America, Canada, Australia and New Zealand. About forty percent of this investment could be termed "direct", as it involved managerial control. Much of this was undertaken by "free-standing firms" – British companies, registered under British company law, and with a British office, but operating

French Investment in Russia

Russian industrialization from the 1890s was financed substantially through the import of foreign capital. French residents were the main suppliers, holding in 1914 a third of all Russian bonds and a seventh of all Russian shares. French investors in the 1890s were disillusioned with the low yield available on most domestic securities; Russian shares offered higher dividends, and the rewards that could be obtained were already being demonstrated in the development of the Dnieper region by Belgian capital and German investment in Russian Poland and the Urals. Further encouragement came from the stabilization of the rouble and the lure of orders arising from the state-managed expansion of the railroad system. However, foreign companies operating within Russia were subject to higher taxes than local concerns, so the possibilities of establishing "freestanding" French companies within Russia were restricted. Therefore French investment took place initially through the pioneering Belgian concerns and then through the medium of Russian domestic companies.

French capital contributed to the formation of the southern Russian industrial complex, bringing about vertical integration and the consequent creation of large plants employing technologies superior to those then current in French domestic industry. After 1900 there was increased French investment in the Russian banking system and a rising emphasis on financial holdings in the growing oil industry, usually in the form of shares of either Russian or English companies.

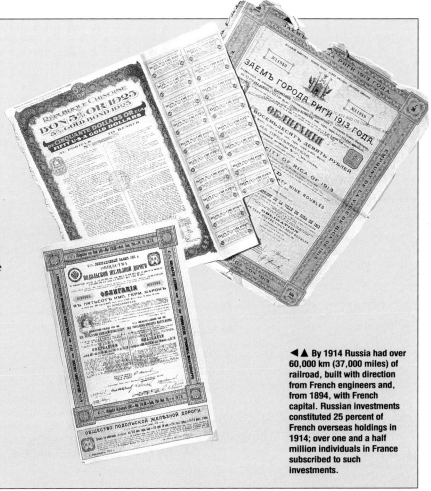

◀▲ By 1914 Russia had over 60,000 km (37,000 miles) of railroad, built with direction from French engineers and, from 1894, with French capital. Russian investments constituted 25 percent of French overseas holdings in 1914; over one and a half million individuals in France subscribed to such investments.

an enterprise in a foreign country. For instance, in many such railroad companies the London board of directors was largely concerned with financial control, while overseas there was a second, local, board, responsible for operation of the line. Such a dual management structure, with clear divisions of function, seems also to have been common in the cases of mining and plantation companies.

French and German foreign investment was for the most part undertaken within Europe, mirroring the greater importance for these economies of intra-European dealings. However, from the 1890s, and especially after 1900, French and German foreign investment became more global in scope, now being undertaken increasingly in the United States, Latin America, Africa and China. Political alliances played a part in this, as in the case of the French lending to Russia from the 1890s, which was very important in Russian industrial development.

It has been held that multinational companies were particularly characteristic of American foreign investment from the 1880s, but in fact British enterprise led in this field. At least 119 British manufacturing firms between 1870 and 1939 undertook direct investment overseas. Early British multinationals were largely involved in engineering, chemicals, food, textiles and metallurgy. Before 1900 most of the foreign activity of British multinationals was in overseas sales offices, but by 1914 it involved overseas production facilities.

◀ Japanese banks began to expand overseas from 1878, when the Dai Ichi Bank opened a branch office in Korea. Its business was taken over in 1909 by the Bank of Korea, renamed the Bank of Chosen in 1911. The Yokohama Specie bank opened branch offices in Manchuria from 1900. Again reflecting the widening of Japan's international interests, the Toyo Takushoku K. K. (Far East Colonial Co.) was established in 1908, as a development bank for Korea.

Debtors and creditors

The growth and increasing intricacy of international dealings led to a change in the underlying pattern of financial settlements. Until the 1890s such patterns consisted of isolated systems, linked only through Britain. Consequently liquidity pressure – a shortage of funds – in one such system could only be transmitted to another via Britain. From the 1890s, however, the whole global system became fully integrated, often bypassing Britain entirely. There were several reasons for this change. One was the rising return stream of substantial annual payments of interest by Britain's foreign debtors. Another was the growing importance of French, and also German, capital exports from the 1890s and their consequent return flows of interest payments. Yet

▼ The central sorting office in the post office of Toronto, Canada. The post remained the most important medium for communications even after the development of the international cable network. Indeed cables were confirmed by letter, a practice that persisted into the 20th century.

another was the spread of industrialization in Europe and the growth of demand, on the part of industrial nations other than Britain, for primary products from non-European sources. Lastly, from the 1890s the demand for manufactures amongst countries that were part of the British Empire came increasingly to be met by American and European concerns. The overall effect of all these developments was that by 1914 industrial Europe, together with the United States, had substantial deficits with the primary producing countries, but were creditors of Britain, which in turn was a creditor of the primary producing world.

Many foreign banks had offices in London and many foreign countries kept sterling balances there. London supplied the liquidity for the increasing scale of international dealings through the provision of trade credit, long-term overseas lending and Britain's continuing import surplus. The United Kingdom before 1914 was an ideal international creditor because of her free trade policy, which allowed debtors to accumulate sterling through exports to Britain. Further, cyclical falls in British long-term lending could be offset by parallel increases in the British import surplus, as happened during the 1890s.

The gold standard and reserve currencies

Confidence in sterling as a stockholding and trading currency was increased during the last quarter of the 19th century by the fall in the gold price of silver, the other monetary metal, which was used substantially in Europe, Latin America and the East. From 1868 until the 1890s the adoption of a bimetallic monetary standard was internationally considered, and the Bank of England went as far as balloting its directors, but finally decided to have no truck with the proposal to establish a firm monetary link between gold and silver. (India, which was on a silver standard, was regarded as a separate problem.) The attitude of London's institutions was influential in leading most of the major economies to adopt the gold standard by the 1890s. Germany did so in 1871 and in 1878 the mints of the European Latin Monetary Union were closed to silver, with the

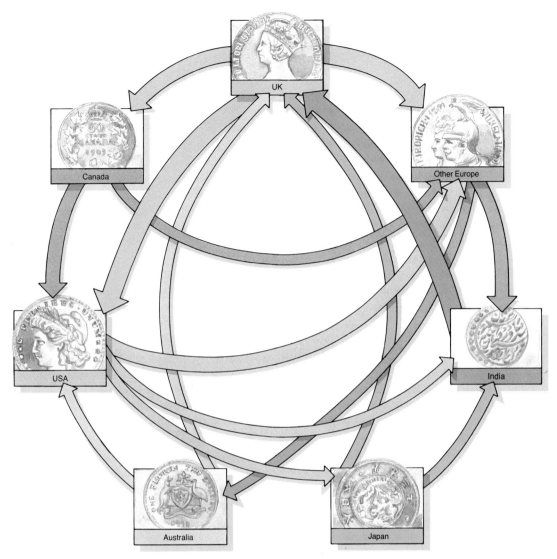

◀ The growing integration of the world economy was particularly marked by the complexity of financial flows which mirrored the movements of goods and capital. From the 1870s world trade became increasingly multinational, with payment deficits and surpluses balanced through dealings with many countries. This diagram broadly indicates the flow of financial settlements between various regions of the world in the years before 1914. Thus Britain's international deficits with North America and Europe were offset by surpluses with India and Australia, which in turn had surpluses with Europe and the United States.

result that Belgium and Switzerland moved onto the gold standard; in 1900 the United States did likewise.

In theory, the gold standard was a mechanism for keeping prices internationally in line. It was based on three factors. First, currencies were allotted gold values, thereby establishing international exchange rates, and currencies were backed by holdings of gold; second, the free movement of gold was permitted between countries; and, third, a country's domestic money supply was more or less automatically linked to the international movement of gold. It was assumed that the money supply of a country losing gold would contract, thereby bringing about a fall in its domestic prices, which in turn would make its internationally traded goods more competitive, raise exports and reduce imports, leading to an inflow of gold. In practice, the institutional structure of the international gold standard was extremely diverse. Only Britain, Germany and the United States were on a full gold standard. Further, the so-called "rules of the standard" were frequently disregarded as international flows of gold were restricted by the operations of certain central banks. In fact it would seem that before 1900 the world was actually using a sterling standard, with a number of countries backing their currencies not by gold holdings, but by holdings

of sterling-denominated securities. Adjustment to international payments problems was generally smooth; in the last resort international payment balances – deficits or surpluses – were accommodated through differential changes in the nations' rates of economic growth.

From the 1890s, while sterling remained the world currency, both the French franc and the German mark came to be held by other countries as reserve currencies. Official monetary reserves in the form of financial securities of other countries had advantages over gold in providing income in the form of interest, and because of their lower transport and transactions costs. But such holdings were also a result of dependency arising from debtor-creditor relationships: they were to become much more common after 1918.

International weights and measures

The role of the Bank of England in the international gold standard was made possible because London was the main gold market for the world, as well as the seat of several major commodity markets. By the late 19th century, Chicago and New York also had important commodity markets. Gradually the bases of measurement came to be standardized in such international commodity dealings, but some trades clung to traditional measures, such as the "long ton". By

The chief streams of British capital flowed into Canada, the United States, and Argentina. Mexico, Brazil, Chile, and other countries in South America also benefited by more or less large British investments. A small flood of British capital poured into South Africa, while Egypt and the colonies on the east and west coasts of Africa were not neglected. India and the Far East vied with Russia and Australia in their endeavours to obtain British capital.

C. K. HOBSON, THE EXPORT OF CAPITAL (1914)

1900 there were two general measurement systems – British imperial and metric. The imperial system prevailed in the English-speaking world, though even there variations occurred, such as the American pint containing only 16 fluid ounces, as opposed to 20 in the British "imperial" system. Similarly, nautical miles were by no means equivalent to an English land mile. On a wider international basis there was a halting adoption of the metric system. Its basic unit of measurement for length was the meter, accepted by the French National Assembly in 1790 and defined as "one ten-millonth of the quarter meridian from the North Pole to the Equator, passing through Paris". owever, the use of the standard meter and its weight equivalent, the kilogram, was not made mandatory even in France until 1840. Wider adoption came but slowly, assisted by the international exhibitions of 1851 (London) and 1855 (Paris). A conference in Paris in 1870 prepared the way for the establishment in 1875 of an International Bureau of Weights and Measures, and 18 countries, including the United States, signed the "Treaty of the Meter".

Improvements in communications
International economic and social intercourse was also improved by agreements over communications. The Universal Postal Union had its origins in a meeting held in Paris in 1863, and in 1874, 22 states signed the Berne Convention which established a uniform postal tariff, together with a formula for disbursing revenue between the countries through which an international postal communication passed. There were parallel international agreements over telegraphy; 20 European states signed the Paris Convention of 1865, and a decade later the International Telegraph Union was formed.

Much postal traffic was carried by the railroad

and the expansion of the railroad system led to the spread of the telegraph network, as well as to the introduction of standardized time. Greenwich Mean Time became the British standard in 1880, although Dublin continued to be 25 minutes behind GMT until 1916. Other countries similarly established comparable local standards, with Paris being the astronomical center in France, Pulkovo in Russia and Washington in the United States. The standardization of world time arose not only from the needs of railroad travelers but also out of the requirements of maritime navigation and the pressure exerted by international scientific congresses.

Scientific cooperation
Standardization involved national pride and international rivalry; it often arose out of a lengthy two-stage process, led by the generation of a scientific consensus and followed by international diplomacy. Formal international scientific meetings began to increase in numbers from the 1850s; the first international health conference took place in Paris in 1851 and the first international physiological conference in 1889. Meetings were often twinned with exhibitions: alongside the Paris International Exhibition of 1900 there were scientific congresses covering mathematics, physics, meteorology, chemistry, botany, geology and psychology, as well as branches of the applied sciences. This increase in formal meetings of the scientific community went hand in hand with closer alliances between national bodies.

Copyright protection and international law
The concerns of science were but one aspect covered by the 25,000 international agreements concluded by 1917. The drawing up of such agreements became more difficult when ideas became property and had earning power. This

▲ Alexander Graham Bell invented the telephone in 1876 and assigned his patents to a company known from 1880 as American Bell Telephone. This acquired the Western Electric Co. in 1882 and established the American Telephone and Telegraph Co. in 1885 to provide long-distance services. By 1893 there were 266,000 Bell telephones in service in the United States, mainly in the business centers of the main cities. Bell's patent rights lapsed in 1893, which led to the rapid emergence of competitors. By 1907 there were over six million telephones in the United States, of which more than three million were Bell.

◄ The Bell system was acquired in 1907 by a New York banking group headed by George F. Baker and J. P. Morgan. Under the management of Theodore Vail, Bell now changed policy, buying up the independent companies and agreeing to supply equipment to non-Bell concerns.

was less the case with copyright, for which reciprocal treaties had been signed since 1797. An International Copyright Union was established by the Berne Convention of 1886 and was further developed by the Berlin Convention of 1908 and the Protocol of 1914. The United States stood apart, although American legislation in 1909 gave copyright to domiciled foreign authors and to authors resident in nations with which the United States had reciprocal treaties.

There were comparable developments in the case of patents, but the Convention of the International Union for the Protection of Industrial Property of 1883, signed by 39 countries, did not override national laws. Consequently, even within the British Empire an inventor still had to file 40 patent applications.

International law grew largely in the same manner as English common law – through the invocation of practice and precedent as authorities for current decisions. This was how the thousands of international tribunals in existence by 1914 generally operated. Greater codification came at the end of the 19th century in the fields of the conduct of war and labor conditions. The Hague Conferences of 1899 and 1906 established a Permanent Court of Arbitration, as well as rules for the treatment of prisoners of war. Articles 4 to 20 of the First Hague Convention laid down that prisoners of war should be well treated – in terms of being fed, housed and clothed on the same basis as the troops of the captor government. While in captivity prisoners could be made to work, but not for military purposes, and under reasonable conditions. Further, prisoners were not to be punished for trying to escape. The Declaration of London in 1909 laid down rules for naval warfare, particularly the conduct of blockades and the treatment of prize and neutral vessels.

These concerns were paralleled by a growing consensus over the need for international action regarding the regulation of working conditions. In 1900 the International Association for Labor Legislation was established in Paris and the two subsequent Berne Conferences of 1905 and 1906 resulted in the signing of conventions for the protection of labor, particularly the prohibition of night work for women and the use of less toxic chemicals where possible, for example advocating white phosphorus in match manufacture. These actions gained increasing international respect, for example in Japan, but the work of the Berne Conference of 1913 was frustrated by the outbreak of war in August 1914.

▲ The use of the telephone grew more slowly in Europe than in the United States. In 1914 Denmark led Europe with 45 telephones per thousand inhabitants; in Germany there were 21, in Britain 17 and in France eight. There had been only 1,370 telephone subscribers in Britain in 1888, when a small but growing trunk network had been established. However, the system was not very efficient or effective, especially the privately run exchanges. The trunk network was progressively taken over by the Post Office from 1892, and municipally run local telephone systems developed from 1899. In the same year the Post Office began to replace private companies, beginning in London.

Tackling Disease

The eradication of communicable diseases became possible from the 1880s as a result of three broad lines of scientific advance. In 1870 Louis Pasteur began to put forward the germ theory, on the basis of studies of the action of microbes upon silk worms; Joseph Lister was meanwhile developing aseptic techniques; and in 1876, Robert Koch established a definite connection between illness and the presence of a microbe, a discovery which led to the subsequent development of the science of bacteriology. These developments brought about the general acceptance that disease was spread by contagion, as opposed to "bad air". The human body was now recognized as the host for many diseases, spread either by direct contact or by food handled by a disease carrier. It was also realized that certain fatal illnesses, like malaria, are transmitted by biting insects.

Major epidemics led to greater insights. A team of American Army surgeons was formed in 1900 after an outbreak of yellow fever. After research carried out in Cuba, they discovered that the disease was transmitted by the mosquito. The remedy was mosquito control, which began in Havana, and the techniques

which were developed were applied in Panama to enable the construction of the Panama Canal. At the same time, studies in India and elsewhere established the role of the mosquito in the spread of first bird and then human malaria. Once more insect control, with swamp drainage, spraying and protective screens for housing, became the method of eradicating the disease, together with the use of quinine as a cure for sufferers.

By the early 20th century it was recognized that the eight most serious tropical diseases – cholera, amebic dysentery, bacillary dysentery, hookworm, malaria, plague, typhus and yellow fever – were all controllable by improvements in sanitation, mosquito control or vaccination. In the temperate world fatalities from diphtheria, scarlet fever, smallpox and typhoid fever had become uncommon, while those from tuberculosis had been greatly reduced. With the retreat of these diseases, cities in advanced countries had become considerably healthier, and the death rate fell rapidly from the 1870s onwards. But even in the Western world, there remained the problems of influenza, pneumonia and syphilis.

Time Chart

	1915	1916	1917	1918	1919	1920	1921	1922
Industry	• May: Beginning of artificial saltpetre manufacture (Ger) • Opening of the World's Fair in San Francisco (USA)	• General Motors Corporation becomes one of the world's leading automobile companies (USA)	• Apr: Leunawerke begin the production of liquid ammonia (Ger)	• Apr: Agreement to deliver corn and other agricultural products from the Ukraine to Germany and Austria • Jul: All industrial enterprises in Russia nationalized	• Regulations for agricultural workers put into force (Ger)	• Introduction of unemployment insurance in British and Austrian industry • German railways placed under government control	• Over 100 enterprises have to close due to lack of materials (Russ) • Rise of Venezuela as an important oil exporting country • Establishment of the Coal Council for organizing the distribution and supply of coal (Ger)	• British Broadcast Corporation (BBC) founded (UK) • Famine in Russia due to bad harvests and political riots
Technology	• H. Junkers develops the first all-metal airplane (Ger) • G. Burstyn constructs the first tank with caterpillar tracks (Aut)	• Mass production of radio valves by Telefunken (Ger) • 15 Sep: Use of tanks in Cambrai (Western Front) by British	• 31 May: F. Fischer produces coal paraffin and coal petrol (Ger) • 1 Jun: Helium extracted from natural gas and used as a substitute for hydrogen in airships (USA)	• 15 May: Regular air mail service begins between New York and Washington (USA)	• Introduction of the assembly line in European car production by Citroën (Fr) • Hoopes produces unalloyed aluminum (USA)	• Building of the first all-welded ship in Birkenhead (UK) • First regular radio service in Pittsburgh (USA)	• 19 Sep: Completion of the first autobahn in Germany, the AVUS	
Finance	• Aug: US banks grant a credit of $500 million to the UK and France	• Legislation regarding the establishment of Joint Stock Land banks and Federal Land banks (USA) • Issue of loans for many countries by Switzerland	• Dec: Decree regarding the control of foreign exchange. Stock exchange reopens (Ger) • Legislation establishes the Banques Populaires (Fr) • Barclay & Co. Ltd acquires the majority of shares of the United Counties Bank and changes its official name to Barclays Bank (UK)	• Apr: Pitman Act and Cunliffe Report. Return to the gold standard recommended (UK) • Formation of the banking group of the Crédit Industriel et Commercial (Fr) • Merger of several large joint stock banks. Treasury opposes any further bank mergers (UK)	• Mar: Support for sterling and the French franc abandoned, followed by depreciation • USA becomes main creditor nation of the world • Establishment of the Banco Central (Sp)	• Stock market collapse in London and New York • Merger among British joint stock banks • Banking legislation in Japan	• Oct: Establishment of Gosbank, the state bank of Soviet Russia • Establishment of the Caisse Centrale des Banques Populaires (Fr) • Beginning of a wave of mergers among the smaller commercial banks (USA)	• May: New law on status of autonomy the Reichsbank (Ger) • Establishment of Open Market Committee in the U
Economic Policy	• Jan: Establishment of a distribution organization for the supply of food (Ger) • Aug: British Chancellor of the Exchequer Lloyd George demands that the economy become a war economy (UK) • Aug: German industrialists demand the incorporation of Poland, Latvia, Lithuania, Estonia and the Ukraine into the German economic sphere	• Jan: Rapid increase in sugar prices. Raising of the tobacco tax and rationing of butter (Ger)	• Apr: Adamson Act: introduction of the eight-hour day for US railwaymen • Jun: Second Liberty Act: fixing of the national debt at $45 billion (USA) • Aug: Price freeze on food (USA) • Oct: US government confiscates all German properties in the USA	• Jan: Strikes in the armament industries (Ger) • Jun: Rationing of bread and other consumer goods in Austria • Jul: Reichstag agrees upon a further 12 billion Marks for financing the war (Ger)	• Jan: Economic crisis in the USA due to the transformation of the war economy into a peace economy • May: Nationalization of the mining industry (Ger) • Sep: German finance minister Erzberger establishes a central tax office, thus strengthening Germany's financial sovereignty • Introduction of the eight-hour day in France, Netherlands and Spain • Steelworkers' strike until 1920 (USA)	• Feb: Legislation on the establishment of works councils put into force • Feb: Rationing of food in Italy • Mar: Beginning of a general strike, especially in the Ruhr (Ger) • Jul: The Spa conference fails to settle finally German reparations	• Mar: Conference on German reparations in London. Amount fixed at 132 billion Goldmarks. • Apr: British miners' strike, demanding a reduction of hours and nationalization of the mines • 5 May: Ultimatum of London demanding a speedy fulfilment of the Treaty of Versailles, threatening Germany with the occupation of the Ruhr • Oct: Beginning of the New Economic Policy (NEP) in Soviet Russia, lasting until 1927	• Feb: Strike of German railwaymen • Jun: International high finance against loan for commercializing the German reparations • Industrialists Stinn (Ger) and de Lubers (Fr) sign an agreement on the participation German industrialist in the regulation of the reparations
International	• Heavy losses for Chile in the saltpetre trade due to the sea war			• Jan: Agreement on mutual financial transactions and support between Germany and Finland • Aug: Agreement on mutual financial transactions between Germany and Russia • Aug: Agreement on economic cooperation between Romania, Germany and Austria	• Jan: Peace treaty conference in Versailles. Controversy regarding German reparations • May: Establishment of the International Labor Organization (ILO) in Geneva • Foundation of the Third International	• Sep: International monetary conference in Brussels. Stabilization of currencies and a return to the gold standard discussed	• Mar: Trade relations established between the UK and Soviet Russia • May: Trade relations established between Germany and Soviet Russia	• Apr: World economic conference in Geneva. Gold exchange currencie recommended • 16 Apr: Treaty of Rapallo between Germany and Soviet Russia regarding economic cooperati • UK imposes an import tax on all German products
Misc.	• 7 May: Sinking of the Lusitania.	• 23 Apr: Easter Uprising in Dublin suppressed (UK) • 16 May: Agreement on the partition of Turkey (UK/Fr)	• 6 Apr: USA declares war on Germany • 7 Nov (26 Oct, Old Style): Bolshevik Revolution in Petrograd (Russ)	• 11 Nov: Armistice signed in Compiègne (Fr).	• 28 Jun: Treaty of Versailles signed by Germany (Fr)	• Jan: Founding of the League of Nations in Geneva • Beginning of the Prohibition (USA)		• Proclamation of the Irish Republic leads civil war (until 1923) • Oct: March on Rom by Mussolini

	1923	1924	1925	1926	1927	1928	1929
	• ...titrust legislation ...nst the misuse of ...nomic power (Ger) • ...ontinued export of corn ...r the famine (USSR)	• Foundation of Imperial Airways (UK) • Foundation of the Deutsche Rohstahlgemeinschaft as the organization of steelworks (Ger)	• Foundation of I.G. Farben (Ger) • Foundation of Chrysler Corporation (USA) • Redistribution of land in Poland at the expense of German proprietors	• Foundation of Lufthansa (Ger) • Imperial Chemicals Industries (ICI) created as counterweight to I.G. Farben (UK) • Formation of a European steel cartel by several European steel companies	• Foundation of Vickers Armstrong (UK)	• General Motors takes over Opel Werke (USA/Ger) • Farmers in the Soviet Union riot over collectivization • Soviet government offers industrial concessions to foreign enterprises	• Foundation of VEBA AG, a mining and electricity company (Ger) • Foundation of Unilever (UK) • General Motors buys a quarter of the shares in the German AEG electricity company (USA/Ger)
	• ...R. Goddard invents the ...d fuel rocket (USA) • ...Jul: First regular air ...e between Moscow ...Gorkiy (USSR) • ...erman company Benz ...duces trucks with diesel ...nes	• Mass production of Leica camera (Ger) • 12 Oct: First Zeppelin flight across the Atlantic Ocean from Friederichshafen to New York (Ger/USA)	• Hydrocarbon synthesis by F. Fischer and H. Tropsch leads to the development of synthetic gasoline	• 7 Jan: First demonstration of television by J.L. Baird (UK) • Wireless telephone service between London and New York set up	• First production of synthetic rubber (USA)	• 8 Feb: First international television transmission from London to New York by J.L. Baird (UK) • H. Geiger and W. Müller invent an instrument for measuring radioactive radiation	• P. Drinker invents the iron lung (USA) • Beginning of tractor production in Stalingrad (USSR)
	• ...yperinflation after the ...upation of the Ruhr by ...nch and Belgian troops • ...ov: Decree on the ...duction of the ...tenmark and the ...ablishment of the ...tenbank. Covering of ...currency by goods ...ead of gold (Ger)	• Aug: Legislation on the introduction of the Reichsmark and a new set of regulations for the Reichsbank put into force (Ger) • Speculation in francs, but a sudden squeeze punishes the speculators (Fr) • Dawes loan issued to reschedule German reparations	• Apr: Restoration of the gold standard with the pound of the prewar parity (Ger) • Apr: Gold Standard Act (USA) • July: Law regarding the revaluation of loans and bonds, issued in Marks, fixing liabilities after inflation • Banking crisis and collapse of many banks (Sp)	• Inflation, followed by a de facto stabilization of the franc at devalued level (Fr) • Jul: New banking legislation, fixing the amount of government borrowing at 400 million Marks (Ger) • Banca d'Italia obtains a note-issuing monopoly (It) • Dec: Suspension of the Latin Currency Union as a result of French inflation	• 13 May: Collapse of the German stock market • Dec: New gold parity for the lira (It) • Dec: Decree by the Soviet government concerning a new organization of gold production (USSR)	• Jun: Devaluation of the franc. Introduction of a gold currency (Fr) • Sep: Currency and Banknotes Act. The figure of fiduciary money in circulation fixed at £260 million (UK) • Establishment of the Banco Exterior de España (Sp) • Central Bank of China, established in 1924 in Canton, becomes the state bank	• Issue of the Kreuger loan of $125 million for 50 years (Ger) • Sep: Collapse of the Allgemeine Österreichische Bodencreditanstalt, and its merger with the Österreichische Creditanstalt (Aut) • 22 Oct: Crash in the Wall Street stock market (Black Friday), and the beginning of the Great Depression
	• ...ep–Nov: ...rganization of the ...netary system ...cussed, so that the ...ering of the currency is ...e substituted by goods ...) • ...ov: Dawes commission ...A) and McKenna ...mmission (UK) ...ablished to decide on ...regulation of ...arations • ...ublication of A Tract on ...netary Reform by J.M. ...nes and Money, Credit ...d Commerce by A ...rshall (UK)	• Apr: Restrictive credit policy adopted by the Reichsbank to defend the exchange rate of the Mark (Ger) • Jul: Beginning of the reparations conference in London. Discussion of the Dawes plan • Sep: Dawes plan put into force. No final regulation of the amount of German reparations. Annual rate of payment fixed • Nov: Strike of Austrian railwaymen	• Jul: British government grants miners special wages and established an arbitration committee to avoid a strike (Red Friday) • Aug: Legislation on protection tariffs for industry and agriculture put into force (Ger) • Aug: Strike of tram and bus employees in Paris (Fr) • Dec: Party congress of the Communist party of the Soviet Union (CPSU) agrees on a transformation of the Soviet Union from an agrarian to an industrial country	• 4–12 May: General strike organized by Trade Union Congress. Miners continue striking until December, when they exhaust their resources (UK)	• Italian Fascist party introduces new labor legislation, the Labor Card • German government warned by the agent for reparations to increase public expenditure • Dec: Party congress of the CPSU agrees on a measures for a socialist economy, the enforcement of industrialization and collectivization of agriculture	• Sep: Young Committee set up to regulate the German reparations • 1 Oct: First five-year plan in the Soviet Union. Concentration on heavy industry	• Jan/Feb: Conferences on the German reparations in The Hague and in Paris. Publication of the Young plan to regulate the reparation payments • Sep: French prime minister Briand proposes the establishment of a United Nations of Europe as a means of overcoming the difficult economic situation • Increase in the rate of unemployment in all European industrial countries
	• ...ov: Establishment of ...Mission Interallié de ...ntrole des Usines et des ...es (MICUM).	• Feb: Agreement between the UK and Germany reduces the reparation tax from 26% to 5% • Aug: Financial agreement between China and Germany • Oct: Germany signs agreements on trade with France and the UK	• Oct: Germany signs agreements on trade with Italy and the USSR	• Oct: First pan-European conference on the unification of Europe • Oct: Empire conference establishes the British Commonwealth (UK)	• Feb: Pilsudski's government approves freedom of movement between Poland and Danzig • May: First international economic conference in Geneva discusses the world economic situation • Aug: International congress of trade unions discusses the reduction of working hours	• Jun: Pan-American conference in Havana discusses the problems of trade between the American countries	• Jul: World congress of women's labor opened in Berlin
	• ...an: French and Belgian ...ops occupy the Ruhr ...er) • ...ov: Revolt in Munich of ...NSDAP under Hitler ...ds in failure (Ger)	• Italian Fascist party wins the elections with a majority of 65% • First Labour party minority government under J.R. MacDonald	• Massacre of demonstrating students in Shanghai by the British police initiates the National Revolution (China)	• May: Coup d'état by J. Pilsudski introduces a moderate military dictatorship in Poland	• Tanaka Memorandum reveals the new Japanese policy of expansion in Asia • UK severs diplomatic relations with the USSR	• Briand–Kellogg pact declaring war to be an unsuitable method of solving international problems is signed by 15 countries	• Austria becomes a presidential republic

Datafile

The war, although a European conflict, affected the entire world economy. The scale of destruction was profound because it was the first major conflict in which the belligerents were either industrial or industrializing economies. The war was expected to be short, but this proved not to be so. Consequently the resources consumed were considerable, leading European nations to draw upon supplies from all over the globe.

As the struggle developed into a war of attrition, it became an opposition of economic resources, and in all belligerent countries the state assumed command over the economy. The war acted as a catalyst in accelerating underlying trends, such as the application and further development of new technologies in weapons of destruction. War also hastened the European adoption of American methods of mass production, which proved beneficial in the 1920s. Outside Europe the war encouraged the development of the United States and Japan as world economic powers.

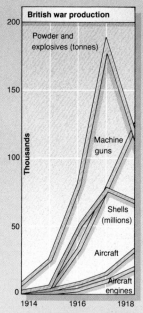

◀▶ In 1914 the British armaments industry consisted of a state-owned sector and 16 private specialist firms, of which ten were small. State production of weapons had been expected to fill the shortfall at the outbreak of any war, providing a bridge for the expansion of private production, but this plan proved to be totally misconceived during World War I as the consumption of munitions rapidly reached totally unforeseen levels. This was true for all belligerents. War production only began to expand once new policies had been introduced. In Britain the Ministry of Munitions took over the whole armaments industry in 1915, and in Germany the War Bureau was created in 1916 to ensure full mobilization.

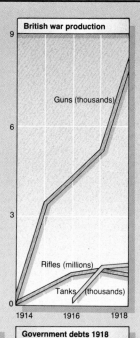

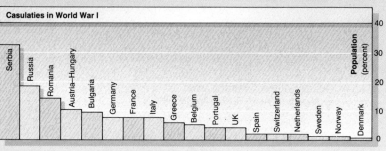

◀ Until 1917 German sinkings of British merchantmen were running at a faster rate than new vessels could be built. Consequently transatlantic supplies were increasingly shipped in American vessels and from 1917 there was a shipbuilding crusade in the United States, doubling the size of the American fleet between 1916 and 1918.

▲ The war had a major demographic effect, beyond the appalling casualties on the battlefield. War deaths prevented marriages and the formation of families. Food shortages and famine had a similar effect. The check to population growth went far beyond the belligerents, having a serious impact upon neutral countries, whose food supplies were cut.

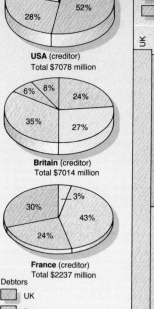

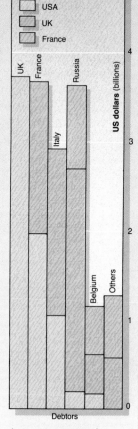

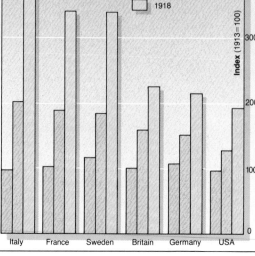

▶ Prices in the world economy had been rising since the mid-1890s, but the war triggered a bout of further inflation which affected the entire world. This inflation had many causes, from the simple shortage of goods and materials to the particular monetary and fiscal policies pursued by individual countries.

▲ All the belligerents borrowed internationally to finance war expenditure. The main lender was the United States, from which the Entente Powers drew supplies of raw materials, foodstuffs and munitions. Britain and France lent money to the governments of their allies to finance the latters' war efforts, in particular Italy and Russia.

▲ Europe emerged from World War I as a major debtor to the United States, completely reversing the position in 1914 when the United States had been in debt to Europe. The settling of these inter-Allied debts proved to be a major problem in the 1920s, a problem complicated by the repudiation of czarist war debts by Soviet Russia.

THE ECONOMICS OF WORLD WAR I

The reasons for the outbreak of World War I are still a matter for debate. Among them was economic rivalry, which from the 1880s heightened tensions between the Great Powers as they jostled in the world market place for manufactures with an increasing number of producers. Manufacturing nations also became anxious about access to sources of supply for raw materials. A considerable number of historians have accepted Lenin's concept of World War I as being an imperialist conflict, arising from the desire to redivide the world into a new pattern of economic and financial spheres of influence. In this atmosphere economic liberalism progressively broke down, to be replaced by policies of protectionism and colonial expansion, and the expression "imperialism" took on a new meaning.

From the 1880s, economic strength had increasingly been regarded as the foundation for international influence, which led to governments taking a direct interest in the well-being of their economies. The first step was the raising of tariff barriers by continental European countries to protect farming against imports from the New World and Russia. This was quickly coupled with

- **Economic rivalry and protectionism**
- **German expansionist policies**
- **Supplying the war effort**
- **The pace of technological change**
- **American economic influence**
- **The Russian Revolution**
- **Settlement and reparations**

▼ Anglo-German naval rivalry was one of the many factors heightening tensions within Europe. Britain was concerned about German intentions, especially after the opening of the Kiel Canal which allowed the German Fleet swift passage from the Baltic to the North Sea. Germany regarded the Royal Navy, as seen in this review at Spithead, as a major threat.

protection for industrialists in order to secure home markets for local producers. Agricultural protection was introduced in France in 1881. Germany initiated agricultural protection in 1879, and although in the early 1890s poor domestic harvests resulted in a shortage of food which forced the temporary suspension of grain duties, from 1900 the government became once more committed to raising agricultural duties. Even within British society there were mounting pressures for the abolition of free trade. As elsewhere in northwestern Europe, these first arose among agriculturalists, but they were soon joined by manufacturers. In the 1906 election the Conservatives campaigned on a platform of tariff reform, but this was decisively rejected and economic liberalism retained its hold in Edwardian Britain.

Tariffs were largely reintroduced after 1880 by those countries that had adopted liberal commercial policies during the mid-19th century. This new trend in commercial policy did not embrace the United States, which had returned to protectionism from the outbreak of the Civil War in 1861, nor Russia and Austria-Hungary, in which economic self-sufficiency largely prevailed. The

reerection of tariffs by the continental European industrial economies from the 1880s went hand in hand with renewed colonial expansion. The main region of colonial division was Africa, but the further development of "informal" economic areas of influence took place in the Middle East and China, largely through state-backed syndicates competing for concessions. It was particularly this latter form of expansion in China to which Washington reacted by trying to promote from 1899 a policy of the "open door" – freedom of access to all markets for all producers.

The economic nature of the war

Many were surprised by the outbreak of a major European war in August 1914. At the beginning, it was expected, drawing upon the experience of the Franco-Prussian War, that there would be a short military campaign, involving a war of movement. Initially those expectations were fulfilled by a series of rapid German successes in both the east and the west, so much so that Berlin began to draw up peace terms in September. However, the Western Front was stabilized and the war in the west became a conflict of attrition, of materiel – the equipment of warfare – and blockade The critical supply lines were the sea lanes, which fed primarily the Allies, but also the Central Powers, with industrial raw materials and foodstuffs. Consequently, in parallel with the grinding horrors of trench warfare, there was a battle on the high seas aimed at constricting the economic resources of the belligerents.

The war of attrition, of industrial might and supply capacity, led to the dismantling of liberal capitalism amongst all the belligerents through the growth of state intervention, which was a pragmatic answer to problems of shortages. Initially the expansion of state control was gradual and piecemeal, but from 1916 it became more general and consolidated, based upon prior experience of trying to ensure the supply of food and munitions.

Restricting supply

During the first few days of the war the mercantile marines of the Central Powers – Germany and Austria-Hungary, shortly to be joined by Turkey and Bulgaria – almost disappeared from the seas, and Germany and her cobelligerents quickly became dependent upon neutral vessels for their growing import needs. The Allies, and in particular the British, mounted a naval blockade to prevent the Central Powers from importing goods from outside Europe. This was coupled with agreements with the European neutrals – Denmark, Italy, the Netherlands, Norway and Sweden – usually through private trading companies but sometimes through quasi-private trusts. Until March 1915, however, these agreements left the neutrals free to export their own native products to the Central Powers, and also allowed the Northern European neutrals to re-export foodstuffs and raw materials to Germany.

German U-boats began to attack Allied commercial shipping in October 1914, although not as part of a deliberate strategy. At first this was done within the codified international rules using an "abridged" procedure which involved boarding, the decision to sink and, if such a decision were executed, allowing time for the crew of the merchantman to disembark. In January 1915 Berlin decided to pursue a strategy of unrestricted submarine warfare, and in February 1915 Germany declared the waters around the British Isles to be a military area in which ships would be sunk without warning. Initially, in military terms, the first U-boat campaign was a success. The monthly sinkings of Allied ships increased to an average of 116,000 gross tonnes during mid-1915. However, it did not strike a mortal blow against the British economy, while the political disadvantages outweighed any logistical damage, since there was strong American reaction to the sinkings of the *Lusitania* and the *Arabic*. This was

▲ The Royal Naval Air Service began to take an interest in heavier-than-air aircraft in 1912, following the first take-off of a plane from the deck of a British warship. However, landplanes were not deployed on British warships until 1917. From then all battleships, battle cruisers and 22 light cruisers carried aircraft; the Grand Fleet had a complement of 100 planes. Generally, larger vessels were equipped with a two-seater aircraft, such as this Sopwith one-and-a-half strutter, on a forward turret and a single-seater fighter on a rear turret.

◄ During the war German submarines sunk more than 11 million tonnes of Allied shipping, of which nearly three-quarters were British. In 1917 alone the Western Allies lost 2.4 million tonnes of shipping to U-boat attacks. From June 1917 Allied westbound shipping was despatched in convoys with, for example, seven convoys leaving every 16 days from Liverpool. Over the course of the war the British sank 178 U-boats.

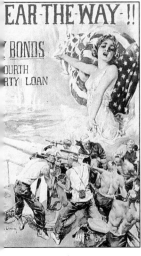

▲ From almost the beginning of the war the European Entente Powers had had to borrow in the United States to finance their purchases of foodstuffs, raw materials and munitions. The mobilization of American finance to defeat the Central Powers became easier when the United States entered the war in 1917. The American government itself now raised dollars for war expenditure through Liberty Bond issues, attracting investors by using modern advertising techniques.

Economic War Aims

The Pan-German League, founded in 1893, was originally a petty bourgeois nationalist agitation society, but came to be a platform for rightwing agriculturalists, landowners and leaders of heavy industry. Their intention was that Central Europe (*Mitteleuropa*), including territory gained in war would "form a large uniform economic area" including Belgium, the French iron ore district of Longwy-Briey, and the French Channel coast to the Somme, with a fortified line to Verdun and a German Mediterranean base at Toulon. There would be a German-controlled Central European Federation which would include Austria-Hungary, Bulgaria, Romania, The Netherlands, Switzerland, Denmark, Norway, Sweden and Finland. German colonies, together with those of Belgium and France, would be attached to this Federation. Further, the League aimed to force Russia to revert to the mid-16th-century frontier, with Poland and the Baltic States being annexed by Germany. In May 1915 the Central Federation of German Industrialists and various other industrial and agricultural interests gave their backing to these plans, which were also supported by various members of the German intelligentsia. Meanwhile, some of the major industrialists had plans of their own. Thyssen wanted to see the southern Russian heavy industry complex and the Caucasus region annexed as part of the *Mitteleuropa* program, which would also give access to Persia and even India. Rathenau of AEG and Gwinner of the Deutsche Bank were keen to promote a Central European Customs Area, with France a member.

They were prepared to permit national autonomy in western Russia, but with indirect German hegemony. The Imperial Government's program of September 1914 aimed at Central European economic union under German leadership, but with the annexation of Longwy-Briey and parts of Belgium. The Peace Treaty of Bucharest gave Germany control of Romanian oil, grain and rail transport, and in March 1918 the Treaty of Brest-Litovsk brought Finland, the Baltic provinces, the Ukraine and parts of the Caucasus within the sphere of influence of the Central Powers.

The Allies had no coherent economic plans comparable to the German *Mitteleuropa* program, but France wanted to recover Alsace-Lorraine and control over Saar coal to support the French steel industry, while Britain intended to establish the empire as a homogeneous economic unit, and was also eager to obtain control over Turkish possessions on the Persian Gulf, principally to obtain oil. Italy, entering the war in 1915, hoped to annex southern Austria and take control over the northern Adriatic. In Paris in 1916 various economic resolutions were passed which aimed at closer Allied cooperation both for the war and the future. The United States had a different view: the "fourteen points" put forward by President Wilson in January 1918 as a basis for peace involved economic freedom and national autonomy, and the settling of colonial questions, like questions of national minorities in eastern Europe, after taking into account the views of the local population.

◀ Oil prospecting seen here in southern Russia, increased in importance from 1900, particularly when navies began to use oil in place of coal. The British Admiralty was offered a Mexican source in 1913, but refused it, turning instead to the Anglo-Persian Oil Co., which had been established in 1909. In 1914 the British government acquired shares in the company. In 1907, Britain had signed a convention with Russia which established their respective spheres of influence in Persia.

sufficient for Berlin once more to revise the rules of engagement for U-boats and in September 1915 to halt sinkings off the Irish coast.

The escalation of German U-boat warfare in February 1915 was used by the Allies as a convenient pretext to impose an unrestricted blockade. By the end of 1915 the Allies had gained the power to ration the imports of the European neutrals. Along with purchasing agreements, this allowed the Allies not only to obtain much-needed foodstuffs and industrial raw materials from the European neutrals, but also to restrict the neutral countries' ability to export any such surpluses to the Central Powers. Further, Allied control of European trade was augmented by a blacklisting of purchasing firms acting on

behalf of the Central Powers, the issuing of "navicerts" at the port of shipment to simplify the interception of shipping, and the intensification of the naval blockade. But it could not prevent the Central Powers from importing ores and timber products from Sweden, ores and fish from Norway, foodstuffs from Denmark and Holland, and oil and grain from Romania.

For their part the Germans intensified their U-boat operations from February 1916. After a period of "restricted" U-boat activity following hostile American reaction to the loss of the *Sussex*, its renewed expansion led to Allied monthly shipping losses exceeding 300,000 tonnes. The third "unrestricted" U-boat offensive, begun in February 1917, increased Allied shipping losses to

866,000 tonnes in April 1917. The Allied reaction to this now acute situation was the belated introduction of the convoy system, increased shipbuilding and improved management and coordination of shipping movements and cargoes.

In some respects unrestricted U-boat warfare from February 1917 was counterproductive for the Central Powers as it led to an almost immediate decline in neutral shipping, which now sought the safety of home ports. The Allied blockade was further intensified by the entry of the United States into the war in April 1917, the establishment of an overall Allied Blockade Committee in March 1918 and the conclusion of a fresh round of agreements with European neutrals during 1918.

Domestic food supplies

The blockade and the U-boat played large parts in the propaganda of the two warring sides but, though the deterioration in diets was an immediate measure of the course of the war to civilians, the war on the high seas played only a marginal role in it. In 1914 Germany was 90 percent self-sufficient in food supplies, as measured by calorific intake, though its agriculture had been import-dependent for a third of its fertilizers and a comparable level of animal feedstuffs, and a million foreign workers had been seasonally employed. However, the mobilization of the German economy for war led to agriculture being stripped of inputs. Military conscription took away labor, and agriculture also lost capital,

horses and fodder, nitrogen fertilizers (nitrogen was needed for making explosives), machinery and fuel. Consequently the productivity of agriculture declined. This loss was aggravated by the conversion of arable to permanent pasture, which produced less food per unit of land. This wartime increase in pasture arose from the German government's failure to control livestock prices from March 1916, which led to the emergence of a premium on meat, as opposed to grain.

Food price controls were introduced in Germany from October 1914 and rationing from January 1915. In May 1916 a Ministry of Food was

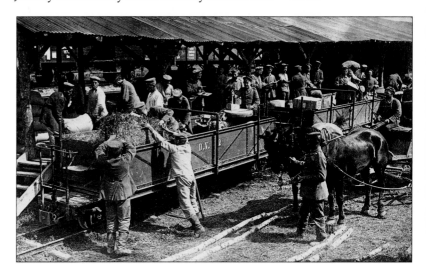

▼ The Western Front required major transport networks, which often took the form of light railways as with this German installation, though local haulage using horses and carts was still needed. The situation was similar on the Allied side. By 1918 over 1600 kilometers (1000 miles) of light railways and tramways had been built in the British sector.

▲ The most acute civilian wartime food situation in the West was in occupied Belgium and northern France. This was recognized by the Allies through special agreements which allowed food for civilian consumption to pass through the blockade. Further, the relief of suffering among the civilian population was undertaken by neutrals, in particular Hoover's American Food Administration.

▲ Troops were encouraged to augment their military rations through "self-help". Behind the front lines allotments developed to provide vegetables in order to eke out basic rations.

◄ The French economy lacked coal and the energy situation became acute during the war, especially for civilians as this queue on the steps of the Paris Opera in 1917 indicates. Coal shortages were coupled with food shortages, so that at the end of 1917 the Allies agreed that France should be supplied with 639,000 tonnes of food a month.

established, paving the way for general rationing, but the entitlement was below subsistence level, producing a growing food crisis. It reached a peak in the winter of 1917–18, following a poor domestic harvest, the effects of which along with increasing transport difficulties and poor distribution, led to a growing black market. These months brought starvation to the people of Germany and Austria–Hungary.

Italy, too, suffered badly during the war, as its supply routes through the Mediterranean for food imports were easily disrupted by blockade. Unlike the relatively prosperous France, the government was less able to organize a distribution netork, and the urban population – in particular – tended to go short. Owing to its free trade policy Britain had for some time been substantially dependent on foreign supplies of food and by 1914 only 35 percent of British consumption was home-produced. Until the end of 1916 food imports held up at about 90 percent of prewar levels, but the consumer was confronted by rising prices – 61 percent higher by June 1916. When food imports declined they became the subject of increasing government control.

British state control of imported foods went hand in hand with the expansion of domestic production through a "plough-up" drive to increase grain output. Unlike Germany, Britain possessed sufficient resources within its war economy to increase inputs – tractors, seeds and fertilizers – into agriculture. As a result the cultivated arable area increased by over three million hectares by 1918, yielding a rise in the domestic production of starch products of more than 40 percent, and adding 24 percent to overall domestic output. Even so, as in Germany, there was a food crisis during the winter of 1917–18, marked in Britain by growing food queues. Ration cards were finally introduced in January 1918 but, unlike in Germany, rationing provided an adequate diet and the "normal", but state-controlled, system of food distribution held up.

Although dietary conditions in working-class districts of German towns and cities were grave by the closing years of the war, in Eastern Europe and Russia they were worse. Before the war

Austria-Hungary had been largely self-sufficient in basic food supplies, Hungary being the breadbasket of the Habsburg Empire. But in wartime agricultural output fell and, in spite of German-style food controls, the empire was faced by a developing urban famine. This exacerbated already inflamed ethnic tensions; in particular, the Hungarian government used the situation to its advantage, erecting what virtually amounted to a food barrier between the two halves of the empire. In any case, as in Germany, state controls were resented in the countryside; they were a further factor in raising the hostility of all minority groups towards Vienna. Growing urban deprivation fueled antiwar sentiments and led to strikes, which became of major significance from January 1918. The final year of the war was marked by the growing power in Austria of the left wing of the Socialist party and the use of the army to commandeer and requisition food supplies for civilian consumption, which led to disputes between Vienna and Berlin over the final destination of grain shipments on the Danube.

Even Russia, the major European food producer, was affected by declining supplies during the war, largely as a result of distribution problems. Agricultural output fell, but not seriously; rather, peasants held back food supplies because of the absolute shortage of industrial goods, while the state was the first buyer in the market in order to meet military needs, so that food did not reach the towns. From as early as the spring of 1915 urban food shortages provoked strikes. Moreover, military requirements also disrupted the transport system, while the distribution system was flawed by an initial war policy of regional autonomy, never successfully reversed.

The supplies for war

Declining dietary standards in central and eastern Europe both fueled political unrest and led to falling labor productivity, in particular with respect to the output of energy in the form of coal. This, in turn, restricted industrial output, including war materiel. In Germany there had been planning and preparations for war, but these had been premised upon a rapid campaign.

Consequently military supplies had been exhausted by October 1914. As a result of pressure from private industry, which initially supplied well over half of German armaments, in August 1914 a War Materials Department was established. As with German food controls, this operated through corporations, of which there were 25 by 1918. Discussions between government and industry on a long-term armaments program began in October 1914 on the basis of the development of mass production. A new armaments drive in late August 1916 – the Hindenburg Plan – aimed to offset forecast German inferiority in troop numbers by increasing the level of their equipment. It was coupled with a substantial overhaul of the machinery of government by the creation of the War Bureau, under which was placed the War Materials Department, the Labor and War Substitutes Department, and the Arms and Munitions Procurement Bureau. This was to ensure full-scale mobilization.

There were high levels of investment in new factories, steelworks and even new Rhine bridges, and labor was allocated by the Patriotic Auxiliary Service Law passed in December 1916. However, from October 1916 onward the program was disrupted, initially by transport breakdowns. The pace of expansion was further retarded by a coal crisis in the winter of 1916–17 and lagging coal production thereafter. Some labor requirements were supplied by men released from the army and the deportation of workers from

Belgium and Poland during the winter of 1916–17. In 1917 the program was further frustrated by a shortage of raw materials that forced newly created capacity to be left idle. In this situation, priority was given to the maximization of current output and, despite the conditions, some production targets were fulfilled. During 1918 material shortages worsened. An attempt was made to assuage growing worker hostility in June 1918 by controlling industrial profits. New production targets were set and new programs launched; but for the first time field commanders were informed that the armaments drive could not meet their requirements.

Like German planners, the British military had expected a short war. As in Germany, private industry could not cope with the sudden deluge of munitions orders which the War Office placed during the autumn of 1914. The British armaments industry required machinery, raw materials and, particularly, skilled factory workers. One answer lay in standardized production, as in Germany, involving the use of unskilled hands. This "dilution of labor" was met by a series of agreements with the craft unions codified in the Munitions of War Act of July 1915, which also allowed the control of wages and restrictions on labor mobility. The British government attempted initially to control and then, more successfully, to coordinate private businesses, while limiting war profits. Armaments came under Lloyd George's new Ministry of Munitions from June 1915, and "national factories" concentrated on the mass production of basic armaments.

Germany could call upon the not insignificant armaments capacity of its allies, in particular the Skoda works in Bohemia, and France, Italy and Russia had substantial weapons capacities, but the Allies could also draw upon the resources of the United States. There Allied orders, channeled through J. P. Morgan & Co., largely created a war industry between 1914 and 1916. The United States supplied armaments best suited to the expertise of its engineering industry – those which could be produced by standardized production. The European Allies manufactured their own heavy weapons and, along with the tank, developed new major field pieces. When the US Army arrived in Europe it drew its light and medium artillery from French sources, the largest

▲ ► Flanders mud posed major problems and by early November 1917, in the battle for Passchendaele, it consumed mules carrying munitions and, at times, even artillery was swallowed up. Large parts of the battlefield had become seas of mud, adding to the horror. In this situation advances by British, Australian and New Zealand troops were slow and difficult. In contrast, men and materiel destined for the Front were conveyed either by canal barge or in purpose-designed heavy lorries.

▲ The barrages that signaled the beginning of major campaigns on the Western Front involved totally unanticipated levels of consumption of shells. At the battle of Verdun in 1916, 23 million shells were fired by both sides during just five months. This demand for ammunition quickly revealed the inadequacies of private industry, and led to greater state control and organization.

field guns from Britain, and aircraft from both Entente Powers.

In all belligerents, women were drummed into work of all kinds in place of men. Factory benches, public transport and office desks all saw higher proportions of women than ever before. In France, almost half the total workforce was female, and in the east a far higher proportion of women working in agriculture was recorded.

War and technological change

The war acted as a catalyst for the acceleration of technological change: Europe saw the widespread introduction of the "American system" – standardized interchangeable parts manufactured in volume with the end product put together on an assembly line. The war also accelerated the

development of new products. Heavy motor vehicles were developed a considerable pool of men with expertise in driving and maintaining road vehicles. Similarly, war needs for communications advanced telephone technology and ship-to-ship, ship-to-shore and air-to-ground radio transmissions. Another advance was the industrial production of synthetic nitrogen. It had started in 1913, but was restricted by the very high costs of processing. Germany's loss of Chilean nitrate imports led to cooperation between government and industry which resulted from mid-1915 in the steady expansion of synthetic production – the "fixing" of nitrogen from the air itself. This provided much-needed nitrogenous fertilizers for agriculture and became a vital component of the armaments drive.

War and the world economy

The war both isolated Europe from the international economy and accelerated the rise to prominence of the United States and Japan. All sectors of the American economy – in farming and in industry – grew and profited from war orders placed by Europeans for munitions, raw materials and foodstuffs. America, together with Canada, had the advantage of proximity to the European conflagration. The North Atlantic was the shortest sea passage and this became increasingly important as shipping space became constricted. The whole of the world, outside Europe, experienced a war-induced export boom, but it had its most powerful impact in North America. The Allied demands for war materiel stimulated the American economy, and at the same time, the absence of European manufactures on world markets allowed American producers to expand their supply to meet non-European demand, so the war both directly and indirectly spurred on the expansion of the United States within the world economy. One of the most visible markers was the increase of American exports, from $2.8 billion in 1913 to $7.3 billion by 1918.

The Allies had increasingly to pay for American supplies by raising loans in the United States and liquidating dollar securities. As a result, the United States changed during the war years from being a net international debtor to becoming the major international creditor. The American government accumulated over $7 million worth of claims on the Entente Powers, while private foreign investment in the United States was reduced from $7.2 billion in 1914 to $4 billion in 1919. American private overseas investment doubled largely replacing British economic influence in Canada and Latin America.

The Aircraft Industry

The development of the aircraft and the rapid emergence of the aircraft industry are striking examples of the technological advances arising from the exigencies of war. Despite the Wright brothers' achievement in making the first powered flight, the United states lost its early lead in aeronautics, and by the eve of World War I the French were the most important practitioners of military aviation in Europe, having turned to aviation production on a large scale in 1909. The Germans concentrated on airships; between 1910 and 1914, five Zeppelins provided a circular service for seven German cities. The British War Office had taken an interest in flying from 1906, but in April 1911 Britain still had only six military aircraft.

The initial wartime role of aircraft was reconnaissance, at first by eye alone, then by photography means, and finally by radio, with the aim of artillery spotting. Such flights were opposed by anti-aircraft fire, which gradually improved in accuracy, and attack by other aircraft. This resulted in a need for specially developed reconnaissance planes, and ultimately for purpose-built medium and heavy bombers. By 1918 the biplane fighter had become a thoroughbred. In the process, and despite the growing application of mass production, they had become costly weapons.

By 1914 Germany had established a lead in aeronautical science, and in 1915 Junkers produced an all-metal aircraft and went on to construct a long-wing cantilever monoplane fighter, which was a complete innovation. Although this technological breakthrough was not immediately exploited, Junkers had established the shape and construction of the future aeroplane. Despite design advances, however, most aircraft on both sides during the war continued to consist of frameworks of wood or metal, braced with wires and covered with doped fabric, and the wings externally braced. The general simplicity of the construction of most aircraft frames allowed mass production, whereas the use of wood framing meant that furniture producers could turn to airframe construction.

Once mass-production began, a bottleneck tended to be occur in the building of engines. Production increased sharply in France, Germany and Britain during the war; the entry of the United States into the war in 1917 did not

◄ Aircraft propeller blades were made of laminations of wood, glued and then shaped with a spokeshave. Completed propellers, after varnishing, had to be very carefully balanced, so as to place a constant load on the aircraft engine. These propellers were destined to be installed on Bristol Fighters, which went into production during the second half of 1916; deliveries began in December. Altogether 3800 were ordered during the course of the war.

◄ Prototypes for the Bristol Jupiter engine began to be available at the end of the war, which revealed the engine's advantages in terms of low weight, fuel economy and ease of maintenance. Its military adoption was long delayed, in part due to the Air Board insisting on type testing following the in-service failures of the Arab and Dragonfly engines in 1918, when both were in full production. The Jupiter was proved after the war by its installation in the Bristol Badger, the Bristol Bullet, the 10-seater Bristol Pullman and the Bristol Racer. It was to enter military service in the Bristol Bulldog of 1927.

significantly alter the balance of the air war. Nevertheless, in August 1918 it was estimated that more than 8000 aircraft were deployed on the Western Front, nearly 3000 of them French machines, and possibly a similar number of German, compared with only 300 American.

One result of the emphasis on aircraft production was the rapid technological development of the industry. Despite the relative insignificance of the United States' contribution to the war in the air, the development of a 400 horse-power engine had immense implications for the civil aviation industry in the 1920s.

The whole organization was, however, welded into one, and the current adjustments of policy and action effected, by the formation of the Allied Maritime Transport Executive, composed of the heads of the French, Italian and British Divisions together with the second American Delegate, the British member being at once Chairman of the Executive and Secretary of the Council.

J. A. SALTER, ALLIED SHIPPING CONTROL (1921)

Japan joined the Allied side but played very little part in the actual hostilities. Instead Japanese exports increased. The market for Japanese cotton exports expanded to include Australia, India and the Dutch East Indies. Japan's iron and steel and engineering industries expanded so that by the end of the war Japanese yards were supplying the United States with ships. The war export boom in Japan generated a balance of payments surplus which was used to increase currency reserves and supply overseas credits, and which led to some direct investment in China.

Shipping difficulties along the longer routes from Latin America, Asia and Oceania meant that primary producers outside North America generally did not experience the same wartime volume increase in exports, but the value of their exports grew from 1915 onward with the terms of trade moving in their favor, so that they accumulated export surpluses. The shortage of European manufactures encouraged import substitution in the form of the creation of manufacturers overseas, the most important beneficiary being the Brazilian cotton textile industry which

had a sizeable prewar base. However, most of the development of local manufacturing in the primary producing countries was high-cost and only sustainable while the war kept out European supplies. This was also the case with some Japanese industrial developments.

The Russian Revolution

War-weariness had its first major effect in Europe in Russia in February 1917 when the czarist regime was overthrown and replaced by a Provisional Government led by Alexander Kerensky and backed by the middle classes and the bureaucrats. Almost immediately the St Petersburg Soviet of 1905 was revived, followed by the creation of similar bodies in other major cities. The Petersburg Soviet was initially a non-party body, having been re-established by factory workers, though it was rapidly to come under the domination of the Menshevik (moderate) wing of the Russian Social Democrat Party.

Aided by the German government, Lenin, leader of the revolutionary Bolshevik wing of the Social Democrats, arrived in Petrograd (formerly St Petersburg) on 3 April and, somewhat to the astonishment of those who welcomed him, he hailed the worldwide socialist revolution. Initially Lenin was alone amongst Social Democrats in perceiving that it would be possible in Russia to proceed rapidly from a bourgeois to a proletarian and peasant revolution. He also believed that the war could be ended by a European socialist revolution which would allow Russia itself to

pass through a socialist revolution. He rejected the Provisional Government and the war and proposed the slogan of "All power to the Soviets".

The tide of events moved in the Bolsheviks' favor. When it became public on 18 April that the Provisional Government had agreed to honor the undertakings to the Allies that had been given by the czarist regime, the government fell. The second Provisional Government contained no Bolsheviks, which meant that the party would not be compromised by collaboration in a bourgeois-socialist coalition; theirs was the only political platform offering peace at any price.

▼ The distribution of revolutionary propaganda fell upon fertile soil in Russia. The offensive of the Kerensky government in July failed as thousands of Russian troops, tired of war, disarmed themselves and fled from the war zone. As Lenin said, they voted with their feet. Within two weeks Russian military gains in Austria-Hungary from two years' campaigning were lost. Moscow factory workers went on strike in August 1917, following the shooting of mutineers at the Front.

▲ The social turmoil within Russia in 1917 did not come as a shock, although the Russian upper classes were unprepared for revolution. The collapse of czarist society had been heralded by the 1905 revolution.

◄ The Russian revolutions of 1917 were relatively bloodless. The only battle line in Petrograd (later Leningrad) was between Kerensky's Provisional Government and the Bolsheviks. Within a day the Provisional Government had been overthrown.

Against a background of increasing unrest and growing chaos over the summer, the Kerensky government was established, although soon threatened by the attempted military coup of Kornilov in August. The cities were filling with returning soldiers, while rural unrest was growing. In this tense situation in late August the Bolsheviks achieved majorities in the Petrograd and Moscow Soviets, but not in the All-Russian Congress of Soviets. In view of the growing social disorder, Lenin in September decided that time was ripe for the seizure of power. He returned to Petrograd in disguise on 9 October 1917 to prepare for armed insurrection. Bolshevik forces went into action on the morning of 25 October and the second All-Russian Congress of Soviets proclaimed the transfer of power to the Soviets (revolutionary workers' councils).

The new revolutionary government faced a dire situation. Industrial production within Russia had been declining since February as a result of owners closing works, of strikes and the establishment of factory committees, while the urban grain supply had almost collapsed. The acute dislocation of the economy was soon joined by a political counter-revolution. By the end of November Cossack armies and other "White" forces were beginning to assemble in southeast Russia.

At the end of the war the revolution did spread to central Europe, with socialist uprisings in Berlin and other German cities such as Munich, and in 1919 in Hungary. It was this Bolshevik threat which led the Allies, and particularly the Americans, to mount a food relief program for devastated Europe. A possible Bolshevik insurrection in Vienna in spring 1919 was countered by a threat to cut off Allied food supplies.

The economic settlement

From 1916 Allied statesmen had begun to recognize explicitly the economic nature of the war; there was even the fear of a military stalemate, with the war continuing in the form of an inter-national economic struggle. An Allied conference in Paris not only established the grounds for greater wartime economic cooperation within the Entente, but began preparations for the anticipated subsequent economic conflict with Germans. These aimed at constricting Germany's international economic influence, while mobilizing supplies for the growth of the Allied bloc. However, particular national interests were too conflicting for the program to be carried forward. The lowest common denominator was the extraction of reparations from Germany and the seizure of German overseas assets. Against this, the "fourteen points" proposed by American president Woodrow Wilson promised a peace involving economic liberalism for all.

Most Allied statesmen looked to a postwar world in which liberal capitalism would be rapidly re-established within their own domestic economies after the dismantling of wartime planning and control measures. For the international economy, given the economic losses, the inflation and sizeable domestic public debts, the severance of extra-European links, the heritage of public debts to America, and the loss of assets in Russia, particularly by the French, they preferred some kind of new order. However, American statesmen would have no truck with a postwar managed world economy – neither the maintenance of forums erected in wartime such as the inter-Allied shipping council, nor their transformation into organs of the embryonic League of Nations. Washington did agree to the provision of further dollar loans, but once the peace treaties were signed, European reconstruction and the rebuilding of the world economy were to be left to private capitalism.

Hostilities in the West ended on 11 November 1918, but the ending of the Great War was followed by "little" wars which continued until the early 1920s throughout Central and Eastern Europe. Then the peoples of Eastern Europe took matters into their own hands and the Habsburg Empire disintegrated through national revolutions. The main business of the Western leaders in Paris was the drawing up of a peace treaty with Germany; those with other members of the Central Powers followed. The Versailles Treaty redrew the boundaries of Germany. France regained the provinces lost in 1871 – Alsace and Lorraine – and so severed the steel industries of these provinces from their supply of German coke from the Ruhr. A new Poland similarly shattered the economic integration of the Silesian coal and steel industries. The boundaries of Czechoslovakia were determined as much by the desire to give the nation economic strength as by an acknowledgment of the patchwork of ethnic settlement in Central Europe. These two, and the other successor states, through hostile tariffs and appropriation of foreign assets, disrupted the integrated and economically self-sufficient unity of the former Habsburg Empire. The treaty also led to disputes, such as those between Czechoslovakia and Poland over the coal-rich area of Teschen, straddling the new boundaries of the new states, which provoked one of Europe's "little" wars. The Versailles Treaty system, by failing to grant

► One of Lenin's basic premises was that the war was imperialist. Even the war itself fed Western capitalists, standing upon the crushed working masses and maintaining discipline by the gibbet. Within Russia, there were fears that the revolution was phoney. Some early propaganda postcards portrayed workers being harangued by speakers, apparently promising a new order with food and work, but in fact working for capitalist masters.

▲ **World War I, which together with World War II has been called the European civil war, did not end in 1918. The Franco-German conflict continued as a dispute over reparations, leading in 1923 to the French occupation of the Ruhr. Berlin responded by directing passive resistance in this most important German industrial area. The occupying forces organized a separate civil and rail administration, seized banks and factories and isolated the Ruhr economically from the rest of Germany. Some French leaders even considered establishing a new independent Rhineland province.**

▼ **The Central Powers defeated Serbia during the autumn of 1915, with French and British forces arriving too late to be of any assistance. Part of the Serbian army retreated through Albania, and 150,000 people were finally taken to safety.**

Japanese Overseas Expansion

Japanese colonial expansion began after the war with China in 1894–95, which led to Japan acquiring Formosa (Taiwan) and the Pescadores. Following the Russo–Japanese War (1904–5), Japan annexed Chosen (Korea) in 1910 and established spheres of economic influence in the Guangdong peninsula and South Manchuria. As a result of World War I, the Chinese treaty port of Jiao Xian was transferred from Germany to Japan, while some former German Pacific island colonies became Japanese mandates under the League of Nations.

Japan not only made territorial gains as a result of the war, but also enjoyed a balance of payments surplus, generated by the war-induced boom, totalling over 3,000 million yen for the period 1914 to 1919. This temporarily transformed Japan into a net international creditor. Some of this wartime windfall was used to make political loans to Chinese local and provincial governments. Japanese colonial trade, which had been insignificant before 1914 and still only accounted for 12 percent of total trade in 1918, rapidly expanded during the 1920s, comprising 20 percent of the total in 1929. Japan exported manufactures to her Asian colonies, taking in return raw materials and foodstuffs to feed the Japanese population, which grew by more than 25 percent between 1914 and 1930. The cultivation of Japanese-style rice was introduced into Korea and Formosa during the 1920s and by the end of the decade these two colonies had a rice output equivalent to an eighth of Japanese home production. However, the growth of cotton exports, particularly of yarn, to China slowed during the 1920s. Japanese development of its Asian colonies involved capital supplied by the state. One of the major enterprises was the South Manchuria Railway Company, which also controlled large-scale industrial undertakings.

clear national self-determination in Central and Eastern Europe, while destroying the economic integration of a region which had developed over the second half of the 19th century, created nationalist movements and established the groundwork for future economic instability. Outside Europe, the division of the overseas territories of the Central Powers amongst the Allies created tensions between the United States, Britain and France, particularly with respect to oil concessions and the development of ocean cables.

Two great matters were not settled in Paris – reparations and the settlement of inter-Allied debts. The first was finally left to the Reparations Commission, resulting in a running conflict with Germany, which ultimately led in 1923 to French and Belgian military intervention. Inter-Allied debts provoked serious disagreement between Washington and Europe. The Americans insisted that Allied dollar war loans be honored under some suitable composition, without any linkage to German reparations. They regarded the preliminaries for European reconstruction as being the conclusion of agreements to settle Europe's dollar debts and the establishment of a moderate schedule for reparations.

German reparations

On 5 November 1918, German reparations following World War I were defined by the American Secretary of State, Robert Lansing, as the repair of all damages inflicted upon the civilian population of the Allies and their property by land, sea or air. Article 19 of the Armistice stipulated the restitution of the currency reserve of the Belgian National Bank, together with all documents, cash and securities removed from German occupied areas. This amounted in total to 8.5 billion francs, and Germany was also liable to pay several billions of gold marks through deliveries of materiel, together with 5000 locomotives, 150,000 railway wagons, and 5000 lorries. Such stipulations mounted in each monthly renewal of the armistice.

Not only was Germany required to pay reparations, but the territory of the Reich was reduced substantially, by 13 percent compared with 1914. As a result Germany lost 12 percent of its population, 16 percent of its coal production and 48 percent of its iron production. The division of territory in the east was the subject of plebiscites and these led to Allenstein, Marienwerder and western Upper Silesia deciding to remain with Germany. However, Danzig became a free city under League of Nations control. In the west the Saar was League-administered until 1935. In addition Germany had to surrender her overseas colonies and give up 80 percent of her prewar fleet. Overseas losses included German commercial concessions in China, Egypt, Liberia, Morocco and Siam, which had been freely negotiated before 1914. These changes dislocated the German economy and made reparation payments more difficult.

The payment of reparations was not unusual. France had made such recompense in 1815 and again in 1871. But the definition of the coverage of reparations caused division amongst the Entente

▲ French troops re-entered Strasbourg on 29 November 1918 after 47 years, but the economic reintegration of the provinces of Alsace and Lorraine took longer. It involved presidential decrees, as well as stipulations in the Treaty of Versailles that Germany granted duty-free entry to goods from the provinces for a five-year transition period. Nonetheless the economy of the provinces remained geared to exporting to Germany, a stance that could be undermined by the reimposition of a German protective customs barrier. Re-establishing French administration led to further cries for regional independence, especially in Alsace. Lorraine's dependence upon Germany was even greater as its steel and metal working industries were based upon Ruhr coking coal.

Powers, with the result that the Treaty of Versailles described only the nature of damages to be made good, which now included aspects of Allied war costs. The precise sum was to be determined by the Reparations Commission by 1 May 1921, together with an appropriate schedule for its payment over the following 30 years. While the Commission was making its calculations, Germany had to pay 20 billion gold marks and deliver immediately 100 billion gold marks in bearer bonds carrying 5 percent interest from 1 May 1921. In addition, Germany had to defray the costs of the Allied army of occupation and Allied food relief. Further, before 1921 Germany had to hand over ships, animals, machinery, coal and chemicals, whose value would be ascertained by the Reparations Commission and offset against Germany's final liability.

The Reparations Commission only came into existence once the Versailles Treaty had been ratified by the Allies and had come into force, on 10 January 1920. However, its prime functions were largely bypassed through direct negotiations between the Entente and Berlin. A conference at Spa between the Allies and Germany

failed to reach agreement, and Allied terms, after a meeting in January 1921 in Paris, laid down German initial payments of 2 billion gold marks, rising to 6 billion after 11 years and continuing for a further 31 years. In addition there were to be annual payments equivalent to 12 percent of the value of German exports for all 42 years, which meant that a part of the reparations settlement would apparently be matched to Germany's payments capacity. German counter-proposals were ignored and when Germany failed to accept the Allied terms, some cities in the Ruhr were occupied in early March 1921.

During the spring of 1921 the reparations question was in chaos. Finally an Entente summit drew up the "London Schedule of Payments", which in effect required Germany to make annual payments of 2 billion gold marks plus 26 percent of the value of German exports, together with the supply of material and labor to make good war devastation and aid Allied economic development. The German government, under Wirth, accepted the London Schedule, partly to prevent the threatened occupation of the whole of the Ruhr and partly because it involved a single sum of only 50 billion gold marks, which had been its one proposal. By various devices, Germany paid the first 1 billion gold marks, but by the autumn of 1921, with inflation mounting rapidly, it was difficult to see how the London Schedule could be maintained. Attempts were made to raise a foreign loan, but German industry would only supply the necessary resources in return for poliical concessions which its own government was unwilling to grant. Some terms for guarantees of reparations payments were agreed between Germany and the Reparations Commission in May 1922 and Germany did make a payment in July 1922, but at the same time applied for a total moratorium for the rest of 1922, whilst maintaining the impossibility of making further payments over the following two years.

The critical factor was, of course, German inflation, but there was an increasing body of opinion within the Reparations Commission that held that the German government was responsible for the fall of the mark through its failure to balance the budget. As a result the Commission was unable to reach a decision about further moratoria. There were mounting disagreements between France and Germany. The rift between France and Britain over the reparations question became open in August 1922, aggravated by rivalry in the Middle East. The British Government stated that it would renounce all financial claims against its Allies and for reparations in return for a general settlement of inter-Allied debts. In view of the deep slump of the early 1920s, London was fearful of any further disturbances of the European economy, and German inflation was rampant: by November 1922 9000 marks were needed to obtain one dollar. But the French premier, Raymond Poincaré, would only accept a reparation settlement involving the cancellation of Allied war debts which also met the cost of the French reconstruction program in the devastated areas. At the Paris Conference of January 1923 the British tabled an almost incomprehensible plan for German economic recovery which included a four-year reparations moratorium, but Poincaré was only prepared to accept such amorphous proposals if they contained a solid kernel of German guarantees to pay reparations. The reparations commission declared that Germany was technically in default on payments and Poincaré, in conjunction with Belgium, despatched forces to the Ruhr. Initially these consisted of a small contingent of engineers to supervise German state economic assets, thereby securing "productive pledges" for reparations payments. But this intervention was countered by a campaign of passive resistance, orchestrated by Berlin, which turned the Ruhr occupation into a full-scale test of national wills.

The costs of German resistance were substantial and totally unhinged the state budget; it was abandoned in September 1923. The reparations problem was once again handed over to experts, but now with full and active American participation. The Reparations Commission established two committees; one had the remit of balancing the German budget, stabilizing the German currency and constructing a new reparations plan,

Helping the Refugees

The aftermath of war saw many civilians homeless and stateless, including around two million people who had fled from the Russian Revolution and civil war, the majority of whom were stranded in desperate straits in central Europe. Various states appealed to the League of Nations on their behalf, but the League itself lacked financial resources. However, in 1921 it set up a Refugee Organization headed by the Norwegian Fridtjof Nansen, who was a well-known Arctic explorer as well as a diplomat. He believed that the European neutral countries had a special role to play in healing the breach caused by the war, and went on to devote his life to helping prisoners of war and refugees. France – which had strong links with Russian and a postwar shortage of labor – and the Scandinavian countries were the only governments to offer aid to the new organization, but Nansen supplemented this by a series of conferences and direct appeals. In conjunction with the Red Cross, he directed famine relief in the Ukraine in 1922, saving many thousand of lives, and also helped the Armenian and Syrian refugees from Turkey. Nansen received the Nobel Peace Prize for his work, and his Refugee Organization was the forerunner of the International Refugees Organization of the United Nations.

▶ The war of movement on the Eastern Front resulted in armies being encircled and large numbers of prisoners being taken. This first happened with the German victories at Tannenberg and the Masurian Lakes in August and September 1914, which halted and reversed the Russian advance into East Prussia. At the Tannenberg the entire Russian Second Army was lost. However, during the Russian summer offensive of 1916, 400,000 prisoners were taken. Comparable situations only developed on the Western Front in the late summer of 1918 with the final Allied advance. The treatment of prisoners was laid down by prewar conventions, but they could be employed by the captor nation as part of the labor force.

◀ Fridtjof Nansen was instrumental in repatriating some half a million prisoners of war from Russia and Siberia and assisting the two million refugees from the Russian Revolution. As the League of Nations High Commissioner for Refugees in the 1920s, Nansen's work had a major result in the so-called "Nansen passport", a certificate delivered by national authorities on the recommendation of the High Commissioners. Eventually it was accepted as a travel document by over fifty countries.

◀ **The Paris Peace Conference was dominated by the "Big Three" – the British Prime Minister David Lloyd George, the French Prime Minister Georges Clemenceau, and President Woodrow Wilson of the United States. Lloyd George was especially concerned that article 231 of the Treaty of Versailles – the so-called war-guilt clause – should be enforced, even though he knew that Germany's resources were inadequate. Clemenceau, too, under pressure from President Poincaré and the French Chamber of Deputies, maintained that Germany would have to pay reparations. Wilson sought a just peace, based on the "fourteen points" he had proposed in 1918 as a basis for a free postwar world.**

while the other was to estimate German capital flight and devise measures for its repatriation. French ascendancy in 1923 was undermined by France's financial weakness in 1924 and consequent French reliance on American bankers to hold up the franc. The Americans had always made clear that their intention was to secure a moderate reparations settlement to pacify Europe and this is what the Dawes plan of 1924 involved. It laid down a schedule of payments for 64 years, beginning at 1 billion gold marks in 1925–26, rising to 2.5 billion by 1928–29 and thereafter indexed to German "prosperity". The necessary resources were to be obtained half from German taxes and half from a mortgage on German industry and railways. The plan was to be initiated by a 0.8 billion gold marks external German loan.

Germany made reparation payments in the late 1920s as a result of American lending to Germany, while the reparations schedule was once more revised by the Young Plan of 1930. The Young Plan was made ineffective by the financial crisis of 1931, when inter-government debts were frozen for a year by the moratorium imposed by President Hoover. In 1932, following the Lausanne Conference, Germany formally ceased paying reparations. Germany's capacity to pay reparations, and the extent to which the German hyperinflation was deliberately caused by the German government in order to shuffle out of reparations, are still matters for debate.

From September 1924 to the time of the Hoover moratorium of July 1931, reparations totalled 10.8 billion marks, but over the same period German foreign indebtedness increased by about 15.5 billion marks, given allowances for foreign direct investment in Germany and German overseas investment during the late 1920s. The Dawes Plan gave foreign, especially American, investors confidence in Germany, and this was increased by Parker Gilbert, the general Agent for Reparations in Berlin and the Transfer Committee. These two organs apparently ensured the stability of the German economy through overseeing public finances and monetary policy, but did not diminish Germany's economic vulnerability.

THE GLAMOR OF TRAVEL

In the early 20th century, especially after World War I, comfortable travel for the well-to-do became big business. Luxury liners crossed the Atlantic, vying for business by advertising their speed, comfort and style; aircraft and airships allowed the rich to move ever more quickly around the globe; and the rail service, in Europe at least, was in its heyday, both for comfort and the comprehensiveness of the network. In the most renowned towns and cities of the world stood luxury hotels, trading on their cosmopolitanism and the quality of their service, which harked back to the more settled world of the 19th century. The rich had a network of glamor, through which they could tour the world without disturbing their illusions or their sense of their inalienable rights of privilege.

The network was an extension of the Grand Tour, itself a tradition whereby young aristocrats completed their education by a leisurely tour around the cultural highspots of Europe. With the establishment of travel agencies such as Thomas Cook's and the publishing of guides to the sights of Europe (such as Baedeker's guides, published from the 1840s), the tour became accessible to a much broader spectrum of people. Cook's first European tour had been organized in 1851, and from 1867 they began to offer hotel coupons. Twelve years later they entered the banking and foreign exchange business, and thus offered their clients a complete travel service.

Luxury rail carriages, the Pullmans, were introduced into Europe from the United States in the 1880s. But the years after 1918 saw a proliferation of Grand Expresses – the Orient Express, which plied between Paris and Istanbul, and similar services such as the Golden Arrow, the Rheingold and the Blue Train. Luxury liners flourished in the years before 1914, and then again after World War I. With the trend towards air travel by people more concerned to arrive quickly than to travel in style, the liners sought new trade by offering leisurely cruises around the cultural highspots of the world. They thus enjoyed a golden summer in the 1930s. For travelers on these ships and trains, traveling could be better than arriving.

The airship attempted to compete in providing a service that combined speed with comfort, and the largest airships could carry more than 100 passengers across the Atlantic in less than three days. Unlike travel by rail or sea, air travel remained almost entirely a luxury activity until World War II and the advent in the early 1950s of the first jet airliners. Prices began to fall in the mid-1950s, and by the mid-1970s only some 20 percent of transatlantic passengers were paying the full fare. As packaged holidays brought the exclusive resorts within the reach of most people in the industrialized countries, the old exclusive hotels were swallowed up in a mass of uniformity and high-rise concrete. Those seeking the glamor of travel had to seek ever more original ways of making a journey an event of thrill and challenge.

▲ Switzerland had become an important tourist resort in the 1860s. Winter sports were developed by Sir Henry Lunn, who, on a visit in 1883, recognized the possibilities arising from introducing skiing from Norway. This 1900s tour is being escorted up the Mont Blanc glacier at Chamonix.

▲ Flying was a glamorous pursuit from the mid-1920s until the early 1950s, with adventurous and dangerous flights in the 1930s by well-off couples receiving substantial press publicity. In the 1930s aircraft were specifically developed, such as the D.H. Moth series, for private touring and many flying licenses were held by society ladies.

▶ International aircraft flights, particularly flying-boat routes involving overnight hotel stays at exotic locations, creamed off the wealthy from the custom of the luxury liners in the 1930s. The ships built for transport were increasingly redeployed for cruising.

► Growing passenger numbers in the 1960s took the edge off the glamor of air travel, particularly through congested terminals. Airports were redeveloped, but often lagged behind traffic growth. Airport design was revolutionized by the new approach taken at Schipol, Amsterdam.

► The rising incomes of the advanced industrial economies during the 1960s resulted in a growing market for travel. The more ambitious young Westerners developed a new "Grand Tour", to the Orient. For many American students this was but an extension of backpacking around Europe.

▲ The availability of international travel has also led to it being used as a vehicle for fund raising for charity. Sponsoring was developed as a way of financing scientific expeditions, as well as more imaginative sports, such as mountain-cycling. This has now been taken a stage further, with commercial and private sponsoring to raise money for a charitable cause.

Datafile

The 1920s was a decade of marked contrasts. Outwardly it was a prosperous time, seemingly confirmed by the growing consumption of new consumer durables and new leisure industries like the cinema. However, the decade was also characterized by economic instability, with marked fluctuations in the level of activity, for example the deep, sharp slump of the early 1920s. The growth of new technologically-based industries contrasted with the depressed state of major manufacturing sectors, established in the 19th century, like textiles and coal. Moreover, not all advanced economies shared equally in the industrial boom. This was most firmly based in the United States and France, but Britain, and Germany to some extent, experienced major structural problems, since the contraction of older manufacturing activity was not fully offset by the expansion of the new. Postwar recovery was uneven among the industrial and industrializing economies, and for most primary producing economies the 1920s was a period of depression, marked by falling prices.

▼ As well as being the world's leading producer of manufactures, the United States was also a major primary producer. American agriculture had a lean time during the 1920s, following the prosperity of the war years. The problems for American farmers stemmed from falling market prices, allied to relatively high production costs after 1920.

▶ Between 1921 and 1929 average real income per head in the United States increased by 37 percent, while industrial production rose by 90 percent. However, the pace of growth was not even, with falterings in 1924 and 1927 and there were major differences between sectors of the economy, and between different social and ethnic groups.

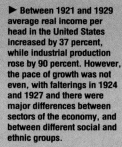

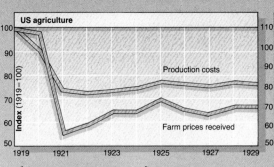

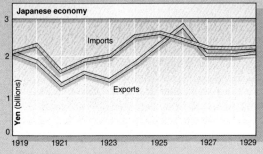

◀ Japan had a balance of payments surplus during World War I, but in the 1920s imports exceeded exports in every year except 1926. Japan's international trading problems were exacerbated by the effects of the Great Kanto earthquake of 1923, which made it necessary to import reconstruction materials. The weak yen encouraged export growth.

▶ German unemployment was high during the 1920s, only falling below 8.5 percent in 1925. The German economy experienced very sharp year-to-year fluctuations, despite its strong recovery after the hyperinflation. The ending of inflation led to a stabilization crisis in 1924, while an outflow of capital in 1926 domestic investment.

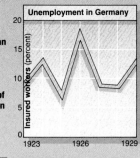

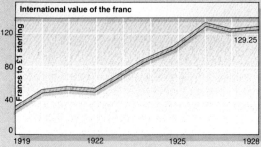

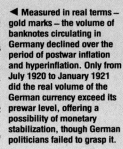

◀ Measured in real terms – gold marks – the volume of banknotes circulating in Germany declined over the period of postwar inflation and hyperinflation. Only from July 1920 to January 1921 did the real volume of the German currency exceed its prewar level, offering a possibility of monetary stabilization, though German politicians failed to grasp it.

▲ France experienced inflation throughout the first half of the 1920s as a result of unbalanced budgets caused by reconstruction expenditure in the devastated regions. There was a steady decline in the international value of the franc, as against the pound. The fall of the franc became a matter of public concern from mid-1923.

▶ After the postwar restocking boom broke in the summer of 1920, unemployment in Britain never fell below 10 percent. One of the major reasons why it remained so high was the difficulties experienced by the old "staple" export industries, especially shipbuilding. There were marked regional variations in unemployment levels.

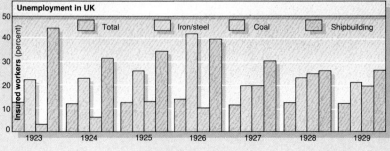

▶ After recovering sharply during the postwar boom, British exports, by value in current prices, remained stagnant throughout the decade. Britain's 19th-century export industries had lost their dynamism and this situation was aggravated both by sterling's return to its prewar parity in 1925 and by rising barriers to trade in the world economy.

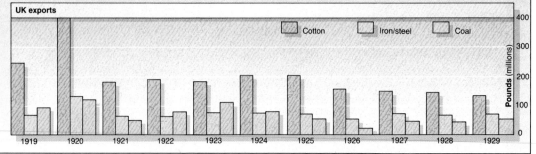

THE POSTWAR YEARS

At the end of World War I the common intention of political and industrial leaders among the liberal-capitalist economies of the West was a "return to normalcy" – putting the clock back to July 1914. In some economic realms this was possible, and the immediate postwar years were marked by rapid dismantling of the systems of state control erected during the war. But it was not possible to return to the world economy of 1914, as the delicate fabric of that entity had been torn apart by the war. Further, war-induced changes occurred at different rates among the economies of the world and consequently there were marked disparities between countries during the 1920s. This lack of homogeneity arose from a range of factors such as the prewar size of "new" industries within an economy and the pace of wartime and postwar inflation. Therefore the basic pattern – of a postwar restocking boom to mid-1920, sharp and severe slump in the early 1920s, followed by recovery and even boom in the late 1920s – varied considerably from country to country.

After the war there was demand for everything, but above all for foodstuffs, industrial raw materials and producer goods. In particular, con-tinental urban Europe east of the Rhine was experiencing famine in varying degrees, while the whole of Europe was short of energy. Consequently, the postwar restocking boom which carried through to the summer of 1920 was experienced most strongly by those industrial economies, such as Britain and the United States, which had intact productive capacity, and by the primary producing countries. The price bubble of this boom broke in mid-1920, by which time supply had got more into balance with demand, while the monetary authorities in Britain and the United States introduced measures to control the expansion of credit.

On the continent of Europe, with a few exceptions like Czechoslovakia and Latvia, inflation continued after 1920. A division can be made among European economies between those that experienced mild inflation until the mid-1920s, like France, and those – in particular Austria, Germany and Hungary – where inflation gathered such a pace that it became hyperinflation, destroying local currencies in 1922 and 1923. High rates of inflation were associated not only with expansion of the money supply, increased public borrowing and balance of payments deficits, but

▼ The 1920s were prosperous years in the United States, although the rich got richer at a faster rate than the poor became less poor. Further, the 1920s boom did not affect all regions equally. Abject poverty persisted amongst the blacks of the South and the whites in the southern Appalachians. City slums contrasted with the growth of a new suburbia characterized by imitation English Tudor houses.

In France in the 1920s motor cars became big business

► Ypres in Belgium was lost to the Germans, but then recaptured by British troops during October 1914. Thereafter the area experienced intense fighting, resulting in as many as a million deaths over the course of the war. The city's cathedral and Cloth Hall became physical symbols of the Entente's determination to resist German aggression. The result of trench warfare on the Western Front was a waste land. Ten *départements* of France had to be reconstructed. In 1923 it was estimated that 13 billion francs would be needed to complete the rebuilding of roads, railroads and canals, filling in trenches and shell holes, and the clearing of barbed wire and unexploded shells.

► The average Frenchman was averse to using checks, preferring cash both for transactions and for savings. Public confidence in the franc in 1920 was increased by the government's agreement to repay loans from the Bank of France.

▼ The Le Mans 24-hour motor race both proved the reliability of the automobile and attracted public attention. Between 1923 and 1938 the four main European car-producing countries manufactured ten million vehicles, with output growing faster than in the United States though from a lower base.

also with weak coalition governments. In these circumstances inflation acted as a common denominator across major interest groups – farmers benefited from high food prices, industrialists profited from the ability to export generated by a depreciating currency, and some sections of workers gained from full employment. Further, inflation shielded economies, to varying degrees, from the acute slump of the early 1920s by expanding their trade through the depreciation of their currencies. However, when inflation in Central and Eastern Europe became hyperinflation, stabilization was often only possible through recourse to external funds, to which there were strings attached dictating the nature of stabilization.

French modernization

The position of French agriculture was weak, but in sharp contrast France experienced an industrial boom during the 1920s, drawing its labor force from rural workers, who for the first time began to move in numbers to the towns and cities. Hydroelectricity, which had a prewar base, was used to power this boom, which led to technical developments in steelmaking and chemical manufacturing.

What best typifies the French industrial boom was the growth of the motor industry, from a prewar base. It was dominated by three firms – Renault, Citroën and Peugeot – which in 1928 accounted for 68 percent of sales of cars in France. Renault had been established in 1899, and by 1914 their works at Billancourt, Paris, occupied 150,000 square meters (1.6 million square feet). War demands expanded the size of the enterprise further and in the 1920s Billancourt became the largest automobile plant in Europe, fed by iron and steel from the former Thyssen works at Handange in Lorraine, one of the provinces now reclaimed from Germany. To Billancourt were added new plants in both the Paris region and the French provinces, while Renault also established assembly lines in six other countries, including Britain and Germany.

In many respects the French boom of the 1920s constituted the belated modernization of the economy, a process which had begun in the 1890s. It was aided by the reconstruction of the devastated northern provinces and by the fall in value of the franc during the first half of the 1920s, due to unbalanced state budgets arising from the financing of reconstruction, which gave French exporters a price advantage, especially as other

80

currencies were progressively stabilized from 1922. However, the financing of reconstruction also posed great problems for the French government. Government finances were heavily dependent on short – and medium-term loans, issued to supply resources for the reconstruction of the war-damaged areas in the expectation that they would ultimately be discharged by German reparation payments. But as the franc continued to fall, it became increasingly difficult to market reconstruction loans, and by late 1922 the French floating debt amounted to nearly eighty billion francs and was a potential source of inflationary pressure. Meanwhile, the vexed question of reparations dragged on. Cutting back government reconstruction expenditure was politically unthinkable, especially as priority had initially been given to industry and so there were still people in the war-torn regions who were living in terrible conditions. Poincaré's decision to occupy the Ruhr in 1923, in protest at what the French viewed as a deliberate German attempt to avoid the payment of reparations, stimulated bond sales for a short period, but eventually the government had to resort to the Bank of France for assistance. The franc continued to decline, but the main public concern was now with the rise in prices, which shot up by 15 percent, more in the case of foodstuffs. By January 1924 the situation had reached crisis proportions.

The mid-1920s in France were marked by continued inflation and the further decline of the international value of the franc. Between May 1924 and July 1926 there were 11 French governments, whose successive finance ministers attempted to deal with the joint problems of inflation and fiscal imbalance. Returning as prime minister in July 1926, Poincaré introduced measures which finally stabilized the franc at a level of one-fifth of its prewar value. This continued to give the French economy an export advantage for both visible and invisible trade until the total collapse of the gold exchange standard in 1931.

Eastern Europe

Apart from Czechoslovakia, the industrial boom of the second half of the 1920s made little impact on Central and Eastern Europe. This was an area of primary production – Europe's own prairies stretching eastward into Russia – and here, as in other areas of foodstuffs and raw material production, incomes were depressed by the fall in prices. The war had made Western Europe more self-sufficient, and all the primary producers suffered in consequence. The resulting economic and social problems were compounded in Central and Eastern Europe by ethnic antipathy, the new political geography set up by the Treaty of Versailles and economic self-sufficiency.

The region had been devastated by the war

▲ The number of motor vehicles in France increased from 125,000 in 1913 to 2.25 million by 1938. In 1938 Renault, Citroën and Peugeot supplied three-quarters of the French market. The technological leader was Citroën, which in 1919 produced France's first popular car, the A-1, and by 1927 was making 400 cars a day, using American methods.

The Italian Corporate State

After an unpopular war, the Italian economy was weak, with huge debts and low industrial production. The early postwar years were marked by inflation, strikes and social disturbances. Taking power in 1922, the Fascists revoked war taxes, liberalized foreign trade policy, and in 1926 passed legislation organizing unions and employers into corporations. The right to strike was abolished. In 1925 trade protection measures were reintroduced in conjunction with the development of the corporate system. Henceforth the Italian economy was to operate under a system of "semi-private and planned capitalism". The larger part of the population was eventually grouped according to occupation into corporations, and a Ministry of Corporations established in 1926, giving the Fascists control over the economy. Postwar state assistance to industry was continued, and the Istituto Mobiliare Italiano was founded in 1931 to provide long-term industrial loans. The Fascists undertook a large program of public works, which were much publicized but which did not significantly reduce unemployment.

▲ The Italian Fascists took power in October 1922, following their virtually unopposed March on Rome. Initially Mussolini organized a broadly based cabinet with representatives from four democratic parties. The Chamber gave Mussolini a grant of "full powers" for a year. The Fascists then subverted and reduced all rival party groupings by methods including violence, and developed a corporatist state which had links with the older managerial and political elite but which destroyed any interest groups attempting either to oppose or to contest with them as a rival. The Fascists utilized the wave of Italian modernism and fully appreciated the propaganda advantages of film. Mussolini laid the foundation stone of the Istituto di Luce, a state-funded film production organization.

◄ A leitmotif of Fascist propaganda was the past glory of Roman civilization, deliberately used to support the building of a modern state. This common strand ran through many Fascist developments, from reestablishing a colonial empire in North and East Africa to reinterpreting classical architecture and social institutions, such as the Forum. Many public works were undertaken under Fascist rule: new bridges, roads and canals were intended to provide work for the unemployed.

and received substantial Allied, mainly American, relief assistance in 1919 and 1920. This had been given as much for political reasons as humanitarian, since not only had food aid been regarded as the best defense against Bolshevism, but its provision also permitted the orderly rundown of American wartime strategic food stocks, so stabilizing price movements. The new national frontiers blocked trade, which was additionally hindered by high protective tariffs. Through these the agrarian states in Eastern Europe attempted to develop industrial sectors, while industrial economies such as that of Czechoslovakia sustained local agricultural production. General antipathy toward Austria prevented Vienna from fully reassuming its role as the financial and commercial hub of Eastern Europe. The problems of trade in the early 1920s were compounded by hyperinflation in Austria and Hungary.

Limited international cooperation

The needs of eastern Europe did prompt mutual cooperative programs undertaken by Western governments in the early 1920s. The Brussels economic conference of 1920, held under the auspices of the League of Nations, produced the Ter Meulen relief scheme and the International Relief Credits Program of 1920. A further economic conference was held in Genoa in 1922, but this had no major practical results. The only advance made in Brussels and Genoa that had lasting impact was the growth of the cooperation between central bankers, led by Montagu Norman of the Bank of England and Benjamin Strong of the Federal Reserve Bank of New York.

Norman had been made deputy governor of the Bank of England in 1918, and governor in 1920. He was therefore heavily involved in plans for postwar financial reconstruction, a three-stage process beginning with the stabilization of hyperinflation in Austria, Hungary and Germany, followed by Britain's return to the gold standard in 1925 and completed by the formation of the Bank for International Settlements during 1929 and 1930. Norman was a committed Atlanticist, and he developed a firm personal friendship with Strong. Both men were in agreement that international bankers had more chance than politicians of guiding the public in the acceptance and execution of policies requiring time and patience for their implementation. However, Norman was unable to call a conference of central bankers in the early 1920s, with the result that this "bankers' diplomacy" was never concerted and consisted of piecemeal initiatives for various programs.

It was however, bankers' diplomacy which gave financial substance to the stabilization programs of the Financial Committee of the League of Nations first for Austria and then Hungary. The bankers were generally believers in liberal capitalism and stressed the importance of "sound money", but this attitude did not take into account the structural problems which had been caused by the fragmentation of the Habsburg imperial economy. The new national boundaries made little economic sense. They separated coal from iron, and spinning mills from weaving sheds; railroad tracks were separated from their junction points and repair sheds, and industrialists from their bankers. Among the vanquished, local industry was opened to the full force of Western competition as a result of the economic clauses of the peace treaties.

◀ The Fiat car plant was a superb example of modernism in Italian architecture, carrying the idea of the mass assembly line throughout the building, so that the whole of the activity within the complex was in the form of a continuous flow. Fascism did not especially accelerate the technological transformation of Italian industry, but it encouraged centralization and thereby assisted the growth of big business. The Fiat works was actually modeled, in terms of the production process, on Ford factories in Detroit. In June 1927 the Fascist government provided tax advantages for mergers. The growth of modern Italian big business, with 266 mergers in 1928 and 313 in 1929, was coupled with a crude interpretation of scientific management, extending the working day from eight to nine hours and imposing wage cuts.

► Inflation aggravated the already dire food situation within German cities and towns. The war had ended with the black market being the main source of food. Some relief was provided by American supplies in 1919 and Western private charity thereafter, especially the work undertaken by Quakers. German agriculture did slowly recover, but farmers and peasants were antagonistic toward the postwar continuation of the state-controlled economy. As a result soup kitchens and other forms of assistance became a common feature of urban life, while in the countryside, in what was called the "paradise of inflation", peasants were paying off their mortgages, rebuilding their farms, and restoring their herds to prewar levels.

German hyperinflation

Germany's own unique monetary experience began in 1921. During the initial years of peace the mark fell on the foreign exchanges, but internal prices rose more slowly, not immediately reflecting the external decline of the currency. This inflation had many roots: postwar shortages and dislocation, a balance of payments deficit, an unbalanced state budget and political instability.

The expansion of the German money supply was fed by the Reichsbank, which gave credits to the government to cover the shortfall of tax revenue as against expenditure, and to industry, initially at very low rates of interest – five percent in July 1922. From the end of 1922, as the mark fell daily on the foreign exchanges, domestic prices were immediately adjusted, with shops closing at noon to alter price tickets. So much money was needed for even simple transactions that it had to be moved in suitcases and perambulators, and its very production caused increasing problems. By August 1923, as many as 30 paper mills were supplying the Reichsbank with paper, to be turned into banknotes by 150 printing firms running 2000 presses night and day.

◄ As German inflation accelerated, prices became astronomic. Price labels had to become larger, just to accommodate the required number of zeros, with four eggs costing 40,000 marks. Carrying sufficient banknotes became an increasing problem: a whole basket of notes was needed in order to complete a very normal, everyday transaction. The shortage of food was an added and particular factor of the inflation, but the losses suffered by city dwellers because of high food prices were gains for those in the countryside.

The summer of 1923 in Germany was one of hopelessness. The mark had largely gone out of circulation to be replaced by dollars, if they were obtainable, or anything which retained its value. Otherwise transactions were made by barter. Many suffered great hardship. Those on fixed incomes, such as war pensions, were quite without financial resources, whereas those who had borrowed during the period of inflation were practically debt-free, because of the depreciation of the currency. On 15 November a new currency, the Rentenmark, secured against the fixed assets of all German industry and agriculture, was introduced. Its stability depended ultimately upon political stability, and the reparations problem was handed over to international committees of nonpolitical experts, which produced the Dawes Plan in April 1924. This was accepted by the Entente Powers in August 1924, and the Reichsmark was introduced on 30 August 1924.

The settling of the two German problems laid the groundwork for general monetary stabilization. Britain returned to the gold standard in April 1925, at the prewar parity of sterling to the dollar. By 1926, exchange rates were stable in 39 countries, and the financial resurrection of the world economy had been largely completed by 1928. Thereafter the only major countries which continued to have floating exchange rates were Japan, Portugal, Romania and Spain.

German recovery

Rebuilding the financial edifice was one thing, installing a mechanism to generate longterm stable growth was another. Initially the machine did not seem to work as liquidity and investment had to be provided by the United States through loans of various maturities to the constituents of the world economy. One of the major recipients was Germany.

Using American funds, often in the form of shortterm loans, German cities were rebuilt and German industry remodeled itself on the American pattern. One feature of the new order was electrification, even of the "older" industrial sectors of the economy such iron and steel and chemicals. This was coupled with advances in fuel economy to increase energy efficiency. Nonetheless, hyperinflation, stabilization, and subsequently rationalization, had a high cost in unemployment. German unemployment during the second half of the 1920s never fell below seven percent of the employed population; it was as high as 18 percent in 1926, and in 1929 – to all appearances the peak year of the decade – it was still 12 percent, some two million individuals.

British structural problems

From 1919 British industry gained in the short run from pent-up frustrated wartime demand. It was in a position to meet these orders before European competitors and provided better quality goods than wartime American or Japanese substitutes. Further, British prices were initially lower than American, an advantage which became greater from March 1919 when the sterling/dollar exchange rate was unpegged and sterling was allowed to float from $4.765 in March

▶ Berlin became famous, if not notorious, for its café society during the 1920s. Hugo Stinnes, the industrialist, was a prime example of those who did well out of the inflation. The contrast between such high living in Berlin's nightspots and the plight of the urban poor became the subject of stark caricatures by artists such as George Grosz, whose "5 o'clock in the Morning" contrasted all-night revelers with those struggling to work in the early hours.

1919 to $3.40 by February 1920. However, the immediate postwar export boom reinforced inflationary pressures within the British economy and gave industrialists a false perspective of what the future held, as it largely provided orders for the old "staple" industries like textiles and coal.

Domestic activity declined first, and the fall in primary product prices from mid-1920 resulted in declining overseas demand too. The effect in Britain was a sharp and severe slump until mid-1922. There then followed the "doldrums", the main casualties being the becalmed, over-capitalized industries of cotton textiles, coal and shipbuilding. The stagnation of these industries resulted in persistent high regional unemployment; total unemployment did not fall below one million throughout the decade. Politicians mistakenly diagnosed the cause as lying in the failure of world trade to recover fully in the 1920s, instead of recognizing that large sections of British industry were manufacturing products that were generally no longer wanted in quantity in the world market place.

The price of Britain's return to the gold standard was also high. The pound was overvalued, which reduced exports and increased imports, and interest rates were high, resulting in deflation. Further, the continuing dominance within the economy of the outmoded staple industries contributed to industrial difficulties. It could be argued that a high pound and high interest rates from 1925 actually accelerated much-needed structural change, but at considerable social cost. Substantial unemployment and industrial discord mounted, to culminate in the General Strike of 1926.

The American economy in the 1920s

The American economy also experienced a sharp depression in 1921, caused by a rapid decline of exports, which was felt first by producers of luxuries such as silk and motor cars. Yet from 1923 the American economy recovered and enjoyed a long boom to 1929, with only minor interruptions in 1924 and 1927. However, it was largely an industrial boom in "new" products – such as automobiles and electrical appliances like radios, irons and refrigerators. "Older" sectors – coal, cotton manufacturing, shipbuilding, shoe and leather manufacturing – either stagnated or declined, as in many European countries, leading to pockets of unemployment.

Like other primary producers, American agriculture experienced severe depression during the 1920s. It had prospered especially during the war, but by 1921 the increase in European agricultural output had made Western Europe more self-sufficient and less dependent on sources of sup-

▲ Modern mass demonstrations against unemployment had begun in Britain during the slump of the mid-1880s. At that time they were a reaction to cyclical unemployment, but society as a whole was unprepared for the deep structural unemployment of the interwar years, which mounted rapidly in the autumn of 1920 after six years of almost full employment during the war and postwar boom. The sudden rise in the number of jobless was put down to political and economic chaos in Europe.

Britain's Return to the Gold Standard

In 1924 the Conservative party won the general election in Britain, and Winston Churchill – who had been secretary of state for war and air between 1919 and 1921 – was appointed chancellor of the Exchequer. One of his tasks was to decide whether Britain should return to the gold standard, since the immediate postwar legislation placing a temporary embargo on the export of gold was about to lapse.

Churchill had little knowledge of economics, and therefore relied heavily on his advisers. The opinion of the Treasury officials and of Montagu Norman, governor of the Bank of England, was that a return would be advisable. This appeared to be backed up by a substantial majority of informed business, financial and political opinion. However, it was opposed by the economist J. M. Keynes on the grounds that a return at the prewar parity of $4.86 to the pound would overvalue the pound by some ten percent; this would reduce exports, increase imports, and lead to continuing high unemployment.

Churchill made up his mind to "return to gold", and gave his announcement as part of his budget speech of 28 April 1925. What his advisers had not foreseen, however, was the German recovery of the late 1920s and the "cheap" exchange rates that were to be adopted by France and Belgium from 1926. As unemployment and industrial unrest grew, Churchill was to come to regret his acquiescence in Britain's return to gold.

▼ Winston Churchill, chancellor of the Exchequer, in 1925.

▲ Skyscrapers were a symbol of American progress and prosperity in the 1920s. Their construction was made possible by the availability of structural steel sections, and in Manhattan, New York, the lack of land on the island which constituted the city's central business district made them an attractive solution. The first such buildings had been put up in the mid-19th century. By 1910 there were 90 buildings in Chicago and New York which had more than ten stories and by 1920 there were 450. They proved to be even more potent as a symbol than as an architect's solution to a particular problem, especially the Empire State Building shown here under construction.

plies outside Europe. American farmers were confronted with a glutted market in which prices fell below the costs of production. In addition, they faced high freight and handling costs. This had particularly harsh consequences since many American farmers had borrowed heavily since 1915, both to purchase land and to buy equipment. Their financial difficulties in turn affected the rural American banks from which they had obtained their mortgages. In reaction to the rise in mortgage debts and the decline in land values, there was an exodus from the rural areas; the farm population fell by an average of over half a million a year during the 1920s. The area of land under production fell by over five million hectares between 1919 and 1924. The American government did intervene, initially with an emergency tariff in 1921 and with the Fordney-Maclumber Tariff in 1922, as well as through the revival of the War Finance Corporation in 1921, an Agricultural Credit Act in 1923, and an Agricultural Marketing Act in 1929; but it could not overcome the underlying problem of world over-production and consequent agricultural depression. However, the low prices of foodstuffs helped the industrial boom, which also benefited

from the decline in the cost of raw materials.

The full development of manufacturing techniques introduced before the war led to increased efficiency, and labor productivity in the United States almost doubled over the decade. It was a model of technical prowess admired universally, even by Soviet Russia. But by the late 1920s the rate of growth of American consumption of the "new" products was beginning to tail off, and this was to have substantial effects upon industries where investment in production capacity had had to anticipate the growth of demand.

While American farmers went into default with their bankers, other primary producing countries sustained their positions during the mid-1920s by borrowing, on either the New York or London markets, since although holding increased stocks of produce was one answer to falling prices, it had to be financed, as did long-term debts already incurred. As in America, industrial consumers of primary products gained from the fall in their prices – the terms of trade moved in favor of the advanced industrial economies – but the diminished incomes of the primary producers meant diminished export markets for industrial producers. The underlying fragile framework

► The Great Kanto earthquake of 1 September 1923 devastated the entire region around Tokyo and Yokohama. Nearly seven hundred thousand households were damaged either by the earthquake itself or by the resulting fires, and the dead or missing totalled 105,000. The government embarked upon a major reconstruction program, earmarking 573 million yen to be spent over six years, while local public bodies contributed a further 230 million yen. Earthquake spending pulled Japan out of the sharp depression of the early 1920s but led to further inflation in the mid-1920s because the import of materials and equipment adversely affected Japan's already weak balance of payments position.

▲ Connections did develop between Bolshevik Russia and the West which led, for instance, to some American relief measures during the famine of 1920–21. During the mid-1920s the New Economic Policy allowed relative autonomy in many areas of the Soviet economy, enabling the further rebuilding of contacts with the Western economies, including the use of foreign engineers and experts and imported capital. When the first five-year plan was proposed, appeals were made to the West for economic assistance, as in this cartoon directly targeted on Western capitalists.

began to collapse at the end of 1927; the countries which were to compose the post-1931 sterling area experienced continuous international payments deficits from 1928 and by April 1930 nine countries, including Canada, Australia and New Zealand, had effectively devalued their currencies and abandoned the gold standard.

Japanese policies

While reconstruction and recovery in Central and Eastern Europe were affected and shaped by inflation and hyperinflation, the Japanese economy suffered an immense blow as a result of the Great Kanto earthquake of 1 September 1923. This caused substantial damage in Tokyo and Yokohama through the fires that followed, resulting in losses worth five and a half billion yen.

The economy underwent an inflationary reconstruction boom in the mid-1920s and the consequent depreciation of the yen on foreign exchange markets stimulated Japanese exports from 1924, while import growth slowed in 1925 and imports actually fell in 1926. The Japanese economy grew in real terms by 50 percent during the 1920s, the most marked trends being the quadrupling of electrical generating capacity between 1919 and 1930 and the expansion of steel production from 584,000 tonnes in 1919 to over two million tonnes by 1929. With these developments heavy industry began to overshadow textiles, but a more important development was the growing dominance within industries of a few firms, usually affiliated to the Zaibatsu. In 1928 these consisted of four industrial–financial conglomerates, of which the most important was Mitsui, which controlled 97 firms with a total capital of 1.6 billion yen.

In 1928 the yen fluctuated wildly on the foreign exchange market. In July 1929 Finance Minister Inouye announced a policy of monetary orthodoxy, involving balanced budgets and a return to the gold standard. The latter was accomplished on 11 January 1930, against a background of buoyant Japanese trade and low interest rates.

The Soviet Union

Soviet Russia was generally isolated from trends in the world economy during the 1920s. Initially the Bolshevik government passed land to local peasant committees which, in turn, largely redistributed it to individuals. The revolutionary land settlement was coupled with the nationalization of the banks, while manufacturing industry came generally under workers' control. However, until 1921 the country was engulfed in civil war and subject to foreign intervention which resulted in dramatic inflation, comparable to the German hyperinflation. Whatever direction took place during these years of "war communism" came through the Bolshevik party apparatus, local soviets and the Red Army. By 1921 agricultural output had fallen to about two-thirds, and industrial output to less than a third, of 1913 levels.

The reconstruction of the economy during the 1920s took place through the New Economic Policy (NEP), which brought to an end rationing and compulsory deliveries by turning distributions over to the market. The hallmark of the NEP in industry was cooperation with bourgeois technicians. It led to a remarkable recovery from the low base reached after the civil war but nonetheless gave rise to problems. As far as agriculture was concerned, individual initiative was encouraged, and a system of market prices was begun to spur the peasants to provide food for the urban population in return for industrial goods. Agriculture came to consist of peasant plots, mainly of medium size, which produced largely for local consumption. Industry suffered from a shortage of investment, which arose from low productivity and high wage costs.

In 1928 Stalin introduced the first five-year plan, which had ambitious growth targets and involved the collectivization of agriculture. This program was designed to operate through the now much stronger Bolshevik party apparatus, using the controls which had been developed by Gosplan, the main economic planning committee of the Soviet Union, in the years since 1921.

The New Economic Policy

By 1921 enforced nationalization and continued food shortages had drastically weakened the Soviet economy. In March 1921 Lenin introduced the New Economic Policy (NEP), which was characterized by relative economic freedom. Economic liberalization led to the emergence of small enterpreneurs – "the Nepmen" – paralleled in the countryside by the well-off peasants, the kulaks. The economy operated through a free market, but this change from "war communism" revealed substantial industrial unemployment and rural underemployment. Although re-establishing market forces, distribution remained a problem and there was an imbalance between high industrial and low agricultural prices. Further liberalization reversed the balance, producing relatively high agricultural prices from 1924. Small-scale private industry was encouraged to provide peasants with consumer goods. Opposition to the NEP within the Party grew from the fear that it would produce a wealthy peasant class with interests opposed to socialism.

▲ From 1920 there had been encouragement for the establishment of collective farms, but in the mid-1920s Russian agriculture flourished under the New Economic Policy with high prices and good harvests. This led within the Party to growing criticism of what appeared to be a pro-kulak policy. From the inception of the first five-year plan, the official attitude of the party changed. The kulaks – rich peasants who hired labor – were no longer regarded as a tolerated necessity, but as a hostile class which had to be destroyed. The campaign for collectivization began in May 1928. It generally required the use of the military, rather than being a democratic viillage decision, as suggested in this propaganda photograph.

◄ By 1927 Russian railroads were carrying as much freight as they had in 1917. The first five-year plan assumed that the existing rail network would cope, but after winter transport crises in the early 1930s, some lines were relaid and re-equipped. Two new routes were constructed, the Turkestan–Siberia railroad, shown here (actually the completion of a line begun under the czarist regime), and a second north–south line, the Karaganda railroad.

THE BLACK ECONOMY

In 1919 the United States Congress passed what became known as the Volstead Act, outlawing the manufacture, distribution and sale of alcohol. Throughout the 1920s and until 1933, the law – more popular in some states than others – made criminals out of millions of citizens who liked their drink. Prohibition also turned the gangster into a respectable criminal, being regarded by many as an honest bootlegger, trying to make a living like any other American.

Gangs had developed over the course of the 19th century, with the growth in the number of saloons, gambling houses and brothels. Gangsters turned to new avenues of criminality in the 1890s, capitalizing on the bitter conflicts between capital and labor. They supplied blacklegs and strikebreakers to the bosses and drew close to organized labor through victimizing those who defied union rules.

The car, the machine-gun and the telephone transformed the organization of gangs through enabling them to spread their influence to embrace whole cities and even states. The income required to equip gangs in this manner was provided by illegal traffic in alcohol. The further growth of gangsterism, and in particular the rise of gang bosses during the 1920s, was seen by many young Italian and Slav immigrants as the American dream being made reality.

During the early years of Prohibition – until 1923 – small gangs were hired by businessmen to protect their breweries and distilleries and to escort deliveries, while businessmen used political influence to gain immunity from the law. After 1923 big city gangs developed to control the illegal trade, either buying fake denaturing plants in order to secure the feedstock of raw alcohol or taking over breweries that produced "near beer", the legal product. Further, they controlled the production in the slum tenements of private illicit alcohol based on corn sugar. Some 3000 private distilleries, worth $50,000, were seized in 1929.

The criminal production and distribution of alcohol, coupled with smuggling from Canada, was tolerated in the urban northeast of America until the late 1920s. Revulsion developed with the move of organized crime into blackmail, "the racket", and the excesses of gang warfare. The economics of bootlegging was undermined by the Depression, the number of speak-easies in New York falling from 32,000 in 1919 to 9000 in 1933, and the private home production of beer and wine. During the Prohibition period, American consumption of wine, largely home produced, increased by 66 percent.

▲▶ Society's ambivalent attitude towards illicit production and distribution of drugs is now frequently the base for organized crime. Drug enforcement agencies of the 1980s – here displaying a haul of smuggled cocaine – are better organized and paid than the Prohibition Bureau.

▶ Modern society has attempted to discriminate between "soft" and "hard" drugs, with marijuana frequently being placed in the former category. Trade in it is barely disguised, and can provide entrepreneurial opportunities for members of outcast social groups.

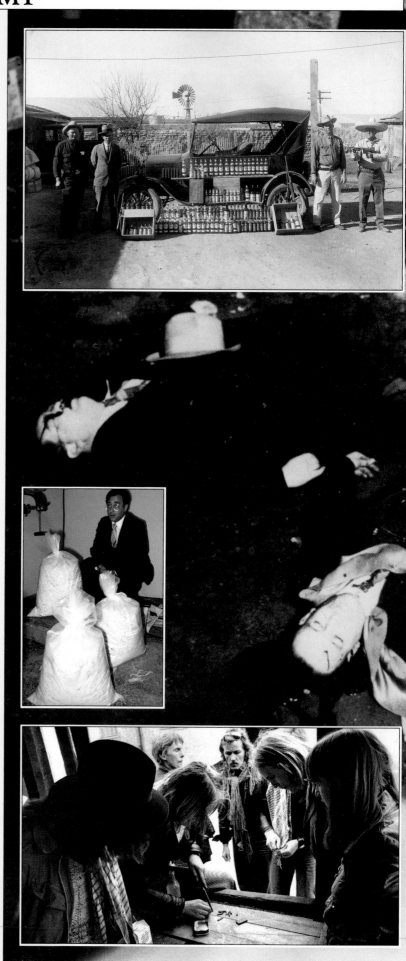

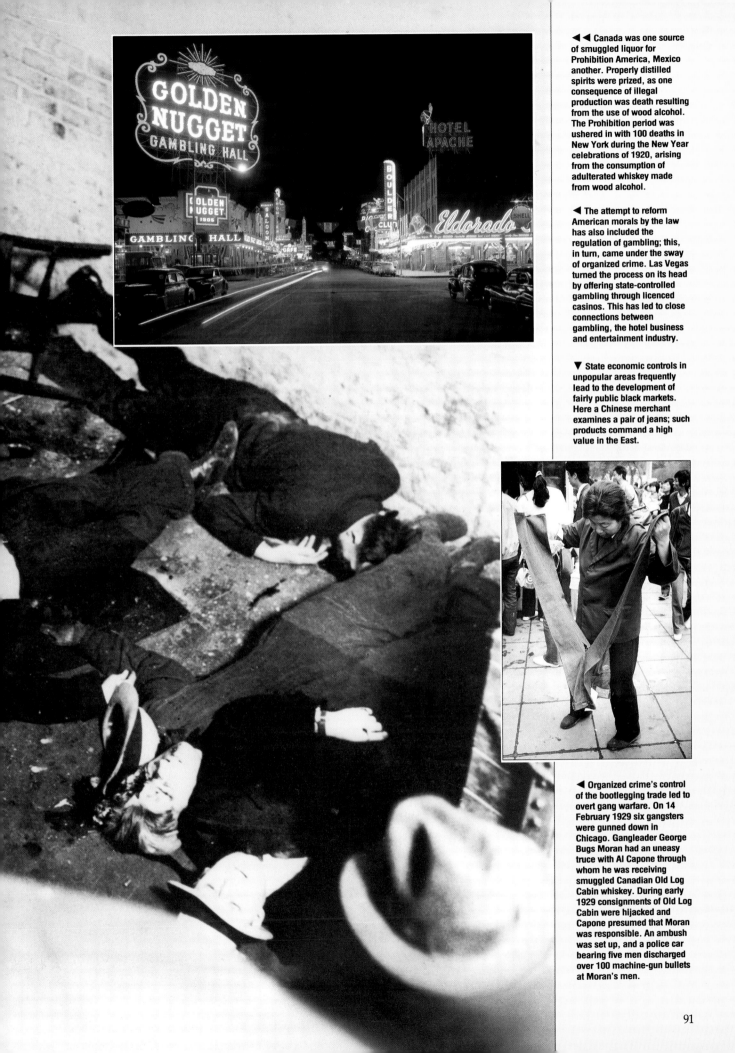

◀◀ Canada was one source of smuggled liquor for Prohibition America, Mexico another. Properly distilled spirits were prized, as one consequence of illegal production was death resulting from the use of wood alcohol. The Prohibition period was ushered in with 100 deaths in New York during the New Year celebrations of 1920, arising from the consumption of adulterated whiskey made from wood alcohol.

◀ The attempt to reform American morals by the law has also included the regulation of gambling; this, in turn, came under the sway of organized crime. Las Vegas turned the process on its head by offering state-controlled gambling through licenced casinos. This has led to close connections between gambling, the hotel business and entertainment industry.

▼ State economic controls in unpopular areas frequently lead to the development of fairly public black markets. Here a Chinese merchant examines a pair of jeans; such products command a high value in the East.

◀ Organized crime's control of the bootlegging trade led to overt gang warfare. On 14 February 1929 six gangsters were gunned down in Chicago. Gangleader George Bugs Moran had an uneasy truce with Al Capone through whom he was receiving smuggled Canadian Old Log Cabin whiskey. During early 1929 consignments of Old Log Cabin were hijacked and Capone presumed that Moran was responsible. An ambush was set up, and a police car bearing five men discharged over 100 machine-gun bullets at Moran's men.

1929 · 1945
THE
DEPRESSION
YEARS

Time Chart

	1930	1931	1932	1933	1934	1935	1936	1937
Industry	• Majority of production in the USSR now industrial (53%) • Foundation of a large iron–coal combine by the building of plants in Magnitogorsk and Kusnezk (USSR)	• May: Opening of a branch of Ford in Cologne (USA/Ger) • Jun: Collapse of the Nordwolle textile company leads to a banking crisis (Ger)	• Feb: Government assistance program for agriculture (Fr) • Collapse of the match company of I. Kreuger (Swe) • Brazilian coffee destroyed to maintain prices (Bra)	• Aug: Crisis in the lace and wool industry (Fr) • Formation of an international steel trust registered in Luxembourg, the International Natural Steel Export Company	• Apr: Extension of import control over all industrial products (Ger)	• Jan: Decision to destroy up to 10 million cotton spindles in the Lancashire cotton industry (UK) • Nov: Nationalization of the French mining industry	• Jun/Oct: Nationalization of the French armament industry and the military airlines • Nov: Debate on nationalization of the British armament industry	• Mar: New assis plan for America agriculture, invol the support of pr by the regulation supply • Jun: Decision t make war prepar in British industry agriculture
Technology	• F. Whittle obtains a patent for his jet engine (UK) • R. Drew invents scotch tape (USA)	• 1 May: Opening of a radio station near Moscow with the greatest range in the world (USSR)	• 9 Aug: R.S. Willows applies for a patent for his discovery of non-creasing fabric (UK)	• M. Knoll, B. von Borries, E. Ruska and E. Brüche develop the electron microscope (Ger)	• R. Watson-Watt builds a radio navigation system (UK) • Industrial production of synthetic silk and staple fiber (Ger)	• Continuous steel casting introduced in the USA and USSR • 13 Apr: Opening of the London–Brisbane air route	• First standard diesel car produced by Daimler Benz (Ger) • H. Focke constructs the first viable helicopter (Ger)	•Feb: Du Pont ap for a patent for ny (USA) • G. Eyston reac 502 km/h in his c Thunderbolt (UK)
Finance	• 7 May: Bank for International Settlements (BIS) established in Basle on capital of $500 million • Jun: Issue of the international Young loan of 1.2 billion Marks, to commercialize the German reparations • Bank of England establishes the Bankers Industrial Development Company (UK)	• 1 Jul: Hoover moratorium on war debts and reparations • 13 Jul: Collapse of the German Danatbank causes a banking crisis. Withdrawal of credits granted from abroad and control of foreign exchange ensues. The bank is placed under the control of the government • 21 Sep: Britain abandons the gold standard. End of the leadership of the pound in the world economy	• Mar: Merger of the Danatbank and the Dresdner Bank (Ger) • May: Establishment of the Exchange Equalization Account (UK) • Jul: Foreign exchange control in Japan. Measures against the withdrawal of capital • Establishment of the National Bank for Commerce and Industry as a successor to the National Credit Bank (Fr)	• 4 Mar: Federal Deposit Insurance Corp. established to protect savers. Security Act allows control over the capital market (USA) • 6 Mar: USA abandons the gold standard. US president Roosevelt is authorized to fix a new gold dollar parity • Devaluation of the yen (Jap) • Establishment of the Institute for Industrial Reconstruction (IRI) (It)	• Jan: New gold parity for the dollar. USA raises the gold price from $20.67 to $35 per ounce after abandoning the gold standard. Gold Reserve Act (USA) • Feb: Establishment of the Export–Import Bank with capital of $500 million (USA) • Devaluation of the Czech crown • Severe control of foreign exchange, and devaluation of Belgian, Italian, Swiss and Danzig currencies	• Prohibition of the universal bank system. Belgian General Society eliminates the General Society Bank as deposit bank. Establishment of the Flemish Credit Bank in Brussels (Bel) • Legislation for the German credit system put into force. Note-issuing monopoly by the Reichsbank after the right of issuing notes by the last private central banks is abolished (Ger)	• Devaluation of the Swiss franc and Italian lira • Devaluation of the French franc and a change in the regulations of the Banque de France. Establishment of the Caisse Nationale de Marches d'État (Fr) • Construction of Fort Knox in Kentucky, where half of the US gold stock is laid down (USA)	• Jan: Devaluatic the yen (Jap) • Jul: Devaluatio the French franc suspension of its parity • Establishment Institut Nationale Credit Agricole in Brussels (Bel) • Note-issuing monopoly for the Central Bank of C
Economic Policy	• Jan: Young plan signed by the German government. Amount of reparations fixed at 38 billion Marks payable in 59 annual rates until 1988 • 16 Jul: First emergency decrees issued by the German government to protect the economy • Reduction in prices for raw materials on the world market	• Jun: Beginning of a sharp deflationary policy by the German government • 11 Jul: Negotiations among the governors of the Reichsbank, Bank of England and Banque de France to counter the German crisis of reparation payments. Failure leads to credit restriction by the Reichsbank (Ger) • Jul: McMillan report demands the maintenance of the gold standard (UK)	• Jan: Establishment of the Reconstruction Finance Corporation, an institute for financing the creation of work and encouraging business activity (USA) • Jun: Conference of London on German reparations. Remaining debt fixed at 3 billion Marks • Aug: Chancellor von Papen announces an economic program for increasing business activity by creation of work (Ger)	• Mar: US president Roosevelt announces his New Deal to overcome the economic depression • Mar: Accession to power of the National Socialist party brings a reorganization of economic associations in a corporative pattern and measures to create work (Ger) • Jul: National Recovery Act enforced to achieve an increase in business activities (USA)	• Sep: Adjustment of imports to the German export possibilities, the "new plan" initiated by H. Schacht • Sep: Industrial league prevents the introduction of the forty-hour week (UK) • Establishment of a corporatist economic system by way of confederations and syndicates of employers and employees as supreme economic associations (It)	• Feb: German minister of finance is authorized to finance governmental creation of work without the consent of the Reichstag • Aug: Economic emergency acts in France to abolish the budget deficit and cause an increase in economic activity • Oct: Establishment of the bureau of industrial cooperation for analyzing the best methods for recovery (USA)	• Mar: Mussolini demands the reorganization of the Italian economy into major corporations (It) • 9 Sep: Tripartite Monetary Agreement signed to reorganize the international monetary system after the collapse of the gold bloc (USA/Fr/UK) • Publication of The General Theory of Employment, Interest and Money by J.M. Keynes (UK)	• On the order of League of Nation Haberler produce study of the theor business cycles, Prosperity and Depression • Oct: Establishm of the Supreme Autarky Council (• Nov: Roosevelt program for incre business activities published, with a increase in house building and publi utilities (USA)
International	• May: French minister of foreign affairs A. Briand publishes his memorandum for the establishment of a United Nations of Europe	• Jul: Conference in London on the German crisis of reparations payments • Sep: Basle standstill agreement for external debts and reparations signed • Sep: Establishment of the Silver Association in London for promoting the bimetallic covering of currencies	• Jan: Establishment of an international bureau for stock exchanges by the International Chamber of Commerce • Feb: Legislation on the final ending of free trade (UK) • Jul: Conference on world trade in Ottawa demands the suspension of all obstacles to trade	• May: Agreement on trade relations between the Soviet Union and Italy and between France and the UK • Conference on the world economy in London demands removal of all trade obstacles, without important results • Oct: Suspension of import tax between France and Italy	• Mar: End of the tariff war between Germany and Poland • Mar: Conference of Valparaiso publishes principles for the regulation of trade relations between the American countries • Dec: American committee for the boycott of German products established	• Feb: Boycott of Germany by the USA. Jewish companies oppose US–German trade relations • Jun: Italy reduces import quotas • Nov: First pan-American economic conference demands an extension of international trade	• Apr: Agreement on trade signed between Germany and the Soviet Union • Jul: Soviet government publishes plans for import restrictions • Dec: Establishment of an Anglo–German company for compensation in trade	• May: Member countries of the C convention conde all obstacles to tra • Jun: Internation Labor Conference publishes a declaration on the introduction of the 40-hour week • Jul: Establishme of a German–Belg Luxembourg economic commi for the promotion trade
Misc.	• Beginning of military expansion in Asia by Japan	• Japan attacks and occupies Manchuria • Westminster Statute settled between the countries of the Commonwealth	• First international disarmament talks of the League of Nations ends in failure	• 30 Jan: Hitler becomes chancellor of Germany. Beginning of the Third Reich • Mar: Coup d'état by Dollfuss in Austria	• First meeting of Hitler and Mussolini in Venice. Political collaboration between the two governments begins (Ger/It)	• 15 Sep: Nuremberg laws initiate racial discrimination against the Jews in Germany	• Beginning of the Spanish civil war • Remilitarization of the Rhineland (Ger)	• Sino–Japanese begins after the M Polo bridge incide

94

...38	1939	1940	1941	1942	1943	1944	1945
...an: German ...ernment urges ...exclusion of ...-Aryans from all ...itions in the ...vate sector ...ug: Construction of ...il pipeline from the ...ntic Ocean to Paris	• Apr: Preparations for war made in France involving the forming of an economic organization and an increase in production • Aug: Transfer of over 30 industrial plants to Manzhouguo (Jap)	• Mar: Unification of British and French war industry and war production • Dec: US department for directing the armaments industries developed (USA)	• Jan: Rise in British military production due to an expenditure of work • Mar: Law passed for an extension of the war economy (UK)	• Jan: US automobile industry transformed into an armament industry • Oct: Foundation of Belgo–European Syndicate for Agricultural, Commercial and Industrial Expansion	• Feb: All enterprises not needed for war production closed (Ger) • Famine in British India	• Nov: Nationalization of French coal mines in the Nord and Pas de Calais *départements* • Nationalization of the Belgian armaments industries	• Jan: Nationalization of Renault (Fr) • Sep: Beginning of the dismantling of German enterprises in the US occupation zone (Ger)
. Schlack discovers ...lon fiber (Ger) ...6 Dec: Opening of ...world's first mobile ...phone station in ...ex (UK)	• P.H. Müller produces DDT (Swi) • 28 Jun: First Atlantic passenger flight by PanAm (USA)	• Testing of mechanical cotton pickers in the USA • Nylon stockings are put on the market (USA)	• Feb: Opening of an air route from Moscow to the Bering Sea (USSR) • L.D. Goodhoe invents the aerosol spray (USA)	• W. von Braun succeeds in launching a guided rocket (Ger) • Industrial synthesis of antibiotics by biological methods (USA)	• J. Cousteau and E. Gagnan invent the aqualung (Fr) • Relay computer Mark 1 enters the market in the USA	• S.A. Wakesman and A. Schatz discover streptomycin as effective antibiotic medicine (USA)	• Testing of the atomic bomb in New Mexico (USA) • DDT used in Greece against the malaria mosquito
...r: After the ...*schluss*, the ...chsmark becomes ...al tender in Austria. ...strian central banks ...en over by the ...chsbank ...May: Devaluation of ...French franc	• Jun: Protest by the board of directors and the resignation of the Reichsbank president Schacht after a law authorizing unlimited credits for the government from the Reichsbank • Sep: Control of foreign exchange, confiscations and reparations determine the international capital markets after the outbreak of World War II	• Administration of foreign exchange in Sweden • Devaluation of the French franc • Devaluation of the pound to £1 = US$4.04 • Investment Company Act and Investment Advisers Act passed (USA)	• 13 Jun: Legislation enforced regarding a reorganization of the banking system under occupation (Fr) • Dec: Agreement between the Federal Reserve Board and the Treasury. Reserve Board declares its cooperation in placing money at low rates of interest at the disposal of the Treasury (USA) • Large loans issued by the USA to the UK and USSR to finance the war effort	• Jan: Establishment of the Central Bank for the Baltic states by the German government • Mar: First issue of banknotes by the Central Bank of the Ukraine, under German control • Notes of the Central Reserve Bank of the government of Wang Ching Wei become the only legal tender in China • Establishment of the Wartime Finance Bank for financing war factories (Jap)	• Jan: Stock markets placed under government control (Ger) • Jan: Establishment of the Deutsche Bank for Eastern Asia, for the furthering of trade relations (Ger) • Dec: Publication of a plan for the establishment of a worldwide Bank for Reconstruction and Development of the United Nations by J.H. Morgenthau (USA)	• Jul: Bretton Woods agreement (USA) to establish an International Monetary Fund (IMF) and an International Bank for Reconstruction and Development (World Bank). • Nov: New parity for the French franc • Currency reform in Belgium • Allies begin to print banknotes for the time of the expected occupation of Germany	• May: Destruction of the German monetary and banking system brought about by the end of the war • Jul: Establishment of the Industrial and Commercial Finance Corporation for financing smaller enterprises (UK) • Currency reforms in France, Austria, Netherlands and Czechoslovakia • Dec: Nationalization of the Bank of France and other large private banks (Fr)
...pr: Creation of a ...rk program at the ...st of $4.5 billion by ...president Roosevelt ...May: French prime ...nister Daladier ...blishes a national ...onomic plan ...Jun: Transformation ...the Japanese ...onomy into a war ...onomy agreed ...Dec: New principles ...foreign exchange ...ntrol in Germany. ...sagreement over ...ancing the war ...ustry	• Jan: Plan for the recovery of financial and economic power. Reduction of public debts (Fr) • Mar: The currency of northern China leaves the pound bloc and joins the yen bloc • Oct: Noiseless war finance begins using treasury bills, bonds and an eightfold increase in cash circulation (Ger) • Dec: Agreement on mutual financial aid with France (UK)	• May: Labor Authorization Law passed, by which all can be forced to work if needed (UK) • Jun: Reestablishment of the eight-hour day and six-day week in Soviet industry • Nov: Ten-year plan for the economic development of eastern Asia published (Jap) • Rationing of goods in the UK and France	• Jan: New wage system for Russian kolkhozes put into force (USSR) • Mar: Lend–Lease law put into force as a mutual financial agreement between the Allies • Apr: US–Canadian agreement on war economy put into force	• Jan: War production claims half of the total national income of the USA • Jan: Establishment of the National Labor Office and the War Production Office • Feb: Common execution of war economy and war production between the UK and France agreed	• Feb: Publication and discussion of the Beveridge plan for social security and social welfare (UK) • Apr: Price controls for all consumer goods (USA) • Plans for reorganization of international capital relations and currencies after the war published by J.M. Keynes and H.D. White	• Jul: Minister of reconstruction Woolton publishes a program for the post-war economy. Stabilization of employment announced (UK) • Jul: Beginning of total war economy in Germany. Introduction of the sixty-hour week in industry • Sep: Conference of Quebec. Discussion of the Morgenthau plan for the deindustrialization of Germany after the war	• Jul: Labour government initiates an austerity policy to rehabilitate the balance of payments (UK) • Jul: Nationalization of collieries, industrial enterprises and joint stock banks (Czech) • Aug: End of the Lend–Lease agreement • Sep: Five-year plan for the iron and coal industry to increase production. Plans for the nationalization of mines and transport discussed (UK)
...Jun: Belgian prime ...nister van Zeeland ...blishes a plan for the ...largement of trade ...d reorganization of ...e world economy to ...unter protectionism ...Jul: Four agreements ...economic relations ...tween France and ...rmany signed ...Dec: Pan-American ...nference in Lima ...rees on further ...velopment of inter-...merican trade	• Mar: Longterm economic agreement signed between Germany and Romania • Apr: "Great German" tariff area established • Sep: Agreement signed on trade relations between Germany and the USSR • Sep: Establishment of a common financial and economic committee by the Pan-American conference in Panama	• Feb: Economic agreement between Germany and the Soviet Union • Apr: Establishment of the United Kingdom Commercial Corporation for promoting trade with Eastern Europe and Asia • Jun: Plan for a Pan-American economic union discussed • Aug: Incorporation of Luxembourg into the German tariff area	• Feb: Conferences of La Plata for the future regulation of trade between Brazil, Argentina, Uruguay, Paraguay and Bolivia • Feb: British government imposes a trade blockade against Romania and Bulgaria • Aug: Japan prohibits ships from sailing to the USA. USA imposes a petrol and crude oil embargo against Japan	• Feb: International conference on social issues in Santiago (Chile) • Jul: Agreement on the delivery of war products and raw materials between the UK and USSR • Dec: German government declares products of occupied regions with the exception of the eastern areas as free of duty	• Jan: Agreement on economic cooperation between Germany, Japan and Italy • May: UN world conference on food in Hot Springs. Declaration on protection of food for all countries • Dec: Establishment of the UN Relief and Rehabilitation Administration (UNRRA) for the reconstruction of all countries affected by the war	• Apr: ILO conference discusses the social security of workers after the war • Jul: Conference in Washington discusses the future of the crude oil policy • Oct: French government under de Gaulle abrogates all signed trade treaties • Dec: US government publishes a plan for the promotion of foreign trade by a reduction of tariffs	• May: Establishment of the Economic and Social Council (ECOSOC) of the UN • May: Establishment of the European Coal Commission in London • Dec: Establishment of the International Monetary Fund (IMF) and World Bank (International Bank for Reconstruction and Development)
13 Mar: *Anschluss* of ...stria into the Third ...eich (Ger) 1 Oct: Incorporation ...the Sudetenland into ...rmany	• 23 Aug: Nazi–Soviet nonaggression pact signed • 1 Sept: German invasion of Poland initiates World War II	• Aug/Sep: Battle of Britain • Defeat of France and the formation of the Vichy regime under Pétain	• 22 Jun: Germany attacks the Soviet Union without warning • 7 Dec: Japanese attack US fleet at Pearl Harbor	• Beginning of British and American bombing raids on Germany • Washington declaration of 26 nations	• Battle of Stalingrad (USSR) • Allies conquer Sicily. Mussolini overthrown (It)	• 6 Jun: Invasion of France by the Allies • Aug–Oct: Conference of Dumbarton Oaks	• 4–11 Feb: Yalta Conference • Capitulation of Germany (7 May) and Japan (2 Sep)

Datafile

The causes of the world economic crisis were varied. They lay partly in the overproduction of both industrial and agricultural goods and in the structural problems experienced by almost all agricultural and industrial countries, particularly the old industrial nations of Western Europe but also in the United States. They could also be found, however, in the monetary sphere: in the mistaken monetary and credit policy of the United States, in the negative effects of the stock market crash, in the incorrect handling of the gold standard, in structural deflation and the problems of international debt. In many countries production sank sharply while unemployment increased. The decline in prices of certain products accelerated; the prices of others began to fall. Stock market prices slumped dramatically and exchange rates were further sharply devalued. The decline in world trade showed clearly to what extent the crisis signified a disintegration of the international economy. International trade did not recover until after World War II.

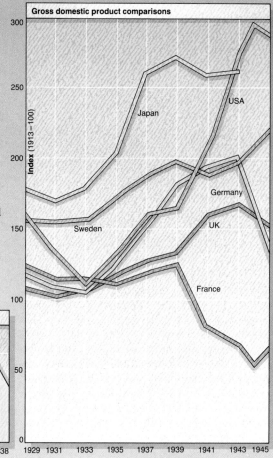

Gross domestic product comparisons

World cotton supplies

World rubber supplies

World tin supplies

World wheat supplies

New York stock market prices

▲ The beginning of the fall in share prices on the New York Stock Exchange in September 1929 was partly an expression of the uncertain economic situation, especially in the United States. It was also itself a cause of the slump into the Depression, resulting in bankruptcy and ruin. Above all, it shattered trust in the capitalist system.

▶ Between 1929 and 1933 world trade shrank by two-thirds. Many countries suffered from the decline in foreign demand, especially the smaller industrial countries and developing countries which exported primary products. The decline was a result of the collapse in national production and restrictive foreign economic policy.

World trade value

▲ During the crisis, all the developed countries had to accept a more or less severe drop in GDP. The upswing in the 1930s, however, varied considerably. A real boom took place only in Germany and Japan. The United States experienced an upswing but 1937–38 saw a renewed crisis. Recovery in Britain was slow, and the French economy stagnated.

▲ Raw materials and foodstuffs were affected by the crisis even more severely than manufactured goods. Production was maintained or even expanded in order to secure some sort of return, despite the fall in prices. Overproduction often accelerated the fall in prices. Government measures to reduce agricultural areas were slow to take effect.

◀ The entire interwar period was one of extremely high unemployment. The Great Depression forced unemployment rates up to a level unique in this century. At the beginning of the 1930s in some countries one in three workers was unemployed, figures that express the extreme wretchedness that the Depression brought with it.

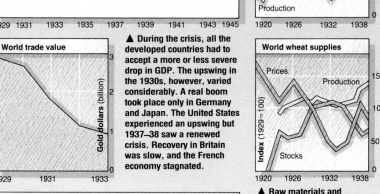

Unemployment in Europe and USA

Norway · Germany · UK · USA

CRISIS AND DEPRESSION

The Great Depression was the biggest crisis ever experienced by the world economy. It hit almost every country: the highly developed countries of Western Europe and the United States; the less developed ones like Canada, Australia, Japan and Argentina; and the underdeveloped countries of Latin America, Asia and Africa just as soon as they became involved in the world market. Many countries experienced the catastrophic breakdown of their national economies, and only a few came through without major damage. The Depression manifested itself in events which had no obvious relevance for many people, such as the complete deterioration of stock prices, the dissolution of the international currency system or the fall of world prices: and also in the immediately felt misery caused by the decline of industrial and agricultural production, the enormous rise in unemployment all over the world and the subsequent reduction in wages. Statistics cannot convey the extent of the effects of the Depression. In 1932, 30 million people were unemployed, while millions more suffered from short hours and extremely low wages in the industrial world alone. The consequences were hunger, higher mortality, apathy and hopelessness, as well as an increase in crime. Political radicalism grew in response to these conditions. As markets for their raw materials and foodstuffs shrank, farmers in developing countries were forced back to subsistence farming despite the fact that people were starving all over the world. In industrial countries farms were abandoned, fertile farm land turned into steppe, and harvests were destroyed in the fields. With the whole world watching, wheat was used to fuel locomotives and coffee was dumped into the sea. And while everywhere in the world people were lining up in their thousands for jobs, newly installed industrial plants decayed for lack of orders.

The world was hit by the Great Depression unprepared. At the end of the 1920s people in the developing nations has no idea of what was coming. Even leading industrialists and businessmen in the West were full of optimism. In the *New York Times* of 29 October 1928, Alfred Sloan, president of General Motors, declared his "conviction that our general economic and industrial situation is thoroughly sound", and at the bankers' conference in Cologne late in 1928 Jacob Goldschmidt, director-general of the Darmstädter und Nationalbank (which finally collapsed in 1931), proclaimed the new revival of capitalism.

Particularly after such claims, the crisis caused a huge loss of confidence in the capitalist system and the liberal world economy. It changed the relationship between state and economy as fundamentally as that between national economies and the world economy.

▼ "The politicians will sit over their breakfast until they are eaten for breakfast themselves." The innumerable conferences which took place all over the world at the end of the 1920s and the beginning of the 1930s produced no concrete results. Instead, they exposed the helplessness with which politicians reacted to the crisis.

The industrial countries

The crisis started in the industrial "center" of the world economy and had its most severe impact there. The GNP of the 16 leading industrial nations fell by 17 percent from 1929 to 1932. In the United States the decline was even bigger, in Western Europe not quite as big. However, in Austria, Poland and Czechoslovakia GNP fell by a fifth. The extent to which the United States was affected can also be seen in industrial production, which fell by 45 percent during this period; in Western Europe the figure was 30 percent.

The effects on international trade were no less serious. The volume of imports of these 16 countries declined by a quarter, the volume of exports even more. As international trade declined, incomes fell in exporting countries, because their markets shrank, and in importing countries, losing their cheapest source. Above all, unemployment increased enormously. As in several European countries, a quarter of the American labor force were unemployed in 1932–33. In Denmark, in Norway, and most significantly in Germany, one in three workers was unemployed. This was the beginning of the process of mass impoverishment characteristic of this period.

Unemployment and poverty

The fate of the unemployed in Belgrade, Brussels, Madrid or Prague was not far different from that of those in Baltimore or Montreal. Early in the morning they went to the employment agency hoping against hope to find some kind of work, at least for this day. Then they waited for hours in long, gray lines, even in snow and rain, usually without success. Lining up for work was followed by lining up for unemployment benefits, if there were any, and then for soup. Certainly, the housewife tried to keep up regular family life, but gradually the atmosphere of poverty spread even to bourgeois homes. Such poverty meant that food had the highest priority over all other necessities, including hygiene. Food was saved for the children. But even worse than material indigence was the feeling of failure and hopelessness. The sheer effort to stay alive dominated everything else. Often it was no longer possible to come up with the rent. Shelters for the homeless were overcrowded. The makeshift homes typical of Depression America also disfigured the cities of Europe and Japan. Shanty towns sprang up in Brussels and Prague. And in Tokyo, along the railroad tracks of Shinjuku, the makeshift shelters of unemployed workers and uprooted farmers joined those left from the time of the 1923 earthquake.

The United States

The United States constituted the dominant part of the industrial "center". It was here that the avalanche began. With increasing speed it took more and more economies into the abyss. In fact, the American economy had shown signs of weakness even before 1929. Investment opportunities were no longer unlimited, as demand fell off during the second half of the 1920s, especially for housing and durable consumer goods. In agriculture, at this time still an important factor in the national economy, real incomes had stopped growing; falling farm prices in the world market posed big problems for American farmers, too. The buoyant bull market at the New York Stock Exchange in 1928 had produced record speculation, and it eventually culminated in the great stock market crash of October 1929, which not only reinforced the recession but finally destroyed confidence in the expansion of the 1920s. Even though New York capital markets were brought back under control relatively fast, the slide into the Depression had started.

The effects on the European economies

The world economy was hit by the events in the United States in various ways. The first blow was the curtailment of foreign loans in 1928–29. This was reinforced by the simultaneous reduction of French and British foreign loans. The boom at the New York Stock Exchange and rising interest rates caused the amount of foreign credits extended by the United States to fall by more than 50 percent during 1928. Many of the countries already severely indebted were primary producers and encountered increasing difficulties as prices for their exports, mainly foodstuffs and raw materials, fell sharply. But such producers of

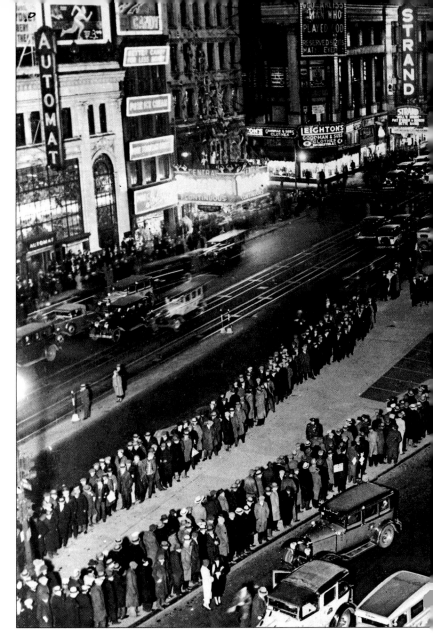

primary commodities were not the only ones to need American capital. Highly developed industrial countries – Germany above all – were also dependent on American credits.

The second blow came with the breakdown of the American economy: foreign loans were further reduced, while import demand contracted significantly. Given the size of the American economy, this was bound to affect the rest of the world, further damaging both exporters of agricultural products and raw materials and industrial nations.

The third blow came in June 1930 when President Hoover signed the Smoot-Hawley Tariff Act, one of the most comprehensive increases in import duty in the history of international trade. The protectionism of this act aggravated the crisis, since debtor countries now found it even more difficult to export goods to the United States in order to earn the dollars necessary to repay their American loans. After the Act American foreign loans dried up completely and American banks intensified their demands for the repayment of outstanding loans.

The crisis was then passed on to European economies through declining American demand

▲ A striking contrast to the glitter of Broadway, New York. Patiently queuing up under the dazzling glare and flicker of the world-famous great white way, hundreds of destitutes lined up every night in Times Square, waiting for the relief kitchen, organized by one of the big newspapers, to open. The situation was similar in all major cities in the 1930s. Everywhere people waited in long queues in order to receive at least one hot meal a day.

for foreign goods, but intra-European trade – more important to the economies of European countries than American trade – was also in decline. The American slump hit Europe at a time when structural problems, insufficient domestic demand, relatively high unemployment, distorted currency parities and problems of international capital integration had already produced an unstable economic situation. As in the United States, a small push sufficed to set off the spiral of recession that kept winding its way farther and farther down. Company expectations of sales and profits were negatively affected by declining demand; thus threatened with overcapacities, companies reduced investments, production and employment. Purchasing power was thus further reduced, limiting opportunities for sales. In many countries investment sank drastically; in some, like Germany, it virtually came to a halt. By the summer of 1932, the economic situation in Europe was grim. Capital and labor were both severely underutilized. Some feared a total breakdown of the economic system.

Financial and monetary collapse

Although the breakdown of the international financial and monetary system did not start in Europe, the European economic situation played a major part. The background was provided by a triangle of debtor-creditor relationships between Germany, the European Allies and the United States, which consisted of reparations, war debts and commercial capital movements: the "debt cycle". Germany needed American capital to fund her war debts, but American capital went to other European countries as well. When the inflow of American capital ceased, European capital exporters – Belgium, France, the Netherlands, Sweden, Switzerland, the United Kingdom – had to curb their capital outflow or even recall foreign capital assets.

▲ The slums of northwestern England, where the textile industry was in depression, were as bleak as those of London's East End. Unemployment and a minimum of state support meant not only economic impoverishment. Many resorted to alcohol which, in turn, put further pressure on family relations.

The Wall Street Crash

The collapse of the New York Stock Exchange in October 1929 has become a symbol of the beginning of the Great Depression. This is to exaggerate its importance, but its consequences should not be underestimated. Before the crash, the sale of shares was often financed with credit. When foreign investors, as well as American banks and institutions outside New York, withdrew their money from the New York market, the crash was triggered. Firms which financed their investments through share issues had to cut back expenditure; production declined and stocks were reduced. And it was not only the professional speculators who took part in share trading: a considerable part of the American middle class had speculated with shares in order to participate in the buoyant market. When the loans with which the shares had been bought could no longer be paid back through the sale of shares, ruin was a not infrequent consequence. The general reduction in consumption caused demand within the United States to fall sharply, along with imports.

▶ An impoverished broker in dire straits.

$100 WILL BUY THIS CAR MUST HAVE CASH LOST ALL ON THE STOCK MARKET

Germany was one particularly weak point in this system of international capital integration. Here, the complicated transformation of commercial capital imports to the export of reparations payments had to take place. In Germany, moreover, short-term foreign credits were turned into long-term industrial assets to a particularly large extent. A sudden withdrawal of capital meant serious trouble for German banks. Problems ccould also arise from the extensive indebtedness of the less well-off European countries and the Third World, in which Western European and North American banks had committed themselves far beyond the financial means of the debtor countries; in a crisis, the servicing of debts was by no means secure. A further weak point was the structure of the American banking system, which consisted of a multitude of minor banks with limited capabilities and small reserves. In a lasting crisis they had to recall their credits in order to survive. Between 1930 and 1933

▲ In the major cities of Asia, as well as those of Europe and the United States, there appeared slum dwellings of the unemployed who could no longer afford to pay rent. Sometimes they lived in wooden shacks, sometimes they sought refuge in old drainpipes, as in this Tokyo shanty town; sometimes on the outskirts of the cities they dug holes in the earth. In such wretched living quarters the standards of hygiene were catastrophic; epidemics spread and mortality rose sharply.

◄ Those countries which produced and exported raw materials and foodstuffs were affected by the crisis almost as severely as the industrialized nations. In Australia during 1930, unemployment rose to 25 percent and in 1931–32 was nearly 30 percent. At times one in three Australians was jobless. From 1931, nominal wages fell drastically and from 1932 real wages declined, even if not so sharply. To accept a loss in real wages was, nevertheless, easier to bear than to receive no wages at all. Public charity was organized but unused to coping with unemployment and homelessness on this scale.

almost nine thousand American banks failed. Finally, the lack of sufficient cooperation between the national central banks created yet another weakness in the system.

The flow of capital back to America triggered a series of crises in German banks between 1929 and 1930. Confidence was not improved by the growing popular support for Hitler's National Socialist party. In 1931 the final collapse occurred. In January, Bolivia defaulted on its foreign debt, with other Latin American countries following suit. Creditors rushed to demand instant repayment of their loans. The major Austrian bank, the Österreichische Creditanstalt, which accounted for over two-thirds of total deposits in the Austrian banking system, failed in May, a collapse that was felt in Czechoslovakia, Hungary, Poland and Romania. In June Chancellor Heinrich Brüning declared Germany's inability to continue the payment of reparations, causing a run on German banks. Except for long-term investments, banks recalled their money from business. It was impossible to refinance debts. To prevent the complete breakdown of the German banking system, the German government had to support the banks by purchasing stock.

The financial crisis in Germany and Central and Eastern Europe soon affected the London money market, which was the conduit for the international flow of capital to the countries in this region. Short-term credits were frozen, since the debtors could not pay. The small gold reserves of the Bank of England, the withdrawal of capital from Great Britain and problems of financial policy undermined confidence in the stability of the pound. In mid-September 1931 the flight from the pound and the consequent outflow of gold had reached such an extent that Parliament had to suspend the obligation of the Bank of England to exchange sterling for gold. Within a few months the pound had fallen by 30 percent against the dollar.

Britain's abandonment of the gold standard was another shock for the world economy, since sterling, together with the dollar, was the major international currency and London was one of the most important money and capital markets. Other countries quickly followed this example, and by the end of 1932 the currencies of 32 countries were no longer on the gold standard. They were engaged in a race of devaluation in the hope that this would give them a competitive edge in world markets. When Franklin Roosevelt's administration took over in the United States in April 1933 and also abandoned gold, the gold standard was at an end as the international currency system. Only a few countries – among them Italy, Poland, France, Belgium, the Netherlands, and Switzerland – held on to gold, thereby increasing the pressure on their economies and their currencies.

A week after Great Britain had abandoned the gold standard, the economist John Maynard Keynes wrote: "There are few Englishmen who do not rejoice at the breaking of our gold fetters ... I believe that the great events of the last week may open a new chapter in the world's monetary history. I have a hope that they may break down barriers which have seemed impassable." In reality, however, there was to be no functioning liberal international currency system for a quarter of a century.

When we consider the magnitude of the losses from which the world suffers during a period of economic stagnation similar to that through which the world is now passing, it is impossible not to be impressed by the almost absolute failure of society up to the present to devise any means by which such disasters may be averted.

LEAGUE OF NATIONS REPORT,
29 SEPTEMBER 1930

German Austerity Measures

In Germany, Chancellor Heinrich Brüning conducted a deflationary policy of austerity in 1930–31 in an effort to balance the budget. Income tax went up by five percent as early as 1930. Taxes on such items as sugar, beer, tobacco and coffee were raised, and a number of new taxes were introduced. Higher contributions to unemployment insurance were imposed. Civil Service pay was cut, along with old age pensions and other social security benefits. Government investment was radically reduced. As a result the volume of the budget decreased by almost a third between 1929–30 and 1932–33; nevertheless, this attempt to save the economy was unsuccessful.

However, the objectives of this policy were not limited to balancing the budget. In Germany, financial policy in the crisis was an expression of the fundamental revision of social policy and thus reflected sociopolitical conditions in the Weimar Republic. The welfare state element in public financial policy, an important feature of social democracy established after 1918, was to be removed. At the same time, Chancellor Brüning's foreign policy intention must be taken into consideration. Primarily, he wanted reparations to be canceled, which ultimately implied the revision of the Treaty of Versailles. Trying to balance the budget was to signal Germany's willingness and, at the same time, its inability to pay.

▶ **Middle-class unemployed demonstrate in Berlin.**

101

Reactions to the crisis

The conservative forces in power in almost all industrial countries maintained an unshaken belief in orthodox remedies, and they reacted to the crisis with the tools of orthodox liberal economic policy. Between 1929 and 1931, most strategies employed to overcome the crisis were based based mainly on deflationary policies of austerity. Restrictive monetary and fiscal policies were intended to prevent the outflow of gold and foreign exchange, curb expenditure and raise revenue to balance public budgets; but instead higher interest rates, higher taxes and reduced public expenditure reinforced the cyclical downturn and aggravated the crisis.

The objective was not only to balance the budget but to restore the prewar liberal-capitalist system by the reduction of state intervention, particularly in the area of social policy. The welfare state element in public financial policy was to be removed.

Yet in another area of policy the reaction was markedly interventionist. The collapse of the gold standard was accompanied by foreign trade policies designed by individual countries to protect their national economies from foreign competition in order to soften the effects of the crisis. These measures ranged from arbitrary currency manipulations to the control of foreign exchange and even its complete management by the government. In the area of trade, governments adopted higher tariffs, import quotas, prohibitions and licencing systems. This resulted in the

◄ When Britain went off the gold standard in 1931, many people obtained good prices for articles made of gold. After Britain suspended gold payments, the pound sterling fell by more than 30 percent against the US dollar, which was still fixed in gold.

further decline of trade and, ultimately, the further disintegration of the world economy.

The less developed countries

Outside of industrial Europe and the United States, most countries – accounting for two-thirds of the global population – were still heavily dependent on the production of raw materials and foodstuffs at the end of the 1920s, even though industrial production was gradually increasing. Exports played a special role for these countries, as their development depended to a large degree on the inflow of foreign capital. In more than fifty countries in southeastern Europe, Latin America, Africa, Asia and Oceania, foodstuffs, agricultural and mineral raw materials accounted for more than half the value of their respective exports. Most countries depended on

▼ The financial crisis in central and southeastern Europe soon affected the London money market. Confidence in the pound faded rapidly. Bank of England messengers had to be quick off the mark with news of changes in the bank rate. Within a few months, sterling had fallen heavily in relation to currencies still on the gold standard.

► The 1930s in Latin America began with a catastrophic loss in the value of native raw materials and foodstuffs on the world market. The fall in demand in the developed countries led to oversupply in the producing countries. As stocks grew massive, the price of coffee sank from 22 to 8 American cents, and in Brazil coffee was shoveled overboard into the sea.

two or three commodities: rubber and tea in Ceylon, coffee in Brazil, sugar in Cuba, rubber in Malaysia. This dependence on foreign markets and foreign capital made such countries vulnerable to any changes in international economic conditions.

Thus, the Depression in the industrial countries soon spread outward to make its impact on agricultural southern and southeastern Europe, on developing countries in the Third World and on newly industrialized countries like Japan, Canada, Australia and New Zealand. Most of all, the Depression hit Latin America and Africa, and, though to a lesser degree, Asia. Latin America's GNP (calculated as the weighted average of the national products of Argentina, Brazil, Chile, Colombia, Cuba and Mexico) declined by 13 percent in 1929–32, whereas Asia's GNP (as the weighted average of the national products of China, India, Indonesia, Korea and Taiwan) actually rose slightly during the same period, before eventually declining a little in 1934.

John Maynard Keynes

John Maynard Keynes (1883–1946) studied mathematics and economics at the University of Cambridge in England. He became a lecturer in economics, and in 1911 took up the editorship of the important English economic publication, *The Economic Journal*, and worked in this capacity to the end of his life. He was also a member of various govermental committees, chairman of an insurance company, journalist and publisher.

Keynes became influential because he combined political-economic practice with theoretical considerations. His main work, *The General Theory of Employment, Interest and Money*, appeared in 1936. With it he accomplished a revolution in liberal economics. The experiences of the Great Depression led him to the view that the capitalist system was not, as classical economics had asserted, stable and tending to equilibrium but, on the contrary, unstable. The state must therefore be active to smooth out business cycles.

▼ No economist of his time was so central to the formation of political and economic decision-making processes. Whether as Great Britain's representative at international conferences, as adviser to the British government, as counselor to American presidents or as a journalist, Keynes personified that direction of economic policy that was no longer helpless in the face of crisis but that urged the state to an active battle against the crisis.

However, national differences were bigger in Asia than in Latin America. Armies of the unemployed did not exist in the cities of the periphery as they did more in the industrial countries, but a process of pauperization took place in rural areas. Japan, Australia and Canada, on the other hand, suffered severe unemployment, even when their national product, as in the case of Australia, did not fall sharply until 1931. As agriculture and industry were hit, farmers who had to abandon their land joined the millions of unemployed industrial workers.

The crisis spread from the center to the periphery as a response to both immediate effects and long-term trends. Primary producers were hit directly by declining demand in industrial countries – a demand that was already stagnating due to improved domestic supplies as a consequence of wartime expansion of farm land and improved agricultural productivity. Natural raw materials were being replaced by synthetics produced in the industrial countries – for instance, fertilizers, silk and light metals; and they were being used more economically. Low population growth and the loss of population in World War I also slowed down demand. Most importantly, an ever-increasing portion of world industrial production originated in countries with agricultural and mineral resources of their own, especially the United States.

But cultivated farm land had been expanded worldwide as a result of World War I, while the exploitation of mineral raw materials had been intensified. For some products, at least, the discrepancy between stagnant demand and growing supply meant potential overproduction. This was true of wheat, sugar, coffee and rubber as well as for tin, lead, wool and cotton. Prices for these commodities declined until 1929, when they fell steeply. Indeed, world market prices in general were falling. On the other hand, demand rose steadily for some products, with prices remaining relatively stable: meat and dairy products, fruit and vegetables, vegetable oils and fats, grains other than wheat, cocoa, copper and oil.

This decline in the volume and prices of exports meant a sharp reduction in export earnings. In 40 countries, mostly in the Third World, they fell by more than fifty percent. Augmenting stocks or destroying them – as happened with coffee, rubber and tin – did not at all affect the fall in prices. Supply reacted particularly inflexibly to declining demand, and even during the Depression production really fell for only a few products. For most, it continued or even increased as producers tried to balance income losses from falling prices. By keeping up or increasing output, prices were pushed down still further. Stockpiles reached an extremely high level. As farmers in many developing countries began to find it impossible to offset income losses by increasing their output, since the domestic market was too small, they retreated into subsistence farming.

A vicious circle

Sinking deeper and deeper into the crisis, the world economy was caught up in a vicious circle: as industrial nations demanded fewer and fewer foodstuffs and raw materials, the export earnings and incomes of primary producers fell. In return, the latter reduced their demand for finished industrial products. Even if this was of only minor importance to the industrial countries, the consequences for primary producers were grave.

Furthermore, the collapse of the international capital market had substantial consequences for less developed countries. Capital inflow ceased in

I was a telephone lineman down in Saskatchewan and I saw farmers as poor as any native in a backward nation anywhere on earth. The Government gave them seed grain, registered grain to plant, and this was to be their next year's crop and if things went right ... but those poor bastards couldn't wait until spring to plant, not when they saw their children starving before their eyes, and they boiled the seed wheat, they made porridge and gruel and bannock out of it, and this is the way some of those farmers got their families through the winter.

B. BROADFOOT,
TEN LOST YEARS 1929–1939.
MEMORIES OF CANADIANS
WHO SURVIVED THE
DEPRESSION

▶ It was perhaps in the 1930s that people began to think for the first time about the consequences of exploiting natural resources, as the agriculturally overexploited prairie lands of North America suffered from drought and erosion. At the beginning of the 1930s there was no rain throughout wide stretches of these lands, and the wind blew the topsoil away in dust storms that became a common sight across the prairies. But the conviction that it was possible to control nature still remained unshaken. Steps were taken to avoid such catastrophes in the future by means of dams on the Mississippi, the regulation of rivers and the planting of hedges and trees.

1929–30. As practically all primary producers were debtors (with the exception of the United States), a surplus in trade now offered the only possibility of meeting their obligations. They were the first to be exposed to the double pressure of falling export earnings and continued high interest payments fixed in terms of gold. The flow of capital was reversed: more capital was now flowing back to the industrial nations than was coming in from them.

Just as in the industrial nations, the immediate political reaction to the crisis in the developing countries was to impose restrictive monetary and fiscal policies and reduce currency reserves, but this liberal policy could not be maintained for very long. Argentina and Australia abandoned the gold standard and both devalued in 1929; other Latin American nations, New Zealand and Spain did likewise. Currency controls, higher tariffs, trade restrictions and more devaluations followed.

These measures could not truly solve the problem of debts. A large number of countries, especially in southeastern Europe and the Middle East, defaulted on their debts. There were no effective sanctions for the default or postponement of debts. Also, creditor countries could resort to moral indignation only to a certain degree, as they themselves were late in repaying their war debts and reparations due to financial difficulties. Nevertheless, the debt problem represented an additional burden for all countries involved.

Causes and explanations

There is no generally accepted explanation for the beginning of the crisis, although its causes have been studied since the 1930s. Some of the possible triggers may lie in overproduction and in unenlightened monetary, credit and foreign trade policies. It may also be that the structural problems brought about by the transition to mass consumption in the 1920s, reflecting changes in technology, population growth and income distribution, were partly responsible. What is certain, however, is that it was not until preparations got under way for a second world war that the Great Depression was defeated.

◄ This poor young black woman standing next to a torn poster of a white woman with a tray of food perhaps reflects the shattering of the American ideal of a free but also humane society. The Great Depression revealed anew that it was the poor and the poorest who were particularly affected by economic crisis. The poverty lasted longest in the southern states with their plantation economy where "King Cotton" ruled. The white small farmers were almost as poor as the black agricultural workers, whose subjugation was reminiscent of slavery.

▼ The agricultural depression of the 1920s in the United States was followed by further disaster as drought claimed the prairies. Huge clouds of dust blew over the land, transforming farmland and pastures into desert. Cattle starved, farmers could no longer repay their debts and had to give up their land. Families moved from the now-barren prairie states like the pioneers before them, to the west and north, where there was land and water. In Canada, too, thousands of farms were abandoned.

Datafile

The events of the 1930s affected world production and international trade in different ways. World production experienced a sharp drop during the crisis, but in the course of the 1930s it increased again vigorously, so that at the end of the decade it lay clearly above the 1929 level. This was above all a consequence of the expansion of industrial production. In the less developed countries, and also in some highly industrialized countries, industrialization accelerated. For world trade, the 1930s signified the end of the liberal era. It was already clear in the 1920s that the rebuilding of a liberal world economy after the chaos of the years 1914–18 was only partially successful, but it was not until the 1930s that it disintegrated.

World trade 1937

- Europe
- North America
- Asia
- Latin America
- Africa
- Oceania

Shares in world manufacturing

▲ The 1930s saw the share of Europe and North America in world trade decline slightly. Newly industrialized countries improved their share.

◀ Among the industrialized nations, only the United States and France suffered losses. Japan and the USSR showed clear gains.

▼ It is striking that the value of most of the settlement flows decreased between 1928 and 1938. Britain suffered the worst reversal, and by 1938 was in deficit with all the regions it traded with.

Balance of trade

The recovery of 1933 from the Depression was anything but dynamic. A few countries that held on to the gold standard, such as France, sank even deeper into the crisis. Countries where the Depression had not been so incisive experienced only a modest upswing. The United States saw considerable rates of growth, but the economy became bogged down again in 1937–38. Properly speaking, among the highly industrialized countries, a real boom took place only in Germany. In terms of the usual macroeconomic indicators – growth, unemployment, trade, prices and so on – the 1930s were a decade of insecurity for most industrial countries, even when the Great Depression was overcome. This can be seen most clearly in the rate of unemployment. In the six years between 1933 and 1938 it averaged 15 percent in the United Kingdom, 16 percent in Sweden, 22 percent in Denmark, and 20 percent in the United States.

In less developed nations the picture was also mixed. South Africa experienced a boom when, after the devaluations, the price of gold rose and gold production expanded from 1931 on. Japan, too, showed dynamic economic development. In Australia, on the other hand, national product grew only modestly. In Canada it grew faster, yet unemployment remained relatively high in both countries. For many people, those were hard years full of bitter memories: ten lost years. As one Canadian recalled, "I never throw away vegetable scraps without thinking, 'I wonder if there is something I can use these for?' That's the Depression thing. You were hungry for so many years, not starving but hungry, and it's like some men I know, some men who have to have three hundred dollars or so in their wallet, just something to fall back on. Because for so many years when they were kids, you understand, or young men, they had nothing. Not a bean." (B. Broadfoot, *Ten Lost Years 1929–1939: Memories of Canadians Who Survived the Depression.*)

The expanding industries

Generally it was the automobile, electrotechnical and chemical industries which sustained the recovery in the highly industrialized countries, while other sectors, such as mechanical engineering, also now developed positively. In terms of motorization, Europe had fallen far behind the United States after World War I; in 1929, with a total of half a million cars, the European automobile industry reached just 11 percent of American production. In the 1930s, however, Europe started to catch up. While American production was hit very hard by the Depression and recovered only slowly, European production, with the exception of France, soon reached full capacity. Together, the four big car-producing

RECOVERY AND ECONOMIC PROGRESS

countries in Europe – the United Kingdom, Italy, Germany and France – averaged a quarter of American output during the 1930s, and in the recession year of 1938 nearly half. As a branch of the economy, the expanding automobile industry required more and more resources as its demands influenced the whole industrial structure. In 1938, for example, the American automobile industry generated the biggest demand for strip steel, bars, sheets, malleable iron, alloy iron, gasoline, rubber, plate glass, nickel, lead and mohair.

Western Europe also recovered at least part of the American lead in other durable consumer goods. Vacuum cleaners, washing machines, refrigerators, record players, radios and telephones – all kinds of household appliances made their way into more and more homes, carrying the expansion in the electrotechnical industry. Apart from the necessary purchasing power, this sort of

▼ **The United States remained unchallenged as the major supplier of consumer durables. The radio, in particular, spread very fast.**

mass production depended upon two preconditions. First, new techniques of mass assembly had to be introduced, with all the corresponding possibilities for increasing production and productivity. Second, sufficient capacities for energy production had to be built up. The spread of household appliances, the rising consumption of electricity for lighting and cooking, and the growing demands of industry led to an enormous increase in electrical generating capacity.

The chemical industry, too, owed its expansion partly to consumer goods. Various kinds of plastics and synthetic fabrics were developed for new consumer industries. In addition, a whole range of other products entered the market permanently, such as artificial fertilizer, pharmaceuticals and dyes. Throughout the 1930s and 1940s, innovation and invention took place in all modern sectors of industry.

▶ Japanese cabinet ministers inspect Japanese-made woollen goods in 1933 – a mark of the importance of the Japanese textile industry, which survived the crisis relatively well. Japan sold woollen goods, as it did cotton, within the boundaries of the British Empire, in South America and in China at state-subsidized dumping prices. The young textile industries in the less developed and underdeveloped countries suffered particularly from this Japanese competition.

▶ After the disintegration of the gold standard, various new currency groupings came into being. These groupings broadly reflected existing patterns of trade and political alliance.

▼ Krupps smelting works, Rheinhausen, Germany. Among the highly industrialized countries, a real boom only took place in Germany. It was based on rearmament, in which the heavy industries were of prime importance. In contrast, the share of consumer goods industries in production as a whole perceptibly declined.

World production and world trade

The 1930s produced different effects on the geographic distribution of world industrial production across individual countries and regions. There were "winners" and "losers". Europe belonged to the former, partly because Germany and some other Western powers built up their arsenals in the second half of the 1930s, and also partly because young industries started to develop in Eastern and Southern Europe. If the Soviet Union is also taken into consideration, the European share rose from just over 40 to over 46 percent, as during those years the Soviet Union's industrialization accelerated. Japan, India, New Zealand, South Africa and Chile were also among the "winners". Nonetheless, the overall share of

the Third World countries rose only a little, from about seven to eight percent. The United States was the only real "loser".

While world production resumed its rise after 1932 and suffered only a slight reverse in 1937–38, the 1930s marked the end of an era for world trade. Apart from the two world wars, no decade in the 19th or 20th centuries had seen world trade so persistently stagnant. In the decade between 1927 and 1937, trade in primary products increased slightly, while that in manufactures decreased. An increase in trade in mineral raw materials was entirely responsible for the growth in the share of primary products.

As early as the 1920s economists believed they could give good reasons for the declining importance of world trade. Technological progress was to make possible the substitution of synthetics for natural raw materials and a more economical use of the latter. The spread of industrialization was to enable more and more countries to produce necessary industrial goods themselves. With income rising, a smaller portion would be used to import goods and a bigger share would go into service industries. Rising economic instability in industrial nations and the growing political emancipation of developing countries would lead to more restrictive trade policies in an effort to minimize the risk of the global economy's getting away from national control. Not every economist believed in the diminishing foreign trade

Currency Blocs c.1930

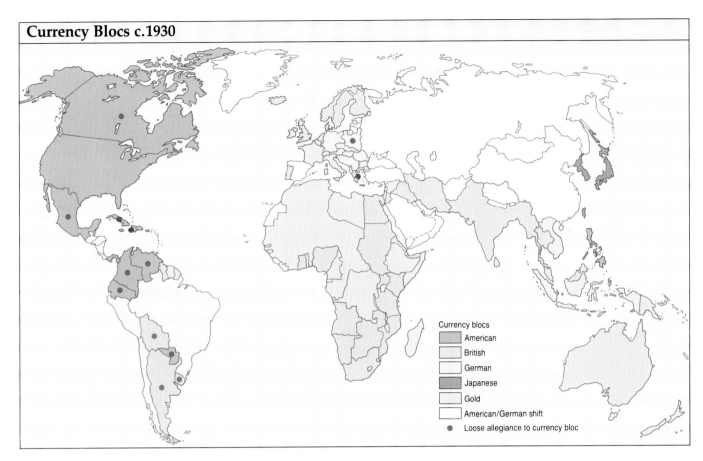

Currency blocs
- American
- British
- German
- Japanese
- Gold
- American/German shift
- ● Loose allegiance to currency bloc

hypothesis, which was to be refuted by the period after World War II. But it was generally accepted that world trade would have to suffer from national protectionism in a world without an international currency system and without an arrangement for international trade in capital and goods.

New currency groupings
With the retreat from the gold standard, a number of regional currency systems came into existence, largely reflecting trading and political links. The sterling bloc united Great Britain with Portugal, Scandinavia, Estonia and Latvia, as well as the Commonwealth countries. A dollar bloc was formed around the United States, including Canada and some Latin American countries, while a yen bloc was set up in Southeast Asia. The gold bloc was made up of countries that held on to the gold standard even after 1932: France, Belgium, Italy, Switzerland, Poland and The Netherlands; in 1936 it dissolved again, when France went off gold. The area in central and southeastern Europe that was dominated economically by Germany could be called a Reichsmark bloc. The currency areas could be seen as an expression of global economic disorder: there was no longer any generally accepted world currency system.

The reduced flow of capital
The collapse of the international capital market was no temporary phenomenon either. It took almost a quarter of a century before it completely functioned again. Investment was determined more by political considerations that by those of

profit. What capital still flowed tended to go to those countries with whom close links already existed – from London to the Commonwealth and other members of the sterling bloc, from France to other members of the gold bloc. It also flowed between Sweden and other Scandinavian countries, between the United States and Canada, and between the Latin American countries. Less and less was invested in the underdeveloped debtor countries, but more in other industralized creditor countries; less in Europe and more in the United States; less by private and more by public institutions.

Efforts at stabilization
In the 1930s international cooperation was at a low point. In the summer of 1933 a World Economic Conference was held in London, but this turned out to be a complete failure. No agreement was reached to fix new exchange rates, to cut tariffs, or to adopt stabilizing measures, despite the emphatic recommendation of the newly elected President Franklin D. Roosevelt that the Conference "must establish order in place of the present chaos by a stabilization of currencies, by freeing the flow of world trade, and by international action to raise price levels". It was the last attempt before the outbreak of World War II to solve international problems by international cooperation. By the beginning of July, Roosevelt was advocating a unilateral move, the "compensated" or "commodity" dollar, on the grounds that the "sound internal economic system of a nation is a greater factor in its well being than the price of its currency in changing terms of the currencies of other nations".

▼ As motorization accelerated, American oil companies began to drill for oil in other regions of the world and to acquire the rights to the exploitation of such oil fields. Here, Canadian Indians sell land rights to oil companies for exploration.

109

▲ Guns or butter? More arms or more trade? It was already clear to critical contemporaries in 1933 that the new regime in Germany was not concerned with job creation and better living conditions, but with rearmament.

▶ The New York World's Fair of 1939 served as a symbol of the nation's industrial and economic power.

▲ "Work and bread", the slogan of the German National Socialist party, lured people with promises of satisfying the most basic needs. In the face of the massive impoverishment during the crisis, this was both clever and dangerous. Such promises were only partially kept. By the middle of the 1930s Germany had, indeed, achieved full employment, but the standard of living remained very low. The regime could, in fact, offer little more than work and bread.

The adoption of bilateralism

Instead of international cooperation, national protectionism increased in the form of currency management, arbitrary currency manipulation, tariff walls, import quotas and prohibitions. Increasingly, bilateral agreements – between pairs of trading partners – replaced traditional trade agreements, saving diminishing currency reserves by reducing the need for settlement in gold or scarce foreign exchange. Such agreements frequently involved either direct exchanges of goods of equal value, or settlements made through special clearing accounts in terms of the two countries' own currencies. Thus, the multilateral system of trade was dismantled in favor of bilateralism, and despite criticism of this development from some quarters, the restrictionism of international trade continued, amidst general skepticism and uncertainty concerning the future development of international trade.

Since bilateral agreements were no alternative to multilateral cooperation, however, various countries tried to reach closer cooperation in trade policies on a regional level. Agreements were made in Southeastern Europe, by Scandinavia, The Netherlands, Belgium and Luxembourg (the so-called "Oslo-group"), and by Italy, Austria and Hungary (the Rome Agreement of 1934). The United States entered into liberalization agreements with several Latin American countries that also concluded similar agreements among themselves. Most importantly, the Commonwealth agreement made in 1932 created the Imperial Preference System, under which Commonwealth countries benefited from lower tariffs and easing of import restrictions, while countries outside were subject to increased restrictions. The amount of trade within the various regions grew sharply as a result.

Cartels and commodities

In the interwar period, falling prices, potential overcapacity and restrictive trade relations led to the proliferation of international cartels in manufactured and semifinished goods such as steel, chemical and electrotechnical products, as well as oil and aluminum. The cartels were supposed to regulate production quantities, stabilize prices, organize sales, and, if possible, secure monopoly profits, as one member of the cartel acted as monopolist. Ultimately, the international cartels were only mirror images of the national ones. During the 1930s capital concentration and the elimination of competition reached unprecedented heights in many countries.

International commodity schemes were really the only effective form of bilateral cooperation in the 1930s. The governments of countries producing and buying such things as sugar, copper, rubber, coffee and tea tried to stabilize – or even increase – production, prices, sales and ultimately earnings. Unfortunately, these commodity schemes, whether bi- or multilateral, could not replace a liberal international economy. They merely represented emergency measures adopted in order to offset at least the worst consequences of global economic disintegration. They created no trade but merely served to mitigate the

negative consequences of a severe depression on each country's own national economy and to shift its costs to other countries.

Government economic policies

Increasing government control over foreign trade and the partial withdrawal from world trade did not mean that governments decisively changed their policy and adopted anticyclical measures, although orthodox-liberal policy had obviously exacerbated the crisis. But in the United States, the Roosevelt administration turned to new directions with its New Deal policies in 1933. And in Sweden the Social Democrats took up anticyclical monetary and fiscal policies as early as 1932, creating additional purchasing power with public works, work creation programs, the improvement of social benefits as well as other measures. The significance of this policy for the course of the economy is difficult to measure. While recovery was fully under way in Sweden from 1935 on, allowing the policy of budget deficits to be discontinued, the American economy was already set for the next crisis beginning in 1937.

The fascist governments of Italy and Germany reacted to the crisis in a special way, national socialist economic policy being particularly successful with regard to the reduction of unemployment and the growth of the national product. German economic policy after 1933 consistently pursued rearmament, which contributed to the country's recovery.

Japan probably achieved the fastest and strongest recovery from the Depression, a recovery determined by the government's anticyclical polices and reinforced by its emphasis on rearmament. The three measures that were taken in order to counter the problems of foreign trade and weak domestic demand and investment – the

devaluation of the yen, reduction in interest rates, and increased government expenditures – were highly successful: the volume of exports doubled between 1932 and 1935, while the national product rose by a quarter.

In contrast, economic policy in other countries helped to exacerbate the downturn far into the 1930s. The crisis hit France relatively late and less severely. Huge gold reserves had tempted policymakers to stick to the gold standard and thus to fixed exchange rates, and rather than devalue or introduce exchange controls, French governments between 1931 and 1936 tried ineffectually to reduce costs and prices by deflationary policies. It was not until the Popular Front took over the government in 1936 that the gold standard was abandoned, the franc was devalued, and expansionary monetary and fiscal policies were adopted. From 1937 on, the French economy started to recover. Other countries that held on to gold – Belgium, The Netherlands, Switzerland and Poland – pursued similar economic policies.

The less-developed countries
Latin America and Africa were both severely struck by the crisis in 1929–32. Thereafter they experienced a distinct recovery, though income rose more slowly than in the 1920s and 1940s.

In Asia the crisis had only limited effects. The general recovery of national economies throughout the world made the reduction of stocks possible: this occurred most of all tin, wheat, cotton, silk and sugar.

Nevertheless, it was a difficult decade for less-developed countries. Capital inflow from industrial countries was still interrupted. Investment projects could not be continued. Servicing debts, where indeed it was possible, was a strain on the balance of payments. Generally, the debt problem remained unsolved. For the majority of Third World countries, the disintegration of the world market meant worse export opportunities. Although export earnings rose strongly, they did not reach the level of the 1920s again. Producers and exporters of basic foodstuffs suffered less than exporters of more sophisticated consumer products such as coffee. International commodity agreements to limit production usually discriminated against small domestic farmers rather than the big plantations owned by American or European investors. The devaluation of the yen and the growth of Japanese exports posed new problems for a number of Asian and African countries. Recovery was interrupted in 1937–38 by the recession in the United States, which mainly hit primary producers. The increase in

Roosevelt's New Deal

▲ Roosevelt's New Deal in action in this works program in New York. The crisis fundamentally changed the relationship between society, state and economy in the United States. The New Deal became the symbol of a capitalism with a more humane face, of concern for the socially disadvantaged. It set in motion unprecedented state activity in order to overcome economic problems.

During the "Hundred Days" of Roosevelt's first administration, programs were initiated to deal with a number of domestic problems. The National Recovery Act of June 1933 introduced industrial codes on production and prices as well as new regulations to protect labor. The Tennessee Valley Authority was set up in May 1933, investing government with control over the hydroelectric dam and the nitrate plants at Muscle Shoals on the Tennessee River, as well as power production, flood control and shipping on the river. New agencies to carry out relief measures were established. The unemployed were offered jobs in public works, and in agriculture direct payments to farmers were made

to reduce output and raise prices. The legal position of trade unions was improved, helping them to increase workers' wages and purchasing power. The banking crisis was tackled by the introduction of bank deposit insurance. Roosevelt hoped these measures would end the crisis.

The sudden economic downturn in the United States in 1937 caused Roosevelt's liberal advisers to urge him to resume deficit spending. He was hard to convince. J. M. Keynes himself joined in the effort to persuade Roosevelt to change his mind; at present, he said, more spending on public works, and particularly on housing, was needed. But Roosevelt was unmoved by his arguments, preferring to balance his budget.

▲ Havana Stock and Produce Exchange and docks. Like other Latin American countries, Cuba was dependent on the export of a small number of primary products. In 1929, about eighty percent of its export earnings came from sugar; three-quarters of this went to the United States. After 1929 exports fell dramatically, as did American capital inflow. Cuba was economically defenseless, and its subservient position in relation to the United States forced it into a major tariff reduction during the Depression. This damaged the limited industrial sector, with the result that Cuba was alone in Latin America in experiencing an industrial decline in the 1930s.

prices was interrupted, although there was no sharp fall as there had been in 1929 because, among other things, European rearmament programs had created a growing demand for raw materials from overseas. But exports and imports declined, and Latin American GNP stagnated, while Asian GNP dropped by three percent.

For many less developed countries, the 1930s brought a reorientation towards national resources. Partial detachment from the international market seemed the best option for most Latin American countries, and internal development in the form of import substitution replaced external development. Policy changed direction to support this switch. By abandoning the gold standard and stopping debt payments, these countries at least partially avoided deflationary pressures. At the same time, they moved to expansionary monetary and fiscal policies in order to finance domestic industrialization. In Europe, too, the less-developed countries experienced an expansion of industrial production based, among other things, on import substitution.

Colonial policies in Asia

The weaker recovery of Asian developing countries resulted not only from the fact that the crisis had been less severe there, but also from the continuation of restrictive deflationary policies in the colonies of the United Kingdom and The Netherlands. The British Colonial Office demanded that each colony should balance its budget. Thus, harshly austere policies were pursued and taxes ruthlessly collected. In British India customs duties, which had already become the most important source of government revenue, had fallen considerably owing to the decline of foreign trade. This made government even less able to make any tax concessions to farmers. Even the salt tax, chosen by Gandhi as the focus of his campaign against British rule, was not reduced but, owing to the crisis, increased substantially even at the price of increasing anti-government agitation. The specter of government bankruptcy in British India, which would have entailed the bankruptcy of the British government, looked dangerously real. Therefore, any devaluation of the rupee, as demanded by Indian nationalists, had to be averted, lest a panic of creditors caused by devaluation precipitate immediate bankruptcy. Thus, deflationary currency policies were added to austere fiscal policies in order to preserve the overvalued exchange rate of the rupee at any price at all.

China suffered from domestic disturbances in this period and, after 1937, from the war against Japan. The Japanese colonies Korea and Formosa (now Taiwan), on the other hand, profited from the Japanese recovery. In Asia, there were no efforts of industrialization comparable to those of Latin America, though there were spectacular individual cases like the Indian sugar industry. To promote import substitution, protective tariffs and other trade barriers would have been necessary; but these would not have been accepted by the industrial countries without retaliation. Colonial powers conceded protective tariffs only for particular items, if at all, mostly in order to get rid of foreign competition.

African countries
The situation was similar in Africa where British, Belgian, French and Portuguese colonial administrations or the national governments tried to compensate for income losses due to declining foreign trade by raising taxes and reducing expenditure on infrastructure and welfare services. Big developmental projects were stopped, particularly in some West African countries. Increasing government interventionism certainly pointed towards future developments. *Laissez-faire* had never been very strong in Africa, and the drift of official policy in the 1930s was clearly towards an expansion of the public sector and the adoption by the state of responsibility and powers for management of the economic system.

In general, the Depression reinforced protectionist tendencies on the part of the colonial powers and increased their willingness to control colonial national economies more intensely. By 1941 the majority of British colonies were embedded in a system of price controls.

Import-substituting industrialization
The import-substituting industrialization practiced in the less developed countries was concentrated mainly on foodstuffs and textiles, with the remainder divided mainly among the metal-producing, metal-processing and chemical industries. However, no advanced technologies were used in production and no high-value-added manufactures were produced. Certainly there were countries like Brazil that experienced a breakthrough in industrialization in the 1930s, and others like Egypt or Southern Rhodesia that made real industrial progress. But even in Latin America, where a number of countries put their industries on a broader basis. Output growth was accompanied by relatively little fresh investment and technical change. The import-substitution industries were not necessarily low-cost, and the plant and equipment for them had largely to be imported. Moreover, new industries tended to remain enclaves of modernity in a general sea of backwardness, showing few indications that they could become the instruments of a more general structural transformation. Instead, they often tended to reinforce economic dualism.

On the average between 1919 and 1939 more than one-tenth of the men and women desiring work were unemployed. In the worst period of the depression well over 25 per cent were left in unproductive idleness ... War time has taught us valuable lessons ... (that) full employment must be achieved in ways consistent with a free society.

AUSTRALIAN WHITE PAPER, 30 MAY 1945

Saudi Oil

In Saudi Arabia, which was founded as a Kingdom in 1932, the international economic crisis caused the flow of pilgrims from eastern grain-producing countries to break off almost overnight, thus depriving the ruling dynasty of its main source of income. Due to the deterioration of grain prices, Indian, Persian and Indonesian Muslims, who usually made up the majority of pilgrims, had not been able to build up any reserves to pay for the long journey to the holy Islamic shrines at Mecca and Medina. In search of new sources of income, the Saudi Arabian king then opened the country to financially potent American oil companies.

At the same time, the large American oil companies had been particularly hard hit by reforms being carried out in various countries, especially in Mexico, where 17 British and American oil companies were taken over during March 1938 as part of General Cardenas's revolution, which included land redistribution and nationalization of the railways as well as expropriation of the oil companies. To balance these losses, the American companies were looking for alternative areas of exploration, and were only too eager to accept the opportunities offered by Saudi Arabia.

Oil, for which there was a growing demand in Western countries, was one of the few resources available in Saudi Arabia. In view of its own financial position, and the need to secure those in power and maintain a feudal way of life, King Saud granted licenses to the American oil companies and opened the country to them. It was to prove the beginning of the road to riches for Saudi Arabia, which proved to have

enormous oil reserves. However, it was not until the early 1950s that Saudi Arabia, along with other oil-producing countries of the Middle East, began to insist on new agreements with the foreign companies which would give it a property share of the vast profits of the oil industry. In 1951 agreement was reached with the Arabian American Oil Company (ARAMCO) to share its profits with the Saudi government even then, only a small share of the revenue stayed in the country.

▲ King Saud of Saudi Arabia is entertained to luncheon aboard ship by his American hosts. The Depression, allied to a developing sense of nationalism, led to a cautious attempt to promote native national resources and to reduce dependence on Western finance.

THE MILITARY–INDUSTRIAL COMPLEX

In most industrialized countries since 1900 there has developed a close cooperation and mutual dependency of the interests of the military, industrialists and politicians. From this has arisen the so-called military–industrial complex, a juggernaut that has moved under its own impetus to fund and build large programs of weapons manufacture. The impetus of this complex has had profound effects on social, economic and political decision-making.

The complex results from the interdependent interests of five groups in society. First are the politicians, to whom military equipment gives muscle in the international arena. Second, the industrialists themselves may win fortunes from large contracts for researching, developing and building new weapons of war, and who achieve considerable influence in the bargain. Third, the scientists may find funds forthcoming for their research projects funds as part of a military program while unavailable elsewhere. Fourth, the generals, admirals and air marshals have an insatiable demand for new products, and the availability of new technology provides the opportunity to devise new battleplans. Finally a strong defense industry provides a substantial proportion of the workforce with secure employment even in times of depression.

In the period before World War II, Germany was considered the country in which the military–industrial complex was most firmly established, and in the 1930s the Nazi party relied on armaments manufacture to provide secure jobs. By the end of the decade, the Nazis, the military and industry were closely interlinked and a clear separation was no longer possible. After 1945, the conditions of the Cold War meant that the United States and the Soviet Union made an important part of their industry dependent on military expenditure. These are simply the most important examples, however; the military–industrial complex exists wherever weapons are produced.

Although the proportion of total public expenditure accounted for by military spending fell in most industrial countries after World War II, the economic importance of the armaments industry grew. As the state took on responsibility for stable economic development, the jobs in the armaments industry, which relied directly on government contracts, became more important. And, as military technology became more sophisticated, it began to product spinoffs in the form of products for commerical use.

However, the logic of the military–industrial complex was not inexorable. As the armaments of the superpowers were being negotiated away, particularly in the second half of the 1980s, experiments were made in converting military works into factories making civilian products without loss of jobs. Many people argued that civil production had more benefit for humanity, as the products of the arms industry exist only to be destroyed, whether on the battlefield, or as a result of successful arms-control negotiations.

▶▶ Soviet leaders and generals during Red Square parade in Moscow, 1950: in the East politicians, generals and industrialists worked closely together in a military–industrial complex.

▶ John Heartfield's satirical photocollage attacked the emphasis on military production: "Hurray the butter is finished! Göring in one of his speeches: Ore has always made an empire strong. Butter and lard have made people fat at best."

▶▶ World War I was the first war in which arms production became the dominant sector of industry. Here the massive German steel works of Krupp produce gun barrels.

▼ Hitler visiting a shipyard in Hamburg in 1935. The military–industrial complex grew in the 1930s in Germany as in no other country.

Hurrah, die Butter ist alle!

Goering in seiner Hamburger Rede: „Erz hat stets ein Reich stark gemacht, Butter und Schmalz haben höchstens ein Volk fett gemacht".

▶▶ Not only are politics involved in the military-industrial complex, in the course of the 20th century science has also played an increasingly important role in the invention of military weapons. The American "Star Wars" program in the 1980s introduced a great deal of government money into scientific research.

▶ The arms industry is an export industry. How dangerous such export business is has been shown increasingly, since more and more underdeveloped nations have become able to buy modern weapons. This aircraft and concomitant missiles are on display in an airshow of 1976.

ЛЕНИН

Datafile

No war had ever before left its mark on the world economy as did World War II. At the high point, in winter 1943–44, approximately one-third of world production was for war purposes. It was indeed, in the truest sense of the world, a world war. Few national economies remained unaffected by it. World production increased rapidly, but the peoples of the world gained nothing thereby. On the contrary, in most countries the standard of living declined rapidly. Seen purely from an economic perspective, however, there were winners and losers among the countries and continents. Germany, in particular, illustrates how quickly the national economy of a loser could change into prosperity. Nevertheless, in the second half of the 1940s something over half of world manufacturing production came from North America, whilst before the war it had been only one-third. Europe's share fell from almost 40 percent to just about a quarter, while the less developed countries were barely able to maintain their share.

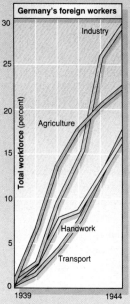

Germany's foreign workers

◀ The German war economy claimed the resources of Europe, including labor. The introduction of foreign workers represented a further form of economic exploitation of other countries. These workers were partly voluntary but principally abducted by force, as many as 14 million people in all.

▼ Naturally, it was production of the leading war requirements such as rubber and aluminum, which primarily increased in the decade between 1938 and 1948. Total energy consumption increased modestly, lifted notably by the American figures. Cement, steel and sawn wood also showed some net increase.

US manufacturing

▲ In the United States – as in other countries at war – the increase in production in the various sectors and the change in the structure of production entailed were naturally determined by the war itself. Aircraft, shipbuilding, explosives, metal manufacture, petroleum and rubber their combined share of the labor force.

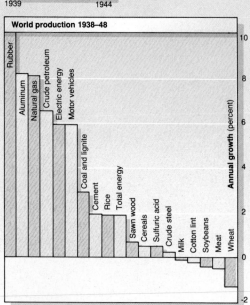

World production 1938–48

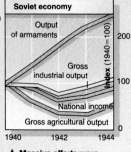

Soviet economy

▲ Massive efforts were necessary, especially after the German invasion of June 1941, to bring about a balanced increase in the output of armaments in the Soviet Union. Half of the industrial capacity was lost to the Germans. The initial fall in agricultural production indicates how difficult the supply situation was, despite Allied support.

To draw up an economic balance sheet of any war seems almost as appalling as war itself. Nevertheless, it has to be said that "gains" as well as "losses" resulted from World War II. For one thing, some countries were not directly involved in the war but received additional stimuli for their national economies from the demand created by belligerent countries. They truly profited from the war. For another, the war also had some genuinely positive effects for countries directly participating in it: economic growth and full employment. Most of all, however, investments were made and capital assets accumulated, which led to the modernization of industry. The acquisition of technological knowhow and the introduction of innovations were important until long after the war. Thus, the new priorities of production established during the war were decisive for future developments. Yet it is important to remember that wartime economic expansion was obtained through the production of goods that were to be immediately destroyed. The vast majority of the populations of the countries involved gained little, with many experiencing a declining standard of living.

The Western Allies' war effort

During the war, world output grew by 15 to 20 percent. But there were big differences in growth between various countries. Nowhere was expansion stronger than in the United States. Between 1939 and 1944, real GNP rose 1.5 times, industrial

THE ECONOMICS OF TOTAL WAR

production tripled, and war production shot up, accounting for 2 percent of total output in 1939 and 40 percent in 1943. In 1942, the United States was already manufacturing more arms than all the Axis countries put together; by 1944 its share had risen to about 40 percent of world armaments production. Overall, the productive capacity of the American economy must have grown by 50 percent.

Between 1941 and 1944, 19 million new jobs were created. At the same time, average plant utilization rose from 40 to 90 hours a week and labor productivity, already high at the start, grew even more. The boom was so strong that consumer spending also rose by 12 percent. Civil production and consumption declined only for durable consumer goods. This meant that all branches of industry profited from the war – most of all, of course, those relevant to armaments. Frequently, these were the most modern ones with bright prospects for future development: aircraft, automobiles, metal-processing, and the mechanical engineering, chemical and electrotechnical industries. The expansion also helped to carry industrialization into new areas in the South and West. At the end of the war, the American national economy was reaching huge productive capacities and high efficiency in comparison with the rest of the world. To an even greater extent than before, the population of America enjoyed by far the highest standard of living in the world.

However, the general upturn in the economy did not have universally beneficial effects. While big industry, fed by government capital and war orders, was growing bigger, small industry was being wrecked by the withholding of priorities and materials. As the investigators for the Senate Committee on Education and Labor in 1943 stated: "Throughout the first two and a half years of our effort one hundred of America's largest corporations have received 75 percent of all war contracts ... This situation ... has been accompanied by the destruction of one small community after another through the shutting down of its factories and the migration of its people."

Like the United States, other more developed countries that participated in the war but were not directly affected by war operations – Canada, Australia and South Africa – also succeeded in combining general economic growth, higher industrial output, especially war production, and improved standards of living. In most belligerent countries, however, this was impossible. For instance, total economic growth, as measured by GNP, was significantly weaker in Britain than in the United States, even though armament and thus industrial production also rose enormously, with basically the same branches of industry expanding. But despite the concentration of resources on arms production, Britain was unable to cover its own demands for armaments. It continued to depend on American deliveries for its supplies. The government used about half the

▼ Corsair fighters with folding wings for use on American aircraft carriers, on a production line at Stratford, Connecticut. The construction of the American military machine was only possible through an immense expansion of the American economy, in particular of its industrial capacities. This expansion contributed to the development of industries, but it also created capacities which brought with them the problem of how they should be used after the war. In the second half of the 1940s almost 50 percent of world manufacturing output was produced in the United States.

▲ The Skoda armament factory in Plzen, western Czechoslovakia, was the largest in Europe, with the two exceptions of Krupp and Schneider Creuzot. Unlike the countries of Eastern Europe, Czechoslovakia was differently exploited; the highly developed Czechoslovakian industry became a tool of the German war economy.

national product for war purposes. In 1943 civil consumption was of necessity roughly 20 percent lower than in 1939.

Continental Europe

Continental Europe was soon ruled by Germany and the European national economies were put to work for the German war effort. In Germany itself, national product increased only modestly until 1941–42, growing much faster thereafter with capacities relevant to the war being expanded almost exclusively after that time. War production peaked in the summer of 1944. After that, it started to fall gradually, and increasingly faster after January 1945, as the fronts collapsed and Allied bombings began to have serious effects. In 1943 the standard of living of individual German

consumers was still higher than the level in Britain. It did not drop until 1944.

The development of the national product is, however, only of limited use as an indicator of German economic capability during the war. Germany used the resources of occupied countries as well as its own. Contributions, occupation levies and other payments accounted for 14 percent of Germany's domestic product between 1940 and 1944, and if the contribution of foreign workers is also taken into consideration this figure must have been 25 per cent higher at least.

Elsewhere in Europe, the impact of the war varied a good deal depending on the extent of fighting and the degree of German exploitation. The worst effects of occupation were felt in Greece, Poland, France, Belgium, The Netherlands and the occupied parts of the Soviet Union. In all these countries output fell sharply, capital was seriously depleted or damaged, labor resources were exploited and living standards declined – in some cases to subsistence levels or even less. Extensive general damage also occurred in those countries where heavy fighting took place. During the occupation, output in France fell to two-thirds and industrial production to just over half of the 1938 level. Occupation levies absorbed one-third of this total, causing consumption to decline to less than half its prewar level. In Belgium and The Netherlands, the experience was similar though not quite so severe. Denmark suffered little serious deprivation, but although in Norway the fall in output was slight, the cost of occupation troops there reduced the living standards of the indigenous population. Countries allied with Germany and nominally independent, such as Finland, Hungary, Romania and Bulgaria, did not do too badly, though their living standards fell as they became increasingly involved in supporting the German war machine. The position of other countries in Eastern Europe was

Albert Speer and German Combat Munitions

When the *Blitzkrieg* ground to a halt just outside Moscow in the winter of 1941–42, Germany explicitly switched to a war economy. Hitler's architect, Albert Speer, was appointed as the Minister of Armaments and Munitions. Speer turned this previously second-rate agency into a super-ministry of planning and controls, achieving an enormous increase in arms production during the following period. His success was based on processing and organization techniques. He utilized the knowhow and organizing talents of the manufacturers themselves, and concentrated production in a few large and efficient companies. A transition took place from the highly time-consuming and cost-intensive serial manufacturing to mass production, thus permitting the use of unskilled as well as skilled labor.

Late in the summer of 1944 production peaked. Thereafter it declined, slowly at first and then increasingly faster. The German war economy broke down by mid-1945.

◀ Albert Speer trying out a new crosscountry vehicle.

much worse. Output declined to very low levels and many people struggled along on subsistence rations or less, while some died of starvation or malnutrition. In those countries such as Poland and Czechoslovakia, where resources and industry were indiscriminately exploited, industrial production ultimately reached a state of virtual collapse.

Soviet industrial production was, astonishingly, slightly higher in 1944 than in 1940, while military output was twice as high and exceeded German war production. Half the industrial capacities had been lost to the German invaders when they attacked the Soviet Union in June 1941, but in the five months after the invasion the most important machines and in some cases entire production plants of 1500 factories were, sometimes under the fire of German artillery, dismantled, loaded on freight cars and moved east. Ten million people were relocated. By the end of the war, the Soviet national economy had been largely destroyed, and only its armament industries were functioning efficiently.

War production in Japan

In Japan war production developed on a similar pattern to that of Germany, that is, the national economy was not completely dominated by the war effort until 1942. From that time on, total production, and especially war production, rose sharply, while war expenditures increased their share of the national product to 50 percent. However, the lack of natural resources caused grave problems which were compounded by the fact that Japan was not a highly industrialized country. The extensive structural changes that had to be carried through meant a forced push towards industrialization at the expense of the people, as the already low standard of living of the prewar period fell even further.

Industrial concentration

Arms production had generally played an increasingly important role since the end of the 1930s in Western Europe and Japan. But it was only after Pearl Harbor on 7 December 1941 and the failure of the *Blitzkreig* strategy that all major

▼ Aircraft carriers, such as this one on convoy operations in 1944, and other warships palpably created a demand for materials and labor. Shipbuilding was an important sector of the war economies of the Allies. American shipbuilding increased between 1939 and 1945 seventeenfold and had the highest growth rate, just behind that of the aircraft industry, and the manufacture of explosives and ammunition.

▶ Britain remained to a large extent dependent on the import of foodstuffs but, contrary to initial expectations, did manage to reduce these imports in the course of the war. The increase in the total net output of calories from British agriculture was achieved by putting more land under the plough and, above all, by growing wheat, potatoes and animal fodder. The regular male labor force declined by a little over five percent, but the actual amount of labor employed in the agricultural sector increased, thanks largely to the formation of the Women's Land Army, a large force of specially recruited female labor.

▼ In Britain, food was grown in surprising places to meet the demand caused by war effort. The British agricultural industry was highly successful, with net output in 1945–46 25 percent above the level for 1936–37. This increase, however, was only possible through limiting variety in the foodstuffs produced, and vegetables, in particular, became rare.

belligerent nations concentrated on the production of war materiel. Between 1942 and 1944, armaments flooded the world. At the peak of production in the winter of 1943–44, about a third of world output was for the war. The international economy was dominated by a war as never before. The process of industrial concentration accelerated: whether in Germany, Britain, the United States or Japan, large corporations were the main beneficiaries of enormously expanding government demand everywhere.

As after World War I, the United States, already the leading industrial power, was involved in the conflict without its industrial structure being damaged at all. By 1946 nearly half of world manufacturing came out of this country alone. The industrial capacity of Third World countries, on the other hand, had reached its all-time relative low. Two-thirds of the global population produced only six to seven percent of manufactures. At the beginning of the 1950s, the geographic concentration of world industrial production reached its peak.

Agriculture and food

The war influenced agricultural production just as much as it did industrial output. At the outset, a suddenly growing demand coincided with a time of much reduced supply. The growing demand

was partly the result of higher employment levels in many countries, with the subsequent growth of incomes and purchasing power; also, soldiers were usually better fed than they had been as civilians. The reduced supply was the result of the agricultural crisis brought about by the Depression, during which governments all over the world had subsidized farmers to take farmland out of cultivation and reduce agricultural output. Problems of supply were not confined to belligerent nations. Leaving aside growing income from increased military spending in countries not directly involved in the war, there was hardly any region of the world without armies creating additional demand for food. The world agricultural market was badly prepared for these sudden changes. In 1938 the biggest part of the global population was fed so badly that even a small rise in demand had considerable consequences on the consumption of certain kinds of food. The problems of supply were made worse by the disruption of international and transcontinental lines of transportation.

The negative effects of the war meant that agricultural production declined drastically in many regions of the world. In the Soviet Union, two-thirds of foodstuffs had been produced before the war in regions now occupied by German troops. In China about 40 percent of agricultural land had been conquered by Japan. Everywhere the reasons for the drop in production were the same: devastation, lack of labor, of fertilizer, of beasts of burden and machines, and the resulting decline of soil cultivation.

However, the war had positive effects too. Agricultural production expanded considerably in some countries: the United States, Britain, Ireland, Australia, Argentina and some others. North America performed particularly well in this field, exporting food to Asia, Europe and the Soviet Union. Even in Europe, the general decline did not preclude increased production of some items, like the potato. Still, this expansion of output could not make up for production losses. Even in 1947–48 world agricultural production was seven percent below the prewar level.

Outside Europe, the greatest production losses were suffered by those countries and regions of the world where agriculture was least productive and people were in danger of starvation even under normal conditions. The highly developed economies with a very productive agricultural sector were able to react much more flexibly than countries with low levels of productivity, which were unable to take advantage of growing demand. Between 1934–38 and 1948–52, annual agricultural output barely rose at all in Africa, the Far East, Latin America and the Middle East. Altogether, the annual average rate of growth was less than one percent in the developing countries during that period; output per head actually fell.

In all developing countries that had contact with foreign armies the economic structure, which was usually rather weak to begin with, was strained by inflation and the rise of black markets. The food reserves of these countries were strained to the limits.

Global numbers do not say much about the

profound changes in the world's agricultural market and output, changes that were a consequence of belligerent nations having to adapt agriculture to the economic necessities of war: sugar beet or potatoes instead of grain, land cultivation instead of livestock breeding. At the same time, the scarcity of cargo space which resulted from the increasing disruption of international transportation led to considerable distortions in the world agricultural market. Despite growing demand, food was destroyed, as in the Depression. Australia and Argentina had to cut back their exports, although they produced a large surplus; and while sugar was rationed and corn production stepped up in the United States, sugar was abundant in the West Indies and corn was burned as fuel in Argentina. As in industrial output, the war caused the distribution of agricultural production to be uniquely imbalanced with North America's share rising dramatically. While around 17 percent of grain exports came from Canada and the United States before the war, the figure after the war was nearly 60 percent.

Raw materials

Developing countries were affected just as much by the course of the war and by Allied control of cargo space with regard to raw materials as with foodstuffs. The production and export of raw materials declined in some countries during the war. In countries such as Burma, Malaya and In-

donesia, the production and export of minerals, oil and tin declined drastically. Many African countries, which sold their exports mainly to Europe, incurred substantial losses. But depending on the strategic importance of the region or the raw materials, some countries were able to profit from the war. The Belgian Congo increasingly exported copper, tin, cobalt, tungsten, zinc and uranium ores. Australia, South Africa and British East Africa also exported more raw materials to the Allies. Overall, more countries

▼ There was hardly anywhere in the world where troops, paramedics and other noncombatants did not appear as additional mouths to feed. This extra demand had negative consequences for the native population. The Allies were concerned to support agricultural production in the underdeveloped countries. However, they had little interest in a genuine improvement in production.

must have profited from war-related additional demand for raw materials than suffered from an equally war-related decline in demand.

Technology and organization

It is widely believed that wars stimulate inventions and promote innovations that positively influence economic development in peacetime. World War II was no exception. Jet engines, rocket and radar are probably the most famous examples, but there were many others, such as silicon and penicillin. Special attention was devoted to developing substitutes for scarce raw materials like rubber and oil. Still, it is not possible to say that the general rate of technological progress increased in the war. Rather, progress was redirected to other areas where, indeed, outstanding results were achieved; but there was hardly any room for long-term research projects and it is by no means certain that the civilian by-products of war-related research and development were equal to what might have been achieved without the pressure of war. Quite often, it was less spectacular innovations which were to be of extraordinary importance to peacetime production. They ranged from the restructuring of plants to the development of fully automated and standardized processes of production, and from improved training for workers to more efficient methods of management.

The war required closer cooperation between the Allies in using available resources and capacities as well as in technological development. This became more and more one-sided as the other Allies copied the technological innovations of American industry. And even though the international exchange of information and the extensive arms trade led to swift technological and organizational progress, this did not mean the adjustment of technological standards. The war proved that only highly developed economies were able to produce complex weapons systems. Even developed countries like Canada or Australia, which built up an extensive arms production, ultimately only took over American or British designs. For most developing countries the war did not really promote development. Scarce raw materials and insufficient technical assistance from industrial countries permitted the expansion of only rather simple industries: textiles, construction materials and foodstuffs, for example. To this extent, the war merely improved

◄ V2 rockets in Peenemünde, Germany, 1944. The V2 was promoted to the German people as their great hope. But though it incorporated advanced rocket technology, it came too late to change the course of war. Notwithstanding it was an example of the numerous promising inventions made before or during World War II.

▼ At a port in Britain a new steel foundry was erected to help supply the steel necessary for the manufacture of tanks and for urgent repair work on ships. Foundry work was almost wholly done by men until the outbreak of World War II. By early 1940s, more than half of the workforce was women. In other highly or less industrialized countries engaged in war, women were called upon to do what had previously been considered men's jobs. Many remained in work after the war.

Foreign Workers in Germany

The recruitment of foreign labor for the German war economy started with the defeat of Poland in 1939. Demand could not be met, although more and more voluntary workers were enlisted and prisoners of war were forced to work during the following period. After the failure of the *Blitzkrieg* strategy in spring 1942, Fritz Sauckel, newly appointed as Plenipotentiary-General of Labor Allocation, employed a systematic approach. In a number of "drives" he concentrated labor from all over the continent in Germany. In the first four months of 1942 an additional one and a half million workers came to Germany and a further million in the following six months. As the resistance of foreign governments increased, the methods of "enlistment" became more brutal. What had started as an exodus of labor ended up as outright deportation. Overall, 14 million foreign workers labored in Germany during the war.

▶ **French workers in Germany in 1944.**

the potential for development and reinforced the desire for self-reliance. For the time being, the gap between North and South widened.

The demand for labor
The war created enormous demand for labor as a result of the build-up of armies and the extraordinary expansion of production in the war economy. The demand was such that unemployment was rapidly reduced everywhere, and other labor reserves had to be tapped in addition: women, adolescents, senior citizens and, especially in Germany, foreign workers. Moreover, war industries proper covered their demand by recruiting from other branches of the economy. Germany was the first country to regulate the labor market by conscription into compulsory labor service and restriction of job mobility. But other countries also limited or suspended the freedom of movement in the labor market. Germany solved its labor problem mainly with foreign workers and prisoners of war, especially those held in concentration camps. An army of slave labor from all over Europe was employed by the German war economy. Similarly, around one and a half million Koreans were working in Japan at the end of the war.

The necessary and enforced integration of women into the industrial labor market produced long-range effects in the postwar period. Even in Germany, where the thorough mobilization of women was avoided for ideological reasons, women worked at their jobs more determinedly after the war than before.

World trade and economic groupings
The effects of the war on world trade were ambiguous. The close cooperation of the Western Allies led to renewed internationalization, while regionalization increased at the same time. As part of the Allied economic bloc, Britain benefited from the Lend-Lease Act of March 1941, whereby huge quantities of food, raw materials and arms were sent to Allied Europe from the United States. Between 1941 and 1945, the value of shipments by sea totaled over twenty-three billion dollars. The two countries also signed an agreement on closer technological cooperation and the coordination of war-related production.

Due to the dangers of long sea routes and the loss of trade with continental Europe, the United States increasingly imported from Latin America and the Caribbean, who were thus associated with the Allied economic bloc. In contrast, other developing countries found it harder to export to the dollar bloc.

Although also affiliated with the Allied economic bloc through Lend-Lease, the USSR was a special case, depending mainly on itself. Continental Europe, too, formed an economic region of a kind. The National Socialists had plans to establish a self-sufficient European economic region dominated by Germany, similar to the American, Soviet or Asian economic regions. Individual national economies were to provide reservoirs of labor and raw materials; the industrial core would be formed by Germany, Alsace-Lorraine, Austria and the western part of Czechoslovakia. Although no such "New Order" was ever established, all the occupied and dependent countries were nevertheless forcibly integrated in various ways into the German economy, through utilization of productive capacities in the southeast, north and west, and relentless exploitation in the east.

Japan organized the Asian-Pacific economic region. Countries occupied by Japan and their economies were controlled neither as completely nor for as long as individual nations in Europe. Here, too, however, the ultimate objective was a greater economic region dominated by Japan. Korea was unusual in having an incipient process of relatively broad industrialization; but otherwise, in newly occupied territories, immediate economic goals were limited to the exploitation of strategic raw materials.

In sum, world trade stagnated between 1938 and 1948, dropping sharply in Europe, less so in

Asia. In contrast, the North American and Latin American shares rose. The war changed the flow of trade and that of capital as well. As in World War I, the United States again became the main creditor of the Allies. Some developing countries were able to reduce their huge foreign debts, even to become creditors rather than debtors.

Government planning, direction and control

Many countries with quite different societies or political, social and economic systems took part in the war. Nonetheless, governments adopted similar economic policy measures to overcome the economic problems of war. They suspended the market mechanism of flexible prices in favor of controls and direction designed to ensure the restructuring of national economies according to the needs of war production. War was no longer predominantly a matter of purely financial costs.

It confronted society and the economy with such a formidable task that all economic resources had to be mobilized. Of course, prices, wages, taxes and credits were still used as financial control mechanisms even in such a strongly planned and directed economy as that of Germany. But more and more branches of production came to be covered by administrative planning and control. Production priorities had to be decided by central agencies, and government institutions had to develop a new sense of identity. Government and economy were no longer two separate sectors of the political-economic system. Instead, they were closely intertwined, with government setting the central targets for the economy, despite inevitable conflicts between specific industrial, company and national interests, and between individual military agencies and ministries.

In 1939 the Soviet Union was the only major

▼ Hamburg after bombing, Germany, 1945. Estimates say that 20 percent of prewar housing was destroyed in Germany and 3–10 percent in other countries. Some air raids were specifically intended to hit the German war economy in strategically important places. There were also air raids, however, which destroyed wide areas of German cities in order to demoralize the population.

▲ Dresden was laid waste by Allied bombing in 1945, but rebuilding began, as was the case in other German cities, immediately after the end of the war. Bricks were made from the ruins in order to get building material for new houses, rubble served to fill in craters caused by bombs, and wood was used to erect primitive emergency accommodation.

The index of armaments production fails to reflect the serious damage done in 1944 to specific segments of the Germany economy – oil, steel, and transportation. This illustrates that the Allies did not attempt to destroy the German economy as a whole or even the war economy as a whole. The bombing offensive sought rather to stop it from operating by damaging key points.

THE UNITED STATES
STRATEGIC BOMBING SURVEY
1946

▶ The atom bombs which fell on Hiroshima and Nagasaki killed 152,000 people and injured another 150,000. In total, over one million Japanese died in World War II. Only few people had, at that time, any notion of the longterm effects of radiation, which continued to claim lives long after the war was over and which brought horrendous suffering to survivors. No-one could have had any concrete idea of how radically the atom bomb would change the world.

belligerent country with an existing system of central planning and direction. In Germany such a system partially existed, with monetary and financial instruments dominating. In Italy and Japan government control of the economy was rather rudimentary. In the United States and Britain a liberal market economy existed despite increased government intervention. In the war years all governments erected a system of central planning, some earlier and more comprehensively than others.

Since the enormous expenditures on the war could only partly be financed by taxes, public debt and money supply rose in belligerent countries. The reduced supply of goods and the increased quantity of money in circulation represented a potential threat of inflation. Price and wage controls were imposed to counter this danger, thus introducing a new element of administrative economic direction. No centrally planned economies of the Soviet variety were formed during the war, but the relationship between government and business changed fundamentally. Experiences accumulated that were to have great impact on postwar economic policy.

Destruction, collapse and reconstruction

No one knows exactly how many people were killed and wounded in World War II. The following figures are probably not too high: 55 million dead, 35 million wounded and 3 million missing. Never before had civilian losses been so high. Air raids, partisan action, mass extermination, labor and concentration camps, flight, deportation and expulsion killed 20 to 30 million people. Europe, particularly Central and Eastern Europe, was hit hardest of all. Here, about 40 million people died. The question of how this loss of people affected Europe economically cannot be answered. Nationally, the problems varied; there were some countries with positive population growth despite high mortality rates. From a national perspective, deportation, expulsion, repatriation, territorial changes or population exchanges were more important than high mortality rates during the war. In Japan and China, too, the loss of people was less important for the economic future than the regional redistribution of the population.

Data on the direct costs of the war produce estimates ranging from 700 to 900 billion dollars. Of these, the United States must have borne about 30 percent, Germany 25 percent, the Soviet Union 14 percent, Britain 12 percent and Japan 7 percent. To estimate the loss and destruction of invested capital is even more difficult. The material damage to a country like the Soviet Union cannot be expressed in terms of money: whole regions were depopulated and devastated. More than 17,000 towns and settlements and over 70,000 villages were completely or partly destroyed, along with many thousands of factories, railroad tracks, hospitals, schools, libraries and collective farms. In Germany and Japan, too, major cities were devastated.

The infrastructure was heavily damaged in Europe and the Far East as well. Transportation completely broke down at the end of the war in large parts of Europe and Southeast Asia. In this area, too, there was large-scale destruction, especially in occupied territories. However, industrial plants were hit less severely. In 1953 a United Nations report concluded that industrial capacity in Europe and even in Eastern Europe (excluding the Soviet Union) was bigger after the war than before, and more suitable for future peacetime production. A similar report produced the same results for Japan. The devastation of agriculture was much more serious.

When war production came to a halt in 1945, the economies of some countries were in a state of general collapse. No one had any idea of how fast the world economy was going to recover. Prospects for the future were anything but bright. At best, there was a chance of progress in a few developing countries where the process of decolonization had accelerated and new possibilities for development had opened up. The future of the North American economy was by no means certain: it was difficult to see how its enormous productive capacities created in war conditions could be kept busy in peacetime. Large parts of the world suffered from hunger and need, poverty and misery.

THE PLANNED ECONOMY

The Soviet Union was hardly affected by the economic crisis which affected most of the rest of the world in the late 1920s and 1930s. After the Revolution of 1917, it had largely withdrawn from the world market. By the end of 1928, Stalin had taken power and embarked on an ambitious program intended to transform the Soviet Union into a modern nation.

Two five-year plans were to form the basis for this enormous restructuring of the national economy. The first, which concentrated on iron and steel production, began on 1 October 1928 and was declared complete on 31 December 1932. It was consolidated and broadened by the second plan, from 1933 to 1937. Both involved the abandonment of the market economy; instead targets for local industry were set by the Supreme Economic Council. Resources were also directed by the state, and despite some confusion and distorted statistics, the achievements were spectacular.

Between 1928 and 1937 industrial production rose by 12 to 18 percent annually. In particular, mechanical engineering expanded strongly, while a number of new industries were introduced. Tractors, trucks, aircraft and so on were mass-produced for the first time, and the number of industrial employees increased from just over four million to nearly 11.5 million during this period. New roads and railroads, as well as new factories, sprang up all across the Soviet Union, as well as power stations to service the new demand. In contrast, per capita personal consumption fell and the production of industrial consumer goods grew much more slowly than that of investment goods.

The relentless collectivization of agriculture – abolishing private property and reorganizing agricultural production into large collective farms, which were themselves set high production targets by the state – was central to Stalin's plans. Between late 1929 and the end of 1931, 20 million individual farms were turned into collectives. Those who would not willingly join were dealt with ruthlessly. The number of people working in agriculture dropped from 71 to 51 million between 1928 and 1937 (many of them dead, others forcibly removed from the land) and grave famines ensued, especially in 1932–33.

Despite the successes of the five-year plans, the system in the 1930s was by no means planned perfectly. Yet the Soviet Union developed into an important industrial power; mass unemployment was abolished and millions of unskilled or poorly trained peasants received basic training in industry. The human costs of this policy, however, were also enormous.

► The first five-year plan placed great emphasis on tractor production. This poster encouraged Soviet tractor engineers to work harder, indirectly to improve the agricultural situation. Without incentives or profit, the economy relied on such propaganda to raise output.

▲ ► China under Communism also experienced a centrally planned economy. During the 1960s, students, bureaucrats and teachers were directed to the fields in order to improve agricultural production, and to avert the dangers of urban unemployment.

▼ The industrial worker in the five-year plan was promoted as a modern hero. The photographs of Arkadi Schaichet – such as this image of a young man in a new cotton factory in Balakha in 1930 – expressed this quality dramatically.

► ▼ Consumer goods including clothing were given far lower priority than heavy industry, and despite such images of enthusiastic labor in textile mills, consumer output fell below 1928 levels through the 1930s and most of the 1940s.

РАЗВЕРНЕМ НАСТУПЛЕНИ

◄ Power and electricity were at the heart of Stalin's industrialization plans. Here the third turbine is being installed in the new hydroelectric power station in Dneprogues. Water and coal were the main sources of energy.

▼ Tractors being delivered to a *kolkhoz* or collective farm in 1930s. The bucolic image hid the reality of starvation, forcible emigration and widespread opposition to collectivization, which led many peasants to slaughter their own animals.

ОЦИАЛИСТИЧЕСКОЕ
В ГОРОДЕ И ДЕРЕВНЕ!

1945 · 1960

THE
REALIGNMENT
OF POWER

Time Chart

	1946	1947	1948	1949	1950	1951	1952
Industry	• Aug: Britain assumes control over the German iron and steel industry • Aug: Establishment of the British Steel Control Board	• Feb: Nationalization of the electricity industry (UK) • June: Agreement reached between UK petrol company Shell and US petrol company Gulf Exploration Company regarding the exploitation of oil fields	• Jan: Agrarian reform in many western German regions • Apr: Beginning of the decartelization of the iron and steel industry in the UK and US occupation zones (Ger) • Oct: Beginning of industrial production of plutonium (USA)	• Jun: division of the Bosch company. Sale of I.G. Farben prepared. Dismantling of synthetic petrol plants (Ger) • Sep: First East German industrial fair, the Leipziger Messe	• Sep: British High Commission prescribes end of dismantling in the British occupation zone (FRG) • Sep: Regulation concerning the division of six German steel companies (FRG) • Beginning of Chinese agrarian reform	• Jan: Beginning of the first five-year plan in East Germany • Apr: First five of 24 new steel corporations founded (FRG) • Dec: Foundation of Farbwerke Hoechst as successor to I.G. Farben (FRG)	• Jan: Farbwerke Baye Leverkusen AG, BASF Hoechst AG founded to continue the work of I.G Farben (FRG) • Jan: First mining collectives founded (FF
Technology	• Construction of the first computer (ENIAC) by J.P. Eckert and J.W. Maunchley (USA)	• Construction of a viable photocopier, patented by C.H. Carlsson (USA) • C.E. Yeager (USA) crosses Atlantic Ocean in a supersonic rocket plane	• Invention of the transistor by J. Bardeen, W. Brattain and W. Shockley (USA)	• Construction of an atomic bomb in the Soviet Union • G. Gabor develops holography (Hun)	• Mechanization of cotton-picking in the USA	• Development of the hydrogen bomb in the USA • 7 Jul: Advent of color television broadcasting in the USA	• Regular airline route from Europe to Japan across the Arctic begir • Completion of the Volga–Don channel V.I Lenin (USSR)
Finance	• 1 Mar: Nationalization of the Bank of England • May: First plans for currency reform in Germany published • May: Division of the three large private banks in Germany (Deutsche Bank, Dresdner Bank and Commerzbank) into 30 successor banks in the western occupation zones • Establishment of the Reconversion Finance Bank (Jap)	• Jul: US loan of $4.4 billion to UK to support the pound. The attempt to make the pound convertible lasts only 6 weeks (UK) • Oct: Establishment of regional central banks in the three western occupation zones (Ger) • Nov: Currency reforms in Austria and in the Soviet Union • Introduction of minimum reserves for Italian banks	• Jan: Devaluation of the franc (Fr) • 21 Jun: Currency reform in the three western occupation zones. Introduction of the Deutschmark (DM). Establishment of the Bank Deutscher Länder, acting as a central bank (Ger) • 23 Jun: Currency reform in the Soviet occupation zone (Ger)	• Sep: Devaluation of the DM. Legislation regarding the introduction of DM balance sheets (Ger) • Sep: Devaluation of the pound. Other currency rates adjusted (UK) • Sep: Further devaluation of the franc (Fr) • Nationalization of the banking system under the Communist regime (China)	• May: Establishment of the Deutsche Notenbank as central bank (GDR) • 1 Jul: Establishment of the European Payments Union (EPU), a combination of clearing central and international credit bank • Stabilization of the yen (Jap) • Establishment of the Cassa per il Mezzogiorno, a special bank for economic and social development in southern Italy	• Jan: Credit principles of the Bank Deutscher Länder put into force. First steps toward the convertibility of the Deutschmark (FRG) • Suspension of the Reconversion Finance Bank. The Japan Development Bank established, to continue the work of the former (Jap) • The Bank of International Settlements demands the convertibility of all currencies	• Jan: $300 million support to the UK from USA for the purpose of armament • Jan: Balance of payments crisis in the sterling bloc countries • Mar: Establishment of three successors to the former main banks Deutsche Bank, Dresd Bank and Commerzba (FRG) • Merger of the last 64 private banks into one large credit institute (China)
Economic Policy	• Jan: Conference on reparations in Paris • Mar: Dismantling of 350 enterprises in the Ruhr, and of 1200 enterprises in the Soviet occupation zone (Ger) • Dec: Agreement on the establishment of a united economic area comprising the British and American occupation zones signed (Ger)	• Jan: Establishment of an economic council for the British and American occupation zones, which in 1948 includes the French zone also (Ger) • Jun: General Marshall's address in Harvard proposing a European Recovery Program (Marshall Plan), accepted by the Western European countries in September • Dec: US president Truman declares a new external economic policy, the "Fair Deal", including economic support for less developed countries (USA)	• Apr: The enforcing of the Marshall Plan begins the economic reconstruction of Europe • Jul: Plans for a tariff union between Belgium, Netherlands and Luxembourg enforced • Beginning of economic reconstruction and the market economy in western Germany	• Jan: Establishment of the Council of Mutual Economic Support (Comecon) in Warsaw by the East European countries • Sep: First government of the Federal Republic of Germany formed under Konrad Adenauer • Nov: US president Truman demands an increase of production and exchange of goods • Nationalization of transport and North Sea ferries (UK)	• First proposal for a European currency in the European Council • Sep: Decision by the government to nationalize the iron and steel industry (UK) • Sep: Establishment of the National Production Authority (USA) • Oct: Italian government decides on a ten-year plan for the economic and social development of southern Italy	• National Union of Mineworkers (NUM) and the National Coal Board agree on better working conditions (UK) • Mar: Revision of the statute of occupation (FRG) • May: The Socialist party demands the nationalization of the steel and chemical industry (Fr) • Nov: US experts report on the economic situation in West Germany (The Hansen Report). Policy of "cheap money" recommended	• Apr: Strikes in the US steel industries. Some steel enterprises broug under government cor (USA) • May: British enterpri close their branches in China and consider the establishment of a new trade organization
International	• Jan: Establishment of the European Coal Organization • Jan: Soviet Union refuses to participate in an international trade conference • Mar: International Monetary Fund (IMF) and World Bank headquarters installed in Washington (USA) • Jul: Credit agreement and far-reaching trade conventions signed between UK and Canada	• Mar: Economic commissions for Europe, Asia and Latin America established by the UN • Mar: Beginning of trade relations between the UK and the western zones of Germany • Sep: Plan for a European tariff union published and discussed • Oct: the General Agreement on Tariffs and Trade (GATT) signed	• Jan: British foreign secretary Bevin publishes a plan for a federation of western European countries • Mar: End of a trade and employment conference in Havana. Set of regulations for an international trade organization dismissed • Apr: Establishment of the Organization for European Economic Cooperation (OEEC)	• Mar: Establishment of a tariff union between France and Italy • Apr: Scandinavian countries discuss the establishment of a Scandinavian tariff union • Oct: West Germany becomes a member of the OEEC • Dec: Negotiations regarding the establishment of a tariff union between France, Italy and the Benelux countries ("Fritalux"). Negotiations fail	• Jan: Beginning of negotiations for a tariff union between the UK and Scandanavia • Feb: OEEC agrees on a liberalization of trade among its members • Sep: British government halts delivery of machinery and strategic material to the countries of Eastern Europe • Sep: UN plan published for economic cooperation between the European and Latin American countries	• Apr: Plan for the establishment of a European organization for agrarian products (Pflimlin Plan) • Jul: End of the conference of Torquay with an agreement containing 147 bilateral tariff conventions (UK) • Sep: West Germany becomes member of the Transferable Account Area (TAA) and GATT	• Jan: West Germany Japan become membe of the IMF and World E • Apr: Import restricti for British and Italian products imposed by government • Dec: Establishment of the "Eastern Committe of West German indus for promoting trade wi Eastern Europe • World economic conference in Moscov Declaration on increas international trade
Misc.	• Beginning of the first Indochina war	• India becomes independent under Nehru • The Truman Doctrine allows military aid for non-communist countries (USA)	• Conference in London links economically the western occupation zones with western Europe (FRG) • 15 May: Independence of Palestine	• Sep: People's Republic of China proclaimed • Formation of the North Atlantic Treaty Organization (NATO) in Washington (USA)	• West German chancellor Adenauer offers German military support for a European Defence Committee	• Mar: The Western allies declare the war with Germany as terminated, but the "Cold War" prevents the making of a peace treaty	• 6 Feb: Elizabeth II accedes to the throne after the death of Geoi VI (UK)

1953	1954	1955	1956	1957	1958	1959	1960
[...]an: Allied agreement [r]estrictions for [Ger]man industry, [limit]ing production [cap]acity (FRG) • [A]ug: Assistance of [Kr]upp and Demag in [con]structing a [st]eelworks in India (FRG/Ind)	• Jan: Restrictions on imports of agricultural products (USA) • Jul: First nuclear power plant in the Soviet Union starts production	• Feb: Agreement between the Soviet Union and India regarding the construction of an iron and steel work in India • Sep: Intensive campaign by the Trade Union Congress (TUC) for the introduction of a 40-hour week (UK)	• Jan: Transformation of the Ford Motor Company to a stock company by the issue of shares (USA) • Jun: The British government agrees to dispose of the Trinidad Oil Company to the US Texas Oil Company	• Apr: The Social Democratic party (SPD) demands public control of the key industries (FRG) • Dec: First nuclear power plant in East Germany begins operation near Dresden	• Jan: First commercial nuclear power plant in the USA in use • May: The Soil Bank program prescribes the laying fallow of arable land (USA)	• Jan: European Coal and Steel Community (ECSC) accepts the merger of Bochumer Verein and Krupp industries (FRG) • Beginning of agrarian reform in Cuba after the revolution	• Jun: UK cuts nuclear power program due to coal surplus • Jul: Passing of a law for pricing agricultural products (Fr) • Jul: Volkswagen company put into private ownership (FRG)
[J.]P. Merill performs [a] kidney transplant	• Jan: launching of the submarine Nautilus, the first nuclear-powered vessel (USA) • Invention of solar cells (USA)	• C. Cockerell patents Hovercraft (UK) • N.S. Kapany develops fibre optics	• First commercial nuclear reactor built at Calder Hall (UK) • First telephone cable between the USA and Europe	• Aug: USSR tests intercontinental ballistic missiles (ICBMs) • 4 Oct: Launch of Sputnik 1 satellite (USSR)	• 1 Feb: Satellite Explorer 1 launched (USA) • Discovery of the laser beam by A.L. Shalow and C.H. Townes (USA)	• Soviet satellite Lunik reaches the Moon • Opening of the St Lawrence Seaway (Can)	• Aug: G.D. Searle Drug markets the first contraceptive pill • First weather satellite Tiros 1 begins operation (USA)
[M]ar: Convention [bet]ween the French [gov]ernment and [the] Bank of France • [M]ar: Change in the [ope]n market policy of [the] Federal Reserve [Boa]rd. Short-term [Trea]sury Bills will be [use]d to influence [inte]rest rates (USA) • [M]ay: Reopening of [we]st German stock [ex]changes • [F]ormation of the [Eur]odollar market	• Jan: London gold market reopens (UK) • Jun: Consultations regarding a European Monetary Agreement after the suspension of the European Payments Union and the introduction of currency convertibility • Foreign exchange law passed for the Bank of Tokyo (Jap) • Establishment of the Australian Bankers' Association	• Mar: Currency reform in China with the introduction of the yuan • Aug: European Monetary Agreement signed • New legislation introduced to regulate the banking system, especially the role of the Austrian National Bank • Formation of the Chase Manhattan Bank and of the First National City Bank as a result of mergers (USA)	• Oct/Nov: Run on the pound after the Suez crisis • Bank Holding Company Act regulates the relations between affiliated banks and their mother company (USA) • Establishment of the International Finance Corporation as affiliated bank of the World Bank	• 26 Jul: Establishment of the Deutsche Bundesbank as central bank by the merger of the former central banks and the Bank Deutscher Länder (FRG) • Sep: Repeated devaluation of the franc (Fr)	• 27 Dec: European Monetary Agreement enforced. Eleven European countries declare their currencies as freely convertible • Dec: Devaluation of the franc (Fr) • Dec: Suspension of foreign exchange control (FRG) • European Investment Bank established as the bank of the European Economic Community (EEC)	• Mar: Establishment of the Inter-American Development Bank by 19 American countries • Mar: drachma declared convertible by the Greek government • Dec: Further devaluation of the new franc (Fr)	• Jul: The Bundesbank places two credits at the disposal of the World Bank for the first time (FRG) • Oct: Increase in the gold price in London, Zürich, Paris and New York • Establishment of the Reserve Bank of Australia, acting as a central bank • Cuba withdraws from membership of the World Bank and IMF
[J]an: First five-year [eco]nomic plan [enf]orced (China) • [M]ar: Release of price [and] wage controls [(US]A) • [1]7 Jun: Uprising in [Eas]t Germany due to [the] poor economic [situ]ation and an [dema]nded increase [in w]orkers' norms [supp]ressed by the Red [Arm]y • [A]ug: Beginning of the [p]rivatization of the [iron] and steel industry [(...)]	• Apr: Randall Commission demands new formation of foreign economic policy and capital investment abroad (USA) • Jun: Four-year plan for the modernization of the economy begins (Fr) • Nov: Plan published for a common Scandanavian market	• Apr: Ten-year plan for the development of the French economy • May: First five-year plan for economic development begins (Ind) • Oct: Government undertakes measures for the reduction of consumption, involving the reduction of imports (UK) • The USSR decides to grant support for developing countries, particularly military and technological aid	• Integration of West Germany into the world capital market. Decision by West Germany to grant economic support to developing countries • May: Plan for the reprivatization of nationalized enterprises published (Aut) • May: Inauguration of the second five-year economic plan. Far-reaching nationalization of industry agreed (Ind)	• Mar: Beginning of a severe strike movement in the railway, shipbuilding and machinery industries (UK) • Dec: Government declares control of prices and wages to counter inflation (Fr) • Dec: Establishment of the National Council for Economy and Labor (It) • Establishment of 92 economic councils (USSR)	• Mar: Program for stimulation of the economy and economic recovery published by the US government • Jun: End of coal and coke rationing agreed (UK) • Nov: Khrushchev demands the abolition of seven-year economic plans (USSR) • Draper commission publishes a report regarding economic support for developing countries (USA)	• Feb: Seven-year industry and agriculture plan enforced (GDR) • Jun: Decree regarding an acceleration of technical progress in industry and mining published by the Soviet government • Jul: Beginning of the economic integration of the Saar basin into West Germany • Oct: Reduction of investment in mining agreed (UK)	• Oct: The state committee for economic expansion demands increasing competition and criticizes economic privileges for business (Fr) • Dec: National economy Plan for 1961 agreed (USSR)
[J]an: European Coal [and] Steel Community [(EC]SC) founded • [F]eb: London debt [agr]eement regarding [Ger]man debts. West [Ger]many is considered [the] legal successor of [the] former German [Rei]ch • [J]ul: GATT [com]mission declares [that] in accordance [with] a liberalization of [trad]e a freeing of the [exc]hange rates is [ne]cesary	• May: OECD publishes principles for the clearing of debtors and creditors positions of its members • Jun: Failure of negotiations toward an increase of trade between East and West Germany • Aug: Establishment of an international trade commission for raw materials by the UN	• Jan: Publication of a plan for West German–French trade relations • Jun: Conference of Messina, a preparation for the establishment of the European Economic Community (EEC) • Sep: Ninth session of the GATT agrees upon revision of the GATT treaty, involving the limitation of government subsidy and fixing of capital investment for developing countries	• Feb: countries of the ECSC agree on the establishment of a common European market and an atomic organization (Euratom) • Jul: Nationalization of the Suez canal by the Egyptian government • Jul: OEEC agrees on a 90 percent liberalization of trade amongst its members • Nov: Plan published for a tariff union between France and Tunisia	• Mar: Establishment of the European Economic Community (EEC), comprising West Germany, France, Italy and Benelux • Sep: Inter-American economic conference in Buenos Aires. Declaration of Buenos Aires demands enlargement of trade • Oct: Conference of the finance ministers of the Commonwealth of Nations discusses the establishment of a free trade area with Canada	• Mar: COMECON agrees upon specialization and cooperation in production • Mar: French prime minister Gaillard publishes a plan for economic cooperation between France and North African (Maghreb) countries	• Jan: Establishment of an Arabian Development Bank by the countries of the Arab League • Mar: Establishment of the International Development Association (IDA) by the World Bank • Nov: Stockholm convention signed between Austria, Denmark, UK, Norway, Portugal, Sweden and Switzerland to form the European Free Trade Association (EFTA)	• May: Stockholm convention of the EFTA countries comes into force • 7 Jul: OEEC becomes the Organization for European Cooperation and Development (OECD), including also the USA and Canada • Dec: Convention of the OECD countries on economic support for less developed countries
[2]7 Jul: Division of [Nor]th and South Korea	• G.A. Nasser becomes president of Egypt. British troops agree to leave the Suez canal zone within 20 months	• Announcement of the Hallstein doctrine, breaking off relations with states acknowledging East Germany (FRG)	• Oct/Nov: Second Arab–Israeli war due to Suez crisis • Oct: National uprising in Hungary repressed by the Red Army	• The Eisenhower doctrine promises military aid against any Communist attacks	• 13 May: Formation of the Fifth Republic under de Gaulle (Fr)	• Communist revolution in Cuba under Fidel Castro • Policy of peaceful coexistence between the USA and USSR	• The "African Year"; decolonization in Africa brings independence for many countries • Beginning of the Sino-Soviet conflict

Datafile

In Europe, both East and West, postwar developments transformed economic and social systems. In the West, prewar patterns changed at least partly in response to the state's assumption of greater obligations to ensure citizens attained minimum levels of material wellbeing. In the lower-income East, Communist governments took over complete ownership of industry and much of agriculture. The rural workforce, however, dwindled.

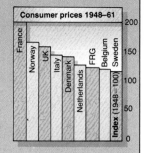

Consumer prices 1948–61

▲ National inflation rates under the Bretton Woods monetary system tended to be similar, to avoid balance of payments crises necessitating expenditure cuts or a realignment of exchange rates. French devaluation in 1958–59 was a response to high inflation, itself a sympton of more fundamental political difficulties.

Social transfers as percentage of GNP 1950

▲ War had encouraged a social solidarity which was subsequently embodied in tax-financed state payments to alleviate need, such as old age pensions and unemployment benefit. Many postwar governments greatly extended the welfare state, but in most other European countries "social transfers" were still a small proportion of GNP.

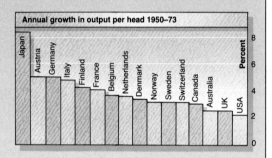

Annual growth in output per head 1950–73

▲ At the two extremes of economic growth among industrial countries were Japan and the United States. The latter was at the technological frontier. Japan was poor and badly war-damaged, and had an enormous range of innovations to absorb. Her growth rate accelerated as the new technologies were adopted by high investment.

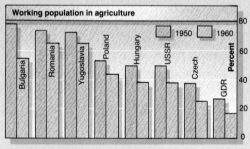

Working population in agriculture

1950   1960

▲ Eastern Europe was still substantially rural and agricultural in 1950. Measured by the proportion of the population working in agriculture, Bulgaria, Romania and Yugoslavia were the most backward economies, Czechoslovakia and East Germany the most advanced. Yugoslavia saw the smallest change in the 1950s.

► Bulgaria, starting with the smallest industrial base, experienced the most rapid rise in industrial output during the 1950s, followed by Romania. East Germany's performance was quite spectacular, for agricultural output increased second only to Romania and the country achieved the third highest industrial growth.

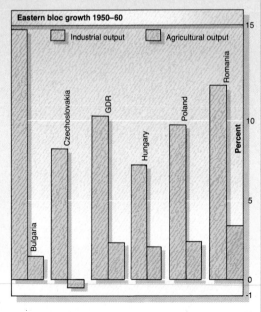

Eastern bloc growth 1950–60

Industrial output   Agricultural output

The United States emerged from World War II not only politically victorious but also economically preeminent. Military demands had eliminated the mass unemployment of the Great Depression by 1941, and – unlike most of the other combatants – the United States did not suffer damage to the physical structures of the economy in the shape of communications, or industrial productive equipment. Even manpower losses were small by comparison with those of the Civil War. By the 1920s it had already become clear that the size of the United States, its resources and its adoption of labor-saving production techniques warranted a claim to be the most powerful economy in the world. Disguised by the Depression and the collapse of the world economy in the 1930s, American economic leadership reemerged triumphantly after the war.

American technological leadership

The greater part of the world's modern manufacturing capacity was now based in the United States, and so too was the bulk of research and development effort. The extensive resources available in a country of such size, coupled with the military demands of the Cold War which followed the rift between East and West after World War II, encouraged the diversion of funds to research and development. In many cases, though, inventions that were to have momentous consequences were neither the product of market-orientated research, nor of the arms race, but were the outcome of a disinterested search for knowledge. For instance, the discovery in 1948 of the transistor at Bell Laboratories was undoubtedly facilitated in part by the finance that the monopoly telephone company Bell were prepared to commit to such research. It was not sheer size that was essential to such successes – indeed, huge institutions can suffer badly from organizational inflexibility. Much smaller companies in Germany and Britain were involved in the manufacture of early mainframe computers and jet engines; but their subsequent development required a corporation willing and able to commit enormous sums of money. Hence IBM and Boeing came to do for the mainframe computer and the passenger jet aircraft what it was impossible for a British or German company to do. Of course the German economy at the end of the war was in no position to develop new technologies and throughout this period could not commit government funds for technological military support in the way the United States did – though that may actually have been in the country's longer-term interests. The relatively slow growth rates of both the British and the American economies may be a consequence of distortion arising from the demand for "hi-tech" military equipment. Nuclear

132

POSTWAR RECONSTRUCTION

American economic leadership

Technological research and development

The German "economic miracle"

The new migration of labor

State provision of social services

The reconstruction of Eastern Europe

weapons research is a case in point. Extremely expensive, such a policy could only be justified by emphasis on their value as a "deterrent" and on the importance of "spin-offs" for the civilian economy in fields such as electricity generation. As the ensuing decades have shown, the costs and environmental hazards of nuclear power meant that in this instance the benefits of military "R and D" – research and development – were rather low.

The immediate postwar position of the United States, and to a lesser extent the United Kingdom, gave them technological leadership. Of one hundred major innovations between 1945 and 1960, American companies accounted for 60 and British firms for 14. As technological leaders, both countries had to spend more on research and development than other countries, in order to maintain a given pace of economic development; their growth rate was inevitably slower since, unlike other countries, they could not advance technological frontiers by copying.

▼ The Cold War gave the West an added incentive to accelerate the economic development of poor countries. Pakistan's Warsak hydroelectric project, Peshawar, shown here in 1959, was financed almost entirely by Canada.

Needing to absorb some nine million refugees expelled from territory seized by the Soviet Union and Poland or fleeing the Communist regime of the newly created German Democratic Republic, West Germany was at first obliged to imitate rather than innovate. The wasting of the German economy by bombing and fighting is well summed up by their description of the year 1945 as "year zero"; it seemed to those who had survived the rigors of wartime existence that society was so devastated and living standards so minimal that matters could only improve. In this situation, there was little alternative for many Germans, who were obliged to make the best of uncongenial circumstances, to work hard and pragmatically, in order that life should become just a little more bearable.

Recovery and re-equipment

Not only Germany but other war-shocked European economies, along with that of Japan, responded with remarkable economic dynamism

to their immediate postwar impoverishment. The common factor in their economic success, extensive wartime destruction and the consequent need to start afresh, prompted some people to extol the gains that resulted from eliminating obsolete capital equipment and replacing it with plant embodying current "best practice" techniques. The implication that the best form of foreign aid is bombing is an absurdity that goes hand in hand with the failure to realize that even equipment designed without benefit of current best-practice techniques will usually be of some value. The element of truth in the hypothesis is most probably that war destroyed some attitudes and institutions that were acting as brakes on economic advance, and created others that were more favourable. Sweden's rapid economic growth raises some doubts over the universal applicability of this theory: as a noncombatant in both world wars, Sweden can only be made to fit this pattern by pointing to the country's late industrial start and consequent delay in producing obstructive organizations.

Unemployment versus inflation

A second possible reason for this dynamic economic growth may have been pressure of demand. Companies were more prepared to invest in expensive machinery incorporating modern techniques if they believed that governments were willing and able to maintain a high level of spending, either through armaments or social provisions or both. This spending increased the chances that there would be buyers for the new products. Governments in their turn were now much more concerned to maintain full employment, and Keynesian economic theory provided ideological support for the view that it was within their power to do so. As long as there were unemployed resources in the economy, it was believed, government spending in excess of

receipts from taxation should not drive up prices, but instead should draw those resources into work and increase output. In fact, the correlation between unemployment statistics and "unemployed resources" was less than perfect and if inflation did rise when unemployment fell to politically acceptable levels, it was ignored for as long as possible.

How long inflation could be neglected depended on the balance of payments position. Once holders of internationally mobile capital – multinational companies and banks – began to feel that price rises were threatening to make an exchange rate untenable, they would pull their

money out of that country and the resulting balance of payments crisis would trigger a government policy reversal. Each country imposed its own national individuality upon this pattern; Italy and Britain had the highest propensity to push up prices, and West Germany the lowest. The United States was so large that the rest of the world was prepared to hold dollars as a currency in which to conduct international transactions, regardless of American policy and rate of inflation. Nonetheless, the adherence of all major economies to a fixed exchange rate or "par value" regime required that over a run of years their rates of inflation should be approximately equal. The fixed-rate regime encouraged the belief that fiscal and monetary expansion would not raise prices to any considerable extent, but would only be taken to the point where they expanded output and employment. In some respects these expectations were self-fulfilling: wage earners did not expect price increases in their wage claims during these years, and therefore did not trigger inflation.

The role of the trade unions

By contrast with the interwar years, the trade unions responsible for these wage claims exercised considerable power. Through the political parties which they controlled or influenced, they were able to reform social policy in general as well as wage policy. In 1957 The Netherlands introduced a centralized wage policy and in the following decade many other countries attempted to do the same as a means of limiting inflation without raising unemployment. At the company level, workplace committees participating in management were legally required all over Europe. Unions were well placed to ensure that their representatives were elected. In Germany, the *Mitbestimmung* system put trade unionists on boards of directors and on the boards of surveil-

lance of coal and steel companies. Such corporatism was anathema in the United States, where revelations of corruption undermined public confidence in trade unions, and legislation passed in 1959 was intended to prevent improper union practices rather than to extend their influence.

Most advanced economies organized their unions on the basis of industries. Thanks to its early industrial start, when industries were organized more loosely, with less capital equipment, Britain's unions grew and persisted much more on lines of craft or occupation. Consequently at any individual British factory a number of

▲ Devastated in the firestorm of a thousand-bomber raid, Dresden required complete rebuilding. The planners shown above were offered a remarkable opportunity to lay out an entire city, subject to the extreme shortage of resources to implement their plans. Though Dresden was among the worst-hit cities, the majority of German towns suffered almost as badly.

Ludwig Erhard and Germany's "Economic Miracle"

As the German Minister of Economics (1949–63) and later Chancellor (1963–66) during Germany's "economic miracle", Ludwig Erhard naturally took some credit for the remarkable recovery from the defeat and destruction of World War II. Erhard's distinctive economic doctrines and political style reinforced the impression among contemporaries that he was responsible in large part for Germany's new found prosperity.

The central idea of Erhard's economic philosophy was "the social market economy": he maintained that he had found a way between "unbridled liberalism" and "soulless state control". Competitive markets, if permitted to do so, would generate the government the revenue necessary to provide a decent living standard for those who, through no fault of their own, but because of age, sickness or war, could no longer directly participate in production.

Erhard's predilection for removing trade and currency controls was supported by the extraordinary productivity growth of the economy, the high propensity of the German public to save, and the stability of prices. Above all, industrial output recovered remarkably

quickly and soon began to exceed prewar levels. By 1953 Erhard was able to say that the man in the street must get it into his head that "refrigerators are not a luxury". Not surprisingly, with such exhortations, Erhard's beaming face, complete with cigar, soon became a symbol of national wellbeing for the German public as it tried to rebuild its prosperity and pride.

◄ On the banks of the Rhine, the ancient city of Cologne was as heavily bombed as most other German towns. Some eighty-five percent of the city was destroyed, yet, miraculously, its famous medieval cathedral survived. As economic recovery proceeded, all around it sprung up modern architecture contrasting strikingly with the elegant Gothic twin spires. The functional lines of the new structures symbolized the commitment of the new Germany to economic advance.

unions were typically interested in employment contracts and wage settlements.

The causes of economic growth
Although buoyant demand probably created a favorable climate for rapid economic growth, variations in growth rates between countries cannot be explained adequately by differences in pressure of demand. Rather, the principal determinants of growth were the technological lag and the ratio of investment to GNP. These two variables reflected entrepreneurial drive in innovating and borrowing new technology, the flexibility of the labor force in accepting new production tasks, work rules and equipment, and a

willingness to move to new plants and new areas. The technological lag measured the opportunity, and the investment ratio, together with the productivity of the investment, demonstrated the extent to which the opportunity was seized. A third explanation for the extraordinary pace of postwar recovery focused on the availability of surplus labor, either as refugees or from agriculture. In agriculture the growth of labor productivity usually outstripped the expansion of demand for agricultural produce and so released workers for jobs in other sectors. Such former agricultural workers fueled the growth of many economies but were not essential, for labor could be attracted out of other sectors, including retailing, or even from other countries, when necessary.

In fact, a good deal of effort in the developed world was devoted to preventing workers leaving the land by a variety of agricultural support policies. Such policies are best explained by the strategic political role of the agrarian voter in many countries. Unlike workers or employers in particular manufacturing industries, farmers and farm laborers are generally the dominant economic group in rural constituencies. Those they elect are therefore obliged to pay particular attention to the interests of the agricultural industry. Considerations such as this explain why in 1956, 60 percent of total American wheat shipments abroad and 80 percent of American cotton were noncommercial. Disaster relief, economic aid and surplus disposal agreements were all means of getting rid of American agricultural produce that

◄ Economic prosperity in Western Europe quickly created a shortage of workers to fill the lower-paid unskilled vacancies in most regions. Rapid population growth and slower economic development in poor countries with imperial or post-imperial links with Europe encouraged migrants from these areas. Pressure on housing and clashes of culture quickly caused friction with some sections of the host country workers. Norman Manley, Jamaica's first Prime Minister, attempted to reduce tension by showing in London a poster from the West Indies warning emigrants to England of possible dangers and disadvantages.

▼ American immigration restrictions imposed in 1954 diverted West Indian migrants to Britain. These Jamaicans arrived in Plymouth on a Panamanian liner in January 1955. European workers were in turn being attracted to Australia, New Zealand, Canada and South Africa.

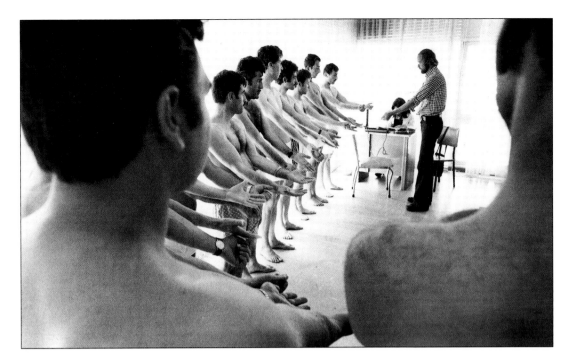

◀ West Germany increasingly drew its supply of unskilled manual workers from Turkey. "Guestworkers" (*Gastarbeiter*) were subject to a number of entry restrictions. They were obliged to prove their medical fitness, ability and willingness to work. Here a Turk is being medically examined by a German doctor in Istanbul. German immigration policy regulated immigration permits to job availability and restricted the right of workers to bring in their families.

would otherwise drive down domestic prices. Both continental Europe and Britain pursued policies with similar objectives at a cost to the consumer and taxpayer of around $3.75 billion in 1961.

The migration of labor

The return to full employment and the adjustment to the postwar regime and boundary changes redirected international migration during the 1950s into channels which had been largely marked out during the 19th century – movement from the populous lands of Europe to the regions of recent European settlement and, within Europe, from agricultural areas to rapidly growing industrial regions. Intercontinental migration from less developed countries followed a different course. The people of India and China no longer faced the opportunities of the 19th century, but in greatly reduced numbers some Asian and African migrants went to Europe. Latin America, before 1914 a major destination for European migrants, now lost population through international migration. Mexicans and West Indians especially headed for the prosperity of the United States. In 1954 the United States reacted by limiting the numbers of West Indian immigrants, who therefore made Britain their destination instead. Restricting Mexican entry was more difficult because of the length of the border to be policed, and consequently the figure of two and a half million official immigrants admitted to the United States considerably understates the true numbers. However, with a total American population of 150 million in 1950, even the complete immigration figures would not show that immigration made a substantial contribution to the American labor supply and population in this period. By contrast, in Australia, Canada and New Zealand migration continued to influence population growth. Almost three-fifths of Australia's population growth between 1947 and 1973 was through immigration and in years of high

immigration about one-third of the Canadian population increase was similarly accounted.

More migrants were still leaving Europe than entering it during the 1950s – a net outgoing figure of about three million people, though this was only a moderate outflow compared with the decades immediately before World War I. Within Europe, first Italy, then Greece, Spain and Portugal supplied workers to the booming North; North Africa and Turkey also ultimately provided new sources of labor for the European recovery. Switzerland alone took almost half of the Italians who migrated within Europe.

The policies of postwar recovery

Between 1950 and 1973 growth of national output per head for those countries in the Organization for Economic Cooperation and Development

◀ Although the conditions under which immigrants worked and the pay they received were generally better than those in their home countries, such workers were typically rather poor in comparison with the majority of host country employees. This double standard raised questions about the ethics of employing immigrant workers. The alternatives were greater mechanization, higher wages in the unskilled jobs, or ceasing production and importing. Only the third option was likely to benefit workers in the countries from which the migrants came.

(OECD) averaged 3.8 percent, compared with a previous best of 1.4 percent for the years between 1870 and 1913. What was the reason for this remarkable performance? Government policies were generally expansionary, and even where this was not so, close involvement in world trade meant that the expansionary policies of other countries exercised a beneficial effect. The United States adopted a Keynesian target with the Full Employment Act of 1946, though foreign aid and military expenditure were probably of greater significance for maintaining total spending until the 1960s. Scandinavia, too, successfully followed the Keynesian recipe of inducing investment in order to stimulate growth and provide full employment, and similar results were achieved by the corporatist policies of France, Italy and Japan. Such approaches were to result in the long boom of the 1960s and early 1970s.

Distribution of incomes and wealth

State provision of social services became more generous and more widespread after the war. However, there remained marked differences in policy in this area between countries, best represented by the views of Lord Beveridge in Britain and Ludwig Erhard in West Germany. Beveridge stood for a universal welfare state, providing similar benefits to all in egalitarian fashion, while Erhard believed in the selective provision of benefits so as not to remove incentives to save and work. Sweden was the most "Beveridgean" country in the world, with high taxation financing payments (known as transfer payments, transfering wealth from richer to poorer) to lower income groups, and especially to the unemployed. Behind such welfare state

philosophies in general lay a concern with relative wealth and income, whereas the policy typified by West Germany – and followed also by France, Italy and Belgium – was primarily interested in raising absolute living standards, regardless of distribution between individuals.

Security of employment proved a major equalizer of incomes, because the incidence of unemployment was traditionally far higher among lower-income families. The transformed labor market after 1945 made the most vulnerable groups better off. A great deal of welfare state legislation was concerned with the redistribution of incomes after tax. Such a policy has two major aspects – taxing the rich more heavily than the poor, and the payment of state benefits or subsidies toward certain items of expenditure which account for a larger proportion of the budgets of poorer families, such as housing, medical treatment and providing a proper diet for children. Measuring the impact of redistribution is extremely complex, but a study of income redistribution in 1960 in the United States showed that taxation took a higher proportion of income as incomes rose, with social security payments and indirect taxation – that is, taxes imposed on goods and services – taking the greatest share. Benefits fell sharply as family income rose, and the principal redistributive effect was from the richest 14 percent of families to the poorest 23 percent.

Nationalizing industry

Income could also be redistributed by requiring industries to charge prices related more to social objectives than to costs or profits. In return the industries would typically be granted monopoly privileges. Telecommunications was an early ex-

The Beveridge Report and the British Welfare State

William Henry Beveridge, First Baron Beveridge, was one of the most influential figures behind the British commitment to full employment and a welfare state after 1945. Beveridge had become the leading authority on unemployment and insurance in the United Kingdom during the years between the wars, when persistent mass unemployment first emerged. The Beveridge Report of 1942 outlined a framework for a comprehensive social security system; it underlay the National Insurance Act of 1946, the creation of the National Health Service, and the provision of family allowances and old age pensions, all carried through by the British Labour governments of 1945–51. Beveridge maintained that a comprehensive social insurance system would remove the five social ills (want, sickness, squalor, ignorance and idleness) caused by unemployment and poverty. He proposed that each person should have a national minimum income financed by weekly insurance contributions from everyone over the age of 16. Everyone would thereby be protected from the consequences of unemployment, sickness, accident and old age. The state would ensure that access to adequate health care facilities, housing and education would be available to all.

Born in Rangpur, India, in 1879, Beveridge lived long enough both to see many of his ideas put into practice and the changes they wrought.

He was a liberal rather than a socialist, concerned to abolish the weaknesses rather than alter the principles of the market economy. In 1960, three years before his death, Beveridge altered the introduction to his book. He now saw inflation, caused by wage awards in excess of productivity growth, as the principal social ill of the time.

▼ Beveridge addressing the Social Security League in 1943, in support of his social security proposals. The Social Security League, chaired by Barbara Wootton, was founded to press for the adoption of the Beveridge Report.

▲ Wealthier consumers in Western Europe were concerned with more glamorous matters than social services. Burgeoning private expenditure was diverted to display, adornment and conspicuous waste, as the austerity years were left behind. The number of women in paid employment began to rise, but some of those remaining at home, as well as those supplementing family income, offered a large and expanding market for "fashion". Those who could afford high fashion were, of course, a small minority.

▶ The supply of coal produced a bottleneck in the reconstruction of Europe, for it was an essential energy source for the capital goods industries. The problem was how to motivate miners to produce more coal when a shortage of consumer goods prevented money from being much of an incentive. In Britain, the newly nationalized coal industry appealed to the miners to work harder for themselves and the people than they had for the former owners.

ample. The "universal service obligation" implied making the same service available to all customers at the same price, regardless of where the customer lived and of the costs of supplying that service. This policy could be justified by pointing to the need to integrate outlying or under-privileged regions into the national economy, to the desire for fairness, or to the wish to promote national cultural solidarity.

The greatest wave of postwar nationalization occured in Britain where, between 1945 and 1951, two million workers were transferred to massive nationalized industries. Electricity, gas, railways, road haulage, steel, coal and passenger air transport were all absorbed into the new organizations. Little thought had been given to the economic goals and organization of these "Morrisonian corporations" (named after Herbert Morrison, the minister primarily reponsible for their establishment). They were instructed to break even after a period of years, but financing these industries came to be seen as an increasing problem.

Elsewhere in Europe nationalization was less ideologically motivated. The French car firm Renault was nationalized for collaboration with the Germans during the war. Renault had to compete with private car companies, yet during the 1950s it paid rather higher wages and achieved lower profits. Profits that might have gone to shareholders (the taxpayers) went instead to employees. In Germany, too, state ownership of companies did not result in new monopoly corporations as it did in Britain. In the motor vehicle (Volkswagen), steel and pig aluminum industries

state involvement was substantial, but the enterprises generally operated like the private businesses with which they competed, although they were expected to preserve jobs when unemployment rose and to contribute toward regional policy. Industries often came into state hands because of employment objectives. The loss of jobs from the British coalmining sector was managed relatively smoothly under state enterprise, whereas the process had provoked bitter disputes in the years between the wars. Nationalization was occasionally expected to achieve the goal of maintaining and enhancing national presences in key technology sectors: Italy's state holding companies IRI and ENI originated between the wars in such aims.

The reconstruction of Eastern Europe

Much of Eastern Europe, especially Poland, Hungary and Yugoslavia, had been devastated by heavy fighting by the end of the war. The difficulties of even the undamaged areas of the economy were exacerbated by the boundary changes of the postwar settlement and by the reorientation of economic relations away from the West and toward the Soviet Union. Manpower losses, both through death and migration, dislocated production. On the farms much livestock had been destroyed and land was made useless by mines or wreckage. Industry was further handicapped by the removal of plant by the victorious Russians. Romania and Hungary, having allied themselves with Germany, were also faced with reparations demands. However, the other countries received generous aid from UNRRA (the United Nations Relief and Rehabilitation Administration), amounting to $1.2 billion, which

▶ During the 1920s, when the French economy experienced boom conditions, large numbers of Poles migrated to Germany. With the economic collapse in the 1930s most returned to Poland. Here in 1949 Poles are producing coke for steel to rebuild the shattered Polish economy. All heavy industry was now owned by the state, so Polish workers in such sectors had the satisfaction of knowing that they were no longer working for the profit of a few wealthy capitalists. As the years passed, however, it became apparent that this was insufficient incentive to continue to improve enterprise productivity. Poland's rich deposits of coal and iron ore were not enough on their own to propel Poland into the ranks of the top industrial nations.

The economy of the GDR has to be developed within a few years in such a way that the superiority of the socialist economic order over the dominance of the imperialist forces in the Bonn state is proved beyond doubt, so that the per capita consumption of our working population of all-important food and other consumption goods equals and exceeds the per capita consumption of the population of western Germany.

WALTER ULBRICHT, 1959

▶ Surprised by Hitler's invasion in 1941, Stalin was determined that buffer states would make a repeat performance impossible. Occupation by Russian troops ensured that Communist governments would come to power in Eastern Europe and remain there, whatever the wishes of the population. Whereas in the years between the world wars the countries of Eastern Europe had fallen into Germany's sphere of economic influence, from the onset of the Cold War they began to be integrated into the Soviet economy. Comecon provided the vehicle for this economic coordination.

was more than opportune in view of the semi-starvation conditions brought about by the war and the poor harvests of 1945 and 1946. In addition the Allied powers supplied credit facilities totalling $458 million between 1945 and 1947, mostly to Poland and Czechoslovakia.

Among postwar policies, the redistribution of land took a high priority. Except in Hungary, some land reform had already begun in the years between the world wars. This process was accelerated by the seizure of German land, which amounted to over one-third of the total in Poland and more than one-quarter in Czechoslovakia. Collectivization was not a major aim of land policy. Rather, the objective was to provide employment for landless peasants or to increase the size of otherwise unviable smallholdings.

Economic dislocation tended to foster centralized control. Food shortages necessitated rationing, postwar inflation encouraged state acquisition of banks and the lack of private capital for investment created a void which the state filled. Two-thirds of industrial capacity in Poland and Yugoslavia was acquired by the state through confiscation or because the original owners had abandoned it. Much of Czechoslovakia's industry had been in the hands of the occupying forces and was therefore taken over by the state. More important as a centralizing force, though, was the prestige and power of the Communists, whose position and popularity now stemmed from the leading part they had played in the resistance movements. Disillusionment with the effects of market-oriented policies in the years between the two world wars gave a further boost to central planning.

By 1948 most East European states had reached their prewar levels of national income. In February there was a Communist coup in Prague and a few months later the Russians blockaded Berlin; the Cold War had begun in earnest. The United States reciprocated by beginning economic war-

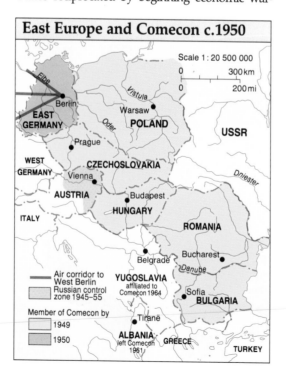

East Europe and Comecon c.1950

Scale 1 : 20 500 000

0 — 300 km
0 — 200 mi

Air corridor to West Berlin
Russian control zone 1945–55

Member of Comecon by
1949
1950

fare against the Soviet Union. NATO – the North Atlantic Treaty Organization – was formed in 1949 and war broke out in Korea in 1950. The Western economic embargo provided a purpose for the Council for Mutual Economic Assistance (CMEA), an organization formed by the Soviet Union and the Eastern European states in 1949 in reaction to the Marshall Plan, which otherwise it would not have found. The embargo also provided the stimulus for the subsequent development of Eastern Europe integrated with that of the Soviet economy. Romanian oil exports to the West, and Czech and Polish timber, earned foreign currency with which the Soviet bloc could buy copper, rubber, tin and wool, materials in which the Russians were deficient.

Soviet industrialization had traditionally concentrated resources by central planning in the heavy industries and armaments while squeezing consumption and agriculture. The spectacular results of this policy were revealed in 1957 with the launching of the Sputnik, the first satellite. Industrial growth was extremely rapid, industrial production approximately doubling during the 1950s, yet by 1960 real national income per employed worker was still well below half the American level, despite remarkable achievements in particular sectors. Almost certainly bureaucracy and the lack of incentive in the central planning system were the cause of the lost opportunities. Yet the planning system was inviolate because it allowed political control of the economy and therefore of other spheres of social life. The cost of the central planning system on Soviet industrial policy was to become clear in 1964 and 1972 when Russia was obliged to make huge purchases in world food markets to remedy the shortfall in domestic agriculture, despite an avowed policy of self-sufficiency.

Charting the course of Russian agriculture is hampered by the selective nature of official statistics, but it appears that the share of the state sector in agriculture continued to rise in the 1940s and 1950s, from 57.5 percent in 1940 to 61 percent in 1950 and 70 percent in 1956. Policy was concerned to ensure that livestock was concentrated in the state sector. Little or no improvement in the per capita availability of farm products occurred between the end of the 1920s, when the mass program of collectivization began, and the beginning of the 1950s. The position in grain was about the same, the amount of potatoes, sugar and cotton had increased substantially and eggs by a little, but there were fewer vegetables, less meat and milk, less wool and flax fibre and fewer sunflower seeds – the major source of vegetable oil for human consumption. During the 1950s a clear improvement occurred in all these categories. Mechanization proceeded rapidly but the resources released for agriculture were insufficient for the demands made upon it, given the collective farm structure. Plan targets were generally wildly optimistic.

Comparison with American agriculture over the same period is illuminating. In 1950 there were five and a half million American farms employing nearly ten million farm workers, 1.8 workers per farm. In the Soviet Union in the same year there were 111,400 collective farms, and 31 million farm workers, 278 workers per farm. By 1970 workers per farm in the United States and the Soviet Union were respectively 1.6 and 558. Between 1950 and 1960 grain produced per farmer increased at the same rate in the two countries, but the United States was to race ahead in the 1960s. Among the major crops, only potatoes showed a Soviet productivity advantage, and that was to be reversed during the 1960s.

The Berlin Airlift

At 6am on 24 June 1948, in an attempt to starve out the Western occupying powers, the Soviet Union completely blocked all ground traffic to the Allied enclave of West Berlin. Two days later the United States Air Force began an airlift of supplies into the beleaguered city and on 30 June the British announced that they too would take part. The air bridge was to last 15 months and cost the Americans $350 million, the British £17 million and the Germans DM 150 million. Over two million tonnes of food, fuel and machinery were flown into West Berlin. Blocks of 70 aircraft were sent from Wiesbaden or Frankfurt every two hours. Each aircraft flew at exactly 170 knots and one minute apart but at four different levels, warned by radar of its distance from planes in front or behind. If a pilot missed his first approach to Berlin's Tempelhof Airport he had to return to base; a second approach risked a collision.

In hindsight, the airlift was an expensive and dangerous mistake. Had the Allies placed tanks at the head of convoys of supply trucks, Moscow would have given orders that they be allowed through. Whether the West could have supplied Berlin forever was not tested; the blockade was called off in May 1949.

▼ Defeating the Soviet attempt to starve the Western Allies out of Berlin demanded a minimum 3,750 tonnes of supplies a day be flown in, including such heavy, low-value items as coal and potatoes. Some of these are shown being stacked in a store in Berlin. Nearly two hundred and eighty thousand flights in total were needed during the Berlin blockade.

◄ Once the Russians had blocked Western land access to West Berlin, the Allies reacted with countermeasures against the Soviet occupied zone. This ragman's cart is being searched as he leaves the American sector of Berlin in 1949 for the Russian sector. The aim was to ensure that goods brought in by the airlift did not get through to the Soviets. The Western embargo on strategic materials was to prove far more effective than the Russian blockade, for the Soviets needed Western goods.

THE TRANSISTOR REVOLUTION

The electronics industry had been made possible by the discovery of the electron in the early years of the 20th century. The first impact of this scientific advance on the technology of everyday life was in the radio. Television, too, was a product of the new electronics in the 1920s, as was radar in the 1930s.

The crucial breakthrough that permitted electronic devices to be manufactured in small, cheap and reliable units was the transistor. This was discovered in 1948, and consisted of a small piece of silicon or semiconductor material, which could replace the large and fragile vacuum tube.

The countries most involved in electronics development in the 1930s and 1940s were the United States, Germany and Britain, and in all three countries World War II provided a stimulus to technical research, with scientists working on radar and computers. German computer research was delayed when several leading computer scientists were called up for military service. The huge American computer corporation IBM relied heavily on government contract work in the years after the war, and by the end of the 1950s the American lead in the industry was clear.

Hearing aids, brought out in 1952, were the first consumer product to benefit from the power of the transistor. By 1954 one million transistors a year were being manufactured. At this stage all transistors were individually wired, but in 1957 the integrated circuit was developed, which allowed transistors to be manufactured with other components on semiconductor chips made of silicon.

The transistor revolution changed the quality of life at many levels; it also brought a new industry capable of dramatic growth. This would benefit both countries such as Germany and the United States with established traditions of science, and those which sought rapid economic advance by investment in new technology and marketing new products, such as Japan.

▲ In 1948 John Bardeen and Walter H. Brattain, working at the Bell Telephone Laboratories, invented the point contact transistor, consisting of a semiconductor chip. Three years later a colleague, William Shockley, invented the commercially viable junction transistor. The three were jointly awarded the shared a Nobel Prize for Physics in 1956.

▶▲ Transistors are small devices of semiconductor material which amplify or control electric current. Simple to manufacture though requiring careful handwork in assembly, they supplanted the vacuum tube almost completely by the 1970s. The need to wire them into position was overcome by the development of the integrated circuit.

▲ The earliest mass consumer product provided by the electronics industry was the radio, which, in the interwar years, spread even more rapidly than the telephone. Until the late 1950s radios, like computers, depended on vacuum tubes. The assembly of radios was light work requiring manual dexterity, and women found this especially suitable work.

◄ The first transistor radios came on the market in the mid-1950s. Like most consumer products that require technological innovation, at first they were comparatively expensive – retailing at a price equivalent to a musical instrument. Eventually, however, mass-production made the battery-powered portable radio accessible to all.

◄ The earliest computers of the late 1930s and 1940s were enormous affairs, but the advent of electronic switching enabled them to become more practical. Before the advent of the integrated memory chip, computer memories were made up of lattices of wires threaded through tiny ferrite rings. Passing a current through these rings could create a field that allowed them to act as an electrical "switch". A bank of such rings, each of which had a precise location and could be "switched" on or off to give a 0 or 1 signal, could store digitized information for future retrieval.

adar, an invention of the s, was developed in me Britain and the United s; in the late 1940s the knowledge was applied to aviation. Radar, as here e Netherlands in 1955, d track the position of aircraft in the area, and ermitted a much higher ity of air traffic.

► In 1957 the Soviet Union surprised the world by launching the first artificial satellite (Sputnik), an achievement made possible only by developments in electronics and miniaturization. By the mid-1960s satellites had become central to worldwide communications networks.

Datafile

International economic cooperation centered on two mutually exclusive blocs, those of the industrial West and of the Communist states. Most of the poorer countries were closely tied to the Western bloc by economic interests if not by political bonds. The Communists' Council for Mutual Economic Assistance, or Comecon, was a considerable integrative force among the Eastern European economies. Soviet resources began to aid both China and the Eastern European satellite countries, although all members of the bloc generated much lower incomes per head than the leader of the Western world, the United States. From the United States to its allies in Europe flowed substantial sums as gifts in the form of Marshall aid (the European Recovery Program), to support rapid recovery after the war. The United States also led the way in tariff reductions to encourage the rebuilding of the world economy. In response to this reduction of trade barriers and to rising incomes, trade expanded strongly.

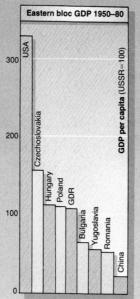

Eastern bloc GDP 1950–80

GDP per capita (USSR=100)

▲ The most prosperous Eastern European economy in 1950, Czechoslovakia, produced less than half the output per head of the United States. On the other hand, compared with the labor productivity of China under Mao Zedong's new regime. Eastern European economies comfortably exceeded Chinese GDP per head.

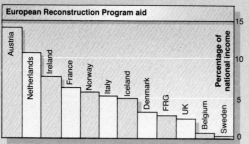

European Reconstruction Program aid

Percentage of national income

▲ Marshall aid or payments under the European Recovery Program were widely distributed. Neutral nations such as Ireland and Sweden were eligible, as were former Axis powers, Germany and Italy. The Communist-controlled states received no aid only because of Soviet objections.

GATT signatories 1947

Australia	Czechoslovakia	Southern Rhodesia
Belgium	France	Syria
Brazil	India	S Africa
Burma	Lebanon	UK
Canada	Luxemborg	USA
Ceylon	Netherlands	
Chile	New Zealand	
China	Norway	
Cuba	Pakistan	

▲ The General Agreement on Tariffs and Trade was signed by 23 countries in October 1947. By 1964 there were 64 signatories. The underlying principle was nondiscrimination. Tariff reductions agreed between any two countries were extended to all other trading partners. But Customs Unions such as the EEC were still permitted.

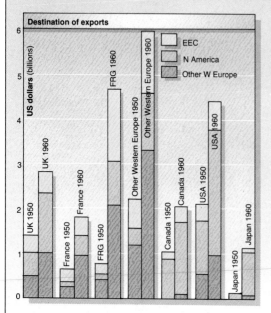

Destination of exports

US dollars (billions)

- EEC
- N America
- Other W Europe

◀ The 1950s saw a massive expansion of trade in manufactures as war damage was made good. West Germany's export growth was most spectacular, with exports of manufactures exceeding those from the United States by 1959. Expansion of EEC markets made an important contribution to Western European prosperity.

No war had been so pervasively destructive of the world economy as World War II, nor had been preceded by such a deep and longlasting depression as that of the 1930s. The need for a new order had never been greater and was not hard to recognize. The ideal shape of the new order was, however, less obvious. Unlike the interwar years, the United States now had no intention of withdrawing into political or economic isolation. American leadership was essential to the new international order, since otherwise individual national interests were likely to pull in such different directions that any consensus solution would be impossible. And since the United States was intending to make the largest financial contribution to the proposed new institutions, and was able to offer other incentives to encourage compliance with its wishes, American proposals were bound to attract more effective support, or at least, acquiescence, than those of other nations.

Without the new framework of international economic institutions, the economic history of

INTERNATIONAL COOPERATION

American supremacy

New international institutions

The IMF and the World Bank

Marshall aid and European recovery

Western European economic integration

Eastern European economies

the world would have resembled much more closely that of the years between the world wars. But American planners who began work in 1942 formed a clear diagnosis of the problems of the world economy in the 1930s, and on that basis the United States advocated the establishment of three new institutions – the International Monetary Fund (IMF), the International Trade Organization, and the World Bank (or more formally, the International Bank for Reconstruction and Development, IBRD) – to supervise world payments, trade and capital movements. The IMF and the World Bank were successfully proposed at the Bretton Woods Conference in New Hampshire in 1944, though plans for an international trade organization proved more difficult to put into effect.

In fact none of the proposed institutions operated immediately from the end of the war as intended, but the onset of the Cold War soon offered an additional incentive for the United States to continue to lead the world economy, and to maintain a free Europe in the face of Soviet

▼ World War II restored to the American economy the prosperity lost in 1929. By the end of the war, on the threshold of the long postwar boom, American economic selfconfidence knew no bounds. Macy's New York department store in 1961 exemplified the new affluence.

expansionism. Marshall aid and West European cooperation in the form of the European Payments Union, the European Coal and Steel Community, and later the Common Market, all depended on the support of the preeminent power of the Western world, despite running counter to American free market ideology.

The International Monetary Fund

Proposals for all three institutions were premised on free indiscriminatory trade and long-term capital movements as a source of international harmony. Fixed exchange rates were to replace floating or unilaterally adjustable exchange rates such as had prevailed in the 1930s, when they had resulted in competitive devaluation and the export of unemployment. (A lower exchange rate meant cheaper exports, higher sales and more jobs; but higher exports were likely to be achieved at the expense of other nations, who had in turn to join the vicious circle of devaluation in an effort to avoid losing exports and consequently jobs.) Given this decision in favor of

▶ Adjustment to the postwar world economy was a lengthy process. Highly dependent upon international trade and with foreign currency expenditure to support military commitments, the British economy in 1949 had to concede that the sterling–dollar exchange rate was unlikely to be sustainable unless very tight exchange and import controls were maintained. On 19 September 1949 the pound was devalued from $4.03 to $2.80. All banks in Britain and the London Stock Exchange were closed to enable the necessary business adjustments to take place. Stock Exchange dealers were obliged to conduct their broking in the street.

▼ All European and many Asian combatant nations, both victors and vanquished, suffered shortages and rationing for a number of years after the end of the war. How extreme these shortfalls were may be judged by the willingness of people to queue. The prospect of being able to buy potatoes in June 1947 tempted more than a thousand people to wait outside this London greengrocer's shop.

fixed exchange rates and no trade controls, an organization and rules had to be established to determine the rates that should be fixed, how they should be maintained, when they should be changed, and to provide appropriate exchange rate support. The International Monetary Fund (IMF) was this organization. Members of the IMF were obliged to set a par value for their currencies in terms of gold or the US dollar. Thereafter these exchange rates might only be altered in the event of a "fundamental disequilibrium" in the balance of payments, a state of affairs which was never clearly defined. Reserves for the support of the par value exchange rate could be obtained from the IMF, although automatic access was only allowed up to 25 percent of the quota that the coun-

try itself made available to the IMF. The size of a country's quota was determined by a combination of national income, trade and international reserves.

The dollar gap

Initial American attempts to put their new international payments system into operation quickly foundered on the disrupted economies of most former belligerent nations and the "dollar gap" that disruption produced. Postwar reconstruction needed modern capital goods which were only available in sufficient quantities in the United States. Equally, most of the world's up to date consumer products were made in America. But as the United States was virtually self-sufficient, it needed little from the rest of the world in exchange for the goods they required. The basis for trade was lacking, unless other countries were able to borrow from the United States in order to satisfy their demand for imports that had to be paid for in dollars. The amount they wanted to borrow each year was the "dollar gap".

A sufficiently high dollar exchange rate might have eliminated the gap, but this option was not considered until 1949 because the gap was judged a temporary problem of the transition from war to peace. In 1947, following American insistence that the British remove exchange controls on sterling, the strength of the unsatisfied world demand for dollars was demonstrated by the fall in Britain's foreign exchange reserves. On 15 July, the Bank of England was obliged to supply scarce dollars for abundant sterling at the official exchange rate of $4.03. By 20 August, the official reserves of dollars were nearly exhausted, and convertibility had to be abandoned.

▲ The American military presence in Europe not only offered security against Soviet invasion but also conferred substantial economic benefits. The American forces' demand for goods and services was translated into a demand for workers.

When the Marshall proposals were announced I grabbed them with both hands. Europe can wait no longer.

ERNEST BEVIN, BRITISH FOREIGN SECRETARY, JUNE 1947

Marshall aid and the European bulwark

American policy had, however, already begun to change. In March 1947, President Truman had pledged American aid to countries that were not committed to Communism, and Secretary of State George Marshall made his first public suggestion for an American-financed European Recovery Program (ERP) in June the same year. Congress was, however, chary of approving the ERP until the Soviet-inspired Communist coup of February 1948 in Czechoslovakia. After that and the Berlin blockade, Congress became convinced that United States security required a "European bulwark" against Communism. This, along with the prospect of a fall in demand for American goods which raised the specter of depression, sufficed to swing American foreign policy behind the Marshall Plan.

Most of the aid made available in this way took the form of American commodities, and although as a percentage of GNP or investment the aid was relatively small, the effect on European domestic national incomes was probably several times greater. It was generally accepted that it removed bottlenecks in European production and lubricated the wheels of international trade and payments, freeing precious dollars for the purchase of vital equipment. An additional bonus for the United States was enhanced American influence on monetary and fiscal policies, and the stimulation of European cooperation.

One form this encouragement took was the establishment of a committee, the Organization for European Economic Cooperation, to draft the formal request for American aid. The OEEC then pursued other collective policies to speed up recovery and liberalize trade. (In 1961 the United

States and Canada were to become full members of its successor, the Organization for Economic Cooperation and Development, OECD). Another mechanism for European cooperation was introduced by the ERP administrators – the European Payments Union, which was designed to make the expansion of European trade simpler, at least on a temporary basis.

Longterm loans and trade cooperation

Recipients of Marshall aid were ineligible to participate in IMF arrangements, and since so many major economies were outside the framework of the Bretton Woods agreement, it was rather irrelevant in the recovery years. That was less true of the IBRD. Member countries contributed capital, in the form of gold or dollars and domestic currency; but the bulk of the World Bank's long-term loans were to be financed from other sources. Yet the Bank could not command low commercial interest rates on the New York market until it had established a successful track record. At first, then, its ability to lend was very limited. Loans were made towards reconstructing Europe, and then the poorer countries received IBRD capital. The new organization was to prove its ability to combine profits with long-term socially valuable investments in poor countries, and justify the concept behind its foundation.

The proposed International Trade Organization (ITO) was not so successful. The Havana Charter to set it up was finally agreed in 1948, but never ratified since various countries kept pressing for certain kinds of trade discrimination. As it turned out, by 1948 the achievements of the first session of the General Agreement on Tariffs and Trade (GATT) had reduced the need for an ITO.

The Marshall Plan

In 1947 the American Secretary of State George C. Marshall, a former professional soldier, returned from an ineffective reparations conference in Moscow convinced that the European economies were in a disastrous state and that the Soviet Union wanted to exacerbate this situation. Only the United States was in a position to take the economic measures necessary for European recovery. In June 1947 Marshall announced the European Recovery Program, which was to be administered by an international Committee for European Economic Cooperation in Paris. The Program was greeted with relief and enthusiasm by the foreign ministers of the non-Communist European states, though the Soviet Union declined an invitation, and insisted that no other Soviet-aligned country should take part.

The ERP ran from 1948 until 1952, during which period over $13 billion was made available to European nations, much of it in the form of food, raw materials and equipment, contributing greatly to Europe's recovery. Although in initiating ERP the United States was concerned to prevent the spread of Communism as well as to aid European recovery, this motivation was . not clearly reflected in the distribution of aid. Ireland, a neutral country during the war and unlikely to be the victim of a Communist coup, between 1 July 1948 and 30 June 1949 received resources equivalent to nearly 8 percent of

national income. On the other hand, West Germany gained only about 2.9 percent of national income. After 1951, Europe as a whole received a further $2.6 billion, mainly by 1953. United States producers also benefited from the expanded demand at a time when there was a possibility of recession. Ill health forced Marshall to resign in 1949, but he was awarded the Nobel Peace Prize in 1953 in recognition of his achievement.

▲ Marshall with reporters in December 1947.

The General Agreement on Tariffs and Trade originated in a recommendation of the Preparatory Committee for the Havana conference at the 1946 London meeting. Negotiations for the reduction of trade barriers were to be held under the sponsorship of the committee and were to lead to the adoption of two major principles, that trade should be multilateral and nondiscriminatory, and that quantitative trade controls should be outlawed. GATT prohibited any preferential trading agreement designed to favor one nation over another. In consequence, Commonwealth Preference – whereby Commonwealth nations had particularly favorable terms of trade with Britain – was a source of friction between the United States and Britain during GATT rounds and held back tariff reductions. Even so, GATT did become a forum for liberalizing trade, and 23 countries signed the Agreement on 30 October 1947. One hundred and twenty-three agreements and 20 schedules covering about forty-five thousand tariff items resulted from the first round of negotiations. By January 1952, the number of contracting countries had risen to 34, in total accounting for more than 80 percent of world trade. The effectiveness of GATT may be judged by the fact that by the mid-1950s American duties were 50 percent below 1934 levels.

European economic integration

Although the Americans objected to Commonwealth Preference, they were prepared to support other discriminatory tariff structures if the arrangements furthered the achievement of foreign policy objectives. European economic integration was believed to create a strong and prosperous barrier to the spread of Communism and was therefore encouraged. In May 1950, the French foreign minister, Robert Schuman, made

The EEC and EFTA

EEC member 1957
EFTA member 1959

Scale 1 : 24 000 000

a speech proposing that all French and West German coal and steel production be placed under a common authority. Other European nations would also be free to join this Coal and Steel Community. Turning their backs on the enmity of the previous 80 years may have been easier for France and Germany because the continental superpowers had demonstrated the irrelevance of intra-European conflict to the world balance of power. The European Coal and Steel Community treaty was signed in 1951 by Italy and the Benelux countries – Belgium, The Netherlands and Luxemburg – as well as by France and the Federal Republic of Germany. The United Kingdom had also been invited to take part in the preparations for the Community; but when France indicated that participation implied acceptance of the goals of a supranational authority, and ultimately of political unity, the invitation was declined.

European integration was taken a step further when the liberalization of trade through GATT slowed down. A country with low tariffs had little to offer in exchange for a reduction in its trading partner's high duties during GATT negotiations, and so after a point further reductions in European tariffs proved hard to achieve. The problem was solved by complete trade integration among the six countries who were already members of the ECSC, and who became signatories to the Treaty of Rome in 1957. The treaty set out the rules for the new European Economic Community – popularly known as the "Common Market" – which had a single common external tariff. However, European integration through the Common Market entailed considerably more

▲ A divided Western Europe was a pawn in the game between the superpowers of the Soviet Union and the United States. Economic coordination was a first step in restoring Europe's pre-1914 world position, but even a single customs union proved impossible in the 1950s and 1960s. Instead the principal economies split into two economic organizations, the European Free Trade Area and the European Economic Community (Common Market).

◄ The economy was the most fundamental weapon of the Cold War, but electorates were weary of the economic burdens of continual conflict. A variety of initiatives with essential American support were implemented to maintain the economic impetus. At the opening ceremony of the 1950 Berlin International Industrial Fair, Paul G. Hoffman, the former Marshall Plan administrator, called upon the Western nations to make themselves strong militarily as well as economically to prevent further Russian aggression. The Common Market provided economic support for NATO.

than a customs union, as the 1962 Common Agricultural Policy demonstrated. A variable levy on imports excluded foreign produce while a refund system allowed agricultural exporters to sell below world prices, which was certainly not in accordance with the spirit of GATT. However, GATT only dealt with trade in manufactured goods.

In another respect also, some EEC countries were determined that the new arrangement would be discriminatory. Britain reacted by proposing a European free trade area within the OEEC, but the French did not relish the intensification of competition in industry and agriculture that would bring, and the French government – apparently unilaterally – announced in November 1958 that the free trade area was out of the question. As a temporary measure, Britain pressed for a European Free Trade Area for those European nations remaining outside the EEC. This arrangement, achieved in 1960, was regarded as temporary because, with the exception of

Britain, the largest industrial economies were already within the Common Market and therefore EFTA was quite clearly a second-best solution for the participants.

Intra-European trade grew more rapidly than world trade as a whole under the influence of reduced trade barriers. Most attempts to calculate the impact of the Common Market have found that gains stemmed from the more efficient arrangement of production. Increased competition may have improved best practice techniques, and reduced product differentiation in industries where there were economies of scale. For instance, small car manufacturers disappeared in France and Germany: whichever firm producing one of a group of similar models attained the largest production runs, or the lowest costs, or both, increased sales at the expense of competitors and achieved still larger cost savings. Companies such as Borgward, Lloyd, NSU and Simca either went bankrupt or were absorbed by larger firms. This cost reduction process may have

▼ One year after the signing of the Treaty of Rome, which set up the Common Market, the 1958 Brussels World's Fair epitomized the new united Europe. The spheres of the Atomium seemed to represent the nations of Europe linked together, as well as atoms in a complex molecule.

In Eastern Europe the centrally planned economies also sought the benefits of economic cooperation

Soviet Resources and Industry c.1950

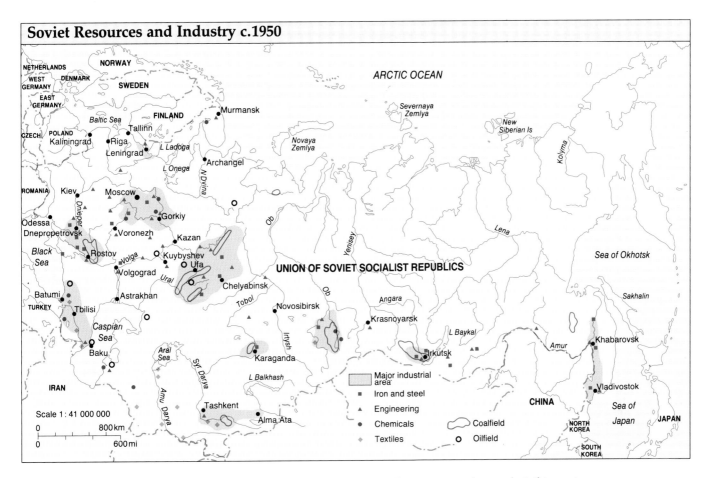

been one reason why the economic growth of EEC countries was high.

Cooperation within Eastern Europe

Before World War II the Soviet Union was the only centrally planned economy and was virtually economically isolated. Occupying and imposing Communist systems upon Eastern Europe after 1945 created a new problem of how to conduct relations between centrally planned economies. Because prices are fixed administratively in such economies, rather than reflecting production costs, it is extremely difficult to be sure that exports are not consuming more resources than are gained by imports. Centrally planned economies therefore tend to opt for more self-sufficiency than comparable market economies. For a country the size of the Soviet Union, this was naturally far less of a problem than for smaller Eastern bloc neighbors, but nevertheless both large and small economies forgo some advantages by not importing the technology of more advanced countries.

Stalin had withdrawn from negotiations on American aid for European reconstruction in 1947 and had also ensured that no other Eastern European government should participate, because the United States would not agree to such aid being unconditional, for fear that it would be used to strengthen Communist governments. In retaliation against the formation of the OEEC, Comecon, or the Council for Mutual Economic Assistance (CMEA), was established in January 1949 to further trade between members of the Communist bloc. By 1953, 80 percent of

CMEA trade was between members – but this was at least partly as a result of Western economic strength, as there was little the West needed from the East. Scarce dollars had to be earned by the export of those few commodities the West could not supply itself, and so throughout the most intense period of economic warfare the Soviet Union continued to ship chrome and manganese ores to the United States. Between the Eastern bloc countries themselves, raw materials such as iron ore were exchanged, and international cooperation in heavy industry and such fields as electricity transmission were developed far more efficiently by Soviet administrators than in the interwar years when Eastern Europe was outside the Soviet umbrella.

▲ The Soviet Union developed its rich natural resources to achieve as much self-sufficiency as possible.

◄ Abundantly supplied with many industrial raw materials like timber, the Soviet Union exported them in return for tropical produce such as sugar, for materials it lacked, including copper, and for advanced technology.

▼ Economic cooperation between the Soviet Union and the other Comecon countries called for cheap, high-capacity transport between them. Rail links were therefore given a high priority.

TOWARD AN INTEGRATED EUROPE

In the aftermath of World War II, a concerted effort was made in Western Europe to avoid the dangers of economic nationalism. The first breakthrough was the creation of the European Coal and Steel Community (ECSC) in 1952, which not only provided some very substantial economic gains in its own right, but pointed the way to the formation of the European economic integration was feasible as well as desirable. Coal and steel were fundamental to European economic development after the war because they were the basis of so many other industries. Yet international boundaries created barriers to a sensible use of European coal and iron ore deposits. Germany was obliged to import half of its iron ore from elsewhere, while France bought one-third of its coal and coke from the Ruhr. Italy had little coal and The Netherlands was short of steel, while Belgium and Luxembourg exported more than two-thirds of their steel output and imported ore from Lorraine and coke from the Ruhr.

After three destructive wars in three-quarters of a century, and doubtful of the value of the Atlantic Alliance, France was keen to strengthen Europe while placing some control on her old enemy, Germany. The need for some form of rapprochement was underlined by the formation of the Soviet-dominated Eastern bloc and the Western European fear of growing Soviet power. The plan for the removal of international constraints upon the European coal and steel industries offered a means of promoting such a strengthening of ties.

Although the scheme was introduced by the French foreign minister, Robert Schuman, and bore his name, it was the brainchild of Jean Monnet, a French economist who was passionately committed to the idea of a united Europe, and who became the first head of the ECSC. Monnet later resigned from his ECSC post in order to form an action committee for European unity, which laid the foundations for the Common Market and earned him the nickname of "Monsieur Europe".

The gains from the organization can be seen from a comparison of the 50 percent growth of American coal prices between 1953 and 1957 with the 3 percent and 10 percent increases respectively in French and German coal prices over the same period. A good deal was saved on transport, for border regions of France and Germany could now import or export instead of trading with more distant locations within the same country. The ECSC also provided housing for workers throughout its member countries.

Once the ECSC was demonstrably a success, the road to the European Economic Community was much easier. In 1957 six nations signed the Treaty of Rome, which laid down the rules of the Community. A policy to harmonize agricultural support was introduced in 1962 and a series of regulations to encourage the mobility of goods, services, people and capital were implemented. The culmination would be the completion of the internal market in 1992.

◀ By the 1980s Western Europeans no longer expected long delays to the movement of people and goods at national frontiers. When Italian customs officers worked to rule in 1984, several thousand lorries blocked the border crossing at Kierfersfelden and at the Brenner Pass. The Dutch truck driver here is protesting at the 20 papers necessary to cross the Brenner Pass.

◄ Steel and coal had long been a source of conflict between France, which lacked adequate resources, and Germany where deposits were rich. By 1949 Germany's much-bombed Ruhr was reviving and the output of steel exceeded 600,000 tonnes a month. One of the biggest steel plants was at Huckingen-Huttenwerk, Duisburg, where a Thomas converter plant is shown. An agreement to share European coal and steel resources in 1952 was the basis of the later Common Market.

▼ The aircraft corporation BAC, of Britain, and Aerospatiale, of France worked together to design and build the supersonic passenger aircraft Concorde, in one of the major international commercial ventures. The first flight was in 1969 and regular services from France and Britain were inaugurated in 1976.

▲ The location of the European Commission headquarters in Brussels, the capital of a small state, avoided jealousies or fears that a German or French location might have aroused. Similarly the name of the European Currency Unit, the ECU was happily ambiguous (inset); it could be taken as an abbreviated English-language term, or as a revival of an ancient French coin.

► First proposed to Napoleon, a tunnel under the Channel between Britain and France has been advocated and attempted on many occasions since then. Only in the late 1980s did technology, capital and international cooperation attain a state sufficiently advanced to make completion probable.

Datafile

Outside Europe and the regions settled by Europeans, economies showed a wide variety of behavior between 1945 and 1960. Measured by their vast populations, the Asian states of India and China might have dominated the world, but low incomes per head left them little political or economic influence outside their regions. Elsewhere economies grew under the stimulus of strong demand at home and abroad and much more optimism than ever before that governments could promote development. With varying effectiveness, governments encouraged primary education as a prerequisite for sustained economic growth, introduced public health programs and adopted interventionist policies towards agriculture, industry and foreign trade.

▶ During the 1950s Asian population growth began to accelerate under the impact of new technologies that permitted the elimination or reduction of disease, and of social reorganization, such as the improvement in peasant incomes that resulted from land reform. Meanwhile European natural increase remained comparatively low. In the Americas, where land was abundant, prosperity encouraged more births and fewer deaths, and immigration to the United States further boosted the population.

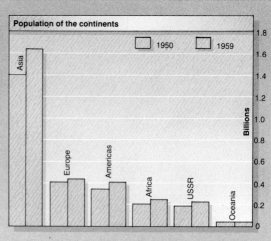

Population of the continents

◀ African economic growth picked up in the 1950s, although it is hard to judge how much because of statistical deficiencies. Even in the 1950s data is none too reliable for these countries. Foreign political domination did not apparently hold down development greatly, for most of Africa was still under colonial rule. Algeria was then still governed by the French, Zimbabwe was a dominion of the British Commonwealth – Southern Rhodesia – ruled by whites, Zaire was the Belgian Congo and Mozambique was a Portuguese colony.

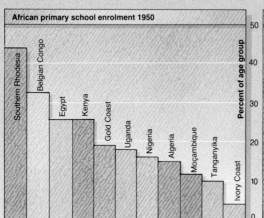

African primary school enrolment 1950

African GDP growth 1950–60

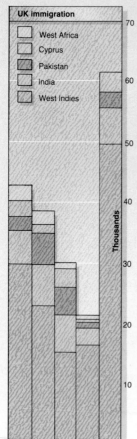

UK immigration

▲ GDP per head is not a wholly satisfactory index of economic progress. Wellbeing depends upon more than production of goods and services valued at market prices or costs. Education, for example, matters. African primary school enrolment figures may not be too reliable, but they offer an alternative indicator of performance.

◀ Although emigrants from Britain were generally skilled, the 1950s saw an inflow of typically unskilled New Commonwealth workers, in response to the strong demand for labor in the Midlands and southeast of the country. As a result of the 1954 US Immigration Act, West Indians came to Britain in increasing numbers.

▶ Redistribution of land in Egypt after the revolution of 1952 eliminated holdings of more than 85 hectares (210 acres). Before this reform more than one-third of all plots were very small, of less than two hectares (5 acres). But even after reform peasant holdings in this very small category still formed a large percentage of all holdings.

▶ Japanese postwar growth was closely tied to the North American market. Although Asia was the largest single destination for Japanese exports throughout the 1950s, North America took a rapidly increasing share. The same modern consumer goods that allowed a penetration of American markets expanded Japanese exports to Europe.

Egyptian landholdings

Japanese exports

Japanese economy 1954

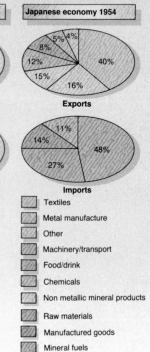

Asia
North America
South America
Europe
Africa
Oceania

Textiles
Metal manufacture
Other
Machinery/transport
Food/drink
Chemicals
Non metallic mineral products
Raw materials
Manufactured goods
Mineral fuels

▶ Being poor in natural resources, Japan imported raw materials, fuel and food, paying for these commodities with exports of manufactures. In 1954 textiles dominated Japanese exports, typically sent to Asian markets. Japan was still a net importer of foreign technology, and a large importer of manufactured goods.

Less than 2 hectares
2–85 hectares
More than 85 hectares

A NEW INDEPENDENCE

Catching up with the West

Foreign investment and aid

Japanese supergrowth

The partition of India

Collectivization in China

Latin American economies

Developments in Africa

The nonindustrialized countries shared few common characteristics in this period except that their economies tended to be poor. Their cultures, histories and economies differed markedly, and the only resemblances were negative ones: in general, such countries were inhabited neither by Europeans nor by people of European descent, nor were they located in temperate zones. Although in 1945 many were European colonies, there were also many – such as the Latin American countries, China, Thailand and Ethiopia – which were not.

Despite the great variations between them, these nations nevertheless frequently accepted similar diagnoses of their economic problems, and similar solutions, chosen by charismatic leaders like Mao Zedong and Gamal Abdel Nasser. The diagnosis was that the production of food, agricultural materials and minerals was no way for a country to get rich – an attitude justified by the economist Raúl Prebisch, who maintained that prices of primary products had deteriorated in relation to manufacturing prices and would continue to do so, with the result that no country could hope to develop by specializing in the export of primary goods. The solution was to concentrate on developing the internal market

▼ The most important food crop in Asia was rice. Typically, small farms were intensively cultivated by the families that owned them. As population expanded agriculture was placed under increasing pressure to raise productivity. The International Rice Research Institute was founded in 1959 to develop higher yield rice varieties and so avert an Asian food crisis.

by stimulating the growth of an indigenous manufacturing sector. Agriculture was to provide the resources for this through collectivization or taxation, although redistribution of land was also recognized as a valuable political weapon to ensure support for the regime among the recipients of the land. In some cases this policy met with economic success, in others less so. World market conditions were then uniquely favorable for "catching up", with a rapid growth of demand in the Western world, as well as the growth of Western development aid. It is difficult to assess what part domestic policies played in achieving the uniquely high rates of growth reached by poorer countries in these years, and how much was a result of world trading conditions.

Prebisch in fact misinterpreted the data he employed to support his theory. He failed to realize that the fall in British import prices, mainly of food and raw materials, during the 19th century was not at the expense of the exporters, but was due to the reduction in transport costs which narrowed the gap between the two sets of prices. Prices paid to supplying countries for their primary produce rose; their terms of trade did not deteriorate. Of course that does not necessarily mean Prebisch's thesis was wrong for the later

period. A large country like India could not hope to achieve the level of export orientation of a small country such as Singapore without a severe deterioration in the terms of trade because of the huge volume of exports that would have to be sold on world markets.

Exploitation by foreigners was generally perceived as a further cause of low incomes in poor countries, and colonial governments were seen as fair game for nationalist politicians trying to rally popular support. Multinational companies, too, were seen as exploiters, often quite rightly – especially where the oil companies were concerned. The major oil companies had operated market sharing arrangements during the interwar years; faced with informed and determined governments, they were unable to rig prices quite as easily after 1945. However, they maintained restrictive practices in selling to poorer countries thoughout this period. The West African Supply Agreement eliminated all competition and kept prices high in small West African markets. Excessive oil prices were charged in the Indian market until 1960; in that year the Indian government was offered cheaper oil by the Soviet Union and formed a national oil company to break the Western companies' control over imports.

Foreign investment and aid

Foreign investment in the nonindustrial areas flowed mainly to Latin America and other regions settled by Europeans, on the 19th-century pattern. India ceased to attract foreign capital on balance as a result of the policy of state ownership or control of industry pursued after independence. In other regions direct investment by multinationals was small, and in conditions which the American government judged unstable it could be perilous for the host government. For instance, nationalization of British Petroleum's oil interests in Iran in 1951 was the cause of a coup assisted by the CIA two years later. In Guatemala, the United Fruit Company was the largest landowner when President Arbenz decided to expropriate the company's uncultivated land as part of a land reform program; the United States overthrew Arbenz in 1954.

Nonindustrial countries were often concerned

about the economic effects of incoming investment as well as the political spinoffs. For instance, much foreign capital was located in mining or other extractive industries. Not only were such projects removing nonrenewable resources from the country at a rate and at prices which might not be in the national interest, but the immediate benefits to the wider economy were generally small. The labor force did not acquire new skills and so was unlikely to establish new businesses or to provide a resource for other indigenous enterprise. Unfortunately, extraction and marketing typically required techniques and facilities not available in nonindustrialized economies; so the alternative to foreign enterprise was sometimes nothing at all.

For the first time government-to-government aid flows became a significant component of the capital inflow to nonindustrialized countries. Political links and trade seem to have been the principal determinants of aid flows. British and French aid was an extension of colonial development grants and was a way of promoting trade and political leverage. American aid was equally politically motivated but with a different ideological basis: the United States felt that it had a moral superiority over the European colonial

▲ Central America and the Caribbean were heavily dependent upon the export of specific crops, such as sugar in the Dominican Republic. Foreign, mainly American, investment paid for the mills, railways and port facilites essential to take their produce out into the wider world. Where foreign investors saw no prospect of profit, industry remained small and backward.

◀ Guatemala's principal export was coffee. Grown in the mountains, the high-quality crops fetched excellent prices round the world. Mechanization gradually displaced manual sorting of coffee beans according to size and appearance. Mechanization created the possibility of a greater variety of jobs, less vulnerable to swings in export demand. At the same time there was the danger that inequality of income would be exacerbated, as the owners of capital grew more prosperous and workers lost their jobs.

powers that warranted more influence and gave it more insight into the political and economic development of poorer countries. American aid was ultimately concerned to gain allies in the Cold War against Communism.

Perhaps the most effective form of foreign aid in terms of the potential for raising living standards began with the establishment with the support of the Rockefeller Foundation in 1946 of the International Maize and Wheat Center in Mexico. New high-yielding varieties of wheat doubled Mexican yields in the 1950s and, from 1956, Pakistan, India and Nepal began to benefit from the new strains. Encouraged by success with wheat, the Rockefeller Foundation joined with the Ford Foundation to establish an International Rice Research Institute in the Philippines in 1959.

Such measures were necessary, for in much of Asia, Africa and Latin American the population was growing at an unprecedented rate and there were ever more mouths to feed, and the food supply could not increase fast enough. Western technological advances had brought new measures, such as chemical spraying to eliminate malaria-carrying mosquitoes, which suddenly and radically reduced mortality, while fertility remained high. In the second quarter of the century, the population growth rate in the southern group of countries in Latin America, Africa, South Asia and Oceania had been 1.5 percent; between 1950 and 1975 it was 2.4 percent. By contrast, in the northern countries of Europe, the United States, the Soviet Union and East Asia, the figure for the same period was only 1.3 percent.

Japanese achievements
Outside Europe and the overseas European off-shoots, Japan had been unique in reaching a degree of industrialization by World War II. But despite remarkable achievements in the field of

▲ Many medical advances were of recent origin, like spraying insecticides to eradicate malaria-carrying mosquitoes, as here in Iran. The impact on population growth in the nonindustrialized world was more dramatic than it had been on the industrial economies during the previous century.

The Cuban Experiment

By 1945 Cuba had achieved low birth and death rates comparable with those of the industrialized economies. One of the highest national incomes per head in Latin America was generated during the 1950s by an economy highly specialized in the production of sugar. Much of the investment in the mills, transport facilities and utilities necessary to export this sugar came from American companies. When Fidel Castro came to power in the 1958 revolution he took over US-owned properties and began to collectivize production. By 1963, 70 percent of agriculture and 100 percent of all other sectors had been collectivized. Unlike his Central American neighbors, Castro chose to refuse American aid, preferring to prove that his regime could accelerate development without it. In this he failed, for dependence on American aid and markets for sugar was replaced by reliance on the Soviet Union, which in effect subsidized Cuba, paying more than the market price for its sugar and selling oil to it for less than current world prices. Between 1966 and 1970 production was severely disrupted by the abolition of farmers' private plots, a heavy emphasis on moral incentives and a reduction in wage differentials.

◄ Some nonindustrial countries deliberately turned their backs on the capitalist road to development. They preferred to reject individual cash incentives and encourage workers by collectivization, public services, greater equality and moral suasion. Cuba increased spending on education and narrowed the gap between rural and urban wages. This Havana mural of heroes Camilo Cienfuegos and Che Guevara was not intended merely to be a decoration. It was an inspiration, an encouragement to cooperate in the achievement of national goals. In the long term the evidence suggests that not all those with skills and professions were persuaded. Many tried to emigrate from Cuba whenever an opportunity was presented.

modern technology to protect or advance national interest. Ideological commitment to common goals within organizations removes much of the need for monitoring and enforcing performance which absorb so many resources in the West.

Another reason for Japan's precocious postwar development was undoubtedly the fact that after 1945 Japan was no longer allowed the heavy military expenditure the country had chosen to bear throughout the earlier part of the 20th century. The result was that between 1950 and 1973 Japanese output per head grew at an average rate of 8.4 percent each year, compared with 5 percent in West Germany, which had the highest growth rate in Europe.

The partition of India

Latin America, India and much of Africa did rather well in economic terms out of the war, experiencing stronger export demands for their products and not suffering from enemy action. India's accumulated foreign exchange reserves were, however, soon dissipated after independence in 1947. Amidst fighting and forced migration on religious grounds, the subcontinent was divided between India and Pakistan. Pakistan gained sovereignty over the food- and raw-material producing areas, while India retained the centers of manufacturing and coalmining. Hostility did not cease with the fighting. Trade barriers between the countries reflected continuing hatreds, forcing India to spend her exchange reserves on importing food.

Both India and Pakistan pursued "import substituting industrialization" (ISI) policies after independence. As large countries they could not hope to prosper solely on the export-oriented strategies later pursued by Singapore, South Korea or Taiwan. In any case, tariff discrimination held back their exports of manufactures to

▲ After 1945, America was the principal export market for Japanese goods like this General Patton toy tank.

◄ Much of the labor force that fueled Japanese supergrowth after World War II came from agriculture. Those that remained provided almost all of Japan's basic food, rice, by the intensive cultivation of poor and scarce soil.

▶ Japan's industrial transformation required an infrastructure including a supply of electrical power. Here as elsewhere the pervasive Ministry of Trade and Industry (MITI) planned and coordinated development.

▼ Expenditure on defense was limited, so Japanese investment and research could be focused on building up a motor cycle and automobile industry which could supply the rest of the world as well as the domestic market.

military technology, Japan had remained a poor country by Western standards. The war threatened to reduce Japanese living standards to below those of her Asian neighbors: two major cities were atom bombed, 88 percent of her 6.5 million tonne merchant marine was sunk, and two-thirds of her massive cotton textile capacity was destroyed. As in West Germany, a refugee problem compounded Japan's postwar disruption. About six million Japanese returned from overseas, only partly offset by the emigration of one million people, mainly Koreans. But equally, like West Germany, Japan rose from the ashes, and continued her prewar economic development at a much faster pace.

Sustained Japanese supergrowth baffled Western observers. After the Meiji restoration of 1868 Japan had shown a remarkable ability to treat Western institutions as a set of social blueprints from which to select the best and most suitable for Japanese conditions. Similarly, after 1945, when the Americans attempted to remodel Japanese society and the economy on Western democratic–liberal lines, pro-trade union legislation was introduced and productivity circles were copied from America. Trade unions in Japan behaved much like company unions, failing to see any divergence of interests between their members and management, as was so often the norm in the West. Productivity circles flourished in Japanese companies whereas a similar attempt to spread them to Britain fell on stony ground.

Various reasons for Japan's startling recovery and growth have been suggested, but it seems probable that at least some of the cause lay in the tradition of loyalty that had always been a marked feature of Japanese culture. After the Meiji restoration, this loyalty had been redirected away from the support of traditional institutions toward the creation of a rich country and strong military and naval forces that could employ

richer countries. They therefore proposed to produce a wider range of manufactures for the domestic market in order to reduce the need for imported manufactures. Under ISI policies, exportable food and raw materials were taxed and the revenue employed to subsidize domestic manufacturing. Farmers were obliged to accept lower after-tax prices for their produce, yet had to pay prices inflated by import restrictions for manufactured goods. Prices of manufactured goods in Pakistan during much of the 1950s and 1960s were double the world market averages. Incentives for farmers were therefore greatly reduced, with the result that migration to urban areas increased and food shortages emerged. Over the 15 years after 1950, Indian agricultural production per head failed to increase, despite an average growth in GDP per head of 1.5 percent per year. What was forgone in the agricultural sector was not offset by gains in manufacturing. India had been slowly increasing world export shares in manufactures during the 20th century, but with independence the movement was reversed. The system of import and investment licencing that gave virtually every firm a monopoly severed the critical link between profitability and economic performance.

A changing China

China had been proclaimed a republic in 1912, but years of internal and external strife had followed. After defeating the Chinese Nationalist armies of Jiang Jieshi and the Japanese invaders, the revolutionary leader Mao Zedong entered

▶ **Pakistan was primarily agricultural but pursued a policy of industrialization at the expense of agriculture. Farm prices were held down, and because investment was discouraged, techniques remained primitive in the 1950s. The most obvious industries to encourage were in agricultural processing, but these were rural, inextricably involved with agriculture itself, so they also remained backward, as in the process of sugar manufacture. First an ox crushed cane in a mill, then the crushed cane was boiled in a vat with soda and the solidified product dried on mats. Pakistan's agricultural output growth in the 1950s was well below population growth, and by 1980 substantial quantities of food had to be imported.**

▶ After 1960 the Pakistan government's policy of squeezing the private-enterprise agricultural sector was relaxed. Farm prices were raised and the distribution of food was increasingly returned to private channels, like this Karachi market stall with its assortment of fruits and vegetables. Irrigation developments from both the Indus river dams and tube wells expanded the cropped acreage. More fertilizer and new seed varieties raised yields, but shortages of capital and finance, and perhaps inadequate information, made it difficult for smallholders to make great improvements.

▼ When Mao came to power in 1949, population growth was accelerating but there was no room to extend cultivation and crop yields were already above average for the nonindustrialized world. The new government therefore faced the problem of producing enough food. Mao's initial attempts to raise productivity were both necessary and successful. Forced labor, reinforced by the required preparation of productivity reports, was the basis of this achievement.

Beijing and declared the People's Republic of China in 1949. Thereafter China pursued a more radical path of development than India, imposing greater burdens on the peasants, although their overall economic performances were quite similar. China was extremely densely populated for an agrarian economy and the peasants were inevitably very poor. Land reform – that is, the abolition of landlords – was announced in 1950, and was probably the most popular policy of the new Communist rulers, calculated to secure the loyalty of the poor peasants. By 1952, 46 million hectares (113 million acres) of China's 107 million hectares (264 million acres) of arable land had been redistributed to give about three hundred million peasants land of their own.

However, in an effort to accelerate Chinese economic development, land reform was soon replaced by a commune system intended to squeeze more labor out of the peasants. Collec-

tivization proceeded in two stages. Early moves introduced cooperative farming, and collectives were granted agricultural credits not available to individual cultivators in an effort to convince peasants of the superiority of the new organization. Peasants were left with a fairly generous allocation of land and livestock. Then in 1957 Mao Zedong visited Moscow, returning determined to bring about full collectivization.

The first five-year plan of 1953–57 was probably the most coherent economic policy that China had under Mao, with a focus on long-term planning and the development of heavy industry. The peasants were collectivized into communes far larger than their Soviet counterparts – they could contain up to twenty thousand households – and different also in that they were committed to industrial as well as agricultural production, and were military as well as production units. The peasants lost what ability they had previously had to control the nature and pace of their work, being deprived of land, implements and livestock. As many as eight percent of adult males were drafted to nonagricultural work, leaving the women to cope with the agricultural labor.

Chinese agriculture understandably suffered from these reforms, and Mao's decision in 1958 to take a "Great Leap Forward" and accelerate modernization proved economically disastrous; food grain output per head had not returned to pre-1958 levels before his Cultural Revolution was to cause another, more severe, decline in 1966.

The economies of Latin America

Latin American countries adopted ISI policies similar to those of India and China, but they started from a higher base income and so might have been expected to achieve more success. Unfortunately their national markets were often too small to support their industrial ambitions.

Latin American economies in this period could

be divided into three groups: those exporting temperate-zone agricultural produce (Argentina and Uruguay), with traditional high, European living standards; economies specializing in tropical agriculture, including Brazil, with revenues and productivity that supported sub-European living standards; and exporters of minerals such as Chile, traditionally believed to have low wages and poor development prospects.

Brazil contrasted strongly with Argentina, achieving five times its growth rate of income per head between 1928 and 1955, and double its rate between 1955 and 1973. As a result Brazil, with one-third of Argentina's income per head in 1928, had drawn level by 1980. Argentinean political difficulties and inappropriate ISI policies were at the core of the problem, yet Brazil also neglected export development between 1947 and 1962. Nonetheless GDP rose at an annual rate of 6 percent. Latin America differed from Asia in having more land which could be brought into cultivation. Brazil doubled the number of its farms and increased its cultivated area by 124 percent between 1950 and 1970. Large estates of more than 400 hectares (1,000 acres) continued to account for a substantial proportion of farmland, mainly pasture, especially in the northeast. The majority of rural workers were small landowners as well. The state played an important role in Brazil as banker and as owner of public enterprises. Seventy percent of investment funds originated from government banks and well over one-third of the assets of the 5,000 largest firms were to be owned by the state by the 1970s. Policy has been fairly pragmatic, allowing multinational companies to prosper. With the emergence of a social insurance system, transfer payments began to constitute a rising proportion of the government's budget.

Developments in Africa

Although situated in North Africa, Egypt most closely resembles China in its long-established population problem. Improvements in irrigation allowed agricultural output to rise above population growth only temporarily, and during the 1950s a falling death rate boosted population growth to over two percent a year. Agrarian reform followed the military coup of 1952 which brought in as president General Neguib, backed by the man who was to hold the true reins of power for the next 18 years, Gamal Abdel Nasser. Nasser's Agrarian Reform law limited the land that any one individual could hold, but required the beneficiaries to pay a portion of the original cost over an extended period. By 1957 all agriculturalists were expected to join cooperatives which were controlled by the government with a view to introducing practices which did not deplete the fertility of the soil and controlled agricultural pests.

During the 1950s, foreign-owned industries and banks, which dominated most of the modern sector, were nationalized. Work began on the Aswan High Dam, which eventually enhanced both the cultivated area and yields. Manufacturing output per worker doubled between 1947 and 1960, but so also did capital per worker, suggest-

The Aswan High Dam

The Aswan High Dam was of enormous symbolic importance to Egypt – a vast project intended to harness the Nile with modern technology and thereby transform the Egyptian economy. For millennia the agricultural economy of the country had been entirely dependent on the River Nile for its very existence. In flood, though, the great river damaged the fields and drowned the workers, while during the summer the water supply was inadequate. The 1902 Aswan dam, some 700 kilometers (450 miles) south of Cairo, was intended to help regulate these seasonal flows, later generating electricity as a byproduct. However, full control of the Nile waters required a much larger construction, and preparatory work on this Aswan High Dam began in 1955. The following year Nasser's nationalization of the Suez Canal led to the withdrawal of Western nations' support for the dam, whereupon Nasser turned to the Soviet Union for finance. In 1960 Nasser laid the foundation stone for the new construction. The rock-filled dam, the tenth largest in the world, was completed in 1970.

More than three kilometers wide and 110 meters (360 feet) high, the dam was designed to hold back Lake Nasser, which extended for nearly five hundred kilometers (over three hundred miles) upstream. Some 2100 megawatts of electricity generating capacity was created and Egypt's cultivable area was increased by one-third. As well as the cost of building the dam, some ninety thousand peasants and nomads had to be relocated, and the ancient temple complex of Abu Simbel had to be repositioned. Among the consequences was an increase in the quantities of salt in the Mediterranean off the Egyptian coast since the flow of fresh water was reduced, with adverse repercussions on fish stocks.

► ▼ **Egyptian economic independence gained a twofold symbol with the Aswan High Dam. First, this massive project, it was intended, would fully control the waters of the Nile for the first time; second, it was financed independently of the West, from Soviet aid. Here are four of the six tunnels being built in the middle of the diversion canal. Relocating the Abu Simbel temple complex was almost as remarkable a technological feat, and caught the imagination of the world.**

ing no overall improvement in efficiency. State control and planning tended to generate overstaffing and mistakes such as the highly uneconomic steel plant at Helwân, but cement and sugar refining were competitive. Real GDP per head rose at 2.9 percent per year through the 1950s.

Sub-Saharan Africa drew upon a very different political and economic tradition from Latin America or Asia. Africa had no nations in the European sense, only tribes, some large enough to constitute empires. African states were therefore typically creations of late 19th-century European empires. Nigeria, for example, remained a British colony throughout the 1950s, though a minority of Africans in Nigeria were elected to European-dominated regional and federal legislative councils. Britain gave substantial development grants of around two to three million pounds each year, but these never amounted to more than five percent of domestically collected government revenue. Continuing wartime government marketing boards for major export crops became a means of taxing agriculture which, probably for that reason, remained primitive. The road network was considerably expanded, and to a lesser extent other transport infrastructure and electrification benefited from

government spending. A considerable advantage came from the discovery of oil in 1958. As national productivity increased, Nigeria became more integrated into the world economy.

South Africa, on the other hand, embarked on its policy of apartheid after the victory of the Nationalist party in the 1948 elections. National income rose rapidly, with manufacturing industry building on the base of the gold and other mines. The urban population also grew, but apartheid meant that the allocation of facilities between black and white areas became grossly uneven.

▲ Rural workers were attracted to all large cities in poor countries by the possibility of jobs, but were usually unable to afford proper living accommodation. Shacks and shanty towns like this one outside Cairo grew up on any available site.

◄ Brazilian economic development was extremely rapid, yet the government palace in São Salvador, Bahia, is reminiscent of the colonial era.

1960 · 1973
THE CONSUMER BOOM

Time Chart

	1961	1962	1963	1964	1965	1966
Industry	• Jan: 60 million rouble credit for Poland to aid the construction of the Comecon pipeline (USSR) • Jun–Aug: Rural protest over the failure of the government to equalize living standards between industry and agriculture (Fr)	• Mar: Central committee and ministerial department of the Politburo decide to improve material incentives in agriculture (USSR) • Nov: US minister of agriculture criticizes agricultural policy of EEC • Agricultural crisis in the Soviet Union	• Mar: Five year supply contract signed between the US Standard Oil Company and the Italian enterprise ENI • May: Krupp manager B. Beitz begins trade negotiations in the Soviet Union (FRG) • Oct: Contract between the Phillips Petroleum Company, the Pan-American Oil Company and Egypt (USA/Egy)	• Jun: Soviet–Polish contract regarding Soviet aid for the Polish petroleum, natural gas and copper industry • Oct: US president Johnson signs the "Food for Freedom" program • Dec: Indonesia places British firms under Indonesian control to prevent the alleged British support for Malaysia	• Feb: West German company, Krupp, and Poland agree on industrial cooperation and on construction of manufacturing plants in Poland • Dec: East German leader Ulbricht announces the establishment of industrial ministries • Plans for land reform in Chile	• Aug: Contract between the Soviet Union and the Italian company Fiat regarding the construction of a motor plant on the Volga (USSR) • Sep: French automobile company Renault builds motor plants in Romania and Bulgaria
Technology	• 12 Apr: Soviet space station Vostok 1 begins operation, manned by the first cosmonaut Yuri Gagarin • W. Haack develops electronic flight security (FRG)	• The satellite Telstar allows TV transmission between Europe and USA • General Motors install the first industrial robots (USA)	• NASA news satellite Relay 1 transmits news exchanges between newspaper offices in UK, USA and Brazil	• Satellite Ranger 8 delivers pictures of the Moon surface at close range (USA) • Development of CT scanning by A.M. Cormack and G.N. Hounsfield (USA)	• First commercial satellite Early Bird begins transmitting TV programmes between USA and Europe	• First Moon satellite Luna 10 begins operation (USSR) • Development of laser radar (Jap)
Finance	• Oct: Gold pool established in London	• 5 Jan: General Arrangements to Borrow (GAB) among the ten major industrial countries decided by the IMF • Mar: First swap agreement between the Federal Reserve Board of the USA and the Bank of France, later also with the Bundesbank • May: Agreement between US Treasury and Swiss National Bank on long term monetary cooperation • New Industrial Development Bank established by the IFC	• May: Special credit of $250 million to support the pound (USA/UK) • Beginning of cooperation between the Deutsche Bank, the Midland Bank, the Banque de la Société Générale and the Amsterdam Bank • The first large loan of the World Bank (in 1947, of $250 million) repaid by the Credit National de France	• Mar: IMF and central banks of Western Europe, USA and Canada support the British pound and the Italian lira with credits • Dec: Prolongation of the European Monetary Agreement agreed until 1965 • Interest Equalization Tax in the USA aggravates the issue of foreign loans and shares	• Sep: Suspension of the 25% covering by gold for the minimum reserves (USA) • Currency reforms and the introduction of new currencies in Brazil, Argentina and Albania • Establishment of the African Development Bank • Merger of the Société Générale, Banque d'Anvers and Société Belge de Banque to form the Société Générale de Banque (Bel)	• Jun: Basle Agreement between UK and several European central banks to finance the short term deficit in the British balance of payments • Aug: The Development Bank of Asia established • Aug: Establishment of the Woschod Commercial Bank in Zürich by the Soviet government (Switz) • Formation of the Banque Nationale de Paris as a result of mergers (Fr)
Economic Policy	• Apr: Reorganization of the economic administrative structure agreed (USSR) • Jul: The committee for the United States of Europe demands a common fund of European currency reserves • Sep: Publication of the Jacobson plan to reform the world monetary system, involving the establishment of a fund of $5 billion.	• Mar: Constitution of the National Council for economic development (UK) • Jul: Fourth economic and social plan enforced (Fr) • Oct: Trade Expansion Act initiated by US president Kennedy • Nov: Khrushchev demands a basic reorganization of the economic structure. Establishment of vertically structured organizations for the control of industry and agriculture (USSR)	• Jan: US president Kennedy publishes a program reducing taxes • Mar: Establishment of the Labor and Economy Council. Suspension of the seven-year plans (USSR) • Jun: EEC commission decides to intensify the common European monetary policy, but postpones monetary integration • Jul: French prime minister Pompidou publishes an economic stability program. End of the price spiral and a tax reform planned	• Mar: Economic Opportunity Act: the establishment of a corporation to counter poverty (USA) • May: Establishment of a committee of experts – the Segre commission – to survey the European capital market • Oct: Labour government imposes 15% import tax to improve the balance of payments (UK)	• Jan: Consumer goods enterprises freed from the constraints of the planned economy (USSR) • Feb: French president de Gaulle and the financial expert J. Rueff demand a return to the gold standard (Fr) • Jun: British prime minister publishes a ten-point economic program for modernizing industry by promoting investment, research and export (UK) • Reform of the world monetary system discussed	• Feb: Establishment of the Ministry of Technology for the modernization of British industry • Feb: New five-year plan in the Soviet Union. Transformation of the first 36 plants into a new centrally guided economic system • Apr: Agreement on economic cooperation between West Germany and Israel
International	• Mar: European Council demands increased cooperation with the OECD • Jun: Legislation regarding the establishment of the Latin American Free Trade Association (LAFTA) comes into force • Jul: 18th session of GATT requests negotiations on tariffs with the EEC, EFTA and LAFTA	• Jun: Council of the EEC decides to carry through the second step to a common market. Twelve decrees are issued regarding the creation of a common agricultural market • Jul: End of the fifth tariff conference of GATT with agreement on the reduction of tariffs	• Apr: Establishment of the Comecon Bank by the Comecon countries • Dec: First Comecon plan for common scientific and technological development enforced • Dec: EFTA countries agree with the demand for a 50% tariff reduction for the coming round of GATT talks • France opposes British application to join the EEC	• Mar: Opening of the UN conference on trade and development (UNCTAD) • May: Opening of the Kennedy round of the GATT talks. 50% tariff reduction demanded • Jun: Romania opposes establishment of a Soviet, Bulgarian and Romanian economic complex in the Danube area • Sep: EEC commission demands the suspension of all internal tariffs	• Jan: US government encourages trade with Eastern Europe • Feb: Decision on the combination of the three European communities, the EEC, ECSC and Euratom • Mar: 22nd GATT discusses the compatibility of regional tariff communities with the aims of GATT as a whole • Nov: An amalgamation of the EEC and EFTA discussed, to avoid the division of Western Europe into two economic communities	• Apr: 23rd session of GATT discusses trade with developing countries and free trade movements • Jun: Establishment of the Asian and Pacific Council (ASPAC) by Asian and Pacidic countries for economic and political cooperation • Jun: The EEC countries agree on a common agricultural market • Dec: EFTA discusses the possibility of joining the EEC
Misc.	• 13 Aug: Construction of the first stage of the Berlin Wall (GDR)	• Oct: US blockade of Cuba after the installation there of Soviet nuclear missiles	• 22 Nov: Assassination of US president Kennedy in Dallas, Texas. Mass demonstrations of the civil rights movement led by Martin Luther King (USA)	• Oct: Soviet leader Khrushchev is ousted by L. Brezhnev (USSR)	• USA officially takes part in the Vietnam War • West Germany and Israel take up diplomatic relations	• Jan: I. Gandhi becomes prime minister of India • Sep: Beginning of the Cultural Revolution in China

67	1968	1969	1970	1971	1972	1973
[...]pr: National aid for the [Fren]ch computer industry • [M]ay: US House of [rep]resentatives authorizes building of the largest [des]alination plant in the [wor]ld • [D]ec: Transformation of [the] first Soviet Kolchoses [into] a new centrally guided [eco]nomic system (USSR)	• 27 Feb: Food and Agriculture Act passed to stabilize the US home market. "Food for Freedom" plan initiated to build up a national food reserve (USA) • 21 Mar: Merger of three British computer firms with government support to form International Computers Limited (ICL)	• Sep: Measures taken to protect agriculture after decontrol of the exchange markets (USA) • Dec: Renault shares distributed among employees (Fr)	• Feb: 20 year contract signed between USSR and West German company Mannesmann regarding the supply of Soviet natural gas to West Germany • Jun: Discovery of rich oilfields in the North Sea • 4 Jul: Libya nationalizes all its oil companies	• 4 Feb: Bankruptcy of the British Rolls Royce company. Government announces a partial takeover (UK) • Feb: US aircraft manufacturer Lockheed in financial difficulties (USA) • Libya nationalizes British Petroleum (BP)	• May: Decision to build a petroleum pipeline from Alaska into the USA	• Jan: Merger of the two British airlines BEA and BOAC to form British Airways (BA) (UK) • Oct: Iraq nationalizes US oil companies Exxon and Mobil Oil • Dec: Peru nationalizes largest US mining concern Cerro de Pasco Corporation
[...]0 Apr: Opening of the [...]m high Moscow TV [and] telephone aerial mast	• Negative effects of thalidomide drug on children discovered • 31 Dec: First commercial flight of a supersonic passenger aircraft (USSR)	• E. Hoff constructs the first silicon microprocessor (USA)	• 12 Jan: First flight of a Boeing 747 • Supersonic passenger aircraft Concorde reaches Mach 2 (twice the speed of sound) (Fr/UK)	• 18 Dec: Completion of the world's largest hydroelectric power station in Krasnoyarsk (USSR)	• 17 Feb: The Volkswagen overtakes the sales record of the Model T (FRG) • Prohibition of DDT in the USA because of environmental damage	• 1 Oct: Opening of a natural gas pipeline from the Ukraine to West Germany
[...]1 Nov: Devaluation of [the] pound. UK receives a [larg]e international credit of [...] billion to support the [pou]nd • Nov: Devaluation of [cur]rencies in Israel, New [Zea]land, Spain and [De]nmark • Nov: Introduction of [mini]mum reserves for [ban]ks (Fr) • [E]stablishment of the [Int]ernational Commercial [Ban]k and the Société [Fin]ancière Européenne	• Mar: Suspension of the 25% covering of banknotes by gold (USA) • Mar: Dissolution of the gold pool as a result of international speculation in gold • 17 Mar: Monetary conference held in Washington to organize the international gold market. A gold price of $35 per ounce agreed for transactions among central banks • Nov: French franc under pressure	• Aug: Devaluation of the franc. Credits from the IMF and some central banks made to support it (Fr) • West Germany becomes the greatest exporter of capital in the world with an amount of DM 23 billion per annum • Apr: Poland demands the transferability of the currencies of the Comecon countries	• Sep: Conference of the IMF in Copenhagen. Three alternatives proposed to reorganize the international monetary relations: freeing of the exchange rates, alteration of the exchange rates step by step, extension of the margins of fluctuations of the exchange rates • Banque Européenne de Crédit à Moyen Terme established by several European private banks	• 16 Aug: US balance of trade shows a deficit for the first time since 1894. Suspension of the convertiblity of the dollar into gold • Dec: declaration of 77 developing countries, demanding participation in decisions on a new world monetary system	• 24 Apr: Currency agreement of the EEC countries enforced. The margin of fluctuation between currencies not to exceed 2.1/4% • Temporary flotation of the pound (UK)	• 12 Feb: Devaluation and flotation of the dollar • 9 Mar: EEC countries decide to introduce a joint float against the dollar • Mar: Temporary closing of exchange markets around the world. End of the Bretton Woods monetary system, and a new system of floating exchage rates comes into being • Nov: Agreement signed allowing central banks to sell gold at market places
[...]May: legislation enforced [en]abling the French [gov]ernment to execute [ec]onomic and social [me]asures by decree • [J]ul: Nationalization of the [Bri]tish steel industry • [J]ul: Transformation of the [las]t Sovkhozes and [rail]ways into a new [ec]onomic system (USSR)	• Jan: Minister president Werner of Luxembourg demands a common European monetary policy • Dec: Publication of Barre plan for the introduction of a European Monetary Union (Fr)	• Jan: Report on the economic situation by the US government. Balance of trade positive for the first time since 1957 • Jan: Nationalization of the British steel industry completed • May: Appeal of 99 European scholars to reform the international monetary system. Free exchange rates demanded • Dec: Conference of the EEC countries in The Hague. Gradual introduction of European economic and monetary union discussed	• Consultations among the EEC countries regarding the introduction of a European Monetary Union (Barre plan) • Jan: National Council for prices and income replaced by the Commission for Industry and Labor force (UK) • Mar: Iceland becomes a member of EFTA • Oct: Werner plan for the introduction of European Monetary Union published • Oct: Council of EEC countries criticizes protectionism in US trade legislature	• Jun: Conference of the EEC countries to discuss a reorganization of the European monetary system and closer economic coopeartion • 25 Jul: Comecon enforces a 20-year plan toward socialist economic integration • 16 Aug: US government declares introduction of a 10% tax and a wage freeze for 90 days due to national emergency. Consultations between US monetary experts and EEC commission to discuss the international monetary and exchange crisis	• Feb: UK Miners' strike. Increase in the rate of unemployment • Apr: Inaugural meeting of a commission for economic and scientific cooperation between the USSR and West Germany • May: West German finance minister Schiller demands a drastic reduction of public deficit spending (FRG) • Oct: Negotiations between the USSR and USA to set up trade relations	• Jan: British prime minster Heath publishes the second phase of his anti-inflation program • 9 Mar: Meeting of the finance ministers and the central bank governors of the "Group of Ten" countries in Paris to discuss the exchange crisis • Apr: The ministers of finance of the EC countries decide to establish a European fund for monetary cooperation • Oct–Dec: OPEC raises the oil price from $3.01 to $11 per barrel. Shock for the Western industrial nations
[...]an: Complete tariff [fre]edom among the EFTA [co]untries comes into force • [M]ay: Conclusion of the [Ke]nnedy round of the [GA]TT talks. Reduction of [tar]iffs demanded • [J]un: Monnet commission [of] the EEC proposes [ec]onomic cooperation [be]tween the EEC, [Co]mecon and the USA • [A]ug: Plan published for [a] second world trade [co]nference and a common [int]ernational trade center	• Feb: UN conference on trade and development opened. Discussion on development assistance and East–West trade • Aug: Romania rejects the proposal to transform Comecon into a supranational organization with a supranational plan • 25 Nov: GATT session agrees on enlargement of trade • Dec: EEC countries agree upon cooperation in scientific research	• Apr: Romania demands the opening of Comecon to non-Communist countries • Jun: Association agreement between the EEC and 18 African countries • Sep: Meeting of the council of EFTA attempts to overcome the economic division of Europe • Oct: East German government demands a greater integration of the economies within Comecon	• Feb: 26th GATT session discusses the problem of enlarging trade in industrial and agricultural products • Jul: Establishment of an International Investment Bank by Commonwealth countries • Jul: CECLA countries formulate their intentions regarding economic relations with the EEC • Oct: UNCTAD conference agrees on a program in favor of developing countries	• Jun: Australia gains membership of the OECD • Jun: First special conference of UN Industrial Development Organization (UNIDO). Developing countries demand that this organization be more independent from the industrial countries • Nov: 26th GATT session defines special rights for developing countries • Austria, Sweden and Norway seek entry to the EEC	• Mar: US finance minister Conally proposes the enlargement of the "Group of Ten" in the IMF • Apr: Comecon bank issues a loan of $60 million to the Eurodollar market • Jun: Interim agreement between the EEC countries and Austria comes into force • Jul: Free trade agreement between the EEC and EFTA countries signed	• Jan: UK, Denmark and Ireland join the EEC • Jun: 27th session of Comecon discusses closer cooperation between its member countries and the machine-building industry • Sep: Conference in Tokyo discusses the necessity of new negotiations in connection with GATT
[...]5-10 Jun: Six-Day War, [the] third Arab–Israeli [co]nflict	• 20-21 Aug: Dubček's "Prague Spring" reform movement suppressed by the Red Army (Czech)	• Aug: Riots in Belfast and Londonderry lead to British military intervention (Irl) • Sep: Military revolt in Libya led by Colonel Muammar Qadhafi	• Salvador Allende becomes president of Chile	• 25 Apr: Establishment of Bangladesh	• 30 Jan: Escalation of the civil war in Northern Ireland leads to "Bloody Sunday"	• Oct: Yom Kippur war, the fourth Arab–Israeli conflict, leads to a worldwide oil crisis

Datafile

The outstanding features of this period for the advanced Western nations were steady prosperity and economic growth. Never before had the world known so high a rate of economic expansion so free of major disturbances. In consequence, for the first time in history the large mass of the population was lifted out of the realm of the elementary curses of humanity, hunger, cold and preventable disease. An expanding net of social services allowed even the weaker members of the community to share in some of the economic goods now available. The population settled down to low rates of increase, so that high overall economic growth was translated into high growth per head.

The main structural changes associated with this expansion were the move out of agriculture and the rise in services and in goods formerly considered luxuries. After traditional needs such as housing and clothing had been met, consumers turned to products made available by new technologies such as electronics, and to leisure pursuits, above all travel.

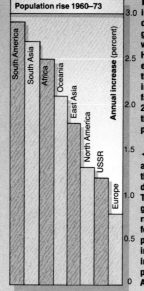

Population rise 1960–73

◀ World population grew at an unprecedented rate, but there were considerable differences between regions. The rich market economies grew only slowly; the fastest rates of increase were to be found mainly among the poorest regions of the world, in Africa and Southern Asia including India. The very poor regions of Latin America grew fastest of all.

▶ Inflation became endemic in the years before 1973. The developed Western nations gave the lead, but others were equally affected. However, prices in the oil exporting countries rose less than elsewhere, while prices in Latin America rose much faster, at an annual rate of 21.8 percent compared with the world average of 5.1 percent in 1960–73.

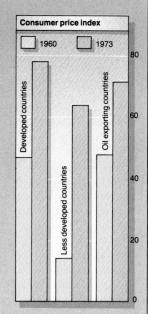

Consumer price index

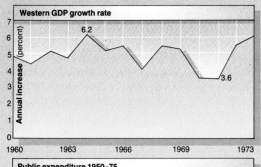

Western GDP growth rate

◀ Economic growth in the advanced countries of the world was remarkably, perhaps uniquely, smooth throughout the period 1960–73. Even the occasional hiccup, as in 1967, when a number of the leading countries faced a recession in demand, and in 1970–71 looked like minor diversions rather than interruptions of a trend.

▶ Asia's population dominated the world scene: over the whole of the period covered, well over half the world's population lived in that continent. By comparison, that of Europe, North America and Oceania combined, where average incomes were highest, formed only about one-fifth of the world's total, and this share tended to decline.

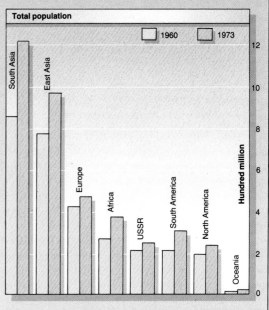

Total population

Public expenditure 1950–75

▲ Public expenditure is made up of several different items, including the costs of government and defense, social welfare costs including education, and transfer payments, such as pensions, among others. It is noticeable that the smaller democracies of northern Europe had the highest rates of public expenditure as a share of national income.

▶ Tourism is a fickle industry, and popular preferences may change rapidly. Korea's rise in popularity started from very low figures, whereas the poor showing of Italy, Spain and Greece relates to their high starting position. Ever more exotic countries were being developed for well-heeled Western and Japanese tourist.

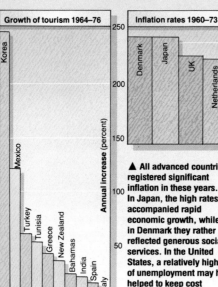

Growth of tourism 1964–76

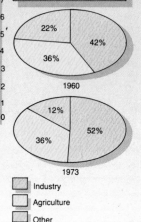

Inflation rates 1960–73

Employment in OECD lands

▲ All advanced countries registered significant inflation in these years. In Japan, the high rates accompanied rapid economic growth, while in Denmark they rather reflected generous social services. In the United States, a relatively high rate of unemployment may have helped to keep cost increases down.

▶ Economic growth in the postwar era was everywhere associated with a decline in the proportion of people working on the land. This was in part made possible by substantial rises in productivity, and in part by a shift to agrarian imports. The share of manufacturing employment remained virtually constant; service industries grew.

PROSPERITY AND OPTIMISM

High employment and increasing affluence

A new lifestyle

Transport and tourism

The education explosion

Social and welfare provisions

Inflation, tariffs and trade

Exchange rates and currency systems

In view of the immense physical and economic damage suffered by the belligerent countries in the course of World War II, it was not surprising that in the immediate postwar years plenty of work was available for all who wanted it. Towns and cities needed rebuilding, and capital equipment had to be brought up to prewar levels. In the early 1950s, the needs of the Korean war kept up the level of demand in Western countries and in Japan. After that, however, it was widely thought that a slump would set in, following a pattern seen at similar times in the past. But that slump never came. Instead, in the years to 1973, the world enjoyed boom conditions and rapidly rising incomes for longer and at a higher level than ever before.

This great boom was worldwide, affecting the Western capitalist countries, the Eastern planned economies and even the poorer and developing nations of what came to be known as the "Third World". As far as the market economies were concerned, it had its origin in the advanced countries of the West – in effect, Western Europe, the United States and Canada, Australia and New Zealand, and Japan – and from there it spread by means of international trade, international capital transfers in the form of loans and investments, and the consequent opportunities to catch up on the latest technological advances. The growth

path was not entirely smooth, and there were years of slower growth, like 1967 and again 1970–71, but these were minor disturbances only, and the faster upward movement was soon resumed. Not all countries advanced at the same speed, as measured by the annual increases in gross national product (GNP) or gross domestic product (GDP), which are taken as representing the sum total of all economic goods and services created. Japan's high growth rate, for instance, was in a class of its own. But even the laggards, like the United Kingdom, year after year achieved rates of growth without parallel in their history.

There is no agreement about the causes of this long period of high employment and fast growth in the West. Certainly, most governments set out to achieve one or both of these aims, and many took as their guide the ideas of the British economist John Maynard Keynes (1883–1946), who believed that the level of employment could be influenced by government action. The apparent success of the boom years even led to the widespread belief that the means of preventing unemployment and stagnation were now known and that national economies could in future be steered at will. Unfortunately, this proved to be wrong, and the causes of the end of the boom have turned out to be as controversial as the causes of its long duration.

▼ The Easter holiday crowds on the beach at Ostend, Belgium, in 1964 show how increased prosperity has brought more leisure as well as the means to travel. In the postwar years, the working population in most Western countries has achieved a higher income and more free time.

▼ Carnaby Street, London, became a symbol for one area of development in the consumer society. Its fashion goods were not necessarily cheap, but they could be afforded by the young wage and salary earners. The emphasis was not merely on brightness and color, but on unconventionality and irreverence. What was new was the independence and spending power of that age group. Whole new industries and distribution agencies were called into being to cater for this new market selling pop records, clothing and holidays abroad. Fashion remained, as ever, at the center of this new lifestyle.

Growth in output and productivity was, as always, not merely the result of technical improvements. It was also accompanied by structural changes, some of which had already been going on for a long time, and continued, or accelerated, in this period. Among the most important of these was the reduction in the share of agriculture, and the rise in the share of services, within the totals of employment and output of each country. This was a pattern to be found in all economies, poor ones as well as advanced ones. There was also a shift out of less productive industries such as textiles into more productive ones such as motor manufacturing, and a relative expansion of industries using newer technologies, including electrical and electronic equipment, chemicals and machine tools. This reflected partly the new technical possibilities, partly the changes in consumer demand. For as incomes rose, the consumption of food in the richer countries increased only slightly, though its composition changed, and the demand for clothing also rose relatively little. Against this, however, expenditure on consumer durables,

luxury goods and relatively fast leisure pursuits rose. The mass consumption of goods formerly available only to the rich, or to the richest countries, was a major feature of this long boom. The rise in ownership of private motor cars is typical of this development. Its widespread use brought about alterations in the location of housing, workplaces and shops; and such increased mobility in turn required more roads, more garages and more filling stations.

Leisure and travel

In all countries, people tended to claim some of the increase in productivity not in the form of more goods, but of more leisure. In all advanced countries in the West total annual hours worked were reduced, on an average by one-ninth, in the period 1960–73. In their free time, people were able to seek new forms of cultural activities, of sports and entertainment. Above all, they took the opportunity to travel farther for their holidays. Increasingly this meant travel abroad, and in Europe and North America, especially to the sun. Every summer, a wave of tourists now descended on the Mediterranean from northern Europe, and on Central America and the Caribbean from North America, arriving by boat, by rail, by car and bus, and increasingly by air.

Mobility and migration

Centers of employment themselves now enjoyed greater freedom of choice of location, now that the source of power was no longer the nearby coalmine or the local waterfall. Instead, the electricity grid now supplied power equally to all parts of most advanced countries. As a result, the new factories were found increasingly in the most pleasant parts of their countries, such as the Mediterranean coast in France, the south coast in Britain, the southern Länder in Germany, and California in the United States. A gap began to open up in some countries, such as Britain and Italy, between the prosperous regions of the country, with their new industries and modern cities, and the older industrial areas, with their grimy towns and declining industries.

People moved to the new jobs within their countries, but there was also a high rate of migration across the borders, from the poorer, less developed countries of Europe to the industrial

▲ With rising standards, consumers began to demand fashion and design. Some retailers profited by offering to a wide public the kind of up-market design in goods for the home that had previously been the preserve of a small privileged class. Some most interesting developments in retail distribution have taken place among those catering for upwardly mobile newly prosperous consumers.

► The ever-increasing streams of summer tourists led to new developments in the areas they visited. The poorer countries around the Mediterranean gained particularly, partly because their prices were still low, from the new opportunities opened up for holidaymakers from the industrial countries of Europe and their families. In many favored spots tourism brought much-needed capital investment and employment, and raised incomes. Hotels and apartment blocks began a new era of development. Spain was one of the first countries in southern Europe to benefit from this new influx of tourism. Cadaqués in Spain was once an exclusive resort for artists; by the 1970s it had begun to cater for a much wider clientele.

The Tourist Industry

Tourism was one of the fastest growing industries worldwide. In the ten years from 1962 to 1972 tourist expenditure probably trebled. In some cases, the very high annual increase in tourist receipts reflected a low starting point, in others they continued to rise from a level that was initially high. Spain, for example, which had received 200,000 foreign tourists in 1930 and 6 million in 1960, welcomed 33 million in 1973. The other "cheaper" Mediterranean countries, including Greece, Turkey, Malta, Israel, Cyprus and Portugal as well as North Africa, also registered large increases. Mexico and the Bahamas had the same experience in the Western Hemisphere. Growth rates were lower in some of the more traditional holiday areas, such as Austria, Switzerland, France and Italy. But in these countries winter tourism was expanding fast. In West Germany, for example, where 565,000 took a winter holiday in 1960–61, this figure reached 3,157,000 in 1975–76. However, even in 1976 the developed countries still took 83 percent of tourist receipts, the developing world only 17 percent. It was a form of expenditure which, on a mass basis, was confined to the richer countries; for some of the poorer it was becoming a vital source of income.

◄ In Europe skiing, once an exclusive sport of the very rich and highly privileged and of a small number of fanatical sportsmen, became a mass sport, as more and more people were able to take a second holiday in the winter, and travel abroad to enjoy it. But the conditions under which skiing took place changed as it attracted more and more people. The journey to the resorts became increasingly overcrowded and uncomfortable, and formerly quiet Alpine villages were turned into busy townships as huge concrete hotels were built to accommodate the tourists.

regions, from the French and British colonies to the mother country and from Latin America to the United States, as well as, in more traditional paths, from Europe to Canada, the United States and Australia. Between 1960 and 1974, Belgium, France, West Germany, Luxembourg, Sweden, The Netherlands, and Switzerland accepted between them a net total of 1,655,000 immigrants. Altogether, the nine countries of the EEC had 10.4 million immigrants inside their borders at the beginning of 1973, more than four percent of the population. In the United States, despite immigration controls imposed in the 1950s, migration represented almost 16 percent of the population increase in the 1960s, and in Canada it was 21.9 percent, not counting the illegal immigrants. Welcoming the immigrants in the period of labor shortage, most Western countries began to introduce restrictions on further immigration in 1973–74, when the boom appeared to be over and rising unemployment raised the specter of anti-foreigner sentiments.

▼ The consumer boom also spread to other continents. São Paulo, the industrial capital of Brazil, with a population of some eight million people at the time, was forced to separate cars and pedestrians to allow the rush-hour traffic to proceed. The cars on the streets were mainly American imports, but Volkswagens were also prominent; increasingly, large multinational companies were building factories in developing countries to produce vehicles on the spot.

The education explosion

It is possible to see the rising provision of education as yet another way in which people made use of the increasing flow of goods and services now available to them. Education may be viewed as being valuable in itself, as well as a way of increasing the productivity of the labor force in the long term. In the postwar boom, there was a veritable explosion in the numbers going to universities or other institutes of higher education.

The United States led in this respect, spending a higher proportion of national income per head than other countries on education, yet keeping its lead even as the rest of the Western world also advanced. This emphasis on education has been seen as an alternative to the provision of other social services, in which the United States was lagging behind, perhaps reflecting the American preference for individual self-help as against social care. In 1960, the United States spent 5.3 percent of its national income on education, compared with 5 percent in Sweden and 4.7 percent in The Netherlands; most of the rest of Europe, as well as Japan, spent between 4.5 and 3.5 percent. In the following years the proportion of secondary scholars among the 10- to 19-year-olds in the 13 developed countries of Western and Northern Europe rose dramatically and the proportion of university–level students among the 20- to 24-year-olds almost doubled.

The expansion of welfare provisions

General social and welfare provisions by the state were also everywhere on the increase. Formerly separate provisions were being consolidated into single, unified schemes, as in Italy in 1965, The Netherlands in 1966, Norway in 1970, Belgium in 1970 and West Germany in 1972.

A specific development which caused much controversy was the support given to regions and to economic sectors suffering from longterm industrial decline. There was widespread consent for sharing out, in the form of aid, some of the benefits of progress among less fortunate groups, such as Belgian coalminers, the inhabitants of the old industrial areas of Britain and of the impoverished South in Italy. There was less agreement on the Common Agricultural Policy (CAP) the European Community's scheme to encourage and enlarge production by offering subsidies to farmers. By the later 1960s it had led to massive overproduction of food and other agrarian products to the point of endangering the finances of the community by its high cost, while it also blocked the export chances of poorer nations into the rich EEC market. Ironically, farming incomes still remained well below national average incomes everywhere, and the subsidies helped rich farmers more than poor ones.

The rise in social provisions was not unexpected, since there is always a tendency for government expenditure to rise disproportionately in booms, only to be cut back again in periods of stagnation. What was unusual was the continuing rise of wages as part of the national income. Normally their share falls in booms and rises in slumps, thus remaining more stable than

The driver is not a member of a class; by the progress of motorization he already represents the mass of the population. ... The car is symbol and instrument of the striving of humanity for new aims which can be achieved only by building good roads.

GERMAN AUTOMOBILE CLUB, 1965

the overall national income, while profits, the other main component, take the brunt of the fluctuations. The reason why wages now continued to rise has probably to be looked for in the longer-term trend of income redistribution in the direction of greater equality. The strengthened social security net, which set a floor to wages, may have played a major part, together with the voting power of wage earners at national elections.

These increases in government expenditure as a share of total national outlay affected all Western countries. By the mid-1970s, it was exceeding the 40 percent mark in most countries. Its momentum was also kept up by the general wish to maintain a high level of employment. This generally meant that any perceived shortfall in overall demand was met by increased government expenditure. Such "Keynesian" methods did indeed lead to high levels of employment throughout the Western world, but they also led to a persistent tendency to rising prices. It seemed that rising incomes and full employment were not to be enjoyed without a measure of inflation.

Inflation, tariffs and trade

Inflation became endemic in the Western world in these years. However, inflation advanced at different rates in different countries, and this was bound to lead to problems in the trading and payments balances between countries. In the

postwar years, statesmen had attempted by international agreements to remove many of the causes of international imbalance which had disrupted the world economy in the 1930s. The International Monetary Fund (IMF) had been designed to make it possible to hold to stable exchange rates between the different currencies, and the General Agreement on Tariffs and Trade (GATT) had tried to remove trade barriers by encouraging and spreading tariff concessions, while inhibiting tariff rises or other obstructions to trade. Both had had some effect, though possibly less than their sponsors had hoped.

Many tariff rates were pushed down in the first flush of enthusiasm, but thereafter they tended to stick. The European Common Market and Free Trade Area were matched by regional free trade agreements in Latin America, the Caribbean, Central Africa, East Africa and Southeast Asia, though several of these had only modest significance.

The liberalization of world trade helped trade to grow faster than production, so that international interdependence increased. But it increased much faster among the industrial nations, in the form of the exchange of manufactures, than between these nations and the developing world, let alone between the developing countries themselves. Capital exports also expanded fast, and a highly significant feature was the growth of

173

"multinational" concerns. About one-sixth of the world's total output of goods and services was at that time produced by the multinationals.

The American balance of payments crisis

Much of the undeniable success of liberalization in the postwar world rested on an unique configuration of the international economy. It depended, in fact, on the huge balance of payments surplus of the United States, which in turn rested on that country's overwhelming superiority in production and productivity. This surplus enabled the United States to finance the operations of the IMF, to provide loans and Marshall aid, to organize development aid in various forms, to make large capital inverstments abroad and still to conduct widespread military operations in many parts of the world as well. Backed by this surplus, the American dollar remained a desirable, "hard" currency throughout those years.

In the course of the 1960s the United States' lead in production fell rapidly as other countries began to catch up on American technology. In those years the growth in GNP and in manufacturing production was consistently lower in the United States than in any other advanced country except Britain. As a result, GDP per man hour fell heavily between 1960 and 1970: a lead of 90 percent over other advanced countries shrank to under 49 percent, and it continued to fall rapidly. Similarly, as a proportion of the total output of the world's market economies, measured as GDP, the figure for the United States fell from 45 percent in 1960 to 34 percent in 1973.

In the early postwar years, the strength of the dollar had made other countries willing to hold it as their national reserve currency, and this in turn confirmed it as a "hard" currency. As the American payments surpluses turned into deficits, the world found itself in the unaccustomed position of having to deal with a weakening dollar. Many transactions were adversely affected. Sterling was devalued in 1967 and the London gold pool, symbol of a common policy on gold, was suspended; the French franc was devalued in 1969 and general monetary uncertainty spread across the world. It was clear that the dollar had become overvalued, and in August 1971 US president Richard Nixon announced that the convertibility of the dollar (into gold) was suspended. Further, a temporary import tax of ten percent was introduced in the United States, and the IMF was asked to consider a new international monetary system.

This unilateral action taken in the interests of the United States while bypassing accepted international channels of consultation marked the end of a major phase of world monetary history, that of the gold–dollar standard. In an effort to prevent monetary chaos, representatives of the ten leading nations met at the Smithsonian Institution in December 1971 and agreed to a devaluation of the dollar against gold by 7.9 percent to $38 per ounce, without restoring the former obligation on the American monetary authorities to sell gold at that rate on demand. They also agreed on a widespread realignment of currency parities

or rates of exchange. Henceforth currencies should be allowed to diverge from those parities by a maximum of ±2.25 percent only, thus providing a new form of stability. At the same time, the US ten percent surcharge was scrapped.

This left the European countries dissatisfied. In March 1972, as the first stage towards a planned single European monetary system, they agreed to keep the permitted deviations from the official exchange rates to half the width of the band allowed under the Smithsonian agreement. However, by June the pound sterling was allowed to "float" free, and several other countries also left the monetary "snake". Others joined, and a bewildering series of changes ensued before the group emerged essentially as a cluster around the Deutschmark. Early in 1973 the dollar was devalued once more, by ten percent, making a total of 23 percent against OECD currencies (except Canada). In March of that year the European Community decided to float as a bloc against the dollar and against other currencies, and in April it agreed to start the Fund for Monetary Cooperation. The dollar itself was now floating and the brief phase of the dollar standard had, in effect, changed into a system of mutual "managed floating", with no firm anchor point for the system as a whole. It was not long before the system was put to the test: in October of the same year the first massive OPEC price rise for oil was announced. A major new source of world instability had emerged.

▲ Multinational companies were increasingly moving their production units into developing countries. Hundred of girls worked in serried ranks for the Philips electronics firm in a factory near São Paulo in Brazil. In the first phases of this transfer across cultures, the multinationals were making use of cheap, willing labor in order to lower their own costs, and were contributing to the movement of population into overcrowded Third World cities marked by poverty, pollution, exploitation and violence. However, in several cases it was just such foreign initiatives which provided the capital, and the knowhow as well as the training, both for workers and managers, on the basis of which native entrepreneurs were gradually able to develop their own economies and to strike out on the path of industrialization and modernization themselves.

The Multinationals

The period saw a sharp rise in the power of multinational corporations, based in one country but with branches in others. They were particularly strong in the extractive industries (notably oil), in manufacturing, and also in the service industries such as banking, retail distribution and hotels. In part, they represented the strength of American production after the war, carried beyond the borders of the home country into an economically weakened world; and American companies furnished by far the largest proportion of the multinationals. However, companies with headquarters in other countries also operated in the same manner. In the early postwar years, Britain was the second most important headquarters country after the United States, but more recently Japan-based companies have expanded fast in all continents. By 1978 the top 20 Japanese multinationals employed a total of 140,000 persons overseas. In the case of some European companies, so many changes have taken place that it is difficult to be certain where the centre of gravity lies or in whose interests the companies are administered. By the 1980s several of the largest multinationals had turnovers equivalent to the GNP of a moderate-sized industrial country.

The objects of expanding abroad were mixed. They included the wish to get inside a tariff barrier, to use cheap labor or cheap raw materials available abroad. There were also potential gains to be had from setting up subsidiaries outside one's own borders by the use of available capital, managerial and technical know-how, or the market created by advertising at home. A growing part of international trade went on within the multinational companies themselves,

supplying member units with raw materials, components and semi-manufactures for which prices could be artificial and unrealistic for the companies' own strategic reasons. There was growing fear in the receiving countries that significant parts of their economies would be controlled from abroad, and might be managed in the interests of foreign shareholders with no commitments to the communities in which the branches were established.

Concerned by these issues, the OECD in June 1976 produced a series of guidelines to member countries, which were intended to ensure that they should "refrain from actions which would adversely affect competition in the relevant market by abusing a dominant position of market power".

▲ Neon lights in Times Square, New York City, in the 1970s advertised brands of multinational products known practically all over the world. Goods were becoming increasingly standardized in more and more countries.

▼ Rio Tinto Zinc (RTZ) is a typical multinational. As it spread from its early mining interests in Spain, Latin America and Africa, it expanded from mining into smelting, making engineering products, construction materials and services, chemicals, oil and gas.

Rio Tinto Zinc: Portrait of a Multinational c.1973

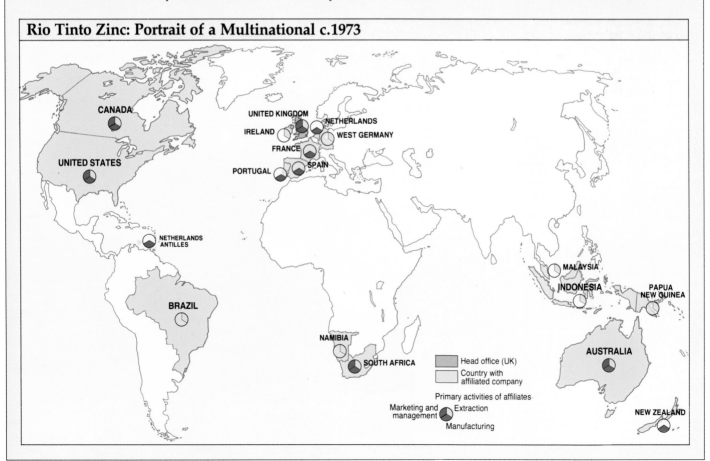

THE CONSUMER SOCIETY

As the basic necessities of life were increasingly well covered by the productive apparatus of the advanced industrial societies, the economic problem shifted from production to the sale of goods and services that can be considered luxuries rather than necessities. There had always been luxuries for a privileged section of the population, and their market had always been uncertain, but bulk products had varied only little. From the early 20th century, even the mass market for the population at large had become uncertain, while producers needed quantity orders to keep down costs of production. One method of bridging this contradiction between a fickle market and high fixed cost was advertising. This began to take up more and more resources, while making itself indispensable to the manufacturers. At the same time, it also began to affect the moral climate: the greed for possessions, the desire to outdo one's neighbor, the quest for luxury were made into acceptable virtues. Purchasing could turn into an end in itself – by the late 20th century the consumer society came into its prime.

Given that there were numerous people with spare income looking for something to spend it on, one method adopted by the advertisers was to create, in the interests of the producers, needs that had not existed before. In some cases, desires were nurtured for entirely new products or services. At other times, they were roused for the latest model, encouraged by built-in obsolescence. The discarded goods, such as second-hand cars, were then disposed of among ever-lower income strata until they landed on enormous scrap heaps, matching the waste of resources at one end with the disfigurement of the landscape at the other.

Moralists and those hostile to capitalism found much to criticize. Yet it could also plausibly be argued that an element of waste was a necessary price to pay for the undoubted drive to progress in the industrialized market economies. Certainly, no alternative proved equally effective, least of all the economies governed by planners with more puritan attitudes as to what constituted the necessities of life. Indeed, there were some indications that those brought up on limited goods without frills, for example in the Soviet Union, were even more easily swayed by glamor than those in daily contact with it.

The emphasis on female consumers, found in the advertising of the 1960s, has given way to a rather more balanced appeal in the 1980s, though the pretty girls were often meant to appeal to male, rather than female, buyers just as the handsome men were to catch the eyes of women. Many of the products and services pushed by the advertisers have lightened the burdens of women as housewives and as producers in the West. By contrast, the women in the East carried many of the burdens of the planning failures on their backs, as they spent their time in queues, struggled with inferior materials, and were expected to engage in full time work outside the home.

▶ Most Third-World large cities contain abject poverty as well as wealth and luxury. The people picking over a rubbish dump in Manila hope to live on the detritus of a consumer society, and their continuous daily activity proves that there is indeed sufficient among what has been discarded by others for families to live on, no matter how offensive and unhygienic the circumstances.

▶ Hairdressing salons were typical of the service element within the consumer economy, requiring frequent repeat visits and emphasizing a certain luxury by the rather lush image and the foreign name (French in English-speaking countries, English in France), which they sported. Curiously, in the inter-war years, most hairdressers cut men's hair, not women's. Women, except for the very rich, had their hair cared for at home.

▶▶ Supermarkets not only lowered the costs of distribution compared with the small corner shop; they also developed new techniques of encouraging purchases, by making it easy to see the whole range available and help oneself to desirable goods.

▼ Naked girls as sales gimmicks for motor cars represent an attempt to make the particular model desirable by the association of ideas, and the abuse of women. By the 1980s, such exploitation of sex was frequently criticized though still used, even if more subtly.

▼ These 1960s women in a Moscow street, looking at high-fashion fur coats in a shop window, were probably not able to afford them. Yet there is clearly an appeal, even in a poor, planned economy, in luxury goods beyond immediate needs; the consumer society reached even the Soviet Union, if only in a limited form.

▲ This advertisement in a Bangladesh street for a Western-style bedroom furniture, expresses the drive to create consumer needs in any circumstances.

Datafile

During this period several countries in the Far East achieved economic growth rates unmatched anywhere else. In the early stages, economic growth at 9 percent or 10 percent a year might be explained by the low starting position, but such an explanation cannot hold once a substantial degree of industrialization has been reached. Undoubtedly one cause of success lay in intensive labor effort, long hours and relatively low wages, which kept costs down and thus allowed the prices of foreign competitors to be undercut. But there were also more positive causes – an eagerness to save, to invest and to innovate; a remarkable adaptability both of managers and workers, together with a willingness to learn new techniques; and the ability to create and maintain a political-legal framework to make modernization and industrialization possible. Japan stands out among the rest of the economies of the Far East, being a larger economy and much earlier in the field. By the 1970s it was a world leader in many product areas.

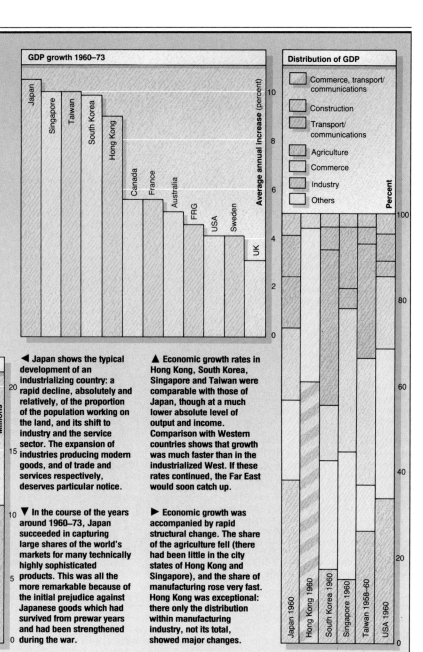

◀ Japan shows the typical development of an industrializing country: a rapid decline, absolutely and relatively, of the proportion of the population working on the land, and its shift to industry and the service sector. The expansion of industries producing modern goods, and of trade and services respectively, deserves particular notice.

▼ In the course of the years around 1960–73, Japan succeeded in capturing large shares of the world's markets for many technically highly sophisticated products. This was all the more remarkable because of the initial prejudice against Japanese goods which had survived from prewar years and had been strengthened during the war.

▲ Economic growth rates in Hong Kong, South Korea, Singapore and Taiwan were comparable with those of Japan, though at a much lower absolute level of output and income. Comparison with Western countries shows that growth was much faster than in the industrialized West. If these rates continued, the Far East would soon catch up.

▶ Economic growth was accompanied by rapid structural change. The share of the agriculture fell (there had been little in the city states of Hong Kong and Singapore), and the share of manufacturing rose very fast. Hong Kong was exceptional: there only the distribution within manufacturing industry, not its total, showed major changes.

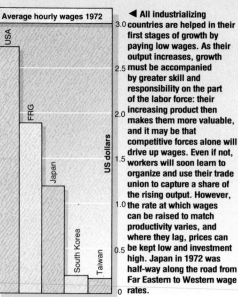

◀ All industrializing countries are helped in their first stages of growth by paying low wages. As their output increases, growth must be accompanied by greater skill and responsibility on the part of the labor force: their increasing product then makes them more valuable, and it may be that competitive forces alone will drive up wages. Even if not, workers will soon learn to organize and use their trade union to capture a share of the rising output. However, the rate at which wages can be raised to match productivity varies, and where they lag, prices can be kept low and investment high. Japan in 1972 was half-way along the road from Far Eastern to Western wage rates.

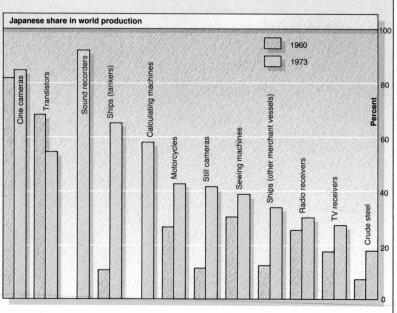

THE RISE OF THE FAR EAST

The successful
economies
Japanese expansion
Tradition and innovation
Education and
organization
The breakthrough to
modernity

Economic growth and general prosperity were found in these years not merely in Europe and North America, but in a modified form all over the world. In one area it was more spectacular still than in the West: a group of Far Eastern countries – South Korea, Hong Kong, Taiwan, Singapore and Japan – succeeded in breaking through to modern forms of industry from low beginnings by an exceptionally steep growth path. The earliest of these, and much the most important, was Japan.

Japanese expansion

The rise of Japan from defeat and devastation at the end of World War II to become the second industrial power among the market economies was remarkable enough. It is even more astonishing when the country's limited natural resources are remembered. Overcrowded, with a cultivable area per head one-fortieth of that of the United States, Japan is also poor in mineral deposits, and was forced to export to pay for necessary imports of raw materials and food. Yet exports were made difficult by anti-Japanese feeling and political changes among its Asian neighbors, its most natural markets, and by over-concentration on cotton textiles, which had little growth potential; the prewar reputation of Japanese goods as being shoddy and imitative did not help, either. Nevertheless, after the immediate tasks of postwar reconstruction were completed, Japan's course towards economic modernization and the economic "miracle" was well and truly set by the mid-1950s. In the period 1960–73 Japan's rates of growth of output and exports were leaving all other advanced countries behind and were in a class of their own. Moreover, while exports had gone at first largely to neighboring countries, before long they also achieved great success in the United States and in Europe, the most sophisticated markets. Similarly, the goods in which Japan scored her greatest successes – ships, cars, motor cycles, cameras, television sets, calculators and electronic equipment – were technically among the most complex products of their day.

Japanese economic prowess was based at first on imitation, but before long Japanese industries proved capable of striking out on their own and getting ahead of the West in certain fields. The causes of this astonishing success have been frequently studied as providing a possible model for others.

One evident cause was the low starting point, which lay well below the technical levels that Japan had reached in the 1930s and 1940s. To regain those levels was not too hard. Moreover, the large agricultural sector – in the later 1940s about half the population worked on the land – provided a useful population reservoir. Agrarian

reform was enforced by the Allied occupation authorities, and agriculture itself became highly efficient. Structural changes, including the relative decline of agriculture as well as of other low-productivity industries like textiles and food processing, gave a further impetus toward a high rate of growth.

The new workforce

An easy labor supply was a striking feature of the Japanese experience. Fed by the massive influx of labor from the land into the cities, it was further helped by the peculiar structure of Japanese industry, frequently referred to as industrial "dualism". A large part of the labor force – some two-thirds in 1962 in all occupations, 62 percent in manufacturing alone – worked in small firms, employing 300 or fewer; indeed, 15 percent of

▼ Fierce competition helped Hong Kong to become one of the most successful economies in the Far East.

▲ Japanese children are introduced early to the intensive study of science. Schools are demanding and highly competitive, and a rich and varied system of further and tertiary education is used by a large proportion of the adult population to acquire additional skills and advance their knowledge of the latest discoveries of science and technology. More than in most other countries, educational achievement in Japan tends to determine occupation and status in later life.

▼ It is common in Japanese offices and factories to engage in communal keep-fit exercises during the working day. Apart from their beneficial effects on health and efficiency, such activities are expected also to foster a corporate spirit and a sense of loyalty towards one's firm and one's superiors. In the larger firms, jobs are regarded as being for life and mobility of labor is low. Promotion and pay increments based on length of service tend to strengthen that attitude. In turn, firms are expected to keep their workers on even in difficult times.

workers in manufacturing were in plants employing nine or less, compared with four percent in the United States. These small firms used little capital and applied older techniques, but survived by paying low wages. The smallest of them paid only 33 percent of the wage rates of the large firms (compared with 67 percent for equivalent businesses in the United States). The differences in productivity were equally striking. Yet the small firms were extremely useful. They acted as subcontractors for the giant corporations who were the real carriers of Japanese economic expansion. They also provided a recruiting ground for newly arrived rural workers, who might, if they were lucky, ultimately join the permanent workforce of the large firm. Meanwhile, this large labor pool helped to keep wages down.

Even in a large company, the workforce for various reasons exercised far less pressure for wage increases than their counterparts in the West. For one thing, trade unions were weak and tended to work within the firms. Perhaps more important were the Japanese tradition of lifetime employment with job security and mutual loyalty, and the widespread *nenko* system of seniority-based wages. It is notable that several of the Japanese export successes, for example electronic goods, were produced with cheap, barely skilled labor.

These exceptionally low wages at any given level of productivity not only kept Japanese exports up, they also helped toward a high rate of saving which, allied to negligible expenditure on defense, gave Japan what was possibly its most distinctive characteristic: much the highest rate of investment in the developed world. Moreover, a smaller share of investment was put into housing in Japan than elsewhere, and there was less older capital stock to be renewed, so that about twice as much – measured as a proportion of GNP – was invested in new productive equipment in Japan as elsewhere. In absolute terms, the input of the new capital in Japan had by 1963 easily surpassed

▲ ▶ The assembly line in this washing machine plant and the steelworks control room are ample evidence that Japan has long ceased to rely merely on cheap labor for being competitive in world markets. Productivity nowadays is based on high investment in modern equipment and the most up-to-date technology. In many areas Japan has become a model for others.

The post-war period has ended; growth as reconstruction is over. Our foremost task is to start building a new Japan, eagerly importing the West's technical innovations.

JAPANESE ECONOMIC WHITE PAPER, 1954

that in France and Britain. Japan also began to make heavy investments abroad. Its direct investment in foreign subsidiaries rose from $1.5 billion in 1967 to $15.9 billion in 1975 (from 1.4 percent to over 6 percent of the world total), and continued to rise fast thereafter.

One particular form of investment which is thought to have contributed very largely to the Japanese success story lay in the field of education. Respect for learning was traditional and the skill of copying from the advanced economies had been practiced since the Meiji era. (Emperor Meiji reigned from 1868 until his death in 1912.) The level of Japanese educational provision and its expansion was among the highest in the world. The high educational standards achieved, together with the success of the larger industrial companies in attracting some of the best graduates, may have contributed to the highly positive attitude to innovation found in Japan.

The government's role
The Japanese government, too, is generally considered to have played a positive role. Among its achievements were the ending of the postwar runaway inflation and the stabilization of the economy thereafter; the provision of much capital (about one-quarter of the total), above all for the larger companies but also for some medium-sized firms; its support for cartels; and the skill with which it kept out foreign manufactured imports while nominally adhering to the GATT rules. Protectionist measures included differential tariff and excise tax rates favoring home producers; restriction of imports by foreign exchange rationing; control of foreign investments; and administrative chicaneries such as frequent changes in obscure technical details demanded of imported automobiles. The government's identification of the major growth industries, beginning with the courageous decision early on to back the heavy industries, was also important. These planning decisions were enforced by favorable conditions for imports of technology and components, by cheap capital, by subsidies and the provision of the necessary infrastructure, and by "administrative guidance" on the part of the responsible ministry, MITI (Ministry for International Trade and Industry).

Traditional and innovation
Beside these general factors, some specific Japanese features have often been noted which might have had positive effects on growth. Among these were the traditional loyalty and lifelong attachment to one's firm and the "family" attitude to one's superiors. Further, although the old *zaibatsu* industrial combines were broken up, new associational groupings, not very dissimilar in structure, known as *keiretsu*, were formed, with one or more banks at the center, much common selling, planning, and again a certain group loyalty as important features. Around 1971, the six leading groupings (Mitsubishi, Sumitomo, Fuji, Mitsui, Dai Ichi and Sanwa) had 387 associated companies between them. Since the banks and the associated companies provided most of the capital, and shareholders only a small

fraction, the managers as a group had a free hand. These groupings drove Japanese growth.

Another factor was the dismissal of the old owner class of the major firms in the course of postwar democratization, and its replacement by able and ambitious professionals unafraid of innovation. Lastly, there was the modesty of the demands made by the employees. The low level of wages has already been mentioned; in addition, Japanese workers worked on average some four hundred hours a year longer than those in other industrial countries. Social expenditure by the state was very low, and the Japanese were slow to take to "luxury" goods like cars. In fact, there seems to have been a cultural lag in the demand by the population for the rising standard of living commensurate with their productivity.

The breakthrough to modernity
Yet the fact that the example of Japan's rapid industrialization was followed very soon after by a number of other countries makes it unlikely that specific Japanese cultural traditions played a major part – unless it can be claimed that a similar role was performed by Chinese and Korean traditions in South Korea, Taiwan, Hong Kong and Singapore. For these countries all showed annual growth rates of GNP of around ten percent a year, and of real GNP per head of around seven percent a year. From almost total postwar dereliction and abject poverty in 1960, incomes caught up rapidly by 1973, South Korea lagging slightly behind, and were to approach those of European states in the next decade. Productivity rises took place in all sectors, but in each case it was manufacturing production which was in the lead. Typically, the greatest successes were achieved with labor-intensive products like electrical goods, plastics and textiles, though shipbuilding was important in Singapore and South Korea, and motor cars soon became a major industry in South Korea.

There were no clear, and possibly no common, causes for this breakthrough into modernity. Apart from South Korea, these countries were very poor in raw materials and energy sources. By their character, they fell clearly into two groups. Hong Kong and Singapore were busy trading ports without hinterland. In the case of Singapore, some 75 percent of GNP and in the case of Hong Kong, some 60 percent was generated within the tertiary sector. In the 1970s Singapore became in the fourth largest port in the world, possessing five kilometers (three miles) of landing shores and, in addition, engaged in commercial activities such as insurance, communication, finance and science consulting. Hong Kong also derived income from tourism.

Taiwan and South Korea had large agricultural sectors with rapidly rising efficiency in this period, growing at well over three percent a year in output while still being able to shed substantial numbers of workers to boost manufacturing employment. In the early stages, the processing of agricultural products and the textile industries were important for both. All had reasonably stable governments, low taxation, and fairly free trade, deeping the prices of imported goods low. Hong Kong received no foreign aid; that received

◄ Mass-produced electrical goods were among the most significant of Hong Kong's export industries. Women workers in this transistor plant, which employed 3500 people in the mid-1970s, were willing to accept low pay, and without protection by trade unions or social legislation they helped the city's exporters to undercut the prices of products of European and American factories. Low wages, however, are not enough by themselves to found modern industries, or the rest of the world would also be industrialized.

"Made in Hong Kong"

The manufacture of articles made of plastics was among the first to be established in Hong Kong after the war – the earliest factory dating from 1947 – and among these toys play a prominent part. Over ninety percent of the output goes abroad, and among the world's toy exporters, Hong Kong occupies first place. Though representing only 0.1 of the world's population, the crown colony was in 1986 responsible for 22 percent of the world's toy exports. An early reputation for shoddy, even dangerous, products has given way to admiration for the ingenuity of design at low prices. Hong Kong toys are geared to a world market, and there is rarely anything to indicate their Chinese origin.

▲ Toys, produced by cheap labor in small firms using relatively little capital, played an important part in Hong Kong's export drive. This Christmas collection at the Trade Development Council's Display Center underlines the fact that much of the city's production has no real base in the home market, as would be normal for industrial countries, but was intended mainly for overseas buyers and consumers.

by the other three petered out in the 1960s. They were all able to attract foreign capital, and showed strong signs of a dual economy, with large, modern factories usually financed from abroad, and a mass of small workshops. They all had, by Third World standards, a well-educated working population, though few craft or industrial traditions; and they all had low, if rising, wages.

Two different explanations have been offered for these success stories. The first is largely economic. According to this view these countries, possessing a cheap labor force in elastic supply, together with weak or docile trade unions, could undercut prices in world markets for goods requiring much unskilled labor but little capital. Input prices were kept low, while high interest rates encouraged saving and led to "correct" decisions, free of the dogmatic government "planning" characterizing the less successful developing countries. Governments further encouraged industry by subsidies and tax concessions. It may not be without significance that the three independent countries in this group had undemocratic dictatorial governments, while in the crown colony some key powers were still reserved for the governor, so that state power could be used to make the way clear for the single-minded pursuit of profitable investment without significant concessions to either public

◀ After Japan, South Korea: motor car production on a large scale, using up-to-date technology, expanded almost tenfold between 1976 and 1986. Much of this was destined for the overseas market, but home sales also rose with rising incomes. By the late 1980s, traffic jams in downtown Seoul began to resemble those of the capital cities of older industrial economies.

opinion or the interests of the poor. The other explanation runs in terms of cultural tradition. According to this, Chinese and Korean culture (three-quarters of Singapore's population is Chinese) favours industriousness, self-discipline and thrift in the general population (though, curiously, only Taiwan had a low consumption ratio), and active enterprise among capital owners. This cultural tradition would also embrace Japan. It may be that the functioning infrastructure and the efficient administration left by the colonial powers, Britain and Japan respectively, also contributed to the "economic miracle".

▼ Hong Kong's modern skyscraper building line provides an appropriate background to the container berths at Kway Chung, which at the time of their opening in 1975 formed the largest and most modern cargo-handling complex in Asia. Hong Kong is a trading as well as an industrial center, with a flourishing service sector contributing a high proportion of GDP.

Datafile

The countries of Eastern Europe, as well as China after the Communist revolution, started out with concepts very different from those of the Western market economies. Nevertheless, there were some remarkable similarities between Eastern and Western Europe, and between China and India. The outstanding difference was the much stronger emphasis on the building up of capital goods industries in the East. Whatever was produced for consumers was quickly sold, since incomes were greater than the output of consumer goods, so that there were shortages everywhere. However, the control that Eastern planners were able to maintain over their economy allowed them to keep prices of necessities, such as bread and housing, low and below cost. By fixing prices they also avoided the inflation current in the West. China, a much poorer country, was able to take only the first steps on the road to modernization. Planning may have made these faster, but subject to more violent swings, than was the case in the comparable economy of India.

▼ In the planned economies of Europe foreign trade played a subordinate role. In this period, these countries became increasingly unable to pay for the needed products of the superior Western technology, possibly a sign of an underlying flaw in their planned growth. The situation parallels the rising debt mountain of the Third World.

▶ In this period, the economies of Eastern Europe grew about as fast as comparable countries in the West and in the Far East, if official statistics are to be believed. It should be noted that the measure used, the "net material product", NMP, is different from the measure favored in the West and tends to exaggerate Eastern European success.

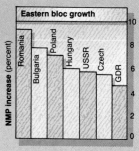
Eastern bloc growth

▼ Steel, cement, and chemical fertilizer are often taken as indicators of economic maturity that are comparable between countries of different traditions and different economic systems. In this respect China and India belonged together, as did the Soviet Union and Japan, both still well below the United States.

Comecon countries – trade deficits with the West

▼ China's economic data are extremely difficult to establish and to compare with those of other countries. In broad outline, however, the irregular growth path shown here, the direct result of violent swings in government policy, may be taken as reasonably correct. The figures do, however, hide enormous regional differences.

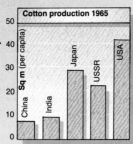
Cotton production 1965

◀ Cotton cloth was a consumer good of major importance in many countries. The gap in production between China and India, and the United States as the most advanced industrialized country, was far narrower than in the case of capital goods. Even here, however, output per head was around five times as high in the United States.

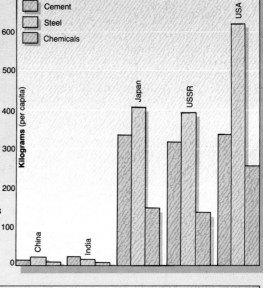
Industrial production 1965

China: phases of growth

Gross industrial output

Gross agricultural output

▼ National income in the Comecon countries tended to fluctuate more than in the West, though the method of calculation may tend to exaggerate the changes in direction. The tendency for the poorest of these countries to grow fastest may be connected with the gains that can be achieved by moving workers away from agriculture.

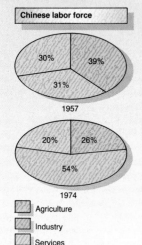
Chinese labor force

1957

1974

Agriculture
Industry
Services

◀ The sharp fall in agricultural employment, together with the slight fall in services, matched by the rise in manufacturing employment, point to a phase of rapid industrialization in China. The trend is plausible, but the ratios may be a result of the unconventional definitions used in the official Chinese statistics.

▶ The strikingly slower growth of real wages than of national income in the Comecon countries is explained by the very large share of national output converted to investment. As in the Soviet Union under Stalin, the generation of workers who lived through the early years of planning were obliged to make sacrifices for a better future.

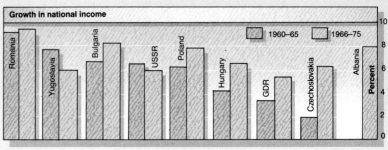
Growth in national income

1960–65   1966–75

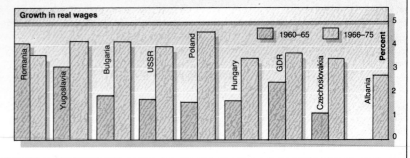
Growth in real wages

1960–65   1966–75

THE PLANNED ECONOMIES

Similarities with the West

Experiments and reforms

Technological development

Comecon and mutual cooperation

The Chinese experience

Those countries which had "socialist" planned economic systems – Bulgaria, Czechoslovakia, the German Democratic Republic, Hungary, Poland, Romania, the Soviet Union and Yugoslavia – showed economic growth rates that were not dissimilar to those of the market economies of the West and Far East. By the standard of the "net material product" (NMP) which was applied in Eastern Europe, annual growth rates for the years between 1960 and 1974 varied from 4.6 percent for the technically most advanced (the German Democratic Republic, GDR) to 9.4 percent for the most backward (Romania).

The measure of NMP tends to exaggerate the rate of growth compared with the GDP measure current in Western calculations, but there is no easy way of comparing the two accurately. The United Nations Economic Commission for Europe translated the data for 1965 into absolute figures of GNP per head, and concluded plausibly that the eight Eastern European countries achieved levels of output ranging from 48 percent to 98 percent of the average of all Western and Southern European market economies. The com-

▼ Consumer goods took second place in the planned economies, the emphasis throughout being on heavy industry and capital goods. As a result, the quality of goods in the shops was poor, service minimal, choice very restricted and queueing common. This Moscow queue waits patiently for ice-cream.

parable figures for consumption were, however, much lower. Moreover, the quality of the goods of the centrally planned economies was low, choice was restricted, supplies were unreliable, service (including that in shops) was poor, transport was overcrowded and housing greatly inferior. These items, which do not enter the official comparisons, make it likely that real income and the standard of living it could buy in the East were considerably lower in relation to the West than the official statistics imply.

In comparison with the West, the planned economies continued to devote more resources to the heavy and investment goods industries. Consequently, the immediate interests of the consumers were neglected in favor of faster future growth, and real wages rose much more slowly than output. Growth was aided by a large exodus from the land. More than a quarter of the total workforce left the land for other occupations between 1950 and 1973, and in Bulgaria this figure was nearly 50 percent. This movement was brought about by a number of factors – by a technological catching-up process, by improvement

in the quality of labor through education, and by a dramatic rise in the number of women in employment.

Experiments and reforms

In the 1960s the supply of free resources was reduced and it became necessary to change from extensive to intensive progress, that is to say from continually increasing inputs to using the given inputs in a better way. This is clearly demonstrable in agriculture. The ploughing up of "virgin" land, initiated in the Soviet Union in 1954, was the last of the extensive campaigns. By 1960 some sixty million hectares (148 million acres) had been sown, and the newly won land carried over 40 percent of the country's grain. But soil erosion and a vast dustbowl effect followed, and the experiment was halted with Nikita Khrushchev's fall in 1964. Instead, more capital had to be applied to the available soil, both to replace labor and to achieve the necessary increases. The number of tractors, for example, more than doubled between 1960 and 1973. Yet despite increased output, the Soviet Union had to import grain in large quantities by the late 1960s.

Faced with the task of dealing with an ever more complex economy, the rigid Soviet planning system, adopted also by the other "socialist" economies, began to show weaknesses. While quite capable of following a set path, such as reaching certain output targets with a given technology, industrial management by bureaucrats reacted poorly to change and to innovation.

A series of reforms initiated by Khrushchev in 1957, which shifted the centers of control from specialist ministries to regional authorities, was reversed by Alexey Kosygin in 1965, but some decentralization was encouraged. Enterprises were permitted to form "associations" with others, as an intermediate layer of authority between the center and the factory. By 1973, there were over eleven hundred of these. Further, the number of planning targets for industrial managers was reduced from 20–30 to only eight. Instead, monetary incentives were introduced, in the form of bonuses to employees, of social expenditure (especially on housing) and of development funds for the works. Cost reductions were also encouraged and a rate of interest, generally of six percent, was charged. By 1970, more than 41,000 enterprises had been converted to the "new system", accounting for about 92 percent of the output and of the workforce.

These reforms found an echo in the other countries of the Eastern bloc. There were formal decisions to steer a new course in East Germany and in Czechoslovakia in 1963, in Poland in 1964, in Bulgaria in 1965, Albania in 1966, Romania in 1967 and Hungary (the "New Economic Mechanism") in 1968. However, little seemed to change as a result, except in Hungary and temporarily in Czechoslovakia, for purely economic rationality could not easily be reconciled with a command economy in which economic targets and methods were fundamentally the subject of political decisions.

Technological development

The failure to come to grips with the latest technology, which was reflected in the waves of reforms and their lack of success, is all the more remarkable since the ruling philosophy placed a

The Space Race

◄▲ Yuri Gagarin, much-decorated hero of the Soviet Union, was the first man in space. The success of the Soviet program of space exploration shocked the West, which had underestimated Soviet technological capability, but it may be that too much of the best Soviet top scientific manpower went into this prestige project.

The development of military rocketry in World War II made it clear that rockets might be developed powerful enough to propel payloads into orbit round the earth and even into outer space. The practical problems were formidable, but in the years after the war both the United States and Soviet Union devoted considerable financial and technological resources to developing programs to overcome them. The Soviet Union succeeded first, and Sputnik I was launched into orbit on 4 October 1957. Sputnik II followed a month later. After sending Luna II to land on the Moon in 1959, the Soviet Union launched Sputnik IV in May 1960. Finally, on 1 April 1961, Vostok I returned after circling the Earth once: in it was the cosmonaut Yuri Gagarin, the first man in space.

These successes caused consternation among American scientists and apprehension among the American public. It became a political necessity to show that American technology could match the Soviet Union's achievements in this field. The space program was stepped up, and in 1962 the first American manned flight took place. In the years to come, both superpowers continued to devote a large proportion of their resources to space technology. Many argued that this was money that could barely be afforded, especially in the Soviet Union; and after the success of the Apollo moon program, both countries cut back on their space exploration programs.

▲ The annual parades in Red Square in Moscow have always included a mighty array of military hardware. The technical equipment of the Red Army is undoubtedly impressive, but it reduced production and productivity available for civilian use far more than comparable expenditure in Western countries. Apart from the use of scarce technical resources, the general burden of the large standing army has also been high, though no exact figures are available, since military expenditure is hidden in many different items in the budget.

high premium on scientific and technical progress. Certainly, the Eastern European countries made great efforts in the educational field, including the universities, and in research and development. The proportions of the total workforce with higher education in the Soviet Union doubled between 1960 and 1973; it more than trebled in East Germany and rose substantially in the rest of the planned economies too. Yet technology remained behind that of the West, and in fact much of the rising import bill which the Eastern bloc countries had to meet in the early 1970s arose from their need for advanced machinery, sophisticated control mechanisms and other "high-tech" goods from the industrialized "capitalist" states. Part of the reason for this may be that a large amount of their research effort was devoted to armaments and to prestige objectives like space travel: some 12 percent of the Soviet national income was spent on defense, compared with nine percent in the United States and six percent or less in Western Europe.

The Eastern investment ratio remained high,

well above that of the West, and investments continued to grow faster than national income. What was unusual among these economies was the very high incremental capital output ratio – that is, the amount of additional capital required to generate a given additional output.

Comecon and economic cooperation

The Council for Mutual Economic Assistance (CMEA, also called Comecon), which had had a rather inauspicious start in 1949, began to be revitalized in the late 1950s and early 1960s. Partly this reflected the need to catch up technically with the West, to switch to producing more consumer goods, and to move away from the Stalinist aim of autarky – independence of the need for foreign commodities. The first international agreement made by the CMEA as an entity was with Finland in 1973.

In 1963 the International Bank for Economic Cooperation was founded to facilitate mutual clearing, using the jointly agreed "transfer rouble", though its effect was limited since trade

◄ The Soviet Union is rich in natural resources, though many of them are in areas difficult of access and far from the European centres of population. Costly investment has been needed to develop them, as in this gas main station in Bukhara, not far from the border with Afghanistan. Transport to major centers of population proved similarly expensive.

► As a major industrial power, the Soviet Union exported manufactured goods, mainly to the less industrialized parts of the world. Heavy goods vehicles like these being loaded at the port of Odessa for the United Arab Republic were typical of this trade. The Soviet Union also supplied technical know-how, helping to build industrial structures such as steelworks in Third World countries.

▼ The natural resources of the Soviet Union were not only developed for domestic use. Oil and gas pipelines were built to convey Soviet products to Eastern bloc countries and to Western European countries as far apart as Finland and Italy. They were among the Soviet Union's main exports and significant earners of much-needed hard currency.

between the member states continued to be conducted by bilateral agreement and in terms of actual goods. Other common institutions were also gradually built up. A rail wagon pool was formed in 1964, followed by coordination or indeed joint enterprises in a number of industries, including the building of rolling mills, iron and steel, chemicals, measuring instruments and space research. From 1973, there was growing collaboration in shipping services on the Danube and in the Baltic. Oil and gas pipelines were built to link Soviet sources with the markets of Russia's Western neighbors. In 1971, the International Investment Bank was set up with a nominal capital of 1000 million transfer roubles: by the end of 1973 it had provided part credit for 33 ventures, at a cost of 588 million transfer roubles. Possibly of greater importance was its ability to take up credits in the West.

Yet the main apparent object of the CMEA, the coordination of economic plans and the expansion of an international division of labor, was not realized, let alone the aim of freer trade between the member countries. On the contrary, in their search for vital machinery imports from the Western countries on credit in the early 1970s, there was a clear tendency for each of the Eastern bloc countries to try and gain some advantage by going it alone. The result was a weakening of CMEA links, and a certain amount of reintegration of the European economy across the East–West divide.

China and modernization

During the 1950s, the industrialization of the People's Republic of China had proceeded at breakneck speed on the Russian model. In 1958, encouraged by this, Chairman Mao Zedong planned to bypass conventional methods by taking what he regarded as a "Great Leap Forward". This was launched with high expectations, but the failure of China's newly established heavy industries, which were carried out with small-scale methods in the villages, combined with a series of bad harvests and the withdrawal of Soviet experts following the political break in 1960, turned it into an economic catastrophe. Agricultural output fell by a quarter to its lowest point in 1960, and industrial output may have fallen even more to its 1962 trough.

As a result, the "Leap" was abandoned and a high rate of growth resumed by traditional methods. Both agriculture and industry made good their losses and by 1965–66 reached their previous peak again, though the population had meanwhile also increased. Much attention was now paid to monetary incentives, to demand and to the market, as well as to economical, efficient production, rather than aiming to maximize output at all costs. But the pattern of growth was interrupted once again by the "Cultural Revolution" of 1966–69, which involved the transfer of production decisions from ministries and experts to groups of revolutionary guards. The Marxist ethos of Mao's revolution contained a strong element of seeing in the peasantry an exploited class that embodied values that were of great significance for the new China. Consequently, millions of skilled workers and specialists were sent to do unskilled work on the farms for the benefit of their ideological education. Agricultural output fell less drastically this time, but manufacturing, transport and foreign trade suffered severely. Finally, about 1970, the "Revolution" was reversed and economic growth resumed once more.

This seesaw between ideology and prosperity in China's progress in the 1950s and 1960s reflects a central dilemma or contradiction in Communist

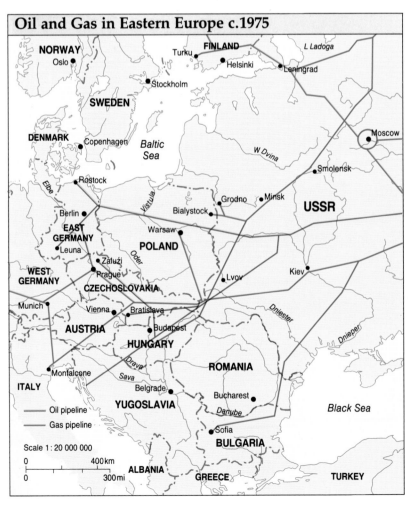

Oil and Gas in Eastern Europe c.1975

Oil pipeline
Gas pipeline

Scale 1 : 20 000 000

▼ ▶ The Chinese economy was still largely agricultural; even in 1975 around three-quarters of the population were still working in the villages. But Mao's revolution was essentially a peasant revolution, and from time to time city intellectuals, like these young graduates, were sent to work in the fields.

economic management which also affected Eastern Europe, especially in agriculture. It was possible to have ideological purity, by collectivization, communes in the villages and other cooperative measures, or to have efficiency and economic growth, but did not prove possible to have both at the same time, once a certain primitive stage was passed. It is noticeable that it was precisely the periods of ideological enthusiasm that showed the worst economic results. Thus GNP in the first five-year plan of 1953–57 rose by 7 percent a year (5 percent per capita), only to fall in the Great Leap Forward of 1958–61 by −3 percent (−5 percent). In the following period of consolidation it rose by no less than 13 percent (11 percent), but during the years of the Cultural Revolution of 1966–69 it dropped again. As soon as that phase was over, growth accelerated once more during 1970–74.

In view of the zigzag course of Chinese economic development, overall growth rates are difficult to establish. Reasonable estimates show that the rates of annual growth of GDP, agriculture and industrial products were all around four percent.

Chinese agriculture remained highly intensive, switching in some areas from one crop a year to two, elsewhere from two to three and in other respects undergoing its "green revolution". In much of the country, rice is the staple food, and it was possible sufficiently to increase output of that crop by better techniques and new varieties, together with using the immensely important enlarged supply of chemical fertilizer, for China to remain essentially self-sufficient in food for her growing population. Thus it was able to maintain a quarter of the world's population on seven percent of the world's cultivable surface. Methods, however, remained primitive, and agriculture had to suffer numerous upheavals on ideological grounds. Equipment belonged to the 19th century rather than the 20th, even though the workers were members of a "brigade" rather than individual peasants.

Some industrial sectors increased rapidly, in the 1960s especially the production of fertilizer, of machinery and of vehicles, as well as of oil and (rather more slowly) of electric power. Others, including textiles and food processing, but also the steel industry, grew slowly. Growth was helped by a massive transfer of population from the land, amounting, according to different estimates, to between 15 and 19 percent of the total working population. For a country as poor as China, the proportions employed in industry were exceptionally high. This can be explained, in part, by the strongly "dual" nature of industry, in which modern large works existed side by side with much, partly rural, small-scale and handicraft production.

The proportion of national income represented by foreign trade remained small, at about four percent of GNP, but it was crucial in bringing in advanced machinery from Japan and from the West. By about 1966 it had made up the losses sustained in the "Great Leap" and it then rose rapidly. Industrial and mineral products rose from about 30 percent of total exports in 1960 to 39 percent in 1975, while "means of production" accounted for between 80 and 90 percent of imports. The "socialist" countries' share in China's trade fell from 64 percent in 1958–61 to a mere 19 percent in 1970–4, while Japan's share correspondingly rose from 3.5 to over 21 percent. Trade connections also expanded with Hong Kong, Western Europe and the United States.

By the standards and from the point of view of

▲ The "Cultural Revolution" involved much enthusiasm among young people and party activists, as well as a very pronounced personality cult. In part a simple struggle for power, it also represented the genuine fear that privileged intellectuals and bureaucrats were drifting into middle-class attitudes of mind, and had to be reeducated by being forced to do hard manual work.

much of the Third World, Chinese economic progress, seen as a whole, had to be accounted a success, in spite of temporary setbacks. The curtailment of freedom for individual peasants, traders and professionals, and the relatively brutal directives, especially during the "Great Leap" and the Cultural Revolution, seemed less abhorrent to people who enjoyed few privileges themselves. The reiteration of the popular, if not populist, character of the Chinese experiment and the repeated, much publicized, attempts to "mobilize" or activate the masses, seemed to be in stark contrast to the procedures of the generally corrupt, selfish and incompetent ruling elites which lorded it over much of the Third World. Against this, the expansion of production capacity in the Chinese industrial sector, especially in the more advanced industries, down to the dispatch of China's own rocket into space in 1971, made a considerable impression. For a number of industries, the technological gap between Japan and China has been estimated at only 15 years in 1966.

The encouragement of partly rural small-scale industry which was a particular feature of the Chinese way to socialism was something which could well appear to be within reach of other less advanced economies. At the other extreme, it was not unreasonable to suppose that it would require a centralized planning machinery, such as the Communist government advocated, before the more impressive large-scale engineering schemes of those years could be carried out. Thus there were large-scale irrigation developments in

Hunan and Fujian provinces; large-scale re-afforestation projects in Hunan, Guangdong, Anhui, Henan and Jiangxi provinces; the completion of water conservancy work on the Grand Canal in Hubei province; electrification schemes, and other ventures. Large canal schemes had, however, been a feature of China's history and China – unlike many other poor countries – possessed a long tradition of literacy and learning, of technical competence and administrative experience, on which the Communist planners could build. Moreover, even a tiny proportion of resources devoted to an advanced sector in a vast country can produce a concentration of impressive achievements.

▶ Industrial growth was slow in the People's Republic of China, and suffered several setbacks. Nevertheless, China also possessed some advanced technology: this worker was employed in a plant making modern electrical generating equipment.

FEEDING THE WORLD

Technical and scientific progress benefited agriculture as well as industry and the services, but in the less developed parts of the world, the gains were largely swallowed by the rapidly increasing populations. Thus between the early 1960s and 1973, world agricultural output rose by 29 percent, and most major regions were near that average, only Africa lagging with about 20 percent; but output per head actually fell in Africa, Latin America and the Middle East; only the industrialized economies kept well ahead of their population growth. Taking them as a whole, the developing countries, which still had an export surplus of grain in 1954, began to be net importers in 1955, and by 1965 their total imports amounted to 16.5 million tonnes; India's imports alone in 1966 were equivalent to one quarter of the whole American crop. The costs of these growing food imports from the developed world became an impossible burden for poor nations to bear.

Increases in their own agrarian output could be dramatic, with the appropriation of Western technology, best exemplified by the "Green Revolution" – a term which found ready acceptance at the time. In its narrow meaning, it referred to the development of high-yielding, fast-growing and adaptable strains of wheat, maize, rice and other food grains, but it could also be taken to refer to every aspect of improved agrarian technology and structure. The first high-yield varieties (HYV) of maize were created in Mexico in a Rockefeller-Foundation-financed research center. By the mid-1960s, maize yield per hectare in Mexico had been doubled and total output trebled. Some new wheat and rice varieties improved yields by up to 350 percent. By 1970 the highest acreages under HYV of rice were Taiwan (74 percent of total production), the Philippines (50 percent), Pakistan (42 percent) and South Korea (40 percent), and for wheat in Mexico (90 percent), Nepal (50 percent), Pakistan (49 percent) and India (33 percent). Proportions elsewhere were much lower, and the new varieties were not without their problems. They needed careful water allocation, weeding, protection from diseases, more mechanization (as the times of ripening were much shorter) and good merchandizing organization, for seeds had to be bought in instead of holding back part of the crop for seed grain as had been traditional. Improved infrastructures, such as roads and irrigation, and structural change, such as larger farms with more resources, were frequently required. All this meant that improved yields tended to benefit the better-off farmers, not the poorest. Also, the poorest countries could not benefit.

The term "Green Revolution" may also have failed to do justice to the steady improvements, including seed experimentation, that had gone on before. Perhaps it comes closest to the truth to say that the "Green Revolution" played its part in the long-term increase of some of the poorer countries' agricultural output, desperately needed to keep pace with their growing populations.

▶ Sacks of grain, supplied by West Germany, being unloaded in a deficit area in Africa. Such aid is often of the most immediate benefit to a population near starvation, and can easily be spared from European farming surpluses. In the long run, however, the deficit countries can only be helped by providing means for them to feed themselves.

▶ Vast mountains of grain and full silos mark the capacity of the United States not only to produce enough for their own population, but also to maintain enormous reserves, artificially kept down by legislation passed in the interest of farmers, which could satisfy the deficit areas of the world. The main problem, however, is that most of the poorest areas cannot afford to buy from North America since they have little or nothing to sell to the outside world.

◀ Large and well-endowed research institutes test different varieties of wheat, many for application in the climatic and soil conditions of the less developed countries. This is one of the most effective ways in which Western science helps the Third World.

▶ New seedlings are being planted in a co-operative farm in Africa. Women in the fields are burdened by their children as they always were, and the watering equipment is elementary. Sometimes new methods have to work within a traditional structure to become socially acceptable.

▲ A well being dug in north-east Mali. Frequently small scale technical improvements, provided by traditional means within the capability of local communities, will be as effective as grandiose schemes drawn up on a national level.

◀ The tin of skimmed milk was no doubt sent to hungry villages as food aid with the best of intentions, but may turn out to be inappropriate and a source of danger. It may give a false impression of nutritional value, while there is a danger of water-borne diseases when the milk is reconstituted from the powder.

Datafile

Poverty still characterized the countries of the "Third World", that is, the countries other than the advanced Western nations, the planned economies and the rapidly expanding economies of the Far East. Extremely rich individuals and groups, as well some as well-to-do cities and regions, could indeed be found in the Third World, but these made the poverty of the rest of the population all the harder to bear.

Rising prosperity in the advanced nations produced two reactions in the poorer countries. One was to make great efforts to break through into modernization, in many cases by economic planning and by other ambitious programs. The other was to apply for aid and loans from the richer economies. By these and other means, the incomes of the less developed world were raised quite substantially. However, in many cases much of the increased output was swallowed up by rising populations. Moreover, the loans they took up required servicing and this caused difficulties where they had not been invested productively.

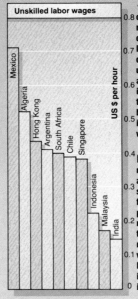

Unskilled labor wages

◀ International comparisons of real wages are difficult to make, since hours and conditions vary and price levels cannot easily be compared. The data used here are therefore approximate, but show wages in the Third World countries to have been considerably below those of the industrialized countries, and with substantial variations.

◀ Like other countries receiving large loans from abroad, India found that the stream of inflowing capital funds was, after a while, partly offset by interest and repayment funds flowing in the opposite direction. The net foreign sums available were therefore declining. Foreign funds must be invested to service the debt in later years.

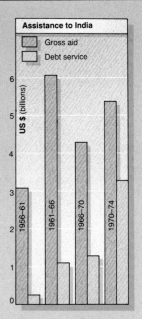

Assistance to India

◀ There were large differences in income per head within the Central and South American region. Some countries, including oil-rich Venezuela and agrarian Argentina, as well as several West Indian islands, had incomes approaching those of parts of Europe, while other regions were little more advanced than parts of Africa.

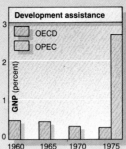

Development assistance

▶ The poorer parts of the world grew at quite substantial rates in this period. Some countries, described here as the "newly developed economies", were able to sustain quite remarkable rates of growth. But at the other extreme population growth swallowed up much of the overall growth of other less developed countries.

◀ Assistance to Third World Countries came from OECD members and after 1973 from OPEC countries, with smaller sums from the planned economies. Aid consisted of gifts, technical assistance and loans on easy terms, as well as favorable trading terms. As a proportion of the donors' own national income, aid tended to decline in this period.

Growth rates

◀ The inflow of borrowings into the less developed countries left their governments with ever larger debt commitments to foreign countries and international agencies. There were great differences among these countries both in the burden of the debt and in its rate of growth. Some had reached levels increasingly difficult to service.

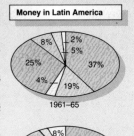

Money in Latin America

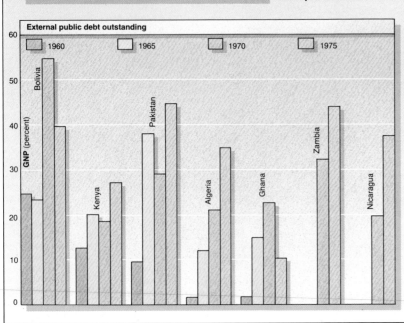

▶ Latin American countries were among the major international debtors. There were important changes in this period. About one-quarter of the loans continued to be granted by multinational companies. As for the rest, consortia of commercial banks from the developed countries replaced the United States government.

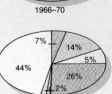

Private inflow
Direct investment
Suppliers
Bonds
Banks

Public inflow
Bilateral – USA
Multilateral
Bilateral (others)

THE THIRD WORLD

The term "Third World" came into increasing use in this period to describe the countries neither in the Soviet bloc nor among the advanced industrial nations. There were considerable differences in per capita incomes among them. Even leaving out the oil-rich states, the richest had incomes per head more than thirty times as high as those of the poorest, and the gap was widening. However, given their low starting point and their primitive economies, statistics of GNP drawn up for poor countries on Western patterns have little meaning. Altogether, despite the convenience of the expression "Third World", there is little to be gained by regarding these nations as a single category.

Latin American inequalities

The countries of Latin America, together with the Caribbean islands, were among the better off, though there were wide differences even between them; several, indeed, approached European levels of income. But expectations in this period that they might break through into advanced levels were disappointed: their growth rates per head were low, and their economies frequently lacked a solid base.

One cause of this relative failure was an extremely high rate of population increase, averaging 2.9 percent a year with a rising tendency, among the highest in the world. Only Argentina and Uruguay were much below that, at 1.5 percent a year or less. Inevitably, this swallowed up much of the quite respectable annual growth rate. Moreover, the economic structure seemed remarkably resistant to change. Emigration from the poorest agrarian regions, which had the highest birth rates, reduced agricultural employment slightly, from 48 to 45 percent of total employment in 1960–73, but industrial employment hardly rose; in some countries it even declined. Instead, the migrants sought to scratch a living from providing unskilled "services", settling in ill-provided shacks on the outskirts of the large cities. Several of these doubled in size in a decade: the population of Mexico City grew from 3 million to 15 million between 1950 and 1980. Official statistics showed unemployment figures of around 6–8 percent; Bolivia had 15–16 percent unemployment in the early 1970s and Colombia 10 percent. In addition, underemployment was widespread in Latin America. In urban areas alone, it stood at 23 percent, and meanwhile agricultural output per head stagnated.

To create modern industries while absorbing all the additional labor would have required large investments, but Latin American savings remained low. Capital imports were needed, and Latin America seemed an attractive place for foreign investors, who were further encouraged by the

▼ The stunning contrast betwen the luxury apartments of the Brazilian rich and the hovels of the poor could be found in every major South American city, where shanty towns have grown up alongside the city proper. Such contrasts are also typical of the large cities, particularly the capitals, of the other poor continents, Africa and Asia. The Third World now enjoys a high degree of mobility, but there is still no escape from mass poverty.

"Alliance for Progress" concept launched by the United States in 1961. Investments averaging $1.6 billion a year flowed into Latin America in 1961–65, rising to $2.6 billion in 1966–70 and $7.6 billion in 1971–75.

The sources of this capital changed significantly in the early 1960s from public authorities, mainly from the United States, to private investors, above all to international bank consortia. And in this lay the roots of one of the major problems of the following era, not only for Latin America; for by the mid-1960s the outflow required for dividends and repayments was beginning to exceed the new borrowings, and the countries concerned were set to slide into a large-scale foreign debt crisis. In fact, neither the political structure of Latin America, nor the attitude and technical competence of the business elite, nor yet that of the workforce, were favorable to modern industrial growth, as the low rate of savings demonstrated.

Yet another difficulty experienced by several of the largest countries in the area lay in their reliance on one, or at most two, major export commodities such as sugar from the Caribbean islands, or coffee from Brazil: as the prices of some to them fell in this period, expansion plans

▶ It is evident that rich and poor countries are not scattered randomly around the globe, but cluster in certain very significant ways. Thus richer countries will be found in the temperate zones, while the poor are mainly, if not solely, in a broad belt north and south of the Equator. Some exceptions (oil in hot countries, deserts in others) do not alter the picture fundamentally. Poverty is therefore not simply the result of wrong policies, but is something that is exceptionally hard to combat in certain geographic areas.

It is machinery that has impoverished India. Machinery is the chief symbol of modern civilization. It represents a great sin. I am not fighting machinery as such, but the madness of thinking that machinery saves labor ... The spinning wheel is also a machine.

MAHATMA GANDHI

▼ India is dependent on the prosperity of its agriculture. Much of the agriculture on the subcontinent is conducted on traditional lines, the labor of the peasants being the main input, and most peasants remain poor and unable to afford modern equipment. Many parts of the country are subject to extreme changes in the weather, excessive rains or drought endangering a rural economy none too well prepared to withstand them. Such improvements as have been possible have ensured merely that output has kept pace with population growth.

had to be cut back. Since the regional economies were largely competitive with each other, there was little to hope for from the expansion of intra-regional trade. The Latin American Free Trade Association (1960) and the Caribbean Free Trade Area (1965) therefore had very little effect, though rather more was achieved by cooperation among the Andean Group (1969) of six countries – Bolivia, Chile, Colombia, Ecuador, Peru and Venezuela.

The oil-rich states

Other groups of countries well above the poverty level but associated with the Third World were the Arab states of North Africa and the Middle East, several countries in Southeast Asia, and the Philippines. The oil-rich countries were in a class of their own. Even in 1973, before the great oil price rise, their GDP per head was approaching – and some cases, notably Kuwait and Saudi Arabia, even exceeding – that of the richest developed economies.

At the other end of the scale, there was poverty-stricken tropical Africa, and there were countries in Southern Asia, such as India, Pakistan and Bangladesh, which the world's development almost seemed to have passed by. Moreover, their low average income figures hid enormous inequalities within their societies. India, which was much the most important country in this group, containing 15 percent of the world's population in 1973, may be taken as an example.

The Indian economy

India began its independence in 1947 with the advantages of a long experience of settled government and a highly educated elite, though their skills tended to be legal and administrative rather than technical. The country set out to develop by means of five-year plans, of which the first ran from 1951 to 1956, in the framework of a "mixed economy" in which some of the basic and heavy industries were to be nationalized.

The momentum of the first two five-year plans was carried over into the third (1961–66), but much of the growth was swallowed up by the

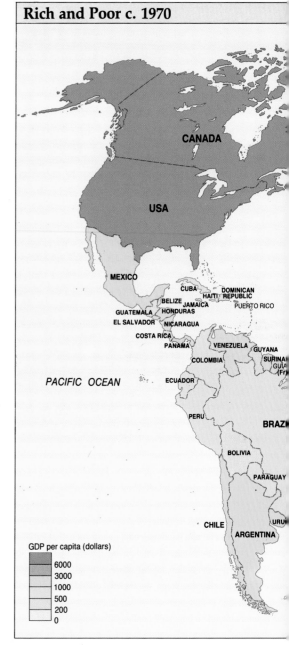

Rich and Poor c. 1970

GDP per capita (dollars)

6000
3000
1000
500
200
0

rapidly rising population. A poor harvest in 1966 helped to weaken the economy to a point where existing plans had to be suspended and the rupee devalued. There followed three years of no-plan fast growth, and a fourth plan period, which once more reduced growth; in 1972–73 growth stopped altogether.

Both agriculture and industry expanded faster than the population, but the fate of the economy was determined by its agricultural sector. Well over 70 percent of the occupied population, with the figures rising, worked in agriculture, producing 52 percent of the national income in 1960–61 and still as much as 43 percent in 1973–74. Its fluctuations and changing fortunes were largely responsible for the fluctuations in the economy as a whole.

From 1965 to 1966 agrarian growth was given a new lease of life by the "high yield varieties" of key crops. This "Green Revolution" was driven forward in India by the Intensive Agricultural

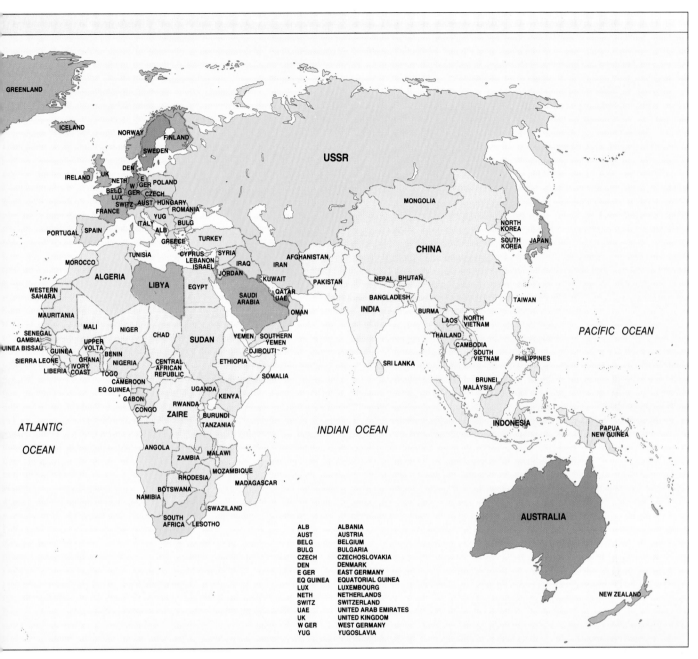

▲ Planting rice by hand, in this case in Sri Lanka, is an example of the primitive form of agriculture still practiced in many poor countries. They lack the capital and the educational facilities for the peasants to use new techniques.

Areas Program (IAAP) of 1965. The program was not an unqualified success, since some of the necessary inputs for the high-yield, short-gestation crop varieties, such as fertilizer and water, were not always available, and it benefited large farmers much more than smaller. Nevertheless, while rice crops were little affected, the productivity of wheat went up by over one-half. The Green Revolution certainly helped to preserve India from starvation.

With regard to industry, the plan allowed for rather more labor-intensive, small-scale, traditional "Gandhian" industry than was the case in most other developing countries. But here also, as in agriculture, results were uneven: expansion was fastest in energy, heavy industry, engineering and chemicals, and slowest in textiles and food processing. Much of the heavy industry remained high-cost, delivering goods at prices above those at which India might have bought in world markets, yet still making huge losses for the state. Other industrial firms, which were run by foreign owners, were accused of taking too much out of the country in dividends.

Domestic savings were bound to be low in a country as poor as India. They ran at some 8–10 percent of NDP. They were helped out by foreign aid and foreign investment, but servicing the debt soon began to eat into the benefits. Because of this, net gains of foreign exchange from capital imports – that is, capital imports less repayments and interest payments – fell from 2.8 percent of national income in 1966–9 to 0.8 percent in the following period, and were bound to fall farther, finally to become losses.

There were, as always happens, some particular causes for India's poor results: poor planning, occasional bad harvests, high military expenditure. But, given the extreme poverty and the high rate of population increase, it is difficult to imagine how much more could possibly have been achieved.

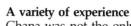

▼ The granting of independence to former African colonies was a political necessity, but it is not clear that it brought much economic benefit. African aspirations, as well as the new architecture exemplified by this Ghanaian independence monument built in 1957, had often little relevance to the most urgent needs. Ghana's undoubted enthusiasm was soon dampened by over-ambitious plans and the almost inevitable rising debt mountain; optimism ended in stagnation and bankruptcy.

Nkrumah's plans for Ghana

A rather different pattern can be seen in Ghana, which in 1957 had been the first African colony to achieve independence. At the time it was the richest and best-educated of the black African territories, and it set out to industrialize with the advice of some of the best development economists in the Western world. Further advantages were an active population, which proved it could react fast to market changes, and a large foreign exchange reserve.

Under its charismatic leader Kwame Nkrumah, Ghana had extravagant plans for a big push of "unbalanced growth" in 1961–65, which was intended to build up a large enough industrial base to supply much of Africa. In 1959 work started on the Volta River project, which was a huge regional scheme involving the construction of a dam to be used for irrigation and for the provision of hydroelectric power. But despite heavy investment in industry on a socialist pattern, the plans failed dismally. Vast foreign deficits were incurred, and by 1966 the country was bankrupt and Nkrumah ousted. His successors had less grandiose concepts, but did not fundamentally change direction, nor did devaluations in 1967 and 1971 and revaluation in 1973 help much. Until 1965, output kept pace with the rise in population; after that output rose more slowly, and in the 1970s it stagnated in absolute terms, so that real income per head fell quite substantially, and Ghana became one of the poorer countries on the African continent. The collapse in the 1960s of the price of cocoa, the country's main export product, contributed to the failure. But among the more fundamental causes were unrealistic, high-prestige planning, inadequate finance, overmanning, technical incompetence and corruption in enterprises that were supposed to be run on socialist principles, and lack of foreign exchange despite aid and the rescheduling of debt.

A variety of experience

Ghana was not the only country in Africa to experience an actual decline in incomes per head, though in the case of Ghana the decline was one of the most spectacular. These were problems that could be found all over black Africa as the newly independent states tried to overcome their economic weaknesses. There was a great variety of experience to be found among Third World

▲ The leaders of the newly independent countries, like Kwame Nkrumah at this conference in Casablanca, tended to adopt a lifestyle not entirely suited to the needs of their economies. Such conferences publicized the case for economic assistance.

▼ Western medical aid must rank among the finest examples of practical humanity in the modern world. Yet the result has not necessarily been a good one. In many areas, the population increase has outrun the technical means of feeding it.

countries. Their overall rates of growth of output, as well as those in agriculture and manufacturing, were in most cases higher than anything they had previously known, but so were the growth rates of their populations. In some of the middle-income countries, output exceeded population growth to such an extent that the economies were rapidly catching up on those of the advanced industrial nations. Others, especially those among the poorest, fell farther behind, at least in per capita terms, though even they registered substantial improvements on traditional standards during this period.

The poorer countries in particular were also marked by striking inequalities of income. Nevertheless, growth was followed everywhere by a rise in real wages, and wages correlated quite well with national income, even where growth largely depended on cheap labor.

Aid and exploitation
The technical advances to make possible this sustained rise in output came almost exclusively from the advanced countries, as did the improvements in health, in education and in administrative methods. From them also came investment funds as well as aid in the form of technical assistance. There were widespread demands that direct aid to foreign countries should be given at the rate of three-quarters or even one percent of the donor countries' national income, but these rates were not often reached; one-third to one-half percent was more common. Even so, together with the special, one-sided trading concessions to some former colonial countries that were granted at conventions in Yaoundé (1964, 1970) and Lomé (1976), and to all under the Generalized System of Preference (GSP, 1968), this aid constituted a form of generosity on an international basis for which there is no historical parallel. However, assistance in the form of loans placed burdens on the poorer economies which they would soon prove unable to bear; and it is also arguable that the longer life that Western medicine was able to bring them led to population increases that overstrained their resources, as birth rates grew and death rates fell.

Doctrines which alleged that it was the advanced countries which caused the poverty of the poor by exploiting them found widespread support in those years, particularly among critics of "capitalism" in the West, and among the elites of the poorest and worst-governed countries in the Third World. Their views were aired at international meetings in which they often had a numerical majority. The high point of their attacks may well have been reached in 1974, at the United Nations meeting in April and at meetings on population in Bucharest, on food in Rome, and on the law of the sea at Caracas. However, the allegations that the rich countries had become rich by exploiting the others, founder on the fact that their trading connections with the Third World countries were much too small to have such an effect. This view also ignores the organized price rises of Third World goods such as tin and oil, as well as the aid flowing into these countries.

Whether Third World poverty was actually caused by the rich countries is, however, a much more complex issue. Some regions were doubtless induced to specialize in commodities which were later subject to strong price fluctuations. Many were inspired by the example of the West to try crash development programs, with disastrous results. In the unstable political conditions prevailing in many countries after independence, others still were persuaded to buy expensive arms – spending an average of some four percent of their national income on them – which helped to keep them poor. Yet all achieved high growth rates, and several of them managed without much difficulty to break through to advanced modernity, quite apart from those fortunate enough to find oil within their borders. The alternative concept of a stable peasantry and a traditional artisan population, untainted by contact with the West, working to supply their own needs and kept down in numbers by high death rates unaffected by Western medicine, can be made to appear attractive. Given the international contacts of the past few centuries and the new patterns of world history, it was, in the 1960s, scarcely a realistic alternative.

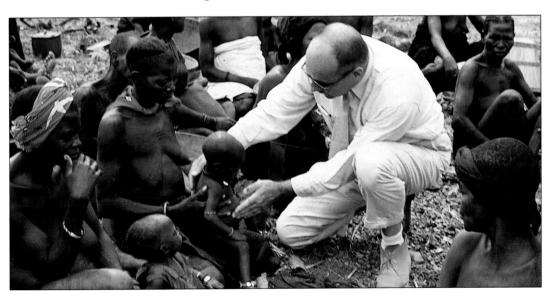

1973 - 1989

THE
WORLDWIDE
NETWORK

Time Chart

	1974	1975	1976	1977	1978	1979	1980	1981
Industry	• Sep: 17 oil companies build a pipeline from the North Sea to the UK	• May: Peru nationalizes Gulf Oil de Peru • 11 Aug: British Leyland nationalized (UK)	• 26 Feb: Contract signed between the British government and oil companies Shell and Esso regarding North Sea oil	• Jun: Merger of French truck producers SAVIEM and Barliot with the Renault group (Fr) • Aug: French national control of the subsidized steel industry commences	• Apr–Nov: China buys US wheat in bulk • Aug: French motor company Peugeot–Citroën takes over Chrysler Europe, becoming Europe's largest car producer	• May: Renault builds a motor plant in Portugal for $400 million (Fr/Port)	• May: US government aid for Chrysler due to decreasing car sales • Sep: Discussion on a joint agricultural policy between UK and France	• Jan–Mar: Introduction of a qu system in the steel industry of the EC countries to reduce production surplus • Sep: Merging of Coneco and DuPon de Nemours (USA)
Technology	• West German–French satellite *Symphony* begins operation	• 1 Oct: US scientists warning about the environmental dangers of CFCs – refrigerant and aerosol propellant gases	• Development of glass fiber cable for use in telecommunications		• First demonstration of compact discs (FRG)	• 28 Mar: Accident at the Three Mile Island nuclear power station due to a defect in the cooling system (USA)	• 5 Sep: Opening of the largest road tunnel in the world, the St. Gotthard tunnel in Switzerland	• 12 Apr: Launch o the first space Shut *Columbia* (USA)
Finance	• Jan: French franc begins flotation for six months • Oct: General Arrangement to Borrow (GAB) of the "Group of Ten" renewed • Nov: Introduction of the currency unit Arcru by Arab countries to recycle income from sale of oil • Dec: US citizens are permitted to buy, sell and own gold for the first time since 1933	• Jan: US Treasury holds its first auction to dispose of a portion of its gold holdings • Feb: Central Banks of the Arab countries establish an Arab monetary fund • Dec: Meeting of the ministers of finance and the governors of the central banks of the "Group of Ten" countries in Paris. They agree to coordinate the sale and purchase of gold by their central banks	• Jun: The "Group of Ten" countries, Switzerland and the Bank for International Settlements (BIS) grant $5.3 million credit to the UK • Sep: Mexican government allows the peso to float due to precarious foreign exchange situation • Suspension of the official gold price by the IMF. Legalization of foreign exchange rate flotation	• 10 Jan: IMF grants the UK a credit of $3.9 billion. The central banks of the "Group of Ten", Switzerland and the BIS agree on a medium-term credit facility of $3 billion to the Bank of England • Apr: New fixing of foreign exchange rates by the Scandanavian countries. Sweden withdraws from the European currency system • Oct: Flotation of the pound (UK)	• Jan: Measures taken by the US government to strengthen the declining dollar and to counter increasing inflation, coordinated with the Federal Reserve Board and other central banks • Mar: Severe foreign exchange restriction in Japan • The West German Bundesbank and US Treasury agree on a duplication of the swap credit lines	• 1 Jan: Introduction of the European Monetary System (EMS) by the EC • Feb: Credit base of the IMF strengthened by the introduction of supplementing credit facilities (Witteveen facility) • May: GAB of the "Group of Ten" renewed for a further five years	• May: Meeting of 115 bankers and governors of central banks from 23 countries to discuss the financing of oil imports • Sep: New currency (shekel) introduced in Israel as a result of inflation • Sep/Oct: Annual meeting of the IMF and World Bank discusses the external debts of the developing countries	• Jan: European Monetary Fund (EM established • Jan: European Currency Unit (ECU introduced • Mar: New fixing o the exchange rates EMS. Devaluation o the Italian lira and th French franc and revaluation of the Deutschmark and th Dutch guilder
Economic Policy	• Oct: US president Ford publishes his economic program to counter inflation and the energy crisis • Nov: US secretary of state Kissinger proposes a "common loan and guarantee facility" by the OECD to recycle $25 billion income from sale of oil • Dec: Declarations of Ayacucho and Guyana demand the economic independence of Latin American countries and economic cooperation	• Jan: Establishment of an oil facility by the IMF to assist countries affected by the oil crisis and to recycle income from sale of oil • Nov: First economic summit of the six major Western industrial countries in France. Declaration on the need for recovery from recession • Dec: Conference on International Economic Cooperation in Paris • Sep: US government begins a $100 billion program to become self-sufficient in energy	• Jun: Second economic summit in Puerto Rico. Consultations and cooperation between the seven major western industrial countries pledged to continue • Oct: Labor party demands the nationalization of banks and assurance companies • Sep: French prime minister Barre publishes a plan to counter inflation	• May: Third economic summit in London. Conference members pledge cooperation on economic problems • May: CIEC decides in Paris to establish a common fund to help stabilize the prices of certain commodities • Bullock report on industrial democracy published. Industry does not accept the report, claiming it gives the trade unions too much power (UK) • Steel industry crisis begins in the EC countries	• Jun: Annual meeting of the OECD. International coordinated action demanded to stimulate the world economy • Jul: Economic summit in Bonn. Common strategy of mutually reinforcing action to promote world economic recovery • Dec: Increase in the oil price of 14.5% by OPEC, in the second round of increases	• Mar: 9% increase in the oil price by OPEC, with a further increase of 23.7% in June • Jun: Fifth economic summit in Tokyo of the seven major Western industrial nations. Secret agreement on trade with China • Jun: 33rd session of Comecon in Moscow. New methods of economic cooperation by the member countries proposed • Jul: US president Carter issues a report on the economic situation in the USA and announces anti-inflationary measures	• Jan: US president Carter imposes restrictions in trade with the USSR as a consequence of its invasion of Afghanistan • May: Sixth economic summit in Venice of the major Western industrial nations. Declarations on the world economy and on Afghanistan • Council of the EC confirms its intention of strengthening the EMS as means of reaching the aim of monetary integration	• Feb: US president Reagan presents his economic program reducing the budge deficit and taxes, an increasing the defen budget (USA) • Mar: 26th party session of the CPSU decides on principle of further economic development • Aug: Declaration o Tegucigalpa. Middle American countries demand to be bette integrated into the world economy
International	• Jul: Conference of Kingston held by 44 African, Caribbean and Pacific countries. Association with the EEC discussed • Sep: Agreement between the six major industrial nations on limitation of the governmental support of export finance • Sep: Comecon takes up informal contacts with the EEC	• Feb: Agreement between the EC and ACP (African, Caribbean, Pacific) countries to regulate trade, financial and industrial cooperation (Lome agreement) • May: UNCTAD conference in Nairobi. Problem of north–south dialog and a program for the use of raw materials discussed • Mar: Second UNIDO conference in Lima. Declaration on industrial development and cooperation • May: Establishment of an $800 million fund for developing countries by the OEEC	• Feb: COMECON publishes a plan for economic cooperation with the EC • May: UNCTAD conference in Nairobi. Problem of north–south dialog and a program for the use of raw materials discussed • May: Establishment of an $800 million fund for developing countries by the OEEC	• Jan: Agreement on financial cooperation between the EC and Egypt, Syria and Jordan signed • Mar: Opening of the UNCTAD conference on the establishment of a fund for raw materials • Nov: Beginning of dialog between the EC and ASEAN countries	• Feb: Agreement between EC and EFTA on the regulation of the steel trade • Mar: Vietnam becomes the tenth member of Comecon • Sep: Agreement between Japan and several Arab countries to regulate the oil trade	• May: OECD demands a greater use of coal from its members in order to reduce the consumption of oil • Jul: OPEC increases its fund for supporting developing countries • Jul: World agricultural conference discusses the UN development program on the problems of developing countries	• Mar: China becomes a member of World Bank, IFC and IDA instead of Taiwan • Jun: Meeting of the ministers council of the OECD countries demands restrictive monetary policy • Jun: UNCTAD conference in Geneva signs agreement on the establishment of an international fund for raw materials	• Greece becomes tenth member of the EEC • Apr: Meeting of th "Group of Five" of th IMF. US criticism of government subsidie in Europe • Jun: Meeting of th minster council of th OECD. Demand for a liberalization of trade and economic cooperation with developing countrie
Misc.	• Watergate scandal initiates impeachment proceedings against US president Nixon (USA)	• 30 Apr: Surrender of South Vietnam to the Communist forces of North Vietnam	• 2 Jul: Unification of Vietnam and its proclamation as a socialist republic		• New leadership in China proclaim a new economic policy of industrialization	• Beginning of the Islamic revolution in Iran under Khomeini • Military interention in Afghanistan by the USSR	• Wave of strikes in Poland. *Solidarność* trade union formed • Beginning of the Gulf War as Iraq invades Iran	• Martial law under General Jaruzelski proclaimed in Polan *Solidarność* banned

2 (1982)	1983	1984	1985	1986	1987	1988	1989
• New principles [m]ergers in the US. ... control over [memb]ers of competing	• Mar: Discussion on leaving farmland fallow because of production surplus and sale problems (USA) • Dec: Mass redundancies in Talbot motor company (Fr)	• Apr: Nippon Kokon (Jap) gains a half share in US National Steel Corporation • Dec: Toxic gas leakage at the US chemical company Union Carbide in Bhopal, India	• Feb: Discussion on the shutting down of the nuclear plant at Zwentendorf (Aut) • Jul: Greece signs a contract for 40 Mirage 2000 with the French company Dassault	• Apr–Oct: Food destroyed in Europe due to contamination following explosion at Chernobyl nuclear plant near Kiev (USSR) • Jul: Fish killed in Mosel River by cyanide poisoning (FRG)	• 18 Sep: Polish cardinal Glemp signs the foundation document of a benefit institution for agriculture sponsored by the Catholic church (Pol)	• Jul: 166 people killed by gas explosion on the British oil rig Piper Alpha in the North Sea • FAO conference in Rome discusses the locust problem in Africa and Eastern Mediterranean	• Strikes by Soviet miners in the Kuzbass and Donbass regions force concessions from the government over pay and conditions
[te]st of Pershing 2 [missi]les by the USA [...gr]ound boring in [U]SA and USSR [reach]es a depth of	• Beginning of the Strategic Defense Initiative (SDI) program (USA) • Development of a microchip with 1 billion bits per qcm (Jap)		• Testing of energy production by means of laser-fired nuclear fusion in Japan and the USA	• 28 Jan: Space shuttle *Challenger* explodes on takeoff killing its seven astronauts • Toshiba/NEC (Jap) and Texas Instruments (USA) develop a four megabit memory chip	• Laying of a glass fiber cable (TAT 8) across the Atlantic Ocean • Beginning of boring of the Channel Tunnel at Calais (Fr/UK)	• Stealth bomber developed (USA)	• 13 Nov: Opening of the LEP particle accelerator (Fr/Switz)
[...]: New fixing of [exch]ange rates in the [.] Devaluation [of the] Belgian and [Luxe]mbourg francs, [D]anish crown, the [...] lira and the [Fren]ch franc, with [reval]uation of the [Deut]schmark and [Dutc]h guilder [De]c: Medium-term [mutu]al financial [supp]ort between the [EC c]ountries prolonged [for a] further two years	• Mar: New fixing of exchange rates in the EMS, with a revaluation of the Deutschmark, the Dutch guilder, the Danish crown and the Belgian and Luxembourg francs, and a devaluation of the French franc, the Italian lira and the Irish pound • Jun: Change of Argentinean currency unit from Peso Ley to Peso Argentino • Dec: New peak of the US dollar in Europe	• Feb: New legislation regarding the control of banks and the credit system (FRG) • Sep: New fixing of exchange rates in the EMS. New calculation of the European Currency Unit (ECU) • Oct: Medium-term mutual financial support between the EC countries prolonged for a further two years	• Jul: Bank of Greece joins the agreement of the European central banks on the EMS, but does not become a part of the exchange rate fixing • Jul: New fixing of exchange rates in the EMS, with devaluation of the Italian lira and revaluation of all other currencies • All international financial institutions allowed to hold ECU	• Jan: Currency reform in Israel. New shekel replaces the old shekel • Apr: New fixing of exchange rates in the EMS, with devaluation of the Irish pound and French franc, revaluation of the Deutschmark, Dutch guilder, Danish crown and Belgian franc • Oct: Annual meeting of the IMF and World Bank. Consultations on the situations of the developing countries and their external debts	• Jan: New fixing of the exchange rates in the EMS. Revaluation of the Deutschmark, Dutch guilder and Belgian franc • 19 Oct: Worldwide stock exchange crash due to disturbances in the international financial markets • 3 Dec: West German Bundesbank and other European central banks decide to reduce the head interest rates to avoid further financial disturbances		• Japanese yen overtakes the US dollar • 16 Oct: Worldwide stock market crash due to failed takeover bid. Markets steadied by US Federal Reserve • Dec: EEC agree schedule for economic and monetary union
[...]: Over three [milli]on unemployed in [U]K [...]: Economic [sum]mit of the seven [maj]or industrial [coun]tries in Versailles [dis]cuss the reasons [an]d consequences [of th]e world wide [rece]ssion [...]: Beginning of a [...]-month price and [wag]e freeze (Fr) [De]c: West German [gov]ernment publishes [pr]ogram toward the [crea]tion of work for the [purp]ose of economic [reco]very	• Jan: British prime minister Thatcher publishes an economic policy aimed at curbing inflation and reducing the budget deficit (UK) • Feb: Soviet leader Andropov announces economic measures to counter the lack of economic discipline • Mar: US president Reagan announces his intention to procure $5 billion for the creation of work (USA) • May: Economic summit of the seven major industrial nations discusses measures for the recovery of the world economy	• Jun: China encourages foreign investment by the establishment of four special economic areas • Jun: Economic summit of the seven major industrial nations in London to discuss the world economic situation • Sep: US president Reagan refuses governmental support for the US steel industry • Consultations by the French government to counter the Lorraine steel crisis (Fr)	• Jan: Chairman of the EC commission J. Delors publishes a plan for the realization of European integration by the establishment of a European market • May: Economic summit of the seven major industrial nations in Bonn. Measures against inflation and a reduction of budget deficits agreed • Jun: Key speech by new Soviet leader Gorbachev on the future of economic development in the USSR. Announcement of the policy of *perestroika* (reconstruction)	• Jan: Sudden collapse in the price of crude oil. OPEC conferences discuss the new situation and demand a reduction in oil output • Feb: Arab League agrees on the establishment of a free trade area due to oil price collapse • Jun: Economic summit of the seven major industrial nations in Tokyo • Sep: Meeting of the "Group of 77" developing countries to discuss their external debt crises	• 22 Feb: Intensive economic cooperation and a reduction of differences in the balance of payments agreed by the major Western industrial nations (Louvre accord) • Feb: EC and the USA plan common measures against Japanese trade restrictions and trade policy • Apr: Conference on external debt among the developing countries discusses a possible suspension of those debts	• Apr: Conference of the "Group of 77" developing countries on the global system of trading preferences • Jun: Economic summit of the seven major industrial nations discusses international debt problems and reduction of agricultural subsidy • Aug: Conference of the "Group of Eight" in Rio de Janeiro on possibilities for economic growth in the Third World	• Polish external debt of $39 billion. Promise of US and EC aid. *Solidarność* prime minister T. Mazowiecki (elected in August after elections in May) in October invites Adam Smith Institute (UK) to advise on privatization
[J]an: IDA reduces [cre]dits to developing [cou]ntries due to lack [of f]unds [O]ct: UN General [Ass]embly demands [tha]t no credits be given [to S]outh Africa by the [De]c: No agreement [rea]ched on quotas of [crud]e oil output after [OP]EC conference	• Jan: Switzerland becomes a member of the "Group of Ten" of the IMF • Jan: EC countries agree on new fishing quotas • Mar: OPEC agrees on a reduction of the oil price to $5 and a limitation of the daily production	• Jun: Third summit of Comecon in Moscow. Declaration on intensified economic cooperation • Oct: New fixing of the quotas of crude oil production by OPEC in Geneva • Nov: Third Lome agreement signed on economic relations between EC and ACP countries	• Jan: Iran, Turkey and Pakistan agree on the establishment of an organization for economic cooperation • Sep: Special meeting of GATT demands a new round of tax and tariff negotiations • Oct: UNCTAD conference in Geneva publishes declaration on economic support for developing countries	• Jan: Spain and Portugal become eleventh and twelfth members of the EEC • May: EFTA demands the liberalization of international trade • Sep: Meeting of the GATT country ministers. Soviet Union requests affiliation with GATT	• 15 Feb: EC commission publishes Delors package, which includes reformation of agricultural policy, establishment of a structure fund and the introduction of new budget principles • Aug: World trade conference UNCTAD demands cooperation between industrial and developing countries	• 25 Jun: Beginning of official relations between the EC and Comecon • Sep: Annual meeting of IMF and World Bank provokes an "anticonference" of those organizations' critics	• Nov: EC discussions on the new situation in Eastern Europe
[Apr:] Argentina [cap]tures the disputed [Falk]land Islands, but [the]se are retaken by [Brit]ain six weeks later	• 21 Jul: Lifting of martial law in Poland • 1 Sep: Korean passenger plane shot down by Soviet air force		• Mikhail Gorbachev succeeds Constantin Chernenko as general secretary of the CPSU, and implements a widespread reform policy (USSR)	• US F-111s bomb Tripoli in reprisal for Libyan terrorist activities (Lib)		• UN ceasefire brings an end to the Gulf War between Iran and Iraq • Large earthquake in Armenia with great loss of life	• 4 Jun: Army crush demonstrations in Beijing (China) • 9 Nov: Berlin wall opened after leader E. Honecker ousted (GDR)

Datafile

So dramatic were OPEC's oil embargo and price rises of 1973–74 that they may be seen as the end of the long postwar boom under American leadership. Higher oil prices redistributed world income away from the West and inaugurated a long period of "stagnation", years of slow or zero economic growth coupled with rising prices. Gradually the industrialized world reduced its demand for oil and developed other sources, until 1986, when oil prices tumbled.

▼ Middle Eastern dominance of the world oil market was well established in 1980. The Soviet Union and China jointly, and Central and South America, owned larger extracted reserves because of the demands of their considerable populations, but their proved reserves were comparatively small.

OPEC members 1973	
Middle East	**Africa**
Abu Dhabi	Algeria
Iran	Gabon
Iraq	Libya
Kuwait	Nigeria
Qatar	**South America**
Saudi Arabia	Ecuador
Far East	Venezuela
Indonesia	

▲ **By 1973, almost as many members of OPEC were located outside the Middle East as within that area. The driving force had, however, been Saudi Arabia, with its huge proven reserves and small population, which had been willing to underwrite output restrictions in order to raise oil prices and OPEC revenues.**

▼ **Other primary commodities became more expensive in 1973 as well as oil. The price effects of the two oil crises in 1973–74 and 1979–80 can be clearly identified, as can the slump of 1985–86. Although commodity prices in general were more erratic than oil prices in the 1970s, in the 1980s their decline was more gradual.**

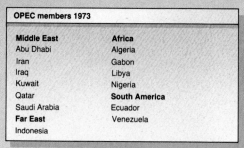

World oil reserves 1980

- Other recoverable
- Proved reserves
- Extracted

Tonnes (billions)

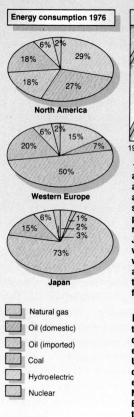

Energy consumption 1976

North America
29% 2% 6% 18% 18% 27%

Western Europe
15% 2% 6% 20% 50% 7%

Japan
1% 2% 3% 6% 15% 73%

- Natural gas
- Oil (domestic)
- Oil (imported)
- Coal
- Hydro electric
- Nuclear

World oil and commodity prices

Other commodities

Oil

Index (1982=100)

1973 1976 1979 1982 1985 1988

◄ **Japan, North America and Western Europe all drew upon coal, hydro and nuclear power, to supply roughly similar proportions of energy, but relied mainly upon oil. Japan was particularly vulnerable to disruptions of world oil supplies since about three-quarters of her total energy in 1976 came from oil.**

► **Vast experience in the application and development of oil extraction technology gave United States firms a competitive advantage in exploiting oil under the North Sea bed. Norway and Britain otherwise allowed their own companies the lion's share of the remaining sites they claimed.**

North Sea oil ownership 1977
5% 1% 7% 2% 13% 43% 26%

- USA
- UK
- Norway
- Holland
- Belgium
- France
- Italy
- FRG
- Canada

The end of the long postwar boom might be dated to the rising unemployment and inflation of 1968–70, or it might be seen as coming with the explosion of primary product prices in 1972. In that year the pressure of demand caused by reflation of all the industrial countries' economies at once reversed the downward trend of the terms of trade between manufactures and primary products. More expensive food and raw materials cut back Western spending power. Measured by rates of economic growth, the depression associated with tight monetary policies and the oil crises of 1979–80 could be regarded as the end of the boom, for on average world growth continued at quite respectable rates during the 1970s. But the most dramatic economic events of the post-World War II years, those of the first oil crises of 1973–74, are the obvious terminal point of the boom. These years appeared to mark a turning point in the economic balance of power between the West and the poorer countries. In the United States the contraction of 1974 was the

THE OIL CRISIS

most severe since the Great Depression of the 1930s, even though it was far less deep and long-lasting. As in the Great Depression, 1973 and 1974 saw the collapse of major banks such as the United States National Bank of San Diego and the Franklin National Bank of New York.

Middle East oil and OPEC

By the 1970s, Western countries in general had come to rely ever more heavily on a regular supply of oil for energy – in heavy industry, transport, and even in domestic applications such as central heating. Britain and France had withdrawn politically from the Middle East in the years after World War II, but were still highly dependent on Middle Eastern supplies of oil, as were other industrialized countries in Europe, as well as Japan. But the new national governments of the Middle Eastern countries – whether under monarchs like the Shah of Iran or military rulers like Colonel Nasser – were determined to regain control over their own resources, especially oil.

The end of the postwar boom

Oil producers and oil consumers

OPEC changes the balance of power

The search for new oil fields

Reducing demand

▼ Control of huge oil refineries such as this, both of crude oil that was pumped into it and the distribution of the refined products, conferred enormous political and economic power.

The Organization of Petroleum Exporting Countries – OPEC – had been formed in 1960 by five oil-exporting countries: Iran, Iraq, Kuwait, Saudi Arabia and Venezuela. Its formation had been triggered by reductions in the prices that the "Seven Sisters" – the major oil companies' cartel which consisted of Standard Oil (New Jersey), Royal Dutch Shell, Mobil Oil, Texaco, Gulf Oil, Standard Oil (California) and British Petroleum – were prepared to pay for crude oil. Throughout the 1960s, OPEC demands for higher prices and greater participation in oil extraction and refining were deflected, deferred or declined. Tired of such exploitation, OPEC gradually acquired technical expertise and began – especially in Libya – to use cartel-breaking independent oil companies such as Occidental to supply outlets and information denied to them by the Seven Sisters.

A Saudi Arabian attempt at an oil embargo in 1967 had failed because the United States was then producing more oil than it consumed and could therefore supply any shortfall. But by 1973

the position had changed radically: the United States had become a net importer of oil. The opportunity for the OPEC countries to change the balance of power had arrived.

In early October 1973 the Arab–Israeli war began. Arab states reduced oil production and imposed embargoes on both the United States, as a supplier of arms to Israel, and The Netherlands, which was closely identified with Israeli foreign policy. World oil supplies fell by approximately seven percent in the following quarter. Within a month the European Community had taken a pro-Arab position on the Middle East, to which the Arabs responded by easing European oil shipments. The Japanese adopted a similar stance. However, oil was still in very short supply in the West, and American, Japanese and German companies bid up oil prices to a peak of $16–17 a barrel, compared with an official pre-crisis price of $3. Inflation in the West rose as governments reacted by implementing policies which were aimed at contracting demand – a completely inappropriate response since price rises were triggered by the external oil shock.

Economic reactions

High oil prices boosted the incomes of net oil producing economies at the expense of consumer states. Since countries measured their incomes in different currencies, redistribution created an international transfer problem. An oil-importing country was not only obliged to give up consuming some other goods and services in order to pay more to oil producers, but it had to pay in foreign currency – dollars. The demand for more foreign currency tended to drive down the exchange rate,

making all imports more expensive and exports cheaper, at least relative to the goods of oil-exporting countries. This balance of payments adjustment to the oil price increases varied in magnitude between countries, not only in relation to the scale of their reliance on imported oil but also in relation to their ability to borrow. Those oil importers with highly developed capital markets, notably Britain and the United States, were destinations for unspent oil money from OPEC members with low "absorptive capacities". Saudi Arabia and Kuwait owned enormous oil deposits but their populations were small, and, unlike Iran or Iraq, they could not immediately spend all their new income on development programs or armaments. So they placed their surplus earnings on short-term deposit in major world financial centers. The capital inflow to London and New York eased or deferred British and American balance of payments adjustment to the higher oil prices.

The switch in expenditure to pay for imports was not generally fully compensated by an increase in demand for exports by the OPEC countries. But the appropriate Western government response, a fiscal policy designed to encourage expansion and maintain output and employment, was not adopted. Western leaders were more worried about inflation than unemployment and so were willing to lose jobs in order to hold down price rises. They failed to realize that inflation in 1974–75 was not driven by too much domestic spending but by rising import costs.

Less developed countries with poor credit ratings were less able to ease the adjustment process by borrowing. Though they needed little oil

▲ Those political leaders in the strongest position to influence oil prices walked a tightrope. The Emir of Qatar was a traditional Arab ruler whose small state happened to possess vast oil deposits. Although such leaders themselves had little interest in alienating the Western world with oil embargoes and high oil prices, the joint threats of Arab socialism in other countries and of the Arab–Israeli wars pressed them into cutting back their oil production.

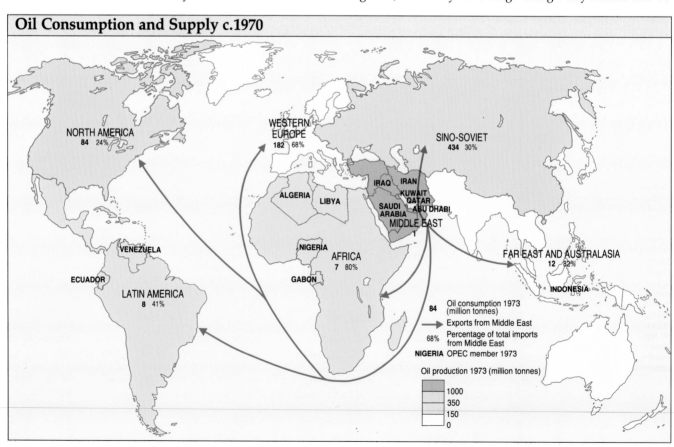

Oil Consumption and Supply c.1970

NORTH AMERICA
84 24%

WESTERN EUROPE
182 68%

SINO-SOVIET
434 30%

IRAQ IRAN
KUWAIT
QATAR
SAUDI ABU DHABI
ARABIA
MIDDLE EAST
1

ALGERIA LIBYA

VENEZUELA

ECUADOR

LATIN AMERICA
8 41%

NIGERIA

AFRICA
7 80%

GABON

FAR EAST AND AUSTRALASIA
12 82%

INDONESIA

84 Oil consumption 1973 (million tonnes)

→ Exports from Middle East

68% Percentage of total imports from Middle East

NIGERIA OPEC member 1973

Oil production 1973 (million tonnes)

1000
350
150
0

Cartels and Commodity Prices

◄ Jamaican bauxite was mined by Western multinationals.

Various other commodity-producing countries tried to band together to emulate OPEC's success, with different results. Six American banana-exporting countries (Colombia, Costa Rica, the Dominican Republic, Guatemala, Honduras and Panama) formed the Union of Banana Exporting Countries in March 1974. An export tax percent on 42 percent of world banana exports, applied by four members of the group, was intended to raise prices. The banana companies reacted strongly. United Brands in Panama began a boycott and Standard Fruit of Honduras stopped buying and exporting from their plantations. In consequence, Panama, Honduras and Costa Rica had to reduce their tax percent by 70–75 percent.

Phosphate suppliers were more successful. Moroccan phosphate rock exporters raised their prices by over 400 percent in 1974. Four other members of the Institute of Phosphates (Algeria, Senegal, Togo and Tunisia) followed, as did the phosphate and phosphoric acid export cartels of the United States. Higher prices encouraged increased supply and reduced demand, however, and Moroccan and American prices fell back dramatically within four years.

Assertion of host-country power over copper resources began at much the same time as with oil. In 1966–67 the Intergovernmental Council of Copper Exporting Countries (CIPEC) had been formed by Chile, Peru, Zaire and Zambia. Five years later all the members except Peru had nationalized all or some of their mines, formerly owned by multinational companies. CIPEC gained confidence in 1972 when American copper companies attempting to block copper sales from nationalized Chilean mines were met by a CIPEC agreement not to provide an alternative supply of copper. Unlike OPEC, CIPEC members produced only just over a third of world output in 1976, although they provided over two-thirds of world exports. On the other hand, poor copper exporters like Zaire, Zambia, and Papua New Guinea relied on copper for 50–95 percent of their export earnings. Nonetheless CIPEC agreed first a 10 percent cut in exports and then a 15 percent reduction in production, though this was not strictly adhered to by members. The cartel was formally abandoned in 1976.

◄ Arab economic and political power in 1973 was based on substantial control of world oil supplies. Exports from the Middle East dominated Western European, Soviet, Chinese, African, Far Eastern and Australasian oil imports. Some of these areas, in particular the Soviet Union, were major oil producers and their oil imports were small. But most were entirely dependent on imports for their oil supplies. Any disruption to those supplies was a real threat to their transport systems.

compared with the industrialized countries, their transport systems had become dependent on oil imports and they were far less able to meet the higher prices. Compared with the maximum of $1–2 a barrel which the oil companies had taken before 1973, the payments now required by OPEC were enormously exploitative, amounting to $10 or more on production costs of 10 to 30 cents. Certain Middle Eastern producers aimed to cushion price rises for selected Muslim countries, and special facilities were made available by Venezuela and Mexico to Central American countries. But for some states the only way out appeared to be the replication of OPEC's coup in other commodities, and various other groupings were formed. The closest approach to another OPEC was the International Bauxite Association. Jamaica led the way in March 1974 by establishing that bauxite revenues should be linked to aluminum prices. Jamaica's revenue jumped by almost seven times. All the other Caribbean producers and Guinea followed suit; only Australia among the principal bauxite suppliers remained aloof.

In general, such policies did not work very effectively because there were too many suppliers and their interests were too diverse. If they managed to agree to restrict output so as to allow prices to rise, it was always in the financial interests of individual countries to renege on the agreement and supply more of the commodity at the now higher price. If all the signatories did so, then the price would fall back to that of the free market. OPEC's unusual solidarity stemmed from the links of a common religion among the principal suppliers and a shared antipathy to Israel, together with leadership by the country most abundant in oil, Saudi Arabia.

▲ Among the larger industrial countries, Britain was unique in having achieved self-sufficiency in oil at the beginning of the 1980s. This position was established by people such as these welders shown at work on the link between two sections of BP's 175km (110-mile) pipeline from the Forties field to Cruden Bay. They are welding from a barge out in the North Sea.

▼ Believing that the economy could not develop solely on the basis of oil exports, Saudi Arabia embarked upon a massive development program intended not only to build oil refineries but other "downstream industries": those relying on oil or cheap energy. The Al Jubail industrial zone exemplified this strategy. Petromin, a Saudi Arabian government agency, and Shell were jointly engaged in the operation.

The response to OPEC

However, even that solidarity was not sufficient to maintain high oil prices for ever. First, recession in the West reduced oil demand; then efforts to economize on oil consumption, either by substituting other fuels or by employing more energy-efficient techniques, became effective. Coal and nuclear power provided alternative primary sources of energy that generated an increasing proportion of electricity during the 1970s. Cars were demanded and produced with smaller, more economical engines, providing a further opportunity for Japanese imports to the United States. General speed limits were introduced to save petrol, and incidentally saved lives. Non-OPEC sources of oil began to expand. The most dramatic development was in the North Sea, where high oil prices and new technology made possible the extraction of so much oil from under the sea that by the beginning of the 1980s Britain was self-sufficient in oil.

In an attempt to avoid a repetition of the events of 1973–74, 16 states formed the International

Energy Agency (IEA) toward the end of 1974. The organization was intended to supervise a system for sharing oil in future emergencies and to reduce the likelihood of such emergencies by encouraging greater self-sufficiency in oil production. In return for sharing the oil of oil-producing member nations – the United States, Canada and the United Kingdom – during emergencies, non-oil-producers accepted in 1976 a minimum selling price of $7 a barrel to protect their investment in new high-cost oil sources.

None of these responses convinced the world that the oil problem had been solved. In 1978 Paul Erdman published his novel *The Crash of '79*, predicting a major war originating in the Middle East, precipitated by the Shah of Iran and the struggle for oil. Fiction proved more accurate than many less entertaining forecasts, for 1979 marked the onset of the second oil crisis, initiated by the overthrow of the Shah of Iran and the disruption of Iranian oil supplies. Oil prices doubled even though the world oil shortfall never exceeded four percent and OPEC production for the year at

tained a new peak. During the first crisis, oil companies had rationed oil supplies and so limited the price consequence of the scramble for oil. By the second crisis they controlled only about one-half of the oil in international trade and could not be so effective. The United States only ceased stockpiling oil in March 1979 and could not access the stocks subsequently because pumps had not been installed. The IEA's emergency sharing system was not activated, despite a Swedish request that it should be, on the dubious grounds that activation might increase the panic. A second opportunity for the IEA to prove itself arose in September 1980, when fighting broke out between Iran and Iraq. By early November oil exports from the two countries ceased, reducing world supplies by slightly more than in the 1979 crisis. Yet oil prices rose from $31 to $40, falling back to $35.5 by the end of the year. Markets were calmer because Saudi Arabia increased production, and the IEA encouraged members to decrease their stocks rather than add to them.

Using oil revenues

OPEC revenues increased to a maximum of $287 billion in 1980, but the new round of price increases stimulated further reductions in demand. OECD countries cut their demand for OPEC oil by 20 percent between 1979 and 1985. By this last date OPEC was supplying as little as 40 percent of the non–Communist world demand for oil, which yielded revenues of only $132 billion. The following year the price of oil fell by almost 70 percent in six months. By 1988 revenues were around $90 billion. Anxious to reduce the economy's dependence on oil, Saudi Arabia had embarked upon massive investment in new industries, such as chemicals, in some of which there was already world excess capacity. As a geographically large country with a small population and a traditional monarch, bordering on populous states with radical governments, Saudi Arabia also felt obliged to acquire the most

sophisticated defense equipment possible. So long as oil prices held up, oil revenues allowed the Saudi government to finance these plans. When oil prices fell again in 1986, Saudi domestic economic strategy became untenable. Saudi Arabia's willingness to adjust its own oil supply in order to maintain agreed prices gradually evaporated as budgetary stringency increased. With the collapse of this pillar of OPEC, the prospect of the cartel wielding market power almost disappeared.

As an oil exporter, the Soviet Union should have benefited from the rise in prices, but the delicate relationship with its oil markets in Eastern Europe made this problematic. The Soviet Union was subsidizing its buffer states by supplying oil at less than world prices. But poor performance by the Soviet and satellite economies made this subsidy an increasingly heavy burden.

▼ New sources of oil were sought and exploited, even in climates as inhospitable as Alaska's, where the oil pipes are covered in frozen snow and the oil-worker has to wear a face mask for protection against the extreme cold. Thanks to the construction of a 1300km (800-mile) oil pipeline, from Prudhoe Bay on the Arctic North Slope to Valdez harbor on the Pacific, Alaska became one of the richest places in the world.

Datafile

During the 1970s the Western world entered a new phase of development; inflation rose along with unemployment, growth of output and productivity slowed. By the end of the decade conservative policymakers were adopting tight monetary policies to deal with what they identified as the principal economic problem. Unemployment, it was increasingly believed, tended to settle at a "natural rate" which could not be shifted by demand management.

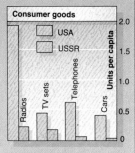

Consumer goods

◄ **Unemployment shot up as inflation began to decline in 1974. In 1979, unemployment rose sharply simultaneously with inflation, but continued rising long after inflation fell. The 1970s eroded the belief that governments could choose the level of spending that gave the desired balance of inflation and unemployment.**

▲ **One measure of economic performance is the ability to provide durable consumer goods. In this respect the Soviet Union showed itself far behind the United States in 1975. Radios, telephones and cars were in short supply. Only in television ownership did the Soviet Union remotely approach American levels.**

Inflation and unemployment

▶ **Inflation is generally an index of political, economic and social tensions. Sometimes these may be largely explained by war expenditures, as in Israel's case. The stability of the postwar settlement in West Germany can be judged by her low inflation rate, while British price increases may reflect the polarized social and economic structure.**

▼ **Unemployment was a waste of opportunity, both for the individual and for society. Sweden and Japan were successful in holding down unemployment rates during the 1970s and 1980s. So far as the official statistics may be believed, Italy was much less so. In almost all countries unemployment rose after 1973.**

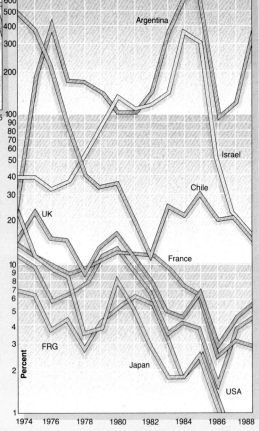

World inflation rates

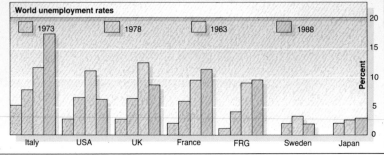

World unemployment rates

Unemployment in the West rose in the 1970s and worsened further in the 1980s. Inflation also accelerated, contrary to what had become the accepted wisdom of the "Phillips curve", whereby it was believed that lower unemployment could be bought at the cost of higher inflation. After the first oil crisis a new term, "stagflation", was coined to account for the coexistence, previously thought impossible, of high inflation and high unemployment. The Keynesian doctrine that a government could spend its way out of a depression became discredited. Instead, monetarist ideas, which emphasized the existence of a "natural rate of unemployment", which could not be reduced by demand management without accelerating inflation, came to be accepted.

More than any other single figure, the American economist Milton Friedman was responsible for this change in attitudes. Friedman argued forcibly that the solution to unemployment did not lie in government policies which aimed to control inflation and unemployment through altering government expenditure and

A NEW TECHNOLOGICAL REVOLUTION

taxes which had the effect of influencing demand for goods and services, but rather in "supply side" policies. These would remove "distortions" and "imperfections" in the labor market, such as minimum wage legislation and high ratios of unemployment benefit to wages.

The American recession of 1974–75 was allowed to take its course without any change in government policy to soften its impact. Monetary policy was tight, and fiscal policy was not used as a control mechanism. Unemployment averaged 8.5 percent in 1975 and remained above 7 percent in the following two years. Policy remained passive, primarily because inflation reached an unprecedented 12 percent in 1974. The entry of more teenagers into the labor force, a reflection of the high birth rates of the early 1960s, and their greater likelihood of experiencing spells of unemployment, account for some of the increase in the numbers of jobless. Nevertheless, the Humphrey-Hawkins Full Employment and Balanced Growth Act passed under the Carter administration in 1978, which enshrined in legislation the earlier target of four percent unemploy-

Recession takes hold in
the West

Unemployment and
social security systems

The black economies

Economic reforms in the
Soviet Union

Technology and the
labor force

Microelectronics and
biotechnology

▼ ▶ **Recession in the West was induced by tight monetary policies. Former car-workers in Detroit queued to cash their unemployment cheques. A more attractive form of support was a public sector job. In Chicago thousands of people crammed the staircases of the Civil Service Commission to apply for such posts.**

ment, was clearly ambitious in aiming to achieve its goal by 1983 or even 1985.

As recession deepened, the typical pattern everywhere was for the numbers of those losing their jobs to increase, while those finding work continued to do so at the same rate as before. The average period of unemployment therefore lengthened. Those joining the unemployment register were likely to be young, unmarried people who had formerly held semi-skilled or unskilled manual jobs with earnings below the national average. In the United States, about forty percent of all teenage unemployment was accounted for by new entrants to the labor force. In Britain, the situation was particularly bad: by 1982 more than half the unemployed had been without work for six months. In the United States and most other countries, the duration of the unemployment was less serious, though very high levels of longterm unemployment were also found in Belgium, Italy and France. In Italy, youth unemployment was particularly high, and Spain and Ireland too suffered especially high unemployment levels.

One of the effects of recession and tight fiscal policies, which kept down wages in the public sector, was an acceleration in the loss of talented people from state-financed areas, especially in medicine, teaching and research, as a growing percentage left for secure employment and well-paid jobs abroad, especially in the United States, or moved to other employment. For the continuing rise in inflation hit consumers' pockets hard as wages and salaries in the state sector failed to keep pace.

▲ Although the Soviet Union's system of central planning ensured full employment, Mikhail Gorbachev's introduction of freedom of discussion and expression, coupled with an increased reliance upon market forces, prompted a public response to Soviet economic problems that would have been quite impossible under earlier Soviet regimes, such as Siberian miners' strike for improved working conditions and accommodation in 1989.

▶ Even in rich countries poverty was not hard to find. The accommodation of these squatters on Venice Beach in the United States contrasts starkly with the high-rise apartments in the background. Rapidly growing, competitive economies generated wealth, but not everybody shared the affluence. Disadvantaged individuals and groups found getting a foothold at the bottom of the social ladder difficult. Sliding down the scale was easy for many of those dogged by ill health, mental problems, addiction to alcohol or drugs, or for single-parent families. How the state social security system coped with such people varied from country to country. Controversy as to whether the benefits of such systems alleviated or perpetuated the poverty problem became intense during the 1970s.

Unemployment and social security systems

Among the reasons put forward for rising unemployment in the West was the form unemployment schemes took. These varied between countries and over time. For instance, in Italy and West Germany benefits were paid by the state; in the United States, employers paid all the cost of the benefit, according to their record of dismissing or laying off workers, so an employer with a good record paid a much lower tax.

Unemployment benefit not only prevented the incomes of the unemployed from falling too low, it was also intended to encourage them to be more selective in their search for work, in the hope that they would be well suited to the job they eventually took, which would improve productivity. But since unemployment benefit in the United States and Britain was around sixty to seventy percent of wages, critics of these allegedly high benefits maintained that, rather than encouraging a search for jobs, such high benefits encouraged idleness and stimulated further unemployment.

The British social security system was generally more comprehensive in providing for the unemployed than those of France or West Germany, but this did not mean that many of those receiving benefit in all three countries were not still very poor. In Belgium, France, West Germany and Italy social security support usually ceased after a given period whereas in Britain it was paid indefinitely. However, in these four

◀ In areas formerly dominated by heavy industry such as coal mining and steel, young people experienced considerable difficulty finding their first job. Traditional employers needed far fewer workers, especially in the recession after 1979. Instead of learning new skills on the job and acquiring work discipline, as they would have done a decade or two earlier, youngsters like these in Swansea, Wales, were inclined to fritter away their time in idleness, enjoying the sunshine whenever they could.

countries family benefits were paid on the basis of numbers of dependents, regardless of income, and tax rates continued to fall as income declined. In Britain, where family income was means tested so that as it increased, eligibility for benefits decreased and a "poverty trap" was the result. A formerly unemployed worker who took a job could find that the increased taxes he was obliged to pay and the benefits lost left him no better off than before.

It was no coincidence that Belgium and Britain experienced worse employment rates than elsewhere. Both countries paid a minimum flat rate benefit, which amounted to about sixty percent of earnings for the first year of unemployment. In 1981 a typical Belgian family with one-half of average earnings would have been 24 percent better off unemployed, and a similar British family would have been neither better nor worse off. France, Denmark and Italy, on the other hand, operated unemployment benefit/income ratio systems which ensured that there was no "unemployment trap", while Germany administered a hybrid system that created a trap only at very low incomes. In all social security systems there was some tension between the demands of economic efficiency, which required the abolition of poverty and unemployment traps, and the dictates of equity, which sought a minimum subsistence rate below which no one, employed or not, should be allowed to fall.

The Nordic bloc was much more successful at keeping down unemployment rates than other European countries: full employment was an important objective of state policy. Finland had the highest rate, of around seven percent in 1987. The rates of Norway and Sweden never exceeded 3.5 percent through the 1980s, and were rarely that high. The oil and gas industries developed in Norway helped, not only as employers but also, perhaps more importantly, in providing a tax yield which helped to fund state measures in

regard to unemployment. Sweden lacked this advantage, so it is even more impressive that the Swedish government helped in achieving the restructuring of the country's industry, and was very active in finding work for and in retraining the unemployed.

In Italy, unemployment benefit was paid as a proportion of lost pay, as in France, so the ratio of benefit to earnings could not reach the high levels of Belgium or Britain. On the other hand, the Italian unemployed might be required to subsist on a very low income indeed. Assessment is difficult, because Italy has a history of massive tax evasion, and the employers' social security contribution of 40.25 percent of wages, was so high as to be a positive encouragement not to pay. A former Italian finance minister has estimated that taxes amounting to seven percent of GDP and 25 percent of actual tax revenue were evaded at the beginning of the 1980s. The Italian black, or informal, economy is generally reckoned to be the largest in Europe, and contributes to enable people to survive, even though official statistics suggest severe impoverishment.

▼ Drug abuse was closely linked with both poverty and crime. Drugs appeared to offer an easier escape from poverty than the job market. Addicts often spent all their money on drugs, leaving nothing for food, clothing or shelter, and frequently turned to crime to pay for more. Their health tended to deteriorate quickly, even if they were not caught up in gang warfare over the supply of illegal drugs. Here a police drug squad in Washington DC picks up an unconscious youth at three o'clock in the morning.

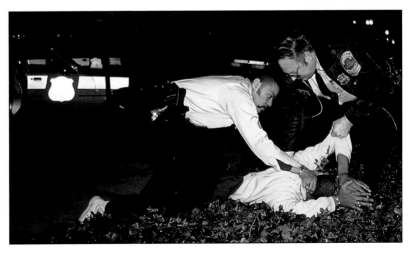

▲ In an attempt to persuade
Soviet agricultural workers to
increase output, the state
allowed them to market
privately the produce of their
small plots. Free markets,
such as this one at Yelon in
Samarkand, demonstrated the
power of private enterprise.
Even here, supply was
constrained by the limited
range of consumer goods and
services that agricultural
workers could buy with their
cash on official markets. More
ominously, the Chernobyl
nuclear disaster of 1986
cast a pall especially over
unregulated growers and
retailers. Buyers could never
be sure of the source of the
fruit or vegetables, whatever
the stallholder said. They
could never be certain their
purchases had not been
contaminated by nuclear
fallout.

Black economies

Increasingly heavy taxation to support complex
and comprehensive social security and defense
systems gave rise in both East and West alike to
expanding "informal" or "black" economies. In
the West this manifested itself in the statistics as
an increasing excess in the amount spent over the
amount calculated from recorded (and therefore
taxable) income as being available for spending.
Originally the discrepancy was merely attributed
to errors of measurement, but by the early 1980s
the divergence had become too large for that explanation to be credible. Estimates for 1980 were
that the alternative economy generated an output
equal to 7.5 percent of GNP in Britain; in the
United States the figure was ten percent, and the
range of estimates for Italy was 15–40 percent. Although the institutions were different, black
economies existed also in the Soviet Union and
other Eastern bloc countries. That of the Soviet
Union itself generated an output of perhaps ten
percent of GDP. Soviet enterprise depended
upon an army of illegal "fixers" to supply the

resources necessary to fulfill plan targets, which
were not available through official channels.

The performance of the Soviet economy

While the West suffered from increasing unemployment and inflation, the Soviet Union remained remarkably free of these ailments. Full
employment was ensured by the centrally planned economy and the social waste of paying to
support unemployed workers was avoided.
Prices were fixed by planners on political criteria
or on a cost-plus basis. Yet the Gorbachev
reforms of 1987 onwards were based upon the
Soviet view that their economy was inefficient
and falling behind the West.

It is difficult to judge whether this view was
correct, for comparison is not simple. One approach is to compute the amount of working time
required to buy goods and services in different
economies. With the exceptions of public transport and rent, all consumer goods needed more
work in the Soviet Union than in West Germany
or the United States in the 1970s and early 1980s.

► Since the first five-year plan, agriculture had been the weak spot of the Soviet economy, squeezed in order to release resources for heavy industry. Farm collectivization had been Stalin's bloody and none too effective means of forcing more work from the peasants. This agricultural show held in the Economic Achievement Grounds, Moscow, was intended both as an encouragement to Soviet farmworkers and as a showpiece. Judged by the Soviet Union's need to import food, exhortation was little more effective than brutality. Farms were too big for adequate management control and their workers, lacking identification with the goals of the enterprise, and any effective incentives, were not interested in boosting productivity.

▼ "We shall fulfill the decisions of the Party Congress" announces the "new" Communist man. Two passers-by take no notice and nor did most of the Russian economy on the eve of Gorbachev's reforms. The centrally planned economy in which the planning bureau, Gosplan, decided what was to be produced, how much and in what quantities, was generally conceded to have failed. Exhortation did not work. People wanted cash incentives and material rewards if they were to exert themselves, but these remained in short supply. On the other hand, unemployment was concealed by overmanning and underproducing.

In 1977 the average amount of house space per person was only 12 square meters, and ownership of consumer durables in the mid-1970s showed the Soviet Union well behind most European countries and the United States. On the other hand, social benefits such as pensions and the guaranteed minimum wage were fairly generous. There were more doctors per head of the population than in the United States or West Germany, and medical care was provided free by the state. Whereas a low-income British family spent 27 percent of that income on housing, fuel and power, a similar Soviet family needed to spend only 5 percent of their income on these items. Life expectancy in 1980 was comparable with that of the United States and Britain, at 70 years old as against 71 and 72 respectively.

The major problem for the Soviet economy was undoubtedly a heavy commitment to defense expenditure. Western estimates of Soviet defense spending in 1982, for example, ranged from 10 to 20 percent of GNP compared with 9.3 percent in 1968. At that earlier date the United States had been spending a similar proportion of a much higher income, but this was reduced to 7.2 percent in 1982. French defense expenditure remained steady at about four percent of GNP at both dates. Military demands on the Soviet economy always took priority over civilian needs and probably exacerbated materials shortages and production bottlenecks. Expenditure for military purposes neither made civilians better off nor enhanced the productive potential of the economy. As weaponry became more technologically sophisticated, an increasing proportion of GNP had to be devoted to defense, if the American effort was to be matched. But the Soviet planning system was increasingly unable to deliver. Hence Gorbachev's "second revolution" – a willingness to reform economic organization (*perestroika*), and in greater openness in the Soviet Union (*glasnost*). Gorbachev's 1987 law on state enterprises was intended to release production units from the clutches of state planners and allow some market

price setting. Seventy large factories were granted the right to trade abroad directly, joint ventures with Western companies were encouraged and cooperatives were allowed. But against the entrenched resistance of Soviet ministers and planing bureaux and against a deep distrust of profits, these reforms made little headway in the first few years, shortages of consumer goods continued and unrest began to mount.

Technological change: the Swedish experience
At the shop floor level, the same new technology that gave advanced Western economies the edge over the Soviet Union was often seen as a major cause of unemployment. Western workers were traditionally inclined to restrict the introduction of the latest techniques if they were able, and expected their trade unions to resist such aims. Economies that continued to grow in the long term either found means of allaying workers' fears or of rendering labor powerless. Sweden chose the first route. The country's centralized industrial relations system, established in 1938, had given Sweden a long period of industrial tranquility. The climate began to alter at the beginning of the 1970s. Technological change, especially computerization, began to give rise to industrial unrest. Information technology penetrated the Swedish economy early on. Sweden quickly developed process control systems, industrial robots, air traffic control systems and computerized office equipment. In the early 1980s computer-aided design and manufacturing systems spread rapidly. Engineering employed nearly half the country's industrial workforce and therefore these changes radically affected work patterns. A legislative reaction began in the early 1970s covering security of employment, the status of shop stewards, the right to board representation, the work environment and industrial democracy. Minimum standards, such as the 1981 regulations on working with VDUs, were laid down.

Sweden's high standard of living and sustained economic growth showed that these measures had been successful in maintaining industrial cooperation while absorbing new technology in the 1970s and the 1980s. Yet by the end of the second decade, large companies like Volvo and Saab were experiencing considerable absenteeism. Their work was not fulfilling and the sense of social obligation or discipline was starting to weaken.

The diffusion and impact of new technology

Although the fundamental breakthrough had been made in the late 1940s and early 1950s, the general public only became aware of microelectronics in the 1970s. The greatest potential lay in communications – in satellites and miniature television cameras and in improving the working of the telephone. But, as it turned out, microelectronics spread faster outside telecommunications, because it was not clear if there really was the demand for improved quality at a higher price. Even teletext and electronic mail, which welded together the techniques of computers and telecommunications, failed to penetrate Western markets as rapidly as had been predicted. Only in France, where the state decided that every household should have a Minitel terminal, did teletext gain much ground outside specialist uses, though it came to be widely used for airline booking in the 1980s.

Independent microelectronic and computer applications showed the most rapid progress. Pocket calculators came into existence using American chips, but in 1971 Japan imported American chips and captured 85 percent of the American calculator market by exporting them back within low-cost calculators. Prices eventually fell so low that calculators became almost throwaway toys, whereas in the 1930s a mechanical calculator had cost as much as two family cars. Digital watches were almost as spectacular and visible a sign of microelectronics but of little fundamental significance for the economy, despite the reduction in watch prices. Of greater significance was the rise of the microcomputer industry. With the falling prices and increasing sophistication of the mass-produced silicon chip, "micros" – computers that could sit on a desktop and needed no attachment with a larger processing unit – could perform many of the tasks of far more expensive mainframe computers. Often built by small companies at low cost, many of them taking advantage of innovations drawn from research and development done by the large computer firms, the rise of the micro bit heavily into the market of the established computer companies. One strategy adopted by the larger companies – among whom IBM remained preeminent – was to concentrate on mainframe computers and largescale business installations, but the need to provide industry standards in the fast-moving world of micros meant that IBM, at least, retained its central role, if not its domination, in this field too.

Microelectronics spread into the motor car industry far more slowly than in other areas since manufacturers at first resisted on grounds of

increased complexity. Only one percent of American Fords contained a microprocessor in 1978. Even so, a small penetration of a large market was worth a great deal. In American motor car production in 1980, the share of semiconductors was valued at $255 million.

The effects of microelectronics on employment were much debated from the mid-1970s. It was feared that mainframe computers would displace clerical labor, but in fact computers generated at least as many new jobs as they destroyed. They required an entirely new production capacity, and created new jobs in retailing, training and providing technical support, as well as creating many jobs in building software, both for mass-market purposes and for specialized tasks suited to individual customers. In general it was the same with the later word processors; there was little evidence of secretarial unemployment. The manufacture and maintenance of telephone exchanges were an exception to this generalization.

Even slower was the development of biotechnology. Biotechnology is a collection of techniques of which the most important is genetic engineering. Originating in Crick and Watson's working out of the structure of DNA in 1953, it was not until the early 1970s that gene transfers were carried out. Biotechnological techniques allow genes from one organism to be inserted into another. Human genes could be introduced into animals whose reactions then provided human growth hormones or other products like Factor VIII, which brought a revolutionary change in the treatment of hemophilia. Around six hundred biotechnology firms started up in the first 15 years after gene transfers became possible, most of them in the United States. The first patent granted for a biotechnology product was for a microbe which could digest crude oil. The first commercial drug, a form of human insulin, was produced at the end of the 1970s. The full impact of biotechnology was only just beginning to be felt in the late 1980s.

◄ Potentially as revolutionary as atomic physics, which, in explaining the structure of matter, confers the power to blow up the world, biotechnology, which is based upon an understanding of the structure of genes, is capable of engineering new life forms. Rosebuds are here being gene-spliced for use in the wine industry – financed by Moët-Hennessy. Uncertainty as to the outcome of the investment and the length of time before commercially viable results were generated meant that companies developing the technology were of necessity farsighted or concerned with other objectives as well as profits.

◄◄ New technology displaced some workers but required that others learn new skills, such as computer programming. Computer-guided robots raised productivity on assembly lines by working faster than men. In this glass factory Swedish-made robots lift French car windscreens on to a conveyor belt. Because they could be reprogrammed, robots increased the flexibility of production. Robots were generally only cheaper than men at high production volumes, so they tended to raise the minimum efficient size of the plant.

▼ Biotechnology's principal contribution in the 1980s was the improvement in strains of plants. This had been carried on for centuries by selective breeding. Biotechnology allowed much faster and more certain results. At the ELF laboratories in France research on the humble sunflower is being done.

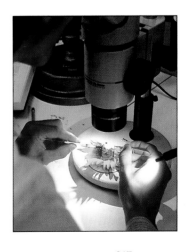

INSTANT INFORMATION

Telegraph and telephone provided instant information over any distance even in 1900, and to these was added radio, effective by 1914. Gone were the days when a fortune could be made by the possessor of a carrier pigeon who knew of the outcome of a battle before anyone else.

The telecommunication explosion of the late 20th century had at least three major aspects: the much increased quantity of information instantaneously available, on monitors and printouts; the enlarged numbers of people able to receive information broadcast on television; and the instant retrieval possibility of stored information. The number of "words supplied" in this way rose by 8 percent a year in the United States in 1960–80, and by almost 10 percent in Japan in 1960–75. By that time, one half of the economic activity of the United States was concerned with the processing of knowledge.

Inasmuch as the economic problem is the problem of uncertainty, the provision of instant information was a key factor. Since costs of knowledge do not vary with size, large firms derived greater advantage from the information revolution than smaller, and so did multinational concerns which, in turn, contributed materially to the international flow of information. For many purposes, the economic distance between countries depended increasingly on the quality and availability of their electronic links rather than on geographic proximity.

Instant information has had some dangerous effects, above all in the case of stock exchanges. These have now become highly volatile, thanks to computer-programed selling which tends to accelerate price falls. This danger has had to be counteracted by an electronic "cutout", to stop transactions in New York when the fall in the Dow-Jones average (the prime indicator of stock prices) exceeds 400 points. Yet, in a typical instance of instability caused by instant information, on 13 October 1989 a sudden fall on the New York exchange by 190 points, or about 7 percent, on the Dow index left the financial world in turmoil; this was a Friday and the westernmost exchange, so nothing could be done until Monday. Then Tokyo opened first, and fell only by 2 percent. Frankfurt, next to open reacted most sharply, partly because many small investors panicked, and partly because foreign holders preferred this market. This left Paris and Brussels in turmoil; but when dealings opened reached London, the worst was over, and after a sharp early fall, the Financial Times share index closed only 70 points, or 3.5 percent down. By Tuesday, things were back to normal throughout the world.

▲ ▶ The teleprinter operator works a machine that was near the technological frontier in the 1930s. Though a great advance over the earlier telegraph tape, it yet seems almost antediluvian compared with the electronic devices available to the office worker of the 1970s and 1980s.

▶ Before the massed monitors in the Hong Kong stock exchange sit operators who are in communication with dealers inside and out. Their access to information allows fast – hence sometimes unpredictable – reactions based on data or VDU screens (inset above).

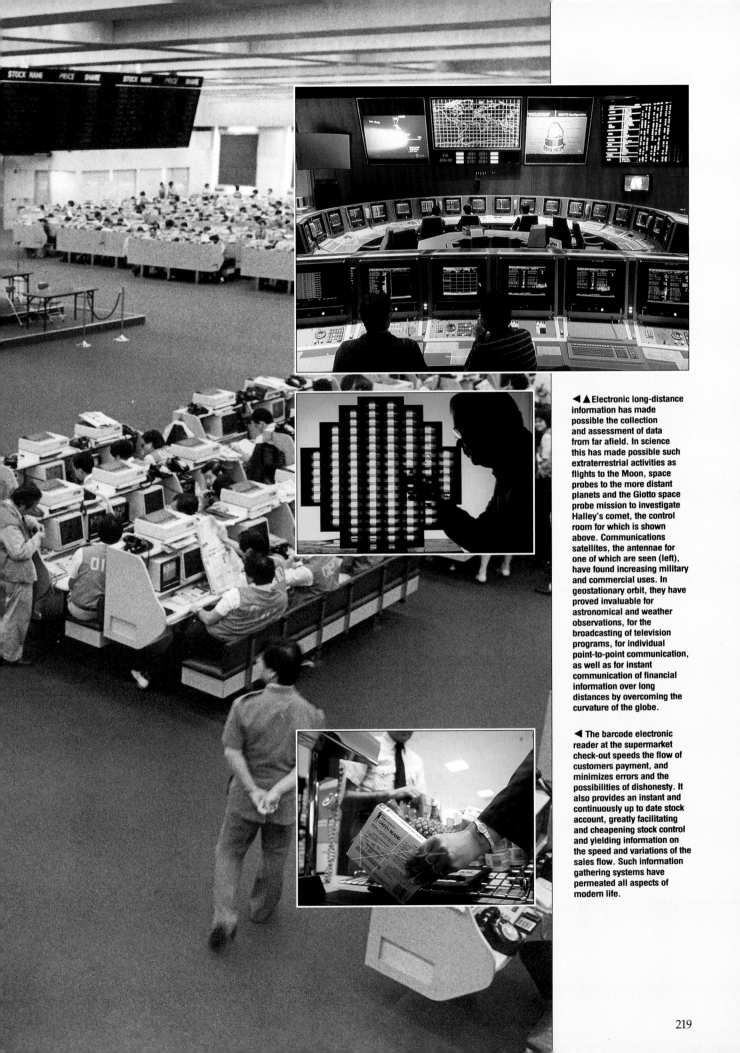

◀▲Electronic long-distance information has made possible the collection and assessment of data from far afield. In science this has made possible such extraterrestrial activities as flights to the Moon, space probes to the more distant planets and the Giotto space probe mission to investigate Halley's comet, the control room for which is shown above. Communications satellites, the antennae for one of which are seen (left), have found increasing military and commercial uses. In geostationary orbit, they have proved invaluable for astronomical and weather observations, for the broadcasting of television programs, for individual point-to-point communication, as well as for instant communication of financial information over long distances by overcoming the curvature of the globe.

◀ The barcode electronic reader at the supermarket check-out speeds the flow of customers payment, and minimizes errors and the possibilities of dishonesty. It also provides an instant and continuously up to date stock account, greatly facilitating and cheapening stock control and yielding information on the speed and variations of the sales flow. Such information gathering systems have permeated all aspects of modern life.

Datafile

Economic growth has it price. Given the high starting level after World War II, the growth of the world economy quickly led to serious pressure on the environment. In the developed world, this was caused mainly by the growth of consumption per head; in the less developed countries, it was caused by the unprecedented increase in population.

Many factors determine the point at which the environment is endangered. Population density is one factor, but soil, climate and the ability to trade also matter. Much of Africa is desert or semi-desert, which must be considered to be overpopulated. Many regions in Asia, too, were overpopulated.

Among the key issues in the debate over the environment were food and energy. Some areas which were traditional sources of food surpluses had now become dependent on imports, and that dependence increased. Energy consumption per head was much higher in the developed world; rising incomes elsewhere put even greater strains on the world's energy supplies.

Population density 1973
Density per sq km

Average crop yields 1975
Tonnes per hectare
- Developing countries
- USA
- World record yields

Maize, Wheat, Soy beans, Sorghum, Rice, Cassava

▲ A major problem for the poorer regions of the globe is the low agricultural yield for which inadequate techniques are partly responsible. Even North American farming did better with extensive methods. Intensive cultivation elsewhere has been able to achieve better results still, but it does not follow that such yields are possible everywhere.

▼ Total land surface is a poor guide to the agrarian possibilities of a region. The cultivable area may be only a fraction of the land surface. Intensive application of capital can make the desert bloom, and new strains can be developed to stand up to extreme conditions. The cultivable frontier is more flexible than is sometimes thought.

World grain trade
- 1981
- 1985

Exports (million tonnes)
Imports (million tonnes)

North America, Australia & New Zealand, Western Europe, Latin America, Eastern Europe & USSR, Africa, Asia

▲ Europe and Asia carry a much larger population per square kilometer than the other continents; parts of them are overpopulated on almost any definition. On the other hand, the low figures for Latin America, the Soviet Union and Africa are averages which hide large uninhabitable regions of desert, mountain or Arctic plain.

◄ North America, and to a small extent Australasia, are now the sole surplus grain regions. The formerly self-supporting or export regions in Eastern Europe and the Soviet Union are obliged to import increasing quantities. Elsewhere, rising population and stagnating technology have widened the gap between demand and supply.

Main food crops 1979

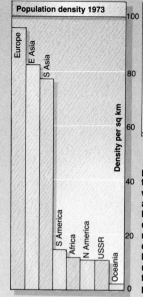

Wheat
35%, 27%, 11%, 10%, 7%, 5%, 5%
- USSR
- USA
- China
- India
- France
- Canada
- Other

Maize
49%, 29%, 9%, 4%, 3%
- USA
- China
- Brazil
- Romania
- S Africa
- Argentina
- Other

Rice
35%, 29%, 16%, 7%, 5%, 4%, 4%
- China
- India
- Indonesia
- Bangladesh
- Thailand
- Japan
- Other

Cultivable land 1981
- Total land area
- Cultivable land

Hectares (millions)

Africa, Latin America, Near East, Far East, North America, Eastern, Europe & USSR, Western Europe, Oceania

◄ Three of the basic food crops of the world are wheat, rice and maize (or sweet corn). Wheat is the main crop in the West, including the Soviet Union and North America, but it also grown extensively in China and other temperate regions. In Europe, its cultivation is labor and capital-intensive, and the area is self-supporting. Canada and the United States provide the export surpluses. Maize production is dominated by the United States, though China is another major grower. In the American economy, it is much used as animal feed in the meat-producing sector. Rice is the basic food of Eastern and Southern Asia. Its intensive production has kept pace with the huge population dependent on it.

Growth in energy use 1980–85
Percent

High income oil exporters, Low income countries, Planned economies, Middle income countries, Upper middle income countries, Industrial market economies

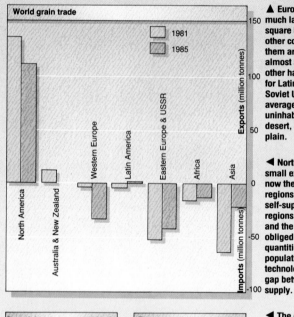

Energy consumption 1985
Kg oil equivalent per capita (thousands)

Industrial market economies, Planned economies, High income oil exporters, Upper middle income countries, Middle income countries, Low income countries

◄ The developed market economies were able, after the oil price shock, to effect considerable savings in their energy consumption, mainly by the introduction of energy-saving techniques. The middle-income countries also did well. It was the poorest societies in which consumption continued to rise fastest, even on a per capita basis.

◄◄ A clear measure of the difference between advanced and less developed economies is their energy consumption per head. Climate may be partly responsible, but most energy is used in industry and transport. The high and rising consumption of the planned economies is due in part to inefficient use rather than to a high income.

THE RESOURCE CRISIS

The general feeling of depression and failure of this period was reinforced by the widespread emergence of fears about the environment and about economic resources on a worldwide scale. The dangers that began to exercise public opinion at this time were mostly of long standing, but had hitherto increased only slowly. Now their exponential growth took on alarming proportions in a number of fields simultaneously, and reinforced the pessimism engendered by economic stagnation and unemployment.

Possibly the most influential publication to catch the mood of the time was a volume entitled *The Limits of Growth* which appeared in 1972. Issued by the Club of Rome, a group of scientists and others called together and financed through the efforts of an Italian industrial consultant named Aurelio Peccei, it summarized in an apparently authoritative way virtually all the current fears about the depletion of resources and the pollution of the environment caused by unrestricted economic growth. An enormous flood of literature, both for and against, confirmed in the following years the widespread concern with the questions the book had raised.

Some developments affected mostly the richer, advanced countries, in which rising incomes caused the strain on environment and resources. Others were problems rather of the less developed or "developing" countries, in which the rapid increase in population gave most cause for concern. However, there were interconnections at many points.

The population explosion
The world's population was indeed growing at the unprecedented rate of 1.9 percent a year. It was not difficult to extrapolate this increase into the future with frightening results. Even assuming that the developing world would go through a "demographic revolution" of the same kind as the advanced countries, so that their falling death rates would be matched by falling birth rates, estimates of the figure at which the total world population would ultimately stabilize sometime in the 21st century ranged from 10.5 to 16.5 billion people – not "standing room only", as some were predicting, but serious enough. Most of this growth would take place among the poorer nations, since Europe, North America and Japan already had almost stationary populations. In some other areas, notably China and India, reductions in the birth rate that had been encouraged by government action were also beginning to have some effect. By 1980–85 world population growth had declined to 1.7 percent a year.

Even at that rate the world's population would double every 40 years, and this implied an un-

precedented pressure on resources. This would be further aggravated by rising incomes as well as by rising urbanization. According to a United Nations forecast made in 1975, 81 percent of the inhabitants of the developed world would live in towns and cities by the year 2000, 41 percent in the developing world, and 50 per cent in the world as a whole; in cities of over 5 million inhabitants there would be 646 million people, of whom 464 millions would be in enormous conurbations in the developing world.

The problem of food supply
The rate of population growth brought the food problem to the fore. Much of the world's cultivable land, it was true, still lay fallow – estimates ranged to well over one-half – and productivity on many acres could still be raised by large amounts. Some estimates put the potential output at 20 times that achieved in the mid-1970s. Even

▼ "The explosive growth of the human population is the most significant terrestrial event of the past millennia." (P. R. and A. H. Ehrlich, *Population, Resources, Environment*).

the United States, a country with plenty of land and a tendency towards extensive rather than intensive cultivation, recorded yields that were double and treble those of the developing world; results in the Far East, and peak performances elsewhere, promised even larger increases. But the necessary fertilizer, machines or drainage represented costs which farmers in the poorer countries could not as a rule afford, while the richer ones among them tended to invest their surplus outside agriculture. Governments, in their turn, frequently pursued perverse policies: they subsidized export cash crops, and kept food prices artificially low in the interest of the city populations, thus discouraging home food production. Food aid from abroad worked in the same direction. Moreover, the infrastructure, especially transport and technical expertise, was usually inadequate in the poorer countries.

In the 1970s and 1980s the developing nations as a whole only just managed to increase their output of food in line with the increase in population; in Africa output per head fell dramatically. Only in the industrialized market economies was output per head rising. These economies, hitherto the main providers of manufactures, were developing exportable food surpluses or sharply reducing their needs of imports of food, while the Third World and Eastern Europe, hitherto the suppliers of primary products, including food, were becoming importers of these commodities. Around 1960, about ten percent of the cereals consumed in Africa, Latin America and the Near East were imported. By the 1970s this had risen to 30 percent. The world still had enough, but the overall balance left unanswered the question of how the poorer countries in Eastern Europe and overseas were going to pay for food from the advanced regions of the world.

In 1979–81 it was estimated that about five hundred million people, including about a quarter of the population of Africa and Southern and Southeastern Asia, were suffering from malnutrition. On current performance, this would rise to one thousand million by the year 2000. In some areas, starvation was an acute problem already. In 1984 the world was shocked into immediate action by reports of starvation in Ethiopia, a catastrophe partly natural and partly artificial. In the Sahel region south of the Sahara, the desert was actually advancing. In the five years between 1968 and 1972 there were four years of drought, but the loss of fertility was made worse by human action. Formerly there had been a stable ecosystem, in which limited numbers of nomadic herdsmen had used the sparse vegetation on the edge of the desert, stocking up occasionally with food and

▲ Drought and the spreading desert have drastically reduced fertile land in Niger as in other parts of Africa in recent years. Climatic conditions may be to blame in part, but in many cases the calamity has been caused by human action, such as the disruption of traditional nomad patterns of pasturing. The countries concerned are too poor and technically too ill-equipped to deal effectively with the environmental disasters that have affected them. They have to be helped by aid from abroad.

▶ Tigrayans from their famine-stricken province of Ethiopia journeyed on foot, carrying their meager possessions, over the mountains to the refugee camps in the Sudan. For those coming from the eastern region the journey took six weeks. Civil war has raged for many years in the area and has aggravated the problem.

The Spreading Deserts

The conversion of fertile land into desert happens in rich countries: the American "dustbowl" of the 1930s ruined many farmers. But in the 1970s and 1980s, deserts were made or grew larger mainly in poor countries, above all in Africa. Apart from climatic change, it was mainly the result of population increase and new technology. Overcropping and the reduction of fallow periods exhausted the topsoil. Rain might then wash it away. On pasture and shrubland, overgrazing and the collection of wood had similar effects. Elsewhere, the sinking of modern wells lowered the water table. Thus the desert advanced in North Africa, in Saharan Africa and in the southern part of the continent.

Famine in Africa drew the attention of the world to the problem. A conference on desertification in 1977 came down in favour of numerous projects designed to reverse the advance of the desert, on the basis of knowledge gained in the West, in the Soviet Union and in China. But by 1984, the United Nations Environmental Program (UNEP) reported that none of these had yet been realized. Some $10 billion had been spent in 1978–83, but almost all of it on infrastructure and preparation, virtually nothing on the desert itself.

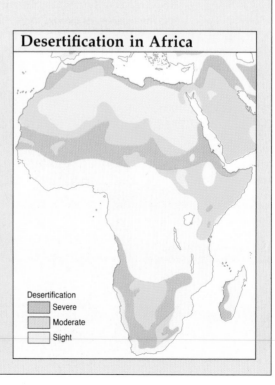

Desertification in Africa

Desertification
- Severe
- Moderate
- Slight

In the course of 1985, millions of African children are likely to die of hunger-related causes. The immediate urgency of saving these children and their families tends to obscure the fact that the survivors of this crisis will inherit a massively degraded environment, barely capable of supporting them without extensive rehabilitation.

INDEPENDENT COMMISSION ON INTERNATIONAL HUMANITARIAN ISSUES, 1984

grazing among the settled farmers further south, whom they also supplied with manure from their animals, and with traded goods. This had been disturbed at both ends when the settled farmers were persuaded to turn to exportable cash crops, and the herdsmen had wells provided which allowed them to increase the numbers of animals beyond the capacity of the grazing lands. For both, the problems were aggravated during later drought years; the output of both groups was cut by half, and the region became a disaster area. By 1984, $14 billion had been committed in aid to eight Sahel countries – $44 a head per annum, equivalent to 17 per cent of these countries' GNP – but no effective method had been found to stop the desertification.

Energy

Next to food, it was energy that was pinpointed as a source of alarm because of the continuing growth of demand. One immediate cause of concern was the oil crisis of 1973–77 itself, but there had been repeated phases of fear over energy supplies, in particular the limited supplies of coal, since the 19th century. Here, though, there was a double potential threat: the exhaustion of supplies, in particular of oil, and the increase of pollution by the emission of carbon dioxide into the air, especially from motor cars, and by the heating up of the streams of water used as coolants for power stations.

Growing populations and their rising incomes did indeed cause the consumption of energy to rise. In 1980, the United States used around ten tonnes of coal equivalent per head a year, the rest of the advanced world around five tonnes, and the developing countries a quarter of a tonne. Yet technical progress also meant a saving in energy consumption: between 1950 and 1978, the consumption of energy per unit of real income had

Alternative Energy

Following the second oil crisis of 1979, efforts to find alternative sources of energy in the advanced countries were stepped up. In spite of the considerable savings in oil consumption in the years 1979–82, and falling relative prices, the momentum continued into the later 1908s. To supplement the traditional sources of water power, mineral fuels, peat, wood and nuclear power, the newly pursued alternatives included the direct conversion of solar power, the biomass, geothermal energy and extracting heat from the oceans, and the use of tidal energy, as well as the return to traditional wind power. Many of these involve enormous capital schemes. Research and development on renewable energy has therefore been largely undertaken by governments or with government support, to the tune of some seven billion US dollars among the 21 member countries of the International Energy Agency in 1977–85 inclusive. Governments also provided subsidies, tax concessions, cheap loans and other incentives.

Direct solar energy, for example for water and space heating, is by now competitive in price in many countries, and its use is expanding. Wind power has proved viable, though only for small units. The biomass, in two forms (waste products, or crops specially grown), is used increasingly either by burning or by conversion into liquid or gaseous fuels. Sugar and maize have been most widely converted. The EEC sugar surplus could provide two percent of the countries' petrol needs, and there is a large potential in other crop surpluses, as well as in specially planted crops.

Among large-scale schemes are tidal projects in Britain and France. Extracting energy from the oceans or from deeper strata of the Earth will require a great deal of further costly research, but may ultimately prove highly competitive.

◀ Solar power allows villages in Niger to receive television programs. A novel technology for using renewable energy sources is coupled with the most up to date electronic technology: the programs, which are broadcast from Niger's state-run television monopoly, are bounced off a satellite. As well as transmitting entertainment, the service is also used for educational programs.

◀▼ Wind-powered electricity generators in California are an example of alternative energy provision in the most advanced industrial countries. In poor countries without coal or oil but blessed with abundant sunshine, such developments offer hope for a breakthrough requiring relatively little sophisticated technology and relatively modest investments of capital.

fallen by 60 percent in the United States and Great Britain. Further, after the oil crisis of 1973–74, its consumption had been curbed very effectively in the advanced market economies, if not in the rest of the world.

The panic over supply was relatively short-lived. Even for oil, the energy source most likely to be exhausted first, the reserves measured in years increased rather than diminished with the passage of time, as rising prices and better technology led to new discoveries. Equally, as the price of oil went up, the exploitation of difficult and marginal sources became more viable. Similarly the estimated reserves of other mineral fuels also went up. Including shale oil, they quickly rose from 102 years to 500 years, not counting nuclear, tidal, solar, wind or other possible alternatives.

Similar revisions were also possible for the estimated reserves of other minerals. Some, like iron or aluminum, were found to exist in practically unlimited quantities; known reserves of others also tended to increase as time passed, through new finds and improved techniques of exploitation, recovery and recycling.

At the same time, some of the newly discovered supplies might need more costly or energy-intensive methods of refining before they entered the market. Optimism about their viability is based on the hope of continuing technical progress. Thus by 1970 the price of coal in the United States had fallen to almost one-fifth of its 1900 level in relation to real wages, that of iron to one-sixth, of copper to one-eighth, and of aluminum to one-thirtieth. Repeated attempts to create world monopolies in metals, like the government-sponsored tin agreement of 1975, seemed to be doomed to failure.

Environmental dangers

Yet the fact that the prophets of doom had so far proved wrong gave no grounds for complacency. At some point, a worldwide catastrophe might prove to be sudden or cumulative and irreversible, and mankind could not afford even one such miscalculation. At least three possible causes of catastrophe were discerned. One was the cutting down of tropical rain forests, particularly in Brazil, West Africa and Borneo: this might fatally interrupt the recycling of the world's oxygen, contributing to the second danger, the accumulation of carbon dioxide in the atmosphere to a point at which not enough heat was reflected outward from the earth, when a "greenhouse effect" would begin to heat up the earth's surface, melting the polar ice-caps. A third danger was damage to the ozone layer, especially that caused by certain ingredients in aerosol sprays. Action to curb this damage began to be taken in the late 1980s. Dealing with the greenhouse effect would require international action on a hitherto unprecedented scale, and there were some signs of agreement between advanced nations on the need for this. As for the first, strict measures would have to be applied to governments which had hitherto been unable to enforce their environmental decrees, even had they wished to do so.

Other, less dramatic, forms of damage were also being brought home to the populations of the industrialized countries. They were largely responsible for the increased awareness of the dangers, and for rising demands for action. The threat to European forests from "acid rain" – acid pollution of the air, and consequently of the water cycle, by chemicals like nitrogen dioxide or sulfur dioxide – began to be noticed in the 1970s. Nitrogenous fertilizers, washed down the rivers, led to the eutrophication of lakes in North America and of large parts of the Baltic, through a complex chain in which oxygen shortage in the water ultimately killed off the fish population. Heavy metals also killed fish around the Japanese coastline and in North America. Rivers and coasts were polluted by the effluvia from the cities and from industry, and ever more European beaches

▼ Tashkent Heliostation illustrates the Soviet Union's interest in developing renewable sources of energy which do not harm the Earth's budget. Some of the southern republics enjoy climatic conditions which make the production of solar energy feasible even at the present state of technology. The efforts that have gone into solar energy research in the Soviet Union, as in the West, do not yet compare with the resources lavished on research on conventional and nuclear energy sources. However, there are indications that both East and West have been induced by signs of environmental damage, particularly the greenhouse effect, to increase their efforts in this direction.

became unfit for bathing. Elsewhere, dams altered the flow of rivers, their scouring action or the deposits they brought with them, In the 1970s, 700 dams a year were being built. Meanwhile, the world's water consumption had risen eightfold between 1900 and the early 1980s, and was estimated to be set to double again by the year 2000. In many areas, the water table was falling to dangerous levels.

Manmade disasters

Occasional disaster lit up a whole scene. One such was the Seveso accident in Italy in 1976, when the chemical TCDD (tetrachloridbenzo-paradioxin) escaped from a factory, poisoning a large surrounding area and injuring numerous people. In 1984, escaping poison gas from an insecticide plant of the Union Carbide Company in Bhopal, India, killed over 2000 people. Another disaster was the explosion in a Soviet nuclear power station in Chernobyl in April 1986 which affected most of Europe. In the same year a fire at a chemical plant near Basle led to a massive pollution of the Rhine. These and other accidents in chemical firms led to the widespread allegation that it was unbridled profit-seeking that endangered humanity, but the danger was no less in noncapitalist economies. There the drive for maximum production at all costs was, if anything, even stronger than in the West. Also, the tradition of citizen initiative was lacking, while bureaucratic power was greater, especially

◀ Coal-fired power stations pollute the atmosphere and contribute very largely to acid rain, which has destroyed large areas of temperate and northern woodlands. Demonstrators in front of the Buschhaus power station in Germany, where damage to forests has assumed large proportions. express a widespread feeling of unease. Installations to reduce the chemical emission from conventional electricity works are expensive to install, but nuclear power stations, an obvious alternative, attract even more protest. Until solar energy becomes more widely available, alternatives are not easy to find.

▼ Effluent pollution in the Rio Martino National Park near Rome shows that progress to improve the environment is slow, even in European countries. Measures are taken more often to cure existing problems than in an effort to seek to prevent pollution occurring in the first place, and the cure is rarely sufficient. Pan-European measures on a cleaner water supply are being adopted, but will take some years to be put into effect.

Industrial Pollution

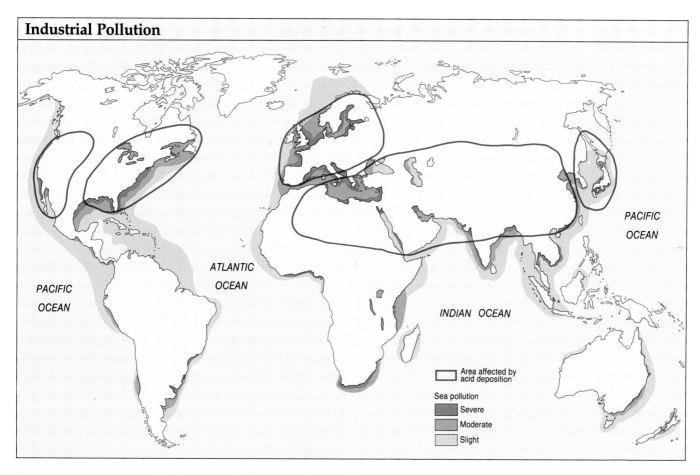

Area affected by acid deposition

Sea pollution

Severe

Moderate

Slight

▲ Acid rain is a product of industrial civilization. Its main causes are the emissions from power stations using mineral fuels, from road vehicles, factories and domestic consumers. The worst concentrations are therefore found in the advanced countries, and especially in those not wealthy enough to afford corrective measures. They do not necessarily affect the exact spots in which the pollution occurs, since it is often carried elsewhere by the prevailing winds. In parts of Central Europe, up to one-half of the woodlands are affected.

▶ Soviet nuclear experts and workmen are keeping a constant check over fields and forests in a 30 km (19-mile) zone around the Chernobyl nuclear power station, where on 26 April 1986 one of the four reactors suffered a meltdown following loss of fission control. The resulting spread of radioactive material was the most serious threat to health arising from nuclear power in Europe to date, and led to more stringent safety regulations in most countries. By alerting the population to the dangers, the catastrophe has led to demands to close down existing stations or, at the least, to stop further building.

if military production was involved. Moreover, Eastern Europe was as yet too poor to afford the costly resources necessary to protect the environment. Examples of environmental failure were the large-scale atomic poisoning at Cheliabinsk in 1958 which went officially unrecorded, massive soil erosion, the poisoning of Lake Baikal in the 1960s and 1970s by two cellulose plants, and, of course, Chernobyl itself. In the 1980s Upper Silesia and the Polish-Soviet Baltic coastlines were considered the most polluted regions of Europe.

The costs of containment

Given enough resources, most of these adverse effects could be contained. Britain's Clean Air Act of 1956 worked wonders in her cities, and the Thames was cleaned up sufficiently to carry fish again. The chemical DDT was prohibited in most countries by the 1970s. Some of the most destructive emissions from motor vehicles, it turned out, could be prevented by a catalyser, developed and applied first in the United States and introduced in the late 1980s also in Europe, though at different speeds in different countries and rarely compulsorily. Increasing numbers of cars were built to run on lead-free gasoline, and while in 1984 this was sold in only one percent of German filling stations, its use spread rapidly since it bore lower taxes and was therefore cheaper, by 1989 a filling station without it had become a rarity. Diesel engines emissions became limited in all European Community countries from October 1989. Finally, substantial reductions in the pollution of the atmosphere by sulfur dioxide from

power stations were agreed to by most Western European countries, with minimum reductions of 40 percent in 1993, 60 per cent in 1998 and 70 percent in 2003. New power stations were obliged to instal smoke-consuming apparatus.

Economists invented the notion of "Measure of Economic Welfare", MEW, in which pollution, congestion and other negatives were deducted from the usual measures of wealth and income, to symbolize the rationality of averting harm as well as of creating good. But the financial costs of counteracting the environmental threats often proved to rise exponentially, and could, in any case, not be afforded by the poorer countries.

Datafile

International economic relations are mainly those of trade and payments, to which, in recent years, has been added aid from richer to poorer nations. Trade, that is the delivery of goods and of the services associated with them, requires payments; if imports are not paid for, indebtedness results. The debt mountain of some countries arose because they absorbed imports without paying for them, or borrowed to finance imports.

Development aid 1980

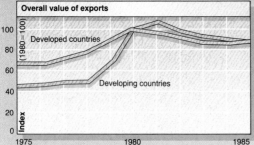

Overall value of exports

▲ The 1970s saw a substantial rise in the price level of exports of the developing countries. This was largely due to the oil price increase which came in two big jumps, in 1973 and 1979. Since 1980–81 prices have fallen again, manufactured prices falling slightly faster than the food and raw materials exported by the developing countries.

► Between 1979 and 1987, there was a remarkable turnround in the developing, capital-importing countries. From deficit in 1979, there is a surplus even after debt charges.

▨ Balance of trade
▨ Net interest payments
☐ Current account

▲ Development aid takes many forms. The totals for 1980 show that the smaller democratic countries of Europe have made greater efforts in this regard than the larger nations. From one point of view, the ratios seem small, especially when measured against the target of 3–4 percent of GNP of the donor country; but it is unique in world history.

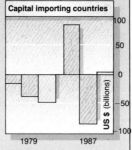

Capital importing countries

◄ The three leading industrial market economies reversed their position astonishingly in the 1980s. Until 1980, the United States still had a positive balance of payments and Japan and Germany a slight negative one; but in the 1980s the huge American payments deficit was financed by the surplus of the other two.

▼ Some developing countries were growing so fast that they were moving out of that category into that of Newly Industrializing Counties (NIC).

Balance of payments

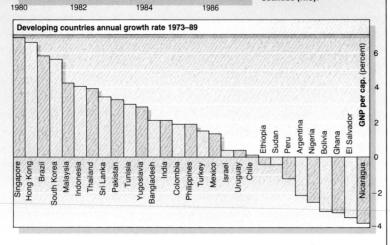

Developing countries annual growth rate 1973–89

The Smithsonian agreement of December 1971, in which the major industrial countries (known as the "Group of Ten": the United States, Japan, Canada, Britain, France, West Germany, Italy, Belgium, The Netherlands and Sweden) had tried to stabilize the exchange rates of their currencies in relation to each other, proved only a temporary stopgap. By 1973, "managed floating" meant that central banks would, at best, try to minimize short-term erratic fluctuations of exchange rates, but that no longer-term stability could be expected. The dollar remained a kind of international reference point, but was itself subject to fluctuations.

Powerful forces made it hard to maintain stability. Large sums were flowing into the OPEC countries after the oil price rises of 1973–74 and 1979, and their recycling by the world's credit mechanism created problems, particularly for developing countries. The so-called Eurocurrency market, a mechanism for switching large short-term funds easily between major centers, added further sources of instability.

In this situation, the International Monetary Fund (IMF) resumed some of its original powers of evening out short-term fluctuations. Under the leadership of the "Group of Five" (the United States, Japan, West Germany, France and Great Britain), it strengthened the role of the dollar as the standard currency against which the others were measured. Gold, on the other hand, was reduced in significance, one-third of the IMF's gold holding being sold and part of the proceeds used to establish a Fund for the developing countries in 1976. In that year, the quota share of the OPEC countries within the IMF was increased, and the total of all quotas raised also. Further, the basis of the "special drawing rights" (SDRs), which had been created to enlarge the lending capacity of the IMF, was changed from gold to a basket of commodities in which the dollar predominated, but no new SDRs were created until 1979. In that year, as well as in 1980 and 1981, US$4 billion annually were added, bringing the total to $21.3 billion.

Towards a European Monetary System

Within Europe, a group of countries had agreed in 1972 to strive to keep their currencies more closely aligned with each other than the Smithsonian rules laid down, varying in effect by only 1.125 percent instead of 2.5 percent above or below par. In 1978 it was decided to strengthen that cooperation still further, and to move towards a full European Monetary System (EMS). Among the innovations were the creation of an European Currency Unit (ECU); an obligation on the central banks of countries achieving payments surpluses, as well as on those countries

INTERNATIONAL RELATIONS

in payments deficit, to take measures to preserve existing parities; and a European Monetary Fund to support the same objective. Though Britain refused to join, and Italy insisted on a wider "band" of six percent within which the lira could fluctuate, the EMS began its active life in March 1979. It had an uncertain start. Its relative exchange rates were changed seven times in four years before the major realignment of March 1983. The "stability" fostered by the EMS was at best relative. It did, nonetheless, provide useful experience for the closer monetary and economic cooperation planned for the future.

Expansionary policies in the United States
The dollar itself remained in a weak position, especially against the Japanese yen and the West German Deutschmark. Together with Switzerland, these countries collaborated with the United States to stabilize the dollar in 1978. Three years later, the United States struck out on its own

under its new president, Ronald Reagan. By a vigorous expansionary policy, fueled by a large budgetary deficit, American output was increased and the country's unemployment cut back. By 1983, the deficit had reached some $100 billion; by 1984 the figure was $170 billion and was still rising. It was approaching four percent of GNP, equivalent to about half the country's net savings.

Given the size of the American economy, such a drastic change of direction was not without significant effects on the rest of the world. Above all, the deficit (or shortfall of savings) within the United States led to a current account deficit in the external balance of payments of enormous proportions, met by a massive inflow (or repatriation) of capital from abroad. Much of this came from Japan and West Germany, where there were more savings than their less than fully stretched economies could absorb. The increasing foreign imbalance and the massive flows of capital be-

▼ The New York Stock Exchange is a highly sensitive indicator of events all over the world, sharp changes in share prices noted here send immediate shock waves round the world.

◀ The products of Western industry reach even the most distant consumers in the Third World. Here, at Senbatic market, in Ethiopia, housewives consider some of the discarded products of Western consumer industries. Perhaps goods will stimulate local initiatives and provide motivation for economic change; but it is difficult to see how the dumping of such cast-offs on the poorer markets of the world can help their development.

▶ China has not only accepted Western technology and American investment; it is considered a reasonable risk even for such advanced financial techniques as the American Express card. It may at present be available to a privileged minority only, but it may also be a sign of things to come.

▼ Brazil has some of the poorest people on Earth, but it also has rich and privileged citizens. It has been the inability of the Brazilian government to control the actions of the rich which has contributed to the country's position as one of the most indebted countries in the world. This enormous indebtedness has in part been caused, and is to some extent counterbalanced, by the capital sent abroad by rich Brazilians who distrust their own economy.

tween these three most powerful Western economies dominated international markets in those years and contributed to their uncertainties.

Any other country in deficit at home and abroad to the extent of the United States would have seen its currency drastically losing in value. Not so the American dollar. High interest rates, reduced inflation and reduced taxes in the United States made the dollar attractive for foreign investors, and far from losing in value, it began an astonishing ascent. By the end of 1983, it had gained 60 percent in real terms on a multilateral trade-weighted basis, and had risen by 40 percent even against the Deutschmark, and by 30 percent against the yen.

By early 1985, there was international pressure to reduce the deficit in the American budget and balance of payments. Some agreement in that direction was achieved at the meeting of the Big Five in New York's Plaza Hotel in September 1985 and in Tokyo in May 1986. Helped also by declining interest rates in the United States, the dollar fell from early 1985 onward as fast as it had risen: within a year, by April 1986, it had lost 20 percent and by May 1987, when the slide was halted, another 13 percent.

The high dollar had itself contributed to the American trade deficit which, in turn, helped to revive growth at least among the advanced industrial countries, though the flow of capital to the United States may have kept down real investment elsewhere. However, the high interest rates ruling in the United States as part of the package increased the burdens on the poorer debtor nations. These nations had taken little part in the deliberations on exchange rates and capital movements. Instead, their interest was focused almost solely on a single issue: how to transfer resources from the richer countries to themselves.

Rich countries, poor countries

Initiatives for what came to be known as the New International Economic Order (NIEO) had begun in the 1960s. Thereafter the developing countries used their voting strength in the United Nations (in 1960, 60 out of 104 votes, in 1980, 115 out of 151) and its agencies, as well as moral pressure on liberal opinion in the West, to keep up the

demand for more money from the West.

The first battles were fought out in 1964 within the United Nations Conference on Trade and Development (UNCTAD), itself the result of pressure by the poorer nations. In 1973 a summit conference of "nonaligned countries", politically rather a misnomer but comprising much the same countries, set forth their claims for more of the world's goods. A "Charter of Economic Rights and Duties of States", launched within the United Nations in 1974–75, emphasized the right of these countries to take over the property of multinationals and other foreign owners on terms decided by themselves. All these demands were broadly supported by the Independent Commission on International Development Issues, made up of distinguished political figures from "North" and "South" (the new synonyms for rich and poor countries). It met between 1977 and 1979 under the chairmanship of Willy Brandt, and early in 1980 issued its *North–South* report, which pleaded for concern for the poorest countries.

To some extent they pushed against open doors. The United Nations and individual Western countries were generally willing to continue aid, especially to the poorest nations. As a proportion of their own GDP, development assistance by OECD members changed very little between 1975 and 1985. In other respects, the political offensive to alter the distribution of the world's goods had, at best, an effect in limited specific areas only. However, in 1973 a major policy change was announced. Instead of as

before supporting projects mainly for improving the infrastructure of creditworthy countries, the Bank would increasingly lend to the poorest for the purpose of reducing their poverty. Using the mechanism of the International Development Association, the World Bank charged no interest for such loans which were repayable only after 50 years: in effect, they bore the character of free gifts and were based on grants by the wealthier nations. (Normally loans by the World Bank bore commercial interest rates and were repayable in 15–20 years.)

Most important of all were the actions of the IMF, which financed various innovatory schemes designed to make loans and credit available to the poorer countries. The result of these measures was that developing countries, which had received less than one-half of the Fund's credits in the 1950s and 1960s, accounted for over ninety percent in the early 1980s. By 1983, some $40 billion of cash flow had been provided for them.

Yet all these international official actions could not prevent serious repercussions from the oil price rises and the recession in the advanced countries on the developing nations. These can be divided into three phases: the impact of the first oil crisis and the consequent stagnation in the West of 1974–79; the second oil price rise and the international debt crisis of 1980–84; and the recovery from both from 1984 onward. It also helps to group Third World countries into three categories: oil exporters, middle-income oil importers and poor oil importers (though for some purposes, the centrally planned economies in Asia, Africa and the Caribbean are best considered separately).

While the OPEC oil price rise suddenly provided the oil exporters with a huge balance of payments surplus, it posed immediate problems for the other countries in the Third World. Not only did their oil imports go up in price, but so did their imported manufactures, since they came from countries which themselves began to suffer from inflation caused, among other things, by the rising oil prices. Further, as their growth slowed, the advanced countries reacted to "stagflation" by erecting obstacles to imports, which made it impossible for the primary producers of the Third World to raise the prices of their exports. Meanwhile rising interest rates were increasing the costs of borrowing. The result of all these factors

was an immediate sharp increase in the current deficits of the developing countries.

Nevertheless, with the exception of the African countries, they held to their policy of growth. This growth could, in view of their external deficits, be kept going only by borrowing ever more abroad, at a rate amounting in 1980 to about five percent of their GNP on average. The huge sums necessary to sustain that rate of borrowing exceeded the lending power of the international institutions, which were limited by their rules, as well as by the difficulties experienced by the advanced countries themselves, the ultimate source of these funds. The gap was closed by private banks which, facing a stagnating demand for their funds at home, were only too eager to place their investments abroad. With the sums obtained in this way, the borrowers were no longer building up the infrastructure or other productive units out of which interest and amortization could be paid, as they had been obliged by the World Bank to do in earlier years. Rather, they used them to maintain a level of income and rate of government expenditure which they were no longer able to afford out of their own efforts. Their annual interest and debt service bill rose, but nothing new was created out of which to pay it. The annual charges thus became an ever heavier burden on the export revenues.

Clearly this kind of economic policy could not continue indefinitely. From 1984, various solutions began to be found for the debt problem. For the very poorest nations, debts were canceled outright or much reduced. For the others, mutually agreed rescheduling lightened the burden without damaging credit standing too much. Between 1980 and 1986 there were 181 debt relief agreements. Above all, by drastic measures, frequently imposed by the international agencies, a basic turnround occurred. Annual new indebtedness was kept down, though at the price of slowing general growth and development, of unemployment and of runaway inflation in countries like Argentina and Brazil.

◄ Possibly the most effective direct help to the less developed nations has been medical aid. Here a nurse, only of only three medically trained people for 35,000 newly-arrived Tigrayan drought refugees in Eastern Sudan, examines a new arrival. In personal, human terms, this kind of aid should clearly have priority. Seen from a wider perspective such aid has contributed to the population increase which has helped to keep the poorer countries poor.

▼ Cattle ranching in Brazil. Many of the loans granted or guaranteed by the World Bank to the poorer and developing countries have been raised for agricultural development. Experience has shown that the careful fostering of sectors such as agriculture, though less spectacular, can be more effective than ambitious large-scale innovatory schemes.

Latin American Inflation

Inflation was endemic in the postwar world, but the inflation rates which developed in Latin American countries in the late 1970s and the 1980s were exceptional and deserve to be regarded as a regional phenomenon. They were linked with the willingness of these countries to continue to accept foreign loans even after the price boom of their own exports, mainly minerals and raw materials, ended in about 1980. Much of this foreign capital went into the public sector: between 1973 and 1983, the private sector debt owed abroad increased only fourfold, but similar public sector debt increased tenfold. Many of the public sector utilities and "key" industries, financed in this way, were unviable from the start, and others became so as incomes ceased to rise after 1980.

The ever larger subsidies required to sustain them brought budgets out of control and public sector deficits soared. Once foreign borrowing ceased to finance them, such deficits were bound to trigger inflationary pressures. Inflation rates varied, with Brazil experiencing 100–200 percent a year in the 1980s, Argentina reaching 1000 percent in 1984–85, and Bolivia 11,000 percent in 1985.

Such rates mostly hurt the working and lower middle classes, but there was no way of reducing them without serious inroads into standards of living. Neither were the methods of income squeezes recommended by the IMF and others politically easy to apply. If subsidies on basic foods, electricity, fares and so on were ended, prices and thus wage demands would rise; if

they were not, deficits would continue to fuel inflation. Only Chile, with its totalitarian government, managed to sustain a regime of austerity and slow growth. Brazil tried a drastic price freeze and a new currency, the cruzado, in 1986, but a consumer boom ensued, there was speculation against the price freeze as goods were hoarded and funds were sent abroad, and inflation was back in 1987. Argentina's drastic "Austral" plan of 1985, including a price and wage freeze, devaluation and a new currency, the austral, also failed. The Argentinean price index (1980=100) stood at 1,000,000 in January 1988, 5,000,000 one year later.

◀ Argentineans protest against high prices. Argentina, in the interwar years among the more comfortably-off nations of the world, lost much ground when the high food and raw material prices of the postwar years collapsed. It also developed one of the worst rates of inflation and one of the highest debt mountains.

▼ Roaring inflation in Argentina has led at times to food riots and to looting, as here in San Miguel. The actual standard of living of the country approaches that of Mediterranean Europe rather than that of Africa, but inflation, as always, hits wage earners particularly hard. The immediate cause of the inflation is unbalanced government budgets, but foreign capital investment has not been able to stem the price rises.

THE DEBT MOUNTAIN

International lending and borrowing became an accepted feature of the postwar decades. Total international indebtedness had been rising slightly, but so had prices, and defaults did not become an issue. This changed quite drastically with the rise in oil prices of 1973–74, and the slow reaction of the developing countries to this crisis. While the industrialized countries rapidly restored their balances of payments by cutbacks and economic slowdown, the developing countries reacted by borrowing more as their current deficits increased sharply.

They were encouraged in this course by the willingness of private bank consortia to lend; whereas in 1970 these had supplied only one-sixth of the lending, and in 1975 one-third, by 1985 they were responsible for well over half of the debts outstanding. By the early 1980s, the growing debt was threatening the trade balance of the poorer countries, and the solvency of the lenders – above all, the debt crisis hit the private banks in the advanced market economies, as well as in the OPEC countries.

The cost of servicing debts, as an average among all non-oil-exporting developing countries, rose from 16 percent of export revenues in 1977 to 20 percent in 1979 and 25 percent in 1982, in some extreme cases approaching half of the revenue from those exports. Drastic cuts reduced their rate of output growth, particularly in Latin America where indebtedness was especially high. Even so, the debts mounted up year by year. The chief creditors, who were by now banks rather than governments, could cancel the debts only at the expense of their shareholders, with negative effects on the economy of their own countries. Even "rescheduling" – stretching the period of repayment and reducing interest rates – harmed the creditworthiness of Third World countries which still needed ever more loans. Either way, catastrophe threatened. The debt issue thus became the major topic of international economic debate in the early 1980s.

Yet the picture was not altogether as bleak as it appeared to many. Much of the debt was owed by oil-producing countries, like Venezuela and the second largest debtor, Mexico, or by middle-income countries with rich resource bases like Argentina or Brazil, the world's largest debtor. Low-income countries owed only about three percent of the debt. Many of the debts were shortterm or renewable. In some countries, capital imports were matched by capital flight abroad: thus Mexican residents held about US$ 3 billion abroad in 1973 and US$ 64 billion in 1984, about as much as the whole of the public section of the country's foreign debt. Moreover, in view of the rapid world inflation in the 1970s, the real burden of debt rose much less than appeared at first sight. From 1984 on, however, the practice of rescheduling and also the complete cancellation of claims against the poorest countries slowed down the growth of international indebtedness, to hardly more than the rate of inflation.

▲ The Mexico Olympic stadium of 1968 is a typical prestige object which adds to the country's indebtedness without contributing much directly to its earning capacity. Other, even less productive objects on which foreign loans have been spent include tanks and presidential palaces.

Debt in 1987 (billion dollars)

100
50
30
20
10
0

Debt as a percentage of total annual exports

◇ Less than 200

◇ 200–400

◇ 400–1000

◇ Greater than 1000

▼ The Nicaraguan civil war, itself a product of poor government, political interference and poverty, drastically impoverished the country even more. Children, and the poor, are often the victims of events over which they have no control.

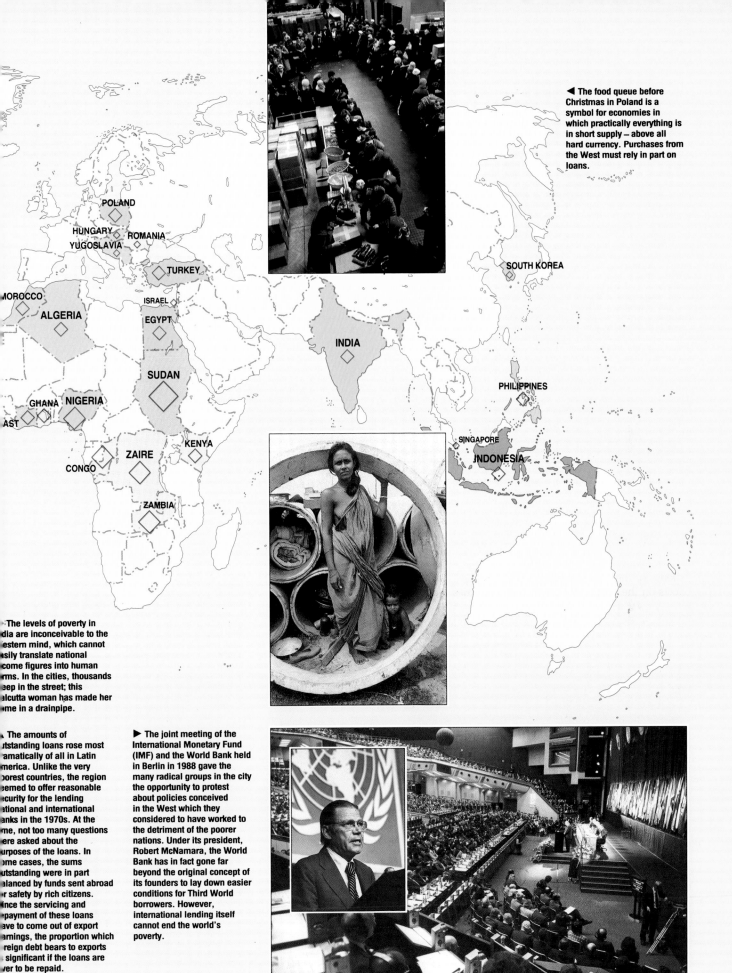

◄ The food queue before
Christmas in Poland is a
symbol for economies in
which practically everything is
in short supply – above all
hard currency. Purchases from
the West must rely in part on
loans.

POLAND
HUNGARY ROMANIA
YUGOSLAVIA
TURKEY
MOROCCO
ISRAEL
ALGERIA
EGYPT
INDIA
SUDAN
GHANA NIGERIA
AST
KENYA
ZAIRE
CONGO
ZAMBIA
SOUTH KOREA
PHILIPPINES
SINGAPORE
INDONESIA

The levels of poverty in
dia are inconceivable to the
estern mind, which cannot
asily translate national
come figures into human
rms. In the cities, thousands
eep in the street; this
alcutta woman has made her
me in a drainpipe.

The amounts of
utstanding loans rose most
amatically of all in Latin
merica. Unlike the very
oorest countries, the region
eemed to offer reasonable
curity for the lending
ational and international
anks in the 1970s. At the
me, not too many questions
ere asked about the
urposes of the loans. In
me cases, the sums
utstanding were in part
alanced by funds sent abroad
r safety by rich citizens.
ince the servicing and
epayment of these loans
ave to come out of export
arnings, the proportion which
reign debt bears to exports
significant if the loans are
ver to be repaid.

► The joint meeting of the
International Monetary Fund
(IMF) and the World Bank held
in Berlin in 1988 gave the
many radical groups in the city
the opportunity to protest
about policies conceived
in the West which they
considered to have worked to
the detriment of the poorer
nations. Under its president,
Robert McNamara, the World
Bank has in fact gone far
beyond the original concept of
its founders to lay down easier
conditions for Third World
borrowers. However,
international lending itself
cannot end the world's
poverty.

BIOGRAPHIES

Agnelli, Giovanni 1866–1945

Founder of Fiat automobile company and leading
Italian industralist. In 1899 he became a founder of
the Fabbrica Italiana Automobile Torino (FIAT)
company. Under Agnelli the company diversified
production to include airplanes, buses, tractors,
diesel engines and ball-bearings with the
acquisition of the RIV company (1907). Fiat soon
developed an international reputation, and during
World War I adapted to military needs, running its
large Turin plants at full capacity. Agnelli became
president of Fiat in 1920. He employed over 30,000
people and favored a paternalistic form of
leadership with an emphasis on workers' welfare.
However, when militant workers occupied the
factory in 1921, he retired and left them to it, soon
to return to his post at their urgent request. He
supported Mussolini, who made him a senator in
1923. Fiat was the chief military supplier in World
War II, and in April 1945, the Italian Committee of
National Liberation removed Agnelli and his top
executives from control, although his family later
maintained a role in the running of the company.

Allende (Gossens), Salvador 1908–73

Chilean president. Politically aware from an early
age and arrested while at medical school for
"revolutionary activities". In 1933 Allende helped
found the Chilean socialist party which broke
away from the Soviet-orientated Communist party.
He was elected to Congress in 1937, served as
health minister (1939–42) and was elected to the
Senate in 1945. In 1970 Allende stood in the
presidential elections for the fourth time and won
narrowly. He aimed to create a Socialist society in
an undeveloped country while maintaining a
liberal parliamentary form of agreement, and so
nationalized the large copper mines, previously
partly US owned, and ended Chile's diplomatic
and economic boycott of Cuba. In 1972 Allende
increased his majority slightly but met with
opposition to his policies. The threat of further
nationalization caused strikes, inflation soared,
food was short and street violence spread. In
September 1973 Allende was killed during a violent
coup by the military and anti-Marxist opposition.

Balfour, Arthur 1873–1957

British industralist. During his early employment
by Seebohm and Dieckstahl of Sheffield, sellers of
crucible steel, a few years' rewarding experience in
the US presaged the activity in overseas trading for
which his own firm was later famous. Returning to
Sheffield in 1897, in 1899 he became managing
director of the company, which, as one of the first
two in Sheffield to develop high-speed steel,
prospered and became Arthur Balfour and
Company, Ltd., in 1915. Balfour served on many
committees and councils, and was a British
delegate at the League of Nations economic
conference in 1927. Chairman of the Industry and

Trade Commission (1924–9) and of the Advisory
Council for Scientific and Industrial Research
(1937–46), he was also a member of the Economic
Advisory Council. A champion of Sheffield and
its industry, Balfour also successfully promoted
overseas trade in his business and as a national
policy. He received several honors, and was
created Baron Riverdale of Sheffield in 1935.

Baring, John 1863–1929

British merchant banker. He entered Baring
Brothers merchant bank, his family firm, in 1883
and was made a full partner in 1890. Baring played
a major role in the successful reconstruction and
recovery of the house after the Baring Crisis of
1890, when the bank's collapse was averted only
by the intervention of the Bank of England, and in
its incorporation as Baring Brothers and Co., Ltd.
Succeeding to the title Lord Revelstoke in 1897, he
became senior director of the bank in 1901. He
cultivated strong overseas connections, the house
specializing in the issue of loan stock in London
for governments, municipalities and railway
companies in the Americas and Russia. After
World War I, issues and commercial credit were
moved away from there and toward Europe.
Revelstoke was director of the Bank of England
and advisor to governments, the Treasury and the
Foreign Office. British representative at the
Committee of Experts to renew the Dawes Plan in
1929, he advocated the establishment of the Bank
for International Settlements.

Beveridge, William Henry 1879–1963

British economist. In 1909, as head of the
Employment Department, he published
Unemployment: a Problem of Industry advocating
improved industrial organization to reduce
unemployment. Winston Churchill, then president
of the Board of Trade, asked Beveridge to create a
national system of labor exchanges, and the
administration of compulsory unemployment
insurance. From 1919 to 1937 he was director of the
London School of Economics. He was chairman of
the Unemployment Insurance Statutory Committee
(1934–44), Master of University College, Oxford
from 1937 and was called into the Ministry of
Labour by Bevin in 1940. In 1941 he chaired a
committee inquiring into social insurance,
resulting in his report of December 1942, which
gained popular support and changed the
understanding of the problem of unemployment.
It demanded benefits without means tests and the
eradication of unemployment, the creation of a
health service and a system of family allowances.
In 1944 Beveridge published *Full Employment in a
Free Society*, influenced by Keynes. During World
War II he took part, at government request, in the
designing of the Welfare State. He became a
Liberal MP briefly in 1945 and, already much
honored, was created a baron in 1946.

Birdseye, Clarence 1886–1956

US businessman and inventor. As a fur trader in
Labrador (1912 and 1916) he was inspired by the
practice of freezing food during the winter owing
to a lack of fresh food. During the 1920s in the US
Birdseye developed a method for quick-freezing
food, and in 1924 helped form the General
Seafoods Company. In 1929 he started to sell his
quick-frozen foods, including fish, fruit and
vegetables, and soon became wealthy. He was not
the first producer of frozen foods but his method,
using two refrigerated metal plates to freeze
packaged food, was efficient, quick, and preserved
the original flavor. In 1929 the company was sold
for $20 million and became the General Food
Corporation, with Birdseye continuing as a
consultant. He was president of Birds Eye Frosted
Foods (1930–34) and of Birdseye Electric Company
(1935–38). He continued to invent and owned 300
patents when he died, including a dehydrating
technique that drastically reduced drying time for
most foods.

Boeing, William Edward 1881–1956

US aircraft designer and founder of The Boeing
Company. He entered aircraft manufacture in 1916
with the establishment of Pacific Aero Products
Company, renamed the Boeing Airplane Company
in 1917. Boeing helped to design the company's
first plane for the US Navy. The company
produced a variety of military aircraft. In 1927 he
also helped to form Boeing Air Transport which
became part of United Aircraft and Transport
Corporation, until 1934 when it was again
incorporated as Boeing. During World War II
Boeing produced such planes as the B-17 Flying
Fortress. The 1950s saw production of commercial
as well as military aircraft, including the Boeing
707, the first US jet airplane, which went into
service in 1958.

Brandt, Willy 1913–

West German politician. He fled Germany after
Hitler's accession, returning when the war ended.
A Social Democrat, he was elected to the federal
parliament (1949), became mayor of West Berlin
(1957–66) and chairman of the Social Democratic
Party (SPD) in 1964. He led the SPD in the
elections of 1961 and 1965 and in 1966 led his party
into a coalition government with the Christian
Democrats, becoming foreign minister and
vice-chancellor. In 1969 Brandt was elected
chancellor in a new coalition government with the
Free Democrats. He revalued the German mark
and concentrated on foreign affairs. He was a
strong campaigner for a united Europe and
influenced the expansion of the European
Economic Community (EEC). In 1971 Brandt
was awarded the Nobel Peace Prize. In 1947 he
resigned after a spy scandal. He sent on to
establish and head the Independent Commission

▲ Andrew Carnegie

▲ André-Gustav Citroën

▲ Charles Gates Dawes

on International Development, known as the Brandt Commission. This distinguished body studied world economic policies, especially regarding developing countries, and in 1980 produced a report, *North–South: a program for survival*, drawing attention to disparities between rich nations and poor, and calling for a redistribution of world wealth.

Bukhárin, Nicholas Ivanovich 1888–1938
Communist leader, economist and Marxist theoretician. He studied economics at Moscow University but did not graduate. In 1906 he joined the Bolshevik party and was made a member of Moscow Bolshevik Committee in 1908. He was imprisoned and then deported in 1911. Bukhárin returned to Russian after the 1917 Revolution, becoming editor of *Pravda*, 1917–29, and being elected to the executive committee of the Comintern. In 1920 he published *The Economy of the Transitional Period* and strongly supported Lenin's New Economic Policy (NEP). A member of the Politburo from 1924, he supported Stalin after Lenin's death, despite distrusting him; but when Stalin abandoned the NEP in 1928 Bukhárin unsuccessfully tried to move party opinion against him. He opposed Stalin's industrialization policy and, in a pamphlet called "Lenin's Political Testament", argued against Stalin's brutal collectivization program. Bukhárin was expelled from the Politburo in 1929, and, although briefly (1934) editor of *Izvestia*, and one of the authors of the 1936 Constitution, his political career had ended. In 1938, after a show trial, he was executed for high treason.

Carnegie, Andrew 1835–1919
Scottish-born US steel industralist. His family emigrated to Pittsburgh in 1848. Carnegie worked in menial positions for the Pennsylvania Railroad Co. (1853–65), became superintendent of the Pittsburgh railroad division and introduced sleeping cars. He successfully invested his savings into oil lands in 1864 and left the railroad in 1865, turning his attention to iron, steel, oil and other business interests. In 1868 Carnegie built the Union Iron Mills at Pittsburgh and in 1873, began to specialize in steel, owning the largest mill in the US. His business operations grew and prospered as he bought sources of supply of raw materials, and transportation lines, and introduced new methods and technology. In 1901 he retired and sold his interests, which became the United States Steel Corporation, to the baker, J.P. Morgan, for $400 million. He devoted his retirement to philanthropy, believing in the distribution to others of the surplus wealth of the rich few. He provided for public libraries throughout the USA and Britain, endowed trusts and institutions and pension funds, Hero Funds and large gifts to Scottish and American Universities.

Castro (Ruz), Fidel 1926–
Cuban revolutionary. Studied law and practiced in Havana. Castro staged an unsuccessful rising against President Batista in 1953 and was sentenced to fifteen years' imprisonment. He was released after an amnesty in 1955 and continued his armed struggle against Batista's draconian regime until, with mounting support, he ended it in 1958. Castro was appointed prime minister in 1959, proclaiming a Marxist-Leninist program of reforms adapted to Cuban requirements. He undertook drastic reforms in industry and nationalized US-owned companies. Far-reaching reforms were also implemented in agriculture and education. A free welfare state system was established, employment was guaranteed and compulsory, ownership was centralized and the media government-controlled. The economy, ideologically soundly based but inefficient, has failed to cope with population growth. The ending of US economic dominance was coupled with the defeat of the attempted US-backed invasion at the Bay of Pigs in 1961. Cuba became dependent on Soviet economic and political aid, and this led to the Cuban missile crisis of 1962. Domestic problems occurred in the production of sugar and tobacco, and thousands of Cubans left for the US. In the 1980s, Castro's disapproval of the Soviet leader Gorbachev's reforming policies cooled relations between their countries.

Citroën, André-Gustave 1878–1935
French engineer and industralist. After convincing the French Army of the need to mass-produce munitions during World War I, he was appointed to construct a munitions plant which became his automobile factory after the war. He began mass-producing a small car, the Citroën, when hostilities ended. Using Henry Ford's production methods, he built one of the largest automobile manufacturing companies in France. He introduced the Citroën Seven in 1934, despite the Depression. However, the company went bankrupt in 1934, and Citroën lost control of it. Also a financier of scientific and geological expeditions, Citroën provided the lighting for the Arc de Triomphe and the Place de la Concorde as gifts to the city of Paris.

Clemenceau, Georges 1841–1929
French premier. After a radical student career and four years in the USA, Clemenceau, now a doctor, became mayor of Montmartre (1870), and entered the National Assembly (1871), resigning from both positions after involvement in the Paris Commune. In 1876, re-elected to the Assembly, he became leader of the far left. In 1880 he started a radical paper, fiercely denouncing colonialism as debilitating to France. His opposition brought down two premiers, gaining him a reputation as a powerful antagonist who would not take office

himself. His unpopularity grew and he was defeated in the elections of 1893. He became an outstanding political writer. In 1902 he became senator for the Var, and then interior minister (1906), premier (1906-09 and 1917–20), and minister of war (1917–18). Running the war in an autocratic and single-minded manner, he inspired popular resistance to Germany, and was a major factor in the Allied victory. Known as "The Tiger", Clemenceau presided at the Paris Peace Conference (1919) defending French interests and pressing for German disarmament. Defeated in the 1920 presidential elections, Clemenceau spent his final years traveling and writing.

Cripps, Sir Richard Stafford 1889–1952
British Labour statesman and postwar chancellor of the Exchequer (1947–50). Very successful academically and as a barrister. In 1930 Cripps was knighted and became solicitor-general in the Labour government. Elected to parliament in 1931 but refused to serve in Ramsay MacDonald's coalition. Became involved in leftwing movements. Expelled from the Labour party in 1939 for his active opposition to Chamberlain's appeasement policy, he sat as an independent MP during the war. Ambassador to Moscow (1940-42) he also went to India in 1942 for unsuccessful negotiations. In the same year he became Lord Privy Seal and leader of the House of Commons. He was transferred to the post of minister of aircraft production. Readmitted to the Labour party when they came to power in 1945, Cripps was appointed president of the Board of Trade, where he initiated an export drive. He became chancellor of the Exchequer in 1947, pursuing a policy of deflation, rationing and emphasis upon balance of payments and investments at a critical time for the British economy. He resigned in 1950 owing to illness.

Dawes, Charles Gates 1865–1951
Chicago banker and US Republican vice-president. Dawes was initially in banking but during World War I he became the outspoken purchasing agent for General Pershing's Expeditionary Force in France. In 1919 he resigned as brigadier general. He was appointed the first director of the budget bureau in 1921 and in 1923 became chairman of the Allied Reparations Commission. The Commission produced the Dawes Plan in 1924 which, with the help of US loans, reorganized German finances. The plan prevented immediate economic collapse in Europe but did not solve the wider question of world economic dislocation. Dawes was vice-president from 1925 to 1929, having played a powerful and positive role in the election campaign. He later served as ambassador to Britain (1929–32) and as president of the Reconstruction Finance Corporation in 1932. In that year he resigned and returned to banking. He was awarded the Nobel Peace Prize in 1925.

◀ Milton Friedman

◀ John Kenneth Galbraith

◀ John Paul Getty

Deng Xiaoping 1904–

Chinese Communist leader. He began his career in the government of the People's Republic of China as vice-premier (1952). His most important role was in the Chinese Communist party (CCP) of which he became secretary general (1954) and a member of the ruling Politburo (1955). Attacked during the Cultural Revolution in the 1960s, Deng was dismissed. However, he was reinstated in 1973 and made deputy premier. In 1975 he was appointed vice-Chairman of the CCP Central Committee, a member of its Politburo, and chief of staff. Deng's push to modernize China alienated Mao and he was again removed from power in 1976, but had returned by July 1977. He opened up Sino-US relations, began attacks on his former opponents and aimed to destroy the cult of Mao and modernize China. Deng followed an "open door" policy to foreign technology and capital and bureaucratic reforms were carried out to facilitate modernization. Named chief deputy premier in 1980, Deng retired soon after but retained his political power. In 1989, the massacre, at his command, of a thousand or more prodemocracy demonstrators, mostly students, in Beijing darkened his reputation.

Ferranti, Sebastian Ziani de 1864–1930

British electrical engineer and inventor. Began his career at Siemens Brothers in 1881 and the following year patented the Ferranti alternator which gained him recognition among electrical engineers. In 1883 he established a business in London which manufactured electrical apparatus. He became chief electrician to the London Electric Supply Corporation in 1887. Ferranti planned and initiated the building of a power station which was to supply electricity to London north of the Thames; this was never completed, owing to the restrictive terms of the Electric Lighting Act of 1888. After 1892 Ferranti concentrated on his private business as a manufacturing engineer and founded Ferranti Ltd in 1896. Between 1882 and 1927 he took out 176 patents, and was a pioneer of high-voltage systems. He was the originator of long-distance transmission of high-power electrical current. He was made a Fellow of the Royal Society in 1927.

Ford, Henry 1863–1947

US automobile industrialist who organized the Ford Motor Company (1903) which in 1908 produced the Model T Ford, the first inexpensive standardized car. Increased demand soon led to the introduction of mass-production methods, which enabled rapid expansion of the automobile industry worldwide. Ford also introduced a new $5 minimum wage for an eight-hour day and profit-sharing plans for employees. He produced motor vehicles for the government during World War I and survived the postwar crisis of 1920–21

but failed to cater to the changing car market, which now demanded style and speed as well as economy; the company lost its dominance of the car market under increasing competition especially from General Motors. In the 1930s Ford took a strong stand against organized labor. He was a pacifist during both world wars and dispatched the "Peace Ship" to Scandinavia in 1915 to seek mediation. Most of his estate was placed in the Ford Foundation (a philanthropic institution) before his death.

Friedman, Milton 1912–

US economist. Friedman worked at Chicago University and for the US Treasury before his appointment as professor of economics at Chicago (1948–79). In 1957, Friedman challenged the accepted Keynesian economic approach with his paper, *A Theory of the Consumption Function*, relating the consumption function to lifetime rather than current income. This challenge continued with the publication of *Studies in the Quantity Theory of Money* (1956) in which Friedman advocated the control of the money supply to control the economy. This work radically altered the perspective of economics and marked the start of the now familiar dichotomy between Keynesian and monetarist approaches. Friedman's other major impact on economics came in 1968 when he declared his theories on "the natural rate of employment", that is, the lowest level of unemployment which the economy can stand without incurring progressive inflation. In 1976, he received the Nobel Prize for Economics.

Galbraith, John Kenneth 1908–

Leading US economist. After teaching at Harvard, he ran the Price Section of the Office of Price Administration. In 1949, Galbraith became Professor of Economics at Harvard University and from 1961 to 1963 was US ambassador to India. In 1952 *A Theory of Price Control* and *American Capitalism: The Concept of Countervailing Power* were published. The former advocated the use of price control and rationing in peacetime as well as during war. In the latter Galbraith contended that giant monopolistic organizations dominate modern advanced economies, contrasting with accepted economic theory and its assertion of the efficiency of competition. In *The Affluent Society* (1958) Galbraith argued that demand for luxury goods is artificially created by the producer; at the same time, funding for public services decreases, because taxation is seen as a disincentive to economic growth. This results in a society with private wealth but public poverty. *The New Industrial State* (1967) protested the domination of "big business". These controversial propositions are now accepted as an alternative to traditional economic theory. He wrote prolifically on other subjects as well as economics.

Getty, John Paul 1892–1976

US oil multimillionaire. After graduating in economics from Oxford University in 1913, he returned to America and entered the oil business. By 1916 he had made his first million dollars. He also headed his father's oil company and inherited $15 million on his father's death in 1930. Merging his father's interests with his own, he went on to acquire over 100 oil companies, building a huge financial empire. Getty was reported to make most policy decisions himself despite the size of his operations. Viewed as an eccentric entrepreneur, he was married and divorced five times, had a reputation for thrift and accumulated a very valuable art collection, much of which was displayed at the J. P. Getty Museum, opened in Malibu in 1954.

Gompers, Samuel 1850–1924

US labor leader and first president of the American Federation of Labor (AFL). Emigrating from London to New York in 1863, he followed his father's trade of cigar making. He was naturalized in 1872, joined the Cigar Maker's International Union on its formation in 1864 and became president of the New York branch. In 1881 Gompers was elected president of the newly formed AFL, a post he held until his death, except in 1895. Under his strong and stable leadership the AFL became the major labor organization in the US. Gompers developed a reputation for conservatism. His goals for the Federation were economic and he distrusted intellectual reformers. He kept the AFL politically neutral. He advocated voluntarism, a principle emphasizing the use of enforcement by economic actions such as strikes and boycotts, and encouraged building trade agreements. A member of the Council of National Defense during World War II, he formed a War Committee on Labor. He was also a member of the commission on International Labor Legislation at the Peace Conference.

Gorbachev, Mikhail Sergeyevich 1931–

Soviet leader. A member of the Communist party Central Committee from 1971, Gorbachev was made a full member of the Politburo in 1980, and became increasingly powerful, ascending to the leadership of the Communist party on the death of Chernenko in 1985. He immediately undertook a campaign against corruption and economic mismanagement in the party bureaucracy. In 1986 he launched the campaign for *glasnost* (openness). From 1987 the state ended its economic monopoly and encouraged private enterprise. Companies were now also allowed to go bankrupt. In the same year Gorbachev announced proposals for an extensive restructuring of the economy, *perestroika* (reconstruction), which aimed to decrease the authority of central government and promote democracy. The twelfth five-year plan (1986–90),

▲ Hermann Göring

▲ Fritz Haber

▲ James Riddle Hoffa

announced in 1985, aimed to increase industrial productivity by increasing labor efficiency and investment in new projects. These aims were achieved, and the industrial sector modernized and encouraged to become self-financing. In agriculture, despite reorganization, reduction of state control and an increase in production, the USSR still has to import large amounts of grain. The lack of success of his agricultural policies, the continuing weakness of the Soviet economy in comparison with those of other major powers, and the desperate shortage of consumer goods, made Gorbachev increasingly unpopular as he occupied the middle ground in Soviet politics.

Göring, Hermann 1893–1946
German industrialist and Nazi leader. Göring met Hitler and joined the Nazi party in 1922. He fled Germany after the unsuccessful Munich putsch in 1923, returning in 1927, when he cultivated contacts in German industry, and re-established contact with Hitler. Elected to the Reichstag in 1928, he became its President in 1932. Rapidly promoted in the Nazi party, by 1935 he was Commander of the Luftwaffe and the most important man in Germany after Hitler. In 1936 he was made minister of economic affairs and became responsible for the four-year plan of the war economy, directing industry and re-arming Germany. From 1937 onwards he amassed a large fortune through the Reichwerke-Hermann Göring, the state-owned giant mining and industrial enterprise created by Hitler in the belief that steel production, vital for rearmament, should be controlled by the state rather than in private hands. In 1939 Hitler named Göring as his successor. After Hitler's suicide Göring surrendered to the Americans, was found guilty of war crimes at Nuremberg but poisoned himself two hours before his scheduled execution.

Haber, Fritz 1868–1934
German physical chemist. Educated in Berlin, he taught physical chemistry at Karlsruhe and pioneered research in electrochemistry. With Carl Bosch he developed the method for the synthesis of ammonia from nitrogen and hydrogen. In 1911 Haber became director of the Kaiser Wilhelm Institute for Physical Chemistry in Berlin. During World War I, the Haber-Bosch ammonia process enabled Germany to manufacture explosives although the Allies prevented access to natural nitrate deposits; the Institute became a major military establishment and Haber played an important part in its development of poison gas. In 1918 he received the Nobel Prize for Chemistry. The Institute developed an international reputation after the war and became the world center for research in physical chemistry. Hitler's rise to power in 1933 forced Haber, a Jew, to emigrate and the Institute was dismantled.

Hammer, Armand 1898–1990
US multimillionaire entrepreneur. Hammer made his first million dollars in his father's pharmaceutical company before 1921, when he qualified as a doctor and went to Russia to help famine victims. Lenin asked him to go into business there. Within a few years he was running the most successful pencil company in the USSR. He sold the company and returned to the USA in 1930 with many art treasures, which he sold to finance successful business ventures, mostly connected with whiskey. In 1956 he retired, but was persuaded to finance the Occidental Petroleum Corporation's drilling of two wells, which struck oil; in 1957 Hammer became Occidental's chairman and chief executive. Expansion and diversification brought the company's gross annual income to over two billion dollars by 1970. Hammer was instrumental in opening up US–Soviet trade links in the 1970s. He is famous also as an art collector and patron.

Hansson, Per Albin 1885–1946
Swedish Social Democratic politician and prime minister. Joined the Social Democratic Youth Association in 1903 and edited its newspaper, *Fram* (1905–09). He joined the Social Democratic party (SPD), and in 1918 was elected to the Riksdag (parliament) serving as minister for defense (1918–26). In 1925 Hansson became leader of the party, campaigning successfully for lower military expenditure but opposing total disarmament. He served on the government's Public Debt Commission (1929–32). In 1932 he became prime minister and formed a coalition with the Agrarian party which allowed him to pass legislation covering such areas as public works construction, agricultural support, pensions, unemployment insurance, financial expansion and tax to finance these programs. His measures were largely successful. Wages recovered by 1936 and unemployment had fallen sharply by 1939. The growing European crisis after 1936 caused Hansson to expand Sweden's defenses and to reject a nonaggression pact with Germany. He formed a coalition government after war broke out and maintained Sweden's neutrality. Hansson formed his last SPD government in 1945.

Hayek, Friedrich August von 1899–
Austrian economist. Studied law, psychology and economics at the University of Vienna, then at New York University (1923–4). He was the first director of the Austrian Institute for Economic Science (1927). From 1931 to 1950 he was Tooke Professor at the London School of Economics. In *Price and Production* (1931) Hayek argued that in a boom rising prices cause a fall in real wages and increased capital investment in equipment to replace labor. As the demand for capital goods rises faster than supply, interest rates rise,

investment falls and the economy turns down. The converse occurs in a slump. This directly opposed the Keynesian viewpoint. Involved in the major economic debates during the 1930s concerning monetary, business cycle and capital theories, he also argued against government intervention in modern economies, as politically undesirable and ultimately ineffective. After the war he took up psychology and social, political and legal philosophy, holding professorships at Chicago (1950), Freiburg (1962), and Salzburg (1969). Awarded the Nobel Prize for Economics (1974), he continued publishing in the 1980s.

Hicks, John Richard 1904–
British economist. Graduated from Oxford (1925), lectured at the London School of Economics (1926–35), became a fellow of Cambridge University (1935–8) and then took up a professorship at Manchester University (1938). In 1946 he moved to a fellowship at Nuffield College, Oxford, becoming professor in 1952 and retiring in 1965. Knighted in 1964, he was joint winner (with Kenneth Arrow) of the Nobel Prize for Economics in 1972. His major works include *A Reconsideration of the Theory of Value* (1934) which introduced an indifference theory to explain consumer behavior as opposed to the traditional marginal utility theory. His celebrated IS-LM analysis appearing in *Mr Keynes and the "Classics"* (1937), was Hicks's method of illustrating why Keynes differed from the "Classical" economists in his approach. This innovative apparatus is now an established means of purveying economic arguments and its versatility is such that differences between Keynesian and monetarist policies may be explained by differing interpretations within the IS-LM framework.

Hoffa, James Riddle 1913–75
US labor leader. Began union activities in the 1930s. Became president of the Local International Brotherhood of Teamsters (IBT) in 1937. Helped organize the Central States Drivers' Council in 1937, became its chairman, then president of the Michigan Conference of Teamsters in 1942. Was elected IBT vice-president in 1957. In the same year Hoffa was charged with attempted bribery, but acquitted. He accelerated the centralization process within the IBT that allowed him to negotiate and sign the first national freight-handling contract in the trucking industry in 1964. Under him the IBT became the largest labor union in the US. In 1967 he began a 13-year prison term for jury tampering, fraud and conspiracy in the disposal of union benefit funds. Hoffa remained president of the Teamsters until 1971, when his sentence was commuted by President Nixon with the provision he would not participate in any union affairs until 1980. In July 1975 he mysteriously disappeared and was officially declared dead in 1982.

Soichiro Honda

Howard Hughes

John Maynard Keynes

Honda, Soichiro 1906–

Japanese businessman. He opened a garage in 1928 and in 1934 established a factory producing piston rings which he had developed. Selling this operation to Toyota after the war he went on to manufacture motorbikes, forming the Honda Motor Company (1948) and becoming its president (1948–73) and director (1973–83). Honda made major technical innovations, and by 1954 the company was one of the five industry leaders and by 1959 had won all of the world's most prestigious racing prizes. Honda designed a more commercial motorcycle, the Honda Supercub, a lightweight, inexpensive model, introduced in 1958. Demand was enormous and by 1959 Honda was the top motorcycle manufacturer in Japan. In 1959 Honda established the American Honda Motor Company, successfully conquered the US and European markets and became the world's largest motorcycle manufacturer. In 1967 Honda began producing cars and trucks, becoming a major international automobile manufacture after the introduction of the Honda Civic in 1973. Honda himself continues involvement in the company as Supreme Advisor (1983–). He has received many honors and awards.

Hoover, Herbert Clark 1874–1964

Republican US president. He studied mining engineering and his subsequent career in mining involved traveling around the world and amassing great wealth. He was actively involved with World War I relief operations in Europe. He served as Secretary of Commerce under Harding and Coolidge. In 1928 Hoover was elected president, entering the White House at a time of great prosperity. However, he soon had to face the "Great Depression". He failed to cope with this crisis, believing the slump to be temporary and mistakenly adhering to accepted economic strategy. Federal expenditure on public works was restrained to avoid a budget deficit. In addition, no effective system of hardship relief was developed, owing to his belief in the responsibility of regional governments and private charities. As the Depression spread to Europe Hoover postponed international debt payments in 1931 and established the Reconstruction Finance Corporation. The presidential election of 1932 brought a decisive defeat by Franklin D. Roosevelt.

Hughes, Howard 1905–76

US millionaire, businessman, film producer and director, and aviator. He inherited his father's tool company at the age of 18 and two years later moved to Hollywood, producing films such as *Hells Angels* (1930) and *Scarface* (1932). Hughes left Hollywood suddenly in 1932 to work as a pilot, then formed the Hughes Aircraft Company and turned to designing, building and flying aircraft. Between 1935 and 1938 he broke most of the

world's air speed records. He abruptly returned to Hollywood, producing his best-known film *The Outlaw* in 1943. He built a large business empire including RKO Picture Corporation, and continued his involvement in aviation, designing for and controlling Trans World Airlines. In 1950 he became a recluse and controlled his vast business interests from secluded hotel rooms.

Ibuka, Masaru 1908–

Japanese industrialist. Educated at Waseda University, he became a research engineer for Japan Audio Optical Industrial Corporation in 1933 and in 1937 was made manager of the radio telegraphy department. Ibuka left the company in 1940 when appointed managing director of Japan Measuring Apparatus Company, Ltd. He moved again in 1945 to become organizer of the Tokyo Telecommunications Engineering Corporation (Sony Corporation since 1956). At Sony he has been president and managing director (1950–71), chairman (1971–76), and honorary chairman and director since 1976. In addition he has been chairman of the Railway Technology Research Institute since 1987, is chairman of the Japanese Committee for Economic Development, a member of the Economic Council and director of several industrial associations. He has received several honorary degrees and awards for his work.

Keynes, John Maynard 1883–1946

English economist. A Cambridge graduate, he became a member of the "Bloomsbury Group" and lecturer in economics. Treasury advisor in both World Wars, Keynes attended the Paris Peace Conference but resigned, voicing his strong opposition to the draft treaty in *Economic Consequences of the Peace* (1919). He became the leading critic of established economic theory and strongly attacked Churchill's restoration of the gold standard in 1925. The Depression inspired his two great works, *A Treatise on Money* (1930) and *General Theory of Unemployment, Interest and Money* (1936). He argued that full employment was not a natural condition but could be achieved by adopting a cheap money policy and undertaking a program of public investment. His views on a planned economy influenced Roosevelt's New Deal administration. In 1943, he proposed an international clearing union, and played an important part in the Bretton Woods Agreements, the establishment of the International Monetary Fund.

Khrushchev, Nikita Sergeyevich 1894–1971

Soviet leader. A member of the Communist party from 1918, he became a full member of the Politburo in 1939. After the German invasion (1941) he directed Ukrainian resistance, remaining in the area after the German retreat (1944) and directing its recovery. In 1949 he returned to

Moscow as first secretary of the Moscow party, and a specialist in agricultural policies, although his plan to create "agro-towns" was unsuccessful. Khrushchev became First Secretary of the Communist party on Stalin's death in 1953 and denounced Stalinism in 1956. He demoted his main rivals and by 1958 occupied the top positions in both party and government. In agriculture Khrushchev advocated increased resources and incentives for collective farming, and oversaw expansion of farming into the virgin lands of Kazakhstan (1954). These programs were largely unsuccessful as were other economic initiatives. Khrushchev's main interest was foreign affairs and he did much to advance Soviet ambitions abroad. However, he was deposed in 1964 and forced into retirement.

Kreuger, Ivar 1880–1932

Swedish businessman and financier. Joint founder of Kreuger and Toll (1908) which rapidly became a large international company, and in 1913, with Kreuger's family's match factories, became a base for the construction of a cartel, Svenska Tändsticks AB (STAB), which by the 1920s, controlled nearly three quarters of the world's match production. After 1914 he used his business and his personality to arrange loans for various governments in return for concessions for match monopolies, subsequently transferring production to the respective countries. He developed an enormous paper financial empire on which he built a corporate structure extending to various types of industry. By 1932 Kreuger was head of a multinational concern, including nearly 400 businesses, was worth hundred of millions of dollars and played a very important role in international finance. His liabilities far exceeded his assets and as the Depression deepened (1931–32) his empire became unstable, his position became increasingly indefensible, and he committed suicide in March 1932. Investigations uncovered frauds, forgeries and financial manipulations; the empire collapsed, a serious setback to the Swedish economy at a time of deep depression.

Krupp family

German industrialists. The Krupp industrial empire, founded by Friedrich Krupp in 1811, became world-famous as a manufacturer of steel and related products. In 1903, under Bertha Krupp, it was incorporated Friedrich Krupp Grusonwerk AG. On Bertha's marriage in 1906, control passed to her husband Gustav, who took the name Krupp. During World War I, Krupp manufactured heavy guns. Gustav, an ardent Nazi supporter, later increased illegal armaments production for Hitler's rearmament program. In 1943 Hitler ordered that the Krupp works be converted into a family holding, and Gustav's son Alfried took control,

Alfried, assuming the name Krupp, expanded the massive empire by accumulating property in countries invaded by Germany during World War II. Krupps used prisoners of war and concentration camp internees as slave labor. Alfried was later tried as a war criminal at Nuremberg, sentenced to 12 years imprisonment and the surrender of his property. He was released in 1951, and his property returned. He restored Krupps to prosperity and by the 1960s it was the largest steel producer in the world and worth over one billion dollars. Gustav was never tried, owing to his senility. Alfried's only son, Arndt, relinquished his succession rights and the Krupp name. In 1967, when Alfried died, the company became public.

Kuznets, Simon 1901–85

US economist. Born in Russia, he emigrated in 1922 to the US where he received his PhD in economics from Columbia University in 1926. Employed at the National Bureau of Economic Research (1927–61), he began studying national income, which led to his comparative study of economic growth in different countries. Kuznets was also professor of economics at the University of Pennsylvania (1930–54), Johns Hopkins University (1954–60) and Harvard University (1960–71). He was elected president of the American Statistical Association (1949) and the American Economics Association (1954) and in 1971 received the Nobel Prize for Economics. One of his major contributions to economics was the recognition of cycles in economic growth (Kuznets cycles). His investigation for differing periods in the US revealed cycles of 15–20 years duration. Kuznets also demonstrated the inverse relationship between national income per head of population and the degree of inequality in the distribution of income.

Lenin, Vladimir Ilych 1870–1924

Russian revolutionary and leader. Living mostly in Western Europe after 1900, he became leader of the Bolshevik wing of the Social Democratic party. Returning to Russia after the 1917 Revolution, he founded the new Soviet state, making peace with Germany and nationalizing all land to be taken over by peasants. The devastation of World War I was followed by civil war (1918–21) with requisitioning of food for the army and industrial workers and the takeover of industry. By June 1918 all large-scale industry was nationalized without compensation, private trade was officially abolished and strikes declared illegal. These restrictive practices became known as War Communism. By 1921 the Communists had won the civil war and Lenin introduced the New Economic Policy (NEP). It aimed to induce economic recovery through the profit motive, by allowing private trade, letting the peasants keep their land, ending grain requisitioning, and

denationalizing all industries and businesses employing under 20 people. Heavy industry remained nationalized but former managers were reinstated. The NEP achieved a period of stability and recovery in which industry and agriculture reached prewar levels by 1926. Lenin died in 1924 without fully witnessing its success.

Lewis, John Llewellyn 1880–1969

US trade unionist. A coal miner from the age of 15, he rose to become president of the United Mine Workers of America (UMWA) from 1920 to his retirement in 1960. A ruthless leader, he expelled many of his opponents. Lewis built the UMWA into a large, united force. In 1935 he established and became president of the Committee for Industrial Organization (CIO). The CIO expelled by the ATL became the most powerful labor union in the world. Initially a supporter of Roosevelt, Lewis clashed with the president, and when Roosevelt won the 1940 elections, Lewis resigned as president of the CIO, but continued to lead war-time strikes, contributing to a wave of antilabor legislation. Postwar strikes, at a time when Europe was desperately short of coal, led to the establishment of miners' pension funds but also the federal seizure of the mines. A subsequent strike, now against the government, defied a court order and led to Lewis and his union being fined heavily.

McNamara, Robert Strange 1916–

US businessman and Democrat politician. Hired as one of a young team to rejuvenate the Ford Motor Company in 1946, he worked his way up with successful plans such as introducing rigorous cost-accounting methods, until in 1960 he became the first non-Ford family member to be president of the company. In 1961 he resigned to join the Kennedy adminstration as secretary of defense, continuing his service under Johnson. McNamara modernized the armed forces, restructured budget procedures and introduced cost-cutting. Initially supporting US military involvement in Vietnam, by 1966 he came to question its escalation. He tried to initiate peace negotiations in 1967 and carried out a major investigation into US involvement which concluded against continued bombing. In 1968 he resigned to become president of the World Bank, a post he held until his retirement in 1981 and in which he showed a great sensitivity toward Third World needs.

Mao Zedong 1893–1976

Chinese Communist leader. Went to Beijing in 1918 and helped found the Chinese Communist party (CCP) in 1921. In 1934, after breaking with Jiang Jieshi, he led the "Long March" from southeast to northwest China. From there he defeated the Japanese and then Jiang's regime. In 1949 Mao proclaimed the People's Republic of

China, becoming its first president. In 1957 he initiated the "Great Leap Forward" to decentralize the economy and encourage continued economic growth. It was a failure, and Mao retired as chairman of the republic in 1959, remaining chairman of the CCP. He reasserted his power in the "Cultural Revolution", peaking between 1966 and 1969 but lasting officially until 1976. Although he was a cult figure, the ultimate effect of his policies on the Chinese economy was disruptive.

Marconi, Guglielmo 1874–1937

Italian inventor and physicist. In 1894 he began experimenting with wireless telegraphy in Italy, then in England where his first patent was filed in 1896. Subsequent demonstrations of sending signals attracted much attention, but little interest in exploiting his work. A cousin of Marconi's eventually helped financially and otherwise to establish Marconi's Wireless Telegraphy Company, Limited. The American Marconi Company was formed in 1899. In 1900 another company was founded to run services between ships and land stations. In the same year Marconi filed a patent allowing various stations to work on different wavelengths without interference. In 1901 he sent signals across the Atlantic. Further innovations led to the first radio message being sent from England to Australia in 1918 and the development of shortwave communication. He spent the rest of his life continuing to develop radio communications, broadcasting and navigation services, both scientifically and commercially. Marconi was awarded the Nobel Prize for Physics in 1909.

Marshall, George Catlett 1880–1959

US soldier and politician. After fighting in France in World War I and serving General Pershing (1919–24), Marshall rose to become Chief of Staff in 1939. He directed the US army throughout World War II and became a general in 1944. Resigning as Chief of Staff in 1945, he was sent to China by President Truman to mediate in the Chinese civil war. In 1947 he became Secretary of State and proposed the European Recovery Program or "Marshall Plan", the plan for US economic and technical aid to Western Europe which played such a successful part in postwar reconstruction and European economic growth. It aimed to restore and invigorate economies, stimulate economic growth and trade, and create stable conditions for democracy. Between 1948 and 1952 Western Europe received $12 billion in US aid. As Secretary of State Marshall also provided aid to Greece and Turkey, recognized Israel and was involved in negotiations leading to the establishment of NATO. He retired in 1949 owing to ill-health but was called back by President Truman as defense secretary during the Korean War. He retired permanently in 1951 and was awarded the Nobel Peace Prize in 1953.

▼ John Pierpont Morgan

◄ Kwame Nkrumah

▼ Julius Kambarae Nyerere

Matsushita, Konosuke 1894–1989

Japanese businessman. At the age of 22 he founded his own concern making sockets and bicycle lamps. Established the Matsushita Electrical Houseware Manufacturing Works in 1918, becoming a major producer of electrical appliances. In 1931 he began producing wireless sets and as business expanded, a variety of domestic electrical products. In 1935 the business was incorporated into Matsushita Electric Industry Companies, Ltd. The 1950s saw Matsushita producing radios, televisions and stereo equipment to meet growing demand. Strong emphasis on research and development, pioneering modern working practices, and an efficient market-research system ensured continued success. The company has constantly diversified production to include innovative products. The majority of sales are to foreign markets and use various brand names. Former president and chairman of the company, Matsushita was an advisory member of the board (1973–89), was active in all areas and was known for his unique business philosophies.

Mellon, Andrew William 1855–1937

US financier and politician. Began his career at his father's banking house, eventually becoming its president. Established himself as an industrial magnate and was one of the richest men in America by the 1920s. Entering politics as a Republican, Mellon was appointed secretary of the Treasury (1921–31). He introduced controversial fiscal reforms in order to reduce the national debt, decreasing tax and economizing in order to encourage business expansion and stimulate investment. As chairman of the World War I foreign debt commission he influenced policy on the US funding of foreign war debts. His insistence on a high tariff hindered repayment of European war debts, and he failed to foresee the Depression. Mellon was US ambassador to Britain in 1932–33. In 1937 he gave the US government an art collection, and much of the money needed to build the National Gallery of Art in Washington to house the paintings.

Messerschmitt, Wilhelm 1898–1978

German aviation designer and producer. Graduated in engineering and became chief designer and engineer of Bayerische Flugzeugwerke from 1926, and its chairman and director in 1938 when it became Messerschmitt Aircraft Manufacturing Works. It produced the Me 109, which set the world speed record in 1939. Messerschmitt made a variety of aircraft and supplied the Luftwaffe during World War II. Held by the US for two years after the war ended, he was banned from producing aircraft until 1958. In 1968–69 he established, and became honorary chairman of, the Messerschmitt-Bölkaw-Blohm company, also producing satellites and missiles.

Monnet, Jean 1888–1979

French political economist and statesman. After beginning his career in the family cognac business, in 1914 he entered the ministry of commerce and helped organize inter-Allied war supplies in World War I. He became deputy secretary general of the League of Nations (1919–23), returned to the family business, then entered international banking in 1925. As head of the Anglo-French Economic Co-ordination Committee in London, Monnet, with Churchill, helped inspire the Franco-British union in 1940 and, after the fall of France, served on the British Supply Council in Washington. After French liberation he led a committee planning the revitalization of the French economy, with the "Monnet Plan" (1947); Monnet himself was in charge of the National Planning Board. He proposed the integration of European iron and steel resources in the "Schuman Plan" of 1950, which resulted in the creation of the European Coal and Steel Community, Monnet serving as the president of its High Authority from 1952 to 1955. His attempts to establish a European Defense Community were less successful. In 1955 he founded the Action Committee for the United States of Europe and became its president (1956–1975).

Morgan, John Pierpont 1837–1913

US financier. Involved in gold speculation and foreign exchange during the Civil War, he went on to specialize in railroad development and organization. By the 1890s he controlled the largest group of railroads in the US. In 1871 he established the New York Firm of Drexel Morgan and Company, known as J. P. Morgan and Company after 1895. The firm became a major source of government finance and one of the world's most powerful banking houses. After purchasing Carnegie's steel interests, in 1901 he formed the United States Steel Corporation, the largest corporation in the world, and controlled shipping lines. Morgan took key decisions on how the government money in his banks was to be used in financial relief in the crisis of 1907. By 1912 he held 72 directorships in 47 large corporations. A noted art and book collector, he donated many works to the Metropolitan Museum of Art.

Nkrumah, Kwame 1909–72

Ghanaian politician. In 1949 he founded the nationalist and socialist Convention People's party (CPP), for which he won massive support with his policy of "self-government now". In 1950, while in prison, he was successful in the Gold Coast's first general elections and was released to become Leader of Government Business. In 1952 Nkrumah was elected prime minister, a post he still held when Ghana gained independence in 1957. Ghana became a republic in 1960 and Nkrumah its president. He played a key role in the Charter of

African States (1961). Economic reforms triggered social unrest, his authoritarianism grew, and several attempts were made on his life. In 1964 Nkrumah became a dictator; his regime was overthrown in 1966 while he visited Peking.

Norman, Montagu Collet 1871–1950

English banker. In 1915 he joined the Bank of England's governors full time. Governor general from 1920, he took the Bank from commercial into central banking and established its authority. During the 1920s' economic crisis Norman worked with the League of Nations and the Dawes and Young committees, helped stabilize foreign currencies and halted British inflation by balancing the budget. The establishment of new central banks abroad was part of his policy and he worked with Strong of the New York Federal Reserve Bank to provide US financial aid. Norman separated economic from political issues and always resisted government intervention. During the Depression, Norman restored confidence in sterling, helped reorganize industry and assisted Austria and Germany. With the outbreak of World War II he planned war finance and exchange controls. Forced to retire in 1944 owing to illness, he was made a peer. Despite the Depression, London never suffered a bank failure during his governorship.

Nyerere, Julius Kambarae 1922–

President of Tanzania. A graduate of Edinburgh University, Nyerere helped form the Tanganyika African National Union (TANU) in 1954, as its president. TANU won the 1958 and 1960 national elections and Nyerere became chief minister in a limited self-government. He became prime minister in 1961, and in 1962 when Tanganyika was declared a republic he was elected President. After 1964 Nyerere developed the new Republic of Tanzania as a one-party state, with elections for MPs. Recognizing the need for economic independence and the poor response to requests for aid, he made the Arusha Declaration in 1967. It stated that TANU leaders should not accumulate personal wealth and power; that economic growth to industrial revolution was inappropriate for Tanzania; and that the country was not to be run for the benefit of the urban population. He nationalized major enterprises and created *ujamaa* villages: farming collectives with voluntary membership and the goal of an egalitarian society producing for use, not profit. He resigned as state President in 1985.

Okita, Saburo 1914–

Japanese economist. Educated at Tokyo University, he joined government service as an engineer in 1937. In 1947 he joined the chief research section of the Economic Stabilization Board and was a member of the UN Economic Commission for Asia and the Far East (1952). Appointed director general

Juan Domingo Perón

Georges Pompidou

Walter Rathenau

of the Planning Bureau (1957) and of the Development Bureau (1962–63), he moved to become president of the Japanese Economic Research Center in 1964, and its chairman in 1973. He was a member of numerous committees on national and international economic policy, including the Pearson Commission on International Development (1969–80), the UN Committee on Development Planning (1965–80) and was Special Advisor to the International Development Center of Japan (1973–79). Foreign minister from 1979 to 1980, he became chairman in 1981 of the Institute of Domestic and International Policy Studies. Okita is president and chancellor of the International University of Japan. Recipient of several honors, he has published many works on the Japanese economy and economic policies.

Oppenheimer, Sir Ernest 1880–1957

South African mining magnate; industrialist and financier. Born in Germany, he moved in 1902 to South Africa as a representative for a London firm of diamond merchants. He soon became a leading figure in the diamond industry and in 1917 established the Anglo-American Corporation of South Africa, Ltd. Oppenheimer founded the Consolidated Diamond Mines of South West Africa, Ltd. in 1919, and then gained control of the pre-eminent De Beers Consolidated Mines. He formed the Diamond Corporation, Ltd. in 1930. He also formed a company in Rhodesia to exploit rich copper deposits. His final project was the opening of goldfields in the Orange Free State, South Africa. By 1957 Oppenheimer owned 95 percent of the world's diamond mines. He was mayor of Kimberley (1912–15) and its MP (1924–38). He was well known as a philanthropist, and was knighted in 1921.

Perón, Juan Domingo 1895–1974

Argentinean president. A colonel in the military coup of 1943, he became secretary of labor and welfare and began organizing workers' support. Appointed vice-president and minister of war in 1944, he was forced to resign in 1945 and imprisoned shortly afterwards. His supporters demanded and obtained his release, and he won the 1946 Presidential elections. Believing Argentina was being used by foreign interests as a supplier and a market at the expense of domestic interests, Perón advocated economic independence, especially from the USA and Britain. Asking increasingly higher prices for the beef that Britain especially needed, Perón used export revenue to finance his nationalization and industrialization policies. At first successful, after his re-election in 1951 these policies ceased to work. Inflation soared. A military revolt in 1955 deposed Perón and he went into exile. His supporters won the 1973 election, he returned and was again elected president, but died in 1974.

Peugeot, Armand 1849–1915

French automobile manufacturer. Peugeot became famous and influential after the success of his machine-tool-manufacturing company. In 1891 he traveled to Germany in search of the ideal two-cylinder engine, finding it being manufactured by Daimler. He returned to France and converted a factory to the production of automobiles. By 1906 he had established factories throughout France. Initially his Sochaux plant concentrated on the production of trucks, demand increasing dramatically during World War II, as for all industrial vehicles, but receding when war ended. Before the war Peugeot cars won many races, including the 1913 Indianapolis 500. The company produced vehicles which had a reputation for sturdiness and innovation.

Phillips, Alban William Housego 1914–75

New Zealand economist. Having entered economics after a career in electrical engineering, in 1958 Phillips was appointed Tooke Professor of Economics, Science and Statistics at the University of London, resigning in 1967 to accept the Chair of Economics at the Australian National University. In 1958 his article *The Relation Between Unemployment and the Rate of Change of Money Wage Rates in the UK, 1861–1957* was published. This gave empirical evidence of a relationship called the "Phillips curve" which showed an inverse ratio between the rates of unemployment and of inflation. Governments would have to choose between the two. The Phillips curve prompted much debate and analysis and is now regarded as insufficiently stable in practice to be a basis for government policy. Much of Phillips' other work concerned the problems of stabilizing economies, known as "optimal control theory".

Pompidou, Georges 1911–74

French premier and president. He left teaching to serve on de Gaulle's personal staff (1944–46). He was a member of the Council of State (1946–57), France's highest administrative–judicial body. In 1955 he joined Rothschild's bank and became its director general in 1959. Pompidou was appointed de Gaulle's chief personal advisor (1958–59) and was prominent in drafting the constitution of the 5th Republic and in planning France's economic recovery. De Gaulle assumed the Presidency in 1959 and Pompidou became a member of the Constitutional Council while continuing his outside business activities. In 1962 he was chosen to succeed Debré as prime minister. His government was defeated in October 1962 but he resumed office after de Gaulle's presidential victory in the same month. He lost his post again in 1968 after civil disturbances. De Gaulle resigned in 1969 and Pompidou was elected president, mainly following his predecessor's policies, but not opposing Britain's EEC entry. He died in office.

Porsche, Ferdinand 1875–1951

German automobile designer. He designed cars for Daimler and Auto Union, becoming director of Austro-Daimler Company (1916) and moving to the Daimler Company in Stuttgart (1923). In 1931 Porsche left to establish his own firm designing sports and racing cars. In 1934 he produced a design for Hitler's project, the Volkswagen ("People's Car"). This mass-produced car broke records on the postwar export market. Porsche designed military vehicles during World War II. After a period of postwar imprisonment by the French, the Porsche sports car was developed and introduced in 1950.

Prebisch, Raúl 1901–86

Argentinean economist. Professor of political economy at Buenos Aires (1925–48), under secretary of finance (1930–32), director of the Central bank (1935–43), from 1950 he worked in the UN, as director of the Economic Commission for Latin America (ECLA), and later as director general of the Conference for Trade and Development (UNCTAD). In an effort to explain and address the problem of underdevelopment in Third World, or peripheral, economies, he developed a four-point theory. The point with which he was most concerned was the tendency to deterioration of peripheral terms of trade. (The others were the increasing center–periphery income gap, inevitable unemployment in the periphery, and the limitation of peripheral economic growth by a permanent trade deficit.) He advocated protective tariffs, increased aid and expansion of the export market for developing countries. Prebisch's theories remain influential, even though the validity of some of his data has fallen into question.

Rathenau, Walter 1867–1922

German industrialist and politician. Headed the large Allgemeine-Elektrizitäts-Gesellschaft (AEG) founded by his father, after 1914. During World War I he instigated and directed the war raw materials department (1914–15), vital to Germany's economic mobilization for war. Rathenau then returned to his business empire. In 1921 as minister of reconstruction, he advocated compliance with Germany's obligations under the Treaty of Versailles. As foreign minister (1922) Rathenau sought reconciliation with the Allies, attempting to meet reparations payments, and signed the Treaty of Rapallo with the Soviet Union (1922), which canceled war debts, gave the Soviet government diplomatic recognition, and strengthened Russo-German economic ties. Despite his success he was increasingly detested in Germany as a Jew, a representative of the Weimar government and for signing the Rapallo Treaty with Communists. An advocate of social democracy, he wrote several books, including *New Society* in 1918. He was murdered in Berlin.

▲ John Davison Rockefeller

▲ Benjamin Seebohm Rowntree

▲ Robert Schuman

Reagan, Ronald Wilson 1911–

US president (1980–88). Hollywood actor from 1937 onward, making over 50 films in the following 25 years. He was a Democrat supporter after World War I, but formally switched allegiance to the Republican party in 1962. Reagan was elected governor of California in 1966 and again in 1970. He increased taxes and cut state government spending. He won the presidential nomination at his third attempt in 1980 and defeated President Carter in the elections. In 1984 Reagan was re-elected for a second term by a large majority. As President, Reagan proposed to strengthen the national economy and increase military power. Making economies in federal government operations, cutting taxes and reducing federal spending in every area apart from the military, he aimed to achieve a reduction in the large US budget deficit, curb inflation and induce economic recovery. Inflation did decrease and there has been economic recovery in line with other Western countries but the budget deficit remains high. Reagan also took a strong and aggressive stance in foreign policy, especially against the USSR and other Communist countries.

Renault, Louis 1877–1944

French automobile manufacturer. After military service Renault persuaded his older brothers to invest in the establishment of an automobile firm, to be called Renault Frères. They sold their cars in 1899 and expanded rapidly. By 1901 Renault was the eighth largest automobile company, and the most important in France. Success was based on the manufacture of a small cheap, reliable car, though after 1905 the taxicab was the largest selling vehicle. Louis and Marcel Renault were successful international racing drivers but after Marcel's death while racing in 1903 this ended. The company was known for its technical and organizational innovations. Louis, more interested in the technical aspects of his business, took out approximately 700 patents for inventions and his transmission system was adopted by many smaller firms. Experience in developing French aviation was later put to use when Renault manufactured military equipment, including aviation engines, during World War I. The company continued growth after the war, but with the liberation of Paris Louis was jailed for collaboration for making military equipment under German occupation. He died in prison, and his company was nationalized.

Robinson, Joan 1903–83

British economist. Graduating from Girton College, Cambridge, in 1925, she lectured in economics at Cambridge, becoming a full professor in 1965 and retiring in 1971. A strong advocate of Keynesian economics, Robinson in her most famous work, *Economics of Imperfect Competition* (1933), analyzed the impact of advertising,

consumer preference and product differentiation on the traditional theory of perfect competition. (Chamberlain developed similar ideas simultaneously and independently.) Her works on Keynes, *Introduction to the Theory of Employment* (1937), and on Marx, *An Essay on Marxian Economics* (1942), helped popularize these two areas of economic thought. After the war, Robinson's work was concentrated on a new Keynesian-type theory of long-run economic growth under capitalism. In her later career she moved increasingly away from, and increased the controversy around, orthodox economic theory.

Rockefeller, John Davison 1839–1937

US industrialist, financier and philanthropist. He established his own food merchant's in 1859. When oil was discovered in Pennsylvania he became involved with oil refining. With his partners he quickly became the largest refiner in Cleveland and organized the Standard Oil Company in 1870 with a capital of $1 million. Rockefeller led the company in its development into the largest oil firm in the USA, symbol of the modern, efficient and ruthless American business corporation, especially with its use of price-cutting offensives used to take over competitors. By 1879 Standard Oil controlled almost all of US refining capacity. To consolidate and be able to operate legally in other states, Rockefeller's concerns adopted a trust agreement putting all stock under the control of a board of trustees. Despite legislation aimed at breaking this organization the Rockefeller enterprises survived under different names but as a single unit. In 1897 Rockefeller formally retired from active leadership. His main concern became the distribution of much of his vast wealth in charitable and philanthropic ventures, helping to establish Chicago University and the Rockefeller Foundation.

Roosevelt, Franklin Delano 1882–1945

US president. An ex-barrister, he entered the senate as a Democrat in 1910, and ran unsuccessfully for vice-president in 1920. Stricken by paralysis in 1921, he maintained his political interest during his convalescence. In 1932 Roosevelt defeated Hoover in the presidential elections. He took immediate decisive action against the economic crisis with the enactment of his "New Deal" legislation. Government reorganized agriculture, industry and finance and undertook new labor legislation, welfare programs and public works using the then radical policy of deficit financing influenced by new Keynesian ideas. The economy began to recover and Roosevelt was re-elected an unprecedented three times. Initially following a neutral policy favoring the Allies during World War II, the US entered the war in 1941 after the Japanese attack on Pearl Harbor and the New Deal was cut short.

Rostow, Walt W. 1916–

US economist. Educated at Yale and Oxford, he taught at Harvard University during the 1940s and became professor of economic history there in 1952. He left Harvard in 1961 to become Deputy Special Assistant in National Security Affairs to President Kennedy. Rostow was Chairman of the Policy Planning Council at the State Department (1961–66) and a US member of the Inter-American Committee to the Alliance for Progress. Appointed Special Assistant in National Security Affairs to President Johnson in 1966, he left in 1969 to become professor of economics and history at the University of Texas. In Rostow's most famous publication *The Stages of Economic Growth: A Non-Communist Manifesto* (1960), he postulated that, having examined the historical records of now industrialized countries, there were definite phases in the relationship between savings rates and capital-output ratios (the productivity of new investment), in which given the prevailing capital-output ratio, savings rose to levels that facilitated "take-off" to steady and increasing economic growth. This theory was heavily criticized and is now regarded as naive. Rostow also wrote the important *The Growth and Fluctuation of the British Economy, 1790–1860* (1953).

Rowntree, Benjamin Seebohm 1871–1954

UK industrialist, sociologist and philanthropist. He joined the family firm of H.I. Rowntree and Company in 1889, was appointed director in 1897 and chairman from 1923 to 1941. He became an authority in the field of scientific management and industrial welfare, becoming director of the welfare department of the Ministry of Munitions (1915–18). Between 1897 and 1898 Rowntree investigated the state of the poor in York and in 1901 published *Poverty, a Study of Town Life* as a result. He published *The Human Needs of Labor* in 1918 and *The Human Factor in Business* in 1921. He undertook a second York survey in 1936 and subsequently published *Poverty and Progress* (1941). Rowntree also worked with Lord Astor on studies of British agriculture.

Schacht, H.H.G. 1877–1970

German financier. Appointed Reich Currency Commissioner and President of the Reichsbank in 1923. Schacht was largely responsible for stabilizing the German mark when it was near collapse in 1923. By 1928 he had achieved eminence as a financier and was re-elected as Reichsbank president. Shortly after he reluctantly signed the Young Plan in 1929, he resigned and became an outspoken critic of German economic policies. In 1933 he resumed the presidency when called back by the Nazis and became the principal director of the German economy for the next six years. Schacht restored the German trade balance by a system of bilateral trade with a number of

▲ Albert Speer

▲ Joseph Stalin

▲ Peter Arkadyevich Stolypin

smaller countries and undertook an expansionist credit policy. His unorthodox methods financed the large Nazi rearmament and public works programs and supplied work for many unemployed. He resigned as president of the Reichsbank in 1939 over a disagreement with Hitler. Charged with high treason and imprisoned by the Nazis, he was acquitted by the Allies in 1945 of crimes against humanity. He subsequently founded a bank in Düsseldorf and was economic advisor to Persia, Syria, Egypt and Indonesia.

Schuman, Robert 1886–1963
French statesman and architect of European political and economic integration. A member of the French National Assembly from 1919, he was arrested by the Gestapo in 1940, escaped in 1942 and became a member of the French Resistance. He returned to Parliament after World War II as a leader of the new Roman Catholic *Mouvement Républicain Populaire* (MRP) and served as minister of finance (1946), prime minister (1947–48, 1948), foreign minister (1948–52) and minister of justice (1955–56). As foreign minister he signed the Atlantic Pact for France (1949) and announced the "Schuman Plan" (1950) to advance European economic and military unity. This led to the creation of the European Coal and Steel Community in 1952, consisting of six western European countries and initiating a succession of economic agreements which resulted in the establishment of the EEC in 1958. In the same year he was elected president of the Strasbourg European Assembly and re-elected to the National Assembly where he stayed until 1963.

Sieff, Israel M. 1889–1972
British industrialist. An economics graduate, Sieff joined the board of Marks and Spencer in 1915, becoming joint managing director, with his childhood friend Simon Marks, and vice-chairman, in 1926. He had a gift for securing high-quality, low-priced suppliers, bypassing wholesalers; and he was the creator of the exemplary human relations system for which the firm is famed. In 1931 Sieff was asked to join the newly founded Political and Economic Planning (PEP), a group formed to inform and assist government and industry. He contributed a practical emphasis, produced its first, brilliant, industrial report, and became PEP's chairman (1931–39) and vice-chairman (1939–64). Sieff had many interests, including music, anthropology, and orchids. In 1966 he was made a life peer.

Sloan, Alfred Pritchard, Jr 1875–1966
US Chairman and President of General Motors. After graduating in electronic engineering in 1895 he joined Hyatt Roller Bearing Company as a draftsman and became its president in 1897. He led the company's rapid progression, quickly

exploiting the increasing market for his product in the expanding automobile industry. Hyatt was purchased by the General Motors Corporation (GM) in 1917 and in 1918 Sloan was appointed a GM vice-president, director and member of the executive committee. He was soon promoted, eventually becoming president and chief executive in 1928. He resigned as president in 1937 and was elected Chairman of the Board. Sloan was given much of the credit for GM's success and its quick recovery from the postwar slump. During his presidency GM became the largest automobile manufacturer and largest single business organization in the world. Through divisions and subsidies he diversified and decentralized production but simultaneously centralized administration. When Sloan retired in 1956, GM accounted for over half US automobile sales. Sloan also supported many philanthropic ventures.

Sorel, Georges 1847–1922
French politician, syndicalist philosopher and engineer. He trained and worked as a civil engineer, becoming interested in social and political issues in his middle age. He retired in 1892 and turned to study, becoming a strong defender of Dreyfus. Influenced by Marx, Nietzsche and Bergson, he formulated a political theory set down in *Réflexions sur la violence* (1908) in which he advocated revolutionary syndicalism. The premise of this movement was that real socialism could only come into being through violent revolution by a proletariat educated by trade unions. In the long term Sorel's views had a greater influence on the right than the left, his ideas being adopted and altered by Italian and German fascists in the 1930s. Disillusioned by syndicalism, Sorel joined a monarchist movement in 1909 and subsequently became a Bolshevik in 1919. In addition to his works on socialism, his writing covered areas including the Bible, Aristotle and the decline of Rome.

Speer, Albert 1905–81
German architect and politician. A qualified architect, he undertook commissions for the Nazi party after joining it in 1931, and became Hitler's chief architect in 1934, when he was commissioned to build the Nuremberg stadium. He was given responsibility for the planned reconstruction of Berlin, which was never achieved. From 1941 to 1945 he was a member of the Reichstag, representing Berlin, and in 1942 became minister of armaments and war production. Speer supervised the conversion of the German economy to capacity war production, greatly improving industrial performance and increasing armaments output three times (1942–44). Production of war materials was maintained by a supply of slave labor from the concentration camps, a system Speer expanded. Toward the end of the war he

openly opposed Hitler and especially the Führer's wish to destroy German industry as the Allies advanced. The only Nazi leader to admit even token guilt for the regime's crimes at the Nuremberg trials, he served 20 years in Spandau prison. Released in 1966, Speer published two memoirs in the 1970s.

Stalin, Joseph 1879–1953
Russian dictator. After Lenin's death in 1924 Stalin, the Communist party secretary, eliminated his political rivals and won control of the Comintern. In the 1930s Stalin carried out the Great Purge of the party and became official head of government in 1940. His chief aims were to consolidate his own position and to achieve rapid economic growth, to be achieved through five-year plans, constructed by the state planning authority, Gosplan. The first and second five-year plans (1928–33 and 1932–37) concentrated on heavy industry and the forced and brutal collectivization of Russia's failing agricultural sector. Industry especially increased output. In 1938, the third Plan was launched to develop a war economy. After the devastation of World War II, a fourth five-year plan was launched (1946–50), industry again being the priority. Heavy industry recovered successfully but there was little investment in new industry and recovery in agriculture was slow, leading to food shortages; nor did agriculture production subsequently increase significantly; collectivization had not been successful. However, by his death in 1953, Stalin had produced a highly industrialized nation, second in output to the USA only. However, collectivization did not work and agricultural production remained low.

Stolypin, Peter Arkadyevich 1862–1911
Russian Statesman. Governor of Grodno (1902) and Saratov (1903), minister of the interior (1906) and prime minister (1906–11) after the elections to the first Duma in 1906. He combined a policy of harsh repression with systematic reforms. He dissolved the second Duma in 1907 and changed the electoral law to restrict franchise and reduce nationalist representation. His agrarian reforms of 1906–11 broke up the commune. They established hereditary land tenure by heads of families and peasants were permitted to leave village communities and establish separate farms, and encouraged to buy and enclose their land. The amount of resources available to peasant land-banks was increased and education and settlement in less populated areas encouraged. Stolypin's aim was to create a prosperous and conservative kulak class of small and medium farmers and generally improve agriculture. The resultant expanded domestic market would eventually be integrated by the industrialization of the country. Stolypin was assassinated by a socialist revolutionary terrorist in 1911.

▲ Margaret Hilda Thatcher

▲ Fritz Thyssen

▲ Orville Wright

Strong, Benjamin 1872–1928

US banker. Starting as a banking clerk in New York, he became secretary of several companies including the Bankers' Trust Company (1903) of which he became president in 1913. He was involved in the investigation and assistance of New York banks in difficulty in the 1907 crisis and was director of a number of companies, including the General Electric Company. In 1914 Strong was appointed the first governor of the Federal Reserve Bank of New York, the largest of 12 regional banks established under the 1913 Act, and it became the pivot of the new system, with Strong exerting considerable influence. US entry into the war in 1917 put the system under strain but this was alleviated largely through Strong's leadership. His postwar conferences with heads of European central banking systems resulted in the vital measures taken for fiscal readjustment and stabilization. Measures that he initiated included loans to Poland, the German Reichsbank and the Bank of England, and the stabilization of the French and Italian currencies.

Strumilin, Stanisláv G. 1877–1974

Russian economist and statistician. Participated in revolutionary activities as a young man, was arrested, imprisoned and exiled, escaping twice. An economics graduate, he worked as a professional statistician for the government and on the wartime fuel distribution committee (1911–14). After the Revolution he began a long career in Soviet statistical and planning bodies, heading statistical offices for the Labor Commissariat and All-Russian Central Council of Trade Unions (1918–23). He became a Presidium member of the State Planning Commission, Gosplan, from 1921, subsequently being appointed chief of the Central Statistical Administration and deputy chairman of Gosplan. Strumilin was largely responsible for the earlier drafts of the first five-year plan. He left Gosplan in 1937 but returned during World War II (1943–51). In 1931 Strumilin was elected a full member of the USSR Academy of Science, becoming head of the Institute of Economics at the Academy. A Communist party member from 1923, he wrote prolifically on economics, receiving two Orders of Lenin and the Red Labor Banner.

Tata, Jamsetji Nasarwanji 1839–1904

Indian industrialist. He joined his father's trading firm in 1858. Recovering from the Indian slump after the American Civil War, they reentered the China trade. Tata then entered the cotton industry, converting the Alexandra Mill in Bombay (1871), building a new mill in Nagpur (1877) and reconditioning other mills. The mills became the pivot of the family fortune and were reputed for their efficiency, advanced labor policies and use of finer grade of fiber. Tata diversified his interest in the 1890s, buying property in Bombay, entering the Bombay money market, building the Taj Mahal Hotel and promoting silk production in Mysore state. Most importantly, in 1901 he began to develop India's first large-scale ironworks, incorporated as Tata Iron and Steel Company in 1907, and later one of the world's largest steelworks. It was the center of a vast and various industrial empire. Tata also planned the hydro-electric plants near Bombay which became the Tata Power companies after his death.

Thatcher, Margaret Hilda 1925–

British Conservative prime minister. MP for Finchley since 1959, after holding ministerial and shadow posts, she was elected leader of her party in 1975. She became the first female British prime minister in 1979. On the right of the party, Thatcher took a strong line on law and order and defense and advocated the end of government control of industry, tax and public expenditure costs and the limitation of trade union power. Economically, she adopted the monetarist policy of controlling the money supply in order to influence the operation of the economy. This and other economic policies resulted in high unemployment and an increasing number of business bankruptcies. Despite her unpopularity, Thatcher's conduct in the Falklands war led to her landslide victory in the 1983 general elections. Her second term was marked by a continuation of monetarist policy and a growing emphasis on liberalizing the economy, marked by the privatization of major public concerns. In 1987 she achieved a record third term in office, and privatization policies continued, unemployment decreased, but inflation and the trade deficit rose sharply. She supported the establishment of a common European market, but stood alone against full European monetary union. She resigned from office in 1990.

Thyssen, Fritz 1873–1951

German industrialist. Son of the wealthy industrialist August Thyssen, Fritz became general director of the Thyssen foundries and in 1928 founded, with his father, the United Steel Works which became the world's largest mining and steel cartel. One of Hitler's first financial supporters, he was regarded as an economics expert and made director of an institute for research on the corporate state after Hitler became chancellor in 1933. He also became a deputy in the Reichstag but by 1935 had begun to doubt the Nazi regime. In 1938 he resigned from the Council of State in protest at Jewish persecution. Although rapid German rearmament was good for business, Thyssen spoke out in the Reichstag against the coming war. With the outbreak of war he fled Germany, forfeiting his nationality, and his property (to the state). Arrested in France in 1940, he spent the remainder of the war in concentration camps. He and his family moved to Argentina, where he died.

Tito (Josip Broz) 1892–1980

Founder and president of Communist Yugoslavia. After adopting Communism, he took part in the 1917 Russian Revolution and on his return to Yugoslavia in 1920, became an activist for the illegal Communist party. During World War II Tito organized the National Liberation Front which alone liberated the country. After the war he became Yugoslavia's first Communist prime minister (1945), becoming president in 1953. Tito applied Marxist principles to industry and trade but left peasants in possession of their land. State control in industry and agriculture was less rigid than in the rest of the Communist bloc. Tito managed to keep Yugoslavia relatively independent of the USSR, politically and economically. Disagreement with Stalin resulted in the stopping of economic aid from Russia; it was instead obtained from the West. Tito pursued new economic policies during the 1960s, lifting price controls and demanding financial self-sufficiency. Tourism was encouraged, Western companies welcomed, and trade links brought new technology.

Toyoda, Kiichiro 1894–1952

Japanese automobile pioneer. In 1933 he established an automobile division within his father's loom business after visiting automobile factories in America. He produced his first prototype vehicle in 1935 and in 1937 the business was incorporated as the Toyota Motor Company, Ltd. Japan's lack of natural resources forced Toyoda to develop highly fuel-efficient engines. In 1940 the Toyoda Science Research Center and the Toyoda Steel Works were established and in 1941 the Toyoda Machine Works, Ltd. After the war, reconstruction led to recovery. Toyota avoided the US- and European-dominated market of large and medium-sized car production, concentrating on the smaller car, of which it produced its first prototype in 1947. However, in 1949, the Japanese economy was severely depressed and Toyoda faced financial and labor difficulties. The Toyota Motor Sales Company, Ltd., was established in 1950 to increase sales, the workforce was reduced to avoid bankruptcy and Toyoda (the president) and all his executive staff resigned. Toyoda died less than two years later.

Voznesensky, Nicholas 1903–50

Russian economist and government official. Joined the Communist party in 1919 and studied economics at Svardlov Communist University and the Economic Institute of Red Professorship, where he lectured from 1931. In 1934 Voznesensky became a member of the Soviet Control Commission and after 1935 worked with Andrey Zhdanov in Leningrad. In 1938 he became chairman of Gosplan, the State Planning Commission, which planned and coordinated

▲ Ahmad Zaki Yamani

▲ Basil Zaharoff

▲ Ferdinand von Zeppelin

economic activities. He advanced to deputy prime minister in 1939 and was chief economic planner in the state defense committee during World War II. From 1943 Voznesensky was a member of the Committee for Economic Reconstruction in Former German Occupied Areas. In 1947 he became a full Politburo member. Early in 1949 he fell into disfavor as a colleague of Zhdanov and lost his seat in the Politburo. He was arrested for supposed involvement in the Leningrad affair and shot. His popular book *The War Economy of the USSR During the Fatherland War* (1947) was declared "anti-Marxist" by Stalin. He received two Orders of Lenin.

Wallenberg, Jacob 1892–1980
Swedish industrialist. Educated in economics in Stockholm, he became assistant manager of Stockholms' Enskilda Bank (1918–27), was appointed vice-managing director and member of the Board of Directors (1920–27) and managing director (1927–46). He then advanced to vice-chairman of the board (1946–50) and became chairman of the Bank (1950–69). In addition, Wallenberg has been appointed chairman of some of Sweden's largest companies, including Providentia and Investor. He was appointed to the board of directors of the Nobel Foundation, was chairman of the Wallenberg Foundation and was a member of the Royal Swedish Academy of Engineering Sciences.

Whitman, Marina Bon Neumann 1935–
US economist. Graduated from Radcliffe College in 1956, received an MA in 1959 and a PhD in 1962, both in economics at Columbia University. Taught economics at the University of Pittsburgh (1962–72), becoming a full professor in 1971. In 1971 Whitman became senior staff economist in international affairs to the Council of Economic Advisors and was appointed by President Nixon to the US Price Commission, the commission's only female member and its youngest. A member of the Council of Economic Advisors (1972–73), she played a key role in producing the economic forecast for 1973. Returning to the University of Pittsburgh in 1973, she was appointed Distinguished Public Service Professor of Economics. In 1979 Whitman resigned to become vice-president and chief economist of General Motors. In addition she was on the overseas board at Harvard College (1972–78); economic advisor for the the US Department of Commerce from 1979; trustee of Princetown University from 1979; member of committees on national and international monetary policies; recipient of the Columbia medal for excellence (1973), and many other honors; member of the Royal Economic Society and American Economic Association; received numerous academic grants and wrote several books.

Wright, Orville (1871–1948) and Wilbur (1867–1912)
US pioneer aviators. Talented and self-taught mechanics, they became interested in aviation through the gliding experiments of Otto Lilienthals and established a bicycle business which financed their early aviation experiments. The brothers developed a three-axis control system for a biplane kite and in 1900 moved on to testing a series of gliders with moveable wing-tips that gave total control. For their experiments they designed a wind tunnel and also undertook much theoretical work. In 1903 they made the first powered airplane flight at Kitty Hawk. The "Flyer II" was flown in 1904 and in 1905 "Flyer III" undertook a flight of 24 miles lasting over half an hour. The Wrights lacked sponsorship but continued to develop aircraft. In 1908 they acquired a licence to produce airplanes in Europe and won a US Army contract to produce the world's first military airplane. In 1909 they gave up their cycle business and established an aircraft production company, of which Wilbur was president until his death. Orville devoted the remainder of his life to research.

Yamani, Ahmad Zaki 1930–
Saudi Arabian politician and oilman. Educated at Cairo, New York and Harvard Universities, he established a private law practice and became director of several companies. Finance minister (1956–58), he was legal advisor (1958–60), to and member of the Saudi Council of Ministers (1960–86) and minister of state (1960–62). In addition he became minister of Petrol and Mineral Resources (1962–86) and director of the Arabian American Oil Company (1962–68). The king ultimately controls oil policy in Saudi Arabia but Yamani was given considerable independence as petroleum minister. He also became chairman of the General Petroleum and Mineral Organization (1963–86) and of the Saudi Arabian Fertilizer Company (1966–86). As secretary general (1968–69) and chairman (1974–75) of the Organization of Arabian Petroleum Exporting Countries (OAPEC) he held great influence in an increasingly powerful organization. During the 1970s Yamani withstood threats from the USA and fellow OAPEC members. However, he lost favor with the Royal family in 1986 after oil revenue fell and was dismissed from government office.

Young, Owen D. 1874–1962
US lawyer and businessman. Young practiced law until 1912 when he was appointed general counsel for the General Electric Company, also serving as chairman (1922–39). He organized the Radio Corporation of America in 1919, becoming honorary chairman of its board of directors (1919–29) and chairman of the executive committee (1929–33). A member of the first committee of experts appointed to advise the Reparations

Commission over currency stabilization in post World War I Germany, he chaired the second international committee of experts in 1929. The plan, which became known as the Young Plan, proposed a new settlement for reparations. Revising the Dawes Plan of 1924, it reduced the amount of reparations due from Germany, established the Bank for International Settlements to handle the transfer of funds and ended Allied control over German economic life. Before the plan got underway the Depression of the 1930s began and after Hitler came to power in 1933 German obligations made under the Treaty of Versailles were not kept.

Zaharoff, Basil 1850–1936
Armaments magnate and financier. Born in Turkey of Greek parents, he worked for his uncle in London (1870–72), leaving after being acquitted of embezzlement. Returning to Greece, he met a financier and diplomat, who successfully recommended Zaharoff for the job of agent to Nordenfelt, the Swedish gun designer. The inventor of the machine gun, H.S. Maxim, joined Nordenfelt in business in 1888 and Zaharoff was their representative in Russian and Eastern Europe. When the Vickers Company of Sheffield acquired the company in 1895, Zaharoff covered an even greater area for the firm and became a millionaire. He extended his fortune by entering shipping, oil and banking. He became a French citizen in 1913. Zaharoff worked as a high-ranking Allied agent during World War I and was knighted in Britain in 1918 for his services, and awarded the Légion d'Honneur. He became very influential in international politics, but always mysterious. He donated much money to universities and other institutions, but was suspected of using his power for his own profit.

Zeppelin, Ferdinand von 1838–1917
German inventor of the dirigible airship. A German army officer, Zeppelin served in the Franco-German war. After retiring in 1890, he spent the rest of his life creating the rigid airship for which he became famous. He produced his first airship, named "The Zeppelin", which was launched in 1900. Although not entirely successful, the launch caught the public imagination and generated funds for the continuation of his work. Zeppelin established a works for airship construction at Friedrichshafen. The poor development of airplane technology was influential in the German government's decision to commission an entire fleet of airships after Zeppelin achieved a twenty-four-hour flight in 1906. In 1910 he founded a passenger service. Over one hundred zeppelins were used for military operations in World War I, but they were too easily shot down so be considered successful to any real extent.

GLOSSARY

Alternative economy
The part of a nation's creation of **goods** and **services** that escapes taxation illegally. Estimates of its size vary greatly. Also known as the "black economy" and the "cash economy".

Autarky
Economic self-sufficiency. An autarkic economy limits its imports and exports by means of bilateral agreements, tariffs and other restrictions.

Balance of payments
The difference between all the payments made from a country to, and to that country from, the rest of the world. It comprises the **balance of trade** and **invisible earnings**.

Balance of trade
The difference between the total values of a nation's imports and exports of **goods** (rather than **services**).

Bankruptcy
The legally established condition of having insufficient money to pay one's debts by their due dates. The bankrupt's assets are liquidated and distributed among the creditors.

Bear market
A market, usually in **shares**, where prices are falling.

Bilateralism
The conducting of trade between two countries under special conditions. This is most important for countries with nonconvertible **currencies**, as any imbalance cannot readily be redressed in trade with others or **multilateralism**.

Bill of exchange
An unconditional written order, promising payment of a specified sum on demand or at a determined date. Bills of exchange are frequently used in international trade.

Black market
Any illegal market. It may be in illegal **goods**, or legal **goods, services** or **currencies** sold above or below a government-stipulated price, and is usually associated with rationing or other stringent government controls.

Boom
A rapid and continuous increase in economic activity and in prices. It is the highest point in a **trade cycle**.

Bull market
A market, usually in **shares**, where prices are rising.

Capital
Any physical **commodity** that can be used in the generation of income. Working capital is used up in the production process. Fixed capital is not, but is subject to depreciation.

Capital formation
Net addition to the stock of **capital**, after depreciation.

Cartel
An association of producers of the same range of **goods**, agreeing to regulate prices by limiting output and competition, to maximize profits.

Capital equipment
Equipment held for use in production.

Cash crop
A crop that is intended to be sold rather than consumed by the grower.

Centrally planned economy
An economy in which every major decision is made by the government rather than through market forces.

Clearing house
An institution usually linked to a stock or commodity exchange in which transactions made in the exchange are registered and settled. It normally also oversees the delivery of the product involved.

Colonial preference
High tariff rates, set by a colonial power, on imports of **goods** of which the colony importing is a major producer, as for instance, (British) Imperial Preference, established by the Ottawa Agreements of 1932.

Council for Mutual Economic Assistance (COMECON)
COMECON was established in 1949 to promote the development of the member nations' economies. Its members in 1990 were: Bulgaria, Czechoslovakia, East Germany, Hungary, Mongolia, Poland, Romania, the Soviet Union, Cuba and Vietnam. Yugoslavia is an associate member.

Commodity
Any physical good that can be traded or consumed, particularly raw materials.

Consumerism
1 Policies that control the standards of products or services for the benefit of their buyers. Such policies may be statutory or voluntary. **2** An economic policy based on a belief that any increase in the purchase of consumer **goods** is desirable.

Currency
The bank notes and coins currently in use. The term is also more broadly used to refer to a particular country's money.

Currency reserve
Metallic or other backing for a **currency**, usually held either by the central bank, or by the "monetary authorities".

Deflation
A sustained fall in the price level; when it coincides with the downswing of the **trade cycle**, output tends to fall and consequently unemployment to rise. Since the 1950s, governments have attempted to deflate economies in order to counteract inflationary pressure.

Demand-side policies
Government policies that affect the general demand for **goods** and **services**, primarily by changes in taxation and government expenditure that affect consumers. See **supply-side policies**.

Depression
A sustained decrease in economic activity (see also **slump**).

Devaluation
An official reduction in a **currency's** value in terms of another **currency**.

Developed countries
The countries with the highest standard of living. Generally, most of their wealth comes from manufacturing and service industries.

Economic dualism
The existence and interrelationship of two major production sectors in an economy, one large-scale, capital- and technology- intensive, the other small-scale and labor-intensive.

Economics
A social science that is concerned with the production of **goods** and **services** and their distribution, exchange and consumption and the links between these activities.

Equilibrium
A situation that will remain unaltered until changed by external forces. A market is in equilibrium when both buyers and sellers are content with the current combination of prices and **goods**.

European Community (EC, in full Commission of the European Communities – CEC)
Formerly the European Economic Community (EEC), this association of European states was established by the Treaty of Rome in 1957. By 1990 it had 12 members: Belgium, Denmark, France, West Germany, Greece, Ireland, Italy, Luxembourg, The Netherlands, Portugal, Spain and the UK.

European Free Trade Association (EFTA)
Founded in 1960, EFTA's members are Austria, Finland, Iceland, Norway, Sweden and Switzerland. Its goals are the abolition of barriers to international trade and close co-operation with the European Community.

European Monetary System (EMS)
Most countries in the European Community belong to the EMS, which attempts to stabilize the value of the members' currency exchange rates.

Exchange rate
The price of a **currency** in terms of another **currency**.

Fiscal policy
Government measures to influence a nation's economic activity by altering taxation, welfare payments and government expenditure.

Free market
A market which is not subject to government intervention or regulation.

Futures market
A market where **commodities** or financial securities are bought or sold for delivery at a fixed date in the future and at an agreed price.

General Agreement on Tariffs and Trade (GATT)
A multilateral treaty; GATT seeks to expand international trade through the abolition of tariffs, quotas and all other trade barriers. Most nations belong to GATT, which was founded in 1948.

Gold standard
The valuation of a **currency** in terms of a fixed amount of gold for which it may be exchanged on demand. Most countries operated on the gold standard in the late 19th century and again between the early 1920s and the mid 1930s.

Goods
Almost synonymous with **commodities** but less used for raw materials.

Great Depression
Another name for the **Depression** of 1929–33.

Gross Domestic Product (GDP)
The **Gross National Product** minus income from abroad (for example, money sent home from migrant workers or rent from foreign property.)

Gross National Product (GNP)
The total monetary value of a nation's output of goods and services over a period of time (usually a year), including income from abroad.

Hard currency
A **currency** that is not expected to fall in value and which is readily exchangeable into other **currencies**. See **reserve currency**.

Horizontal integration
The merger of two or more businesses operating at the same stage of a production process. See **vertical integration**.

Import substitution
Replacement of imports by domestic products which are usually inferior. Governments sometimes place tariffs on imports to encourage import substitution. It is most common in developing countries and in wartime.

Inflation
A continuous rise in prices generally so that the value of money falls.

Interest rate
The price of borrowing **money**, expressed as a percentage per time period (usually per year).

International Monetary Fund (IMF)
Founded in 1945, this agency of the United Nations attempts to promote international monetary co-operation and stabilize the value of **currencies**. It lends money to member countries in the form of **Special Drawing Rights** and also provides economic advice.

Investment
The purchase of capital goods, or the deployment of **money**, in order to generate future income.

Invisible earnings
Earnings from intangible items (**services**).

Keynesianism
Economic theories based on the doctrines of the British economist John Maynard Keynes (1883–1946). Keynesianism advocates controlling the economy through government intervention, especially through **fiscal policy**.

Laissez-faire
(French: let it happen) An economic tenet that the economy is best left to function on its own and that government intervention is harmful.

Lend-Lease
A system adopted in World War II under which the USA gave its allies armaments and food supplies in exchange for deferred payments, property or other material.

Less-developed countries (LDCs)
Also known as "underdeveloped" or "developing" countries or as the **Third World**, countries whose per capita income is less than 20 percent of that of the USA.

Liquidity
The ease with which an asset can be converted into **money**.

Market economy
An economy in which the distribution of goods and services is determined by unfettered demand and supply.

Marshall Aid
More properly known as the "European Recovery Program", Marshall Aid was assistance given by the USA and Canada to Western Europe after the Second World War. It was named after General G.C. Marshall (1880–1959), the then US Secretary of State.

Mixed economy
Any economy where private individuals and enterprises and the government share the significant economic decisions. Most nations are mixed economies to a greater or lesser degree.

Monetarism
A body of economic theory which holds that the money supply is the main determinant of economic activity, particularly inflation, and that the government can achieve its economic goals largely through the control of the money supply.

Money
Anything that will be readily accepted in exchange for **goods** and **services** and in payment of debts. It usually consists of bank notes, coins and cheques.

Money market
An aggregation of credit and deposit markets.

Monopoly
The domination of a market by a single seller of a product. Because there is no effective competition, prices will normally increase.

Multilateralism
International trade in which each nation trades with many other nations rather than with one. See under **bilateralism**.

Multinational corporation (MNC)
A company that operates in more than one country.

Nationalization
The bringing under government control of any industry that was formerly privately owned.

Net National Product (NNP)
The **Gross National Product** minus a deduction to allow for the depreciation in value of any assets.

New Deal
US President Franklin D. Roosevelt's program (1933–39) of building works, social and economic reforms, intended to end the **Depression**.

New Economic Policy
The program introduced in the USSR by V.I. Lenin (1870–1924) in the 1920s to help the country's economic reconstruction after the world and civil wars.

Newly Industrialized Economies (NIEs)
Countries that are neither poor nor rich and which are developing their industrial bases. The **OECD** considers the following to belong to this group as of 1990: Brazil, Hong Kong, South Korea, Mexico, Singapore, Taiwan and Yugoslavia.

Organization for Economic Co-Operation and Development (OECD)
Created in 1961, this association aims to promote economic growth and international trade. The 24 members are all of the European Community and EFTA as well as the following: Australia, Canada, Japan, New Zealand, Turkey and the USA. Yugoslavia is an associate.

Organization of Petroleum Exporting Countries (OPEC)
OPEC was formed in 1960 to advance the interests of its members, which are all oil producers. Its 13 members are: Algeria, Ecuador, Gabon, Indonesia, Iran, Kuwait, Libya, Nigeria, Qatar, Saudi Arabia, the United Arab Emirates, and Venezuela.

Parity
The official exchange rate of a **currency** in terms of gold or the US dollar or another named **currency**; also known as "par value".

Petrofunds
Large surpluses of US dollars and other foreign **currencies** amassed by OPEC members from the 1970s onward.

Planned economy
An economy where the allocation and distribution of resources is directed by the government.

Primary producer
A country that produces mainly raw materials. Most **less developed countries** are primary producers.

Productivity
The efficiency with which resources are used, especially labor.

Protectionism
The policy of restricting imports to protect domestic industry and agriculture. Customs duties, import quotas and selective regulations are the most common types of protectionist measure.

Public company
A company whose **shares** are quoted on the stock market.

Recession
A decrease in economic activity, briefer and milder than a **depression**. Part of the **trade cycle**.

Reparations
Payments deemed due to the victors from the losers after a war as compensation for damage caused, especially from Germany to the Allies after World War I.

Reserve currency
A **currency** that is acceptable internationally and is used by national banks to meet their financial commitments abroad.

Services
Intangible results of economic activity rather than physical **goods**. Accountancy, hairdressing and transportation are all service industries.

Share
A document that represents ownership of a certain amount of financial **capital** in a business.

Silver standard
As **gold standard**, with silver the relevant metal.

Slump
Synonymous with **depression** but a more dated term.

Special Drawing Rights (SDRs)
Established by the International Monetary Fund in 1969 as an internal **currency**, SDRs are distributed to IMF members in fixed quotas and are used for financial transactions between themselves. The value of SDRs is based on a weighted average of the American dollar (42 percent), German Deutschmark (19 percent), and the British pound sterling, French franc and Japanese yen (13 percent each).

Speculation
The buying and selling of any assets, physical or financial, for profit rather than productive purposes .

Stagflation
A simultaneous combination of inflation and increasing unemployment coupled to a slowing down or decrease in economic growth.

Stock
1 The inventory of raw materials and finished **goods** held by a company. **2 UK.** Now almost synonymous with **share**, **stock** was originally the term for a financial security that paid a fixed sum of money in **interest**. **3 US.** A share in company ownership.

Stock exchange
An organized market for **stock** and **share** transactions.

Supply-side policies
Government policies that attempt to boost production (rather than demand) through tax changes. See **demand-side policies**.

Tariff barrier
The imposition of customs duties on foreign imports, usually expressed as a percentage of the delivered price. This is a common form of **protectionism** which **GATT** is attempting to abolish.

Third World
See **less-developed countries**.

Trade cycle
A roughly regular oscillation in the economic activity of a country. It is normally divided into four phases: low output, **boom**, high output, **recession**.

Trade union
An association of workers organized to represent their interests in negotiations with employers.

Transfer payments
Payments made to individuals, usually by government, that are not in exchange for any **goods** or **services**. Student grants, housing benefits and old-age pensions are examples.

Trust
A US phenomenon, developed using state law to transform **cartels** into "near-companies". **Trust** has become very close in meaning to **cartel** or **monopoly**.

Vertical integration
The expansion of a company by either merger or further **investment** to include more stages of the production process. See **horizontal integration**.

Visible trade account
The balance of a country's trade in exports and imports of merchandise without allowing for **invisible earnings**.

World Bank (International Bank for Reconstruction and Development)
Established in 1945 along with the IMF, the IBRD provides long-term loans and technical assistance to member countries to support their economic development.

FURTHER READING

Aldcroft, D H *From Versailles to Wall Street 1919–29* (London, 1977)

Allen, G C *A Short Economic History of Modern Japan* (London, 1962)

Ambrosius, Gerold and Hubbard, William H *A Social and Economic History of Twentieth-Century Europe* (Cambridge, Mass., 1989)

Arndt, H W *Economic Lessons of the Nineteen-Thirties* (London, 1972)

Bairoch, P and Levy-Leboyer M (eds) *Disparities in Economic Development since the Industrial Revolution* (London, 1981)

Batchelor, R A, Major R L and Morgan, A D *Industrialisation and the Basis for Trade* (Cambridge, 1980)

Berend, I T and Borchardt K (eds) *The Impact of the Depression of the 1930's and its Relevance for the Contemporary World* (Budapest, 1987)

Berend, I T and Ranki G *Economic Development in Central and South-Eastern Europe in the Nineteenth and Twentieth Centuries* (New York and London, 1974)

Bergson, A *Productivity and the Social System in the USSR and the West* (Cambridge, Mass., 1978)

Bergstein, C Fred (ed) *Global Economic Imbalances* (Washington D C, 1985)

Blackford M G *The Rise of Modern Business in Great Britain, the United States and Japan* (Chapel Hill N C, 1988)

Blair, J M *The Control of Oil* (London, 1977)

Bloomfield, Gerald *The World Automotive Industry* (Newton Abbot, 1978)

Blumenfeld, H *The Modern Metropolis* (Cambridge, Mass., 1967)

Brandt, Willy et al *North–South: A Programme for Survival* (London, 1980)

Brandt, Willy et al *Common Crisis, North–South: Co-operation for World Recovery* (London, 1983)

Braun, E and MacDonald, S *Revolution in Miniature: The History and Impact of the Semiconductor Electronics* (Cambridge, 1982)

Brunner, K (ed) *The Great Depression Revisited* (Boston et al, 1981)

Buchanan, Ian *Singapore in Southeast Asia* (London, 1972)

Caron, F *An Economic History of Modern France* (London, 1979)

Chaudhuri, Pramit *The Indian Economy, Poverty and Development* (London, 1979)

Clough, S B *The Economic History of Italy* (New York, 1964)

Coffey, P (ed) *Economic Policies of the Common Market* (London, 1979)

Cohn, Stanley H *The Economic Development of the Soviet Union* (Lexington, 1970)

Cole, H S D et al *Thinking about the Future: A Critique of the Limits to Growth* (London, 1973)

Cripps, T F and Tarling, R J *Growth in Advanced Capitalist Economies 1950–1970* (Cambridge, 1973)

Eckstein, Alexander *China's Economic Revolution* (Cambridge, 1977)

Farnie, D A *East and West of Suez. The Suez Canal in History 1854–1956* (Oxford, 1987)

Fearon, P *War, Prosperity and Depression: the US Economy, 1917–1945* (Oxford, 1987)

Feis, H *Europe, the World's Banker 1870–1914* (New Haven, 1930)

Feldman, G D *Iron and Steel in the German Inflation 1916–23* (Princeton, 1977)

Fieldhouse, D K *Economics and Empire 1830–1914* (London, 1973)

Flora, Peter and Heidenheimer, Arnold J (eds) *The Development of Welfare States in Europe and America* (New Brunswick and London, 1981)

Foreman Peck, J *A History of the World Economy: International Economic Relations since 1850* (Brighton, Sussex, 1983)

Galenson, Walter (ed) *Economic Growth and Structural Change in Taiwan* (Ithaca, 1979)

Garraty, J A *The Great Depression. An Inquiry, as seen by Contemporaries and in the Light of History* (New York et al, 1986)

Gatrell, P *The Tsarist Economy, 1850–1917* (London, 1986)

Goudie, Andrew *The Human Impact on the Natural Environment* (Oxford 2nd ed, 1986)

Griffin, Keith *The Political Economy of Agrarian Change. An Essay on the Green Revolution* (Cambridge, Mass., 1974)

Hammarstrom I and Hall, T (eds) *Growth and Transformation of the Modern City* (Stockholm, 1979)

Harberler, G *The World Economy, Money and the Great Depression, 1919–1939* (Washington, 1976)

Hardach, G *The First World War 1914–18* (London, 1977)

Harrison, J *An Economic History of Modern Spain* (Manchester, 1978)

Heilbroner, R L and Singer, A *The Economic Transformation of America* (New York, 1977)

Hirsch, Fred *Social Limits to Growth* (London, 1977)

Hirschmeier, Johannes and Yui, Tsunehiko *The Development of Japanese Business 1600–1973* (Cambridge, Mass., 1975)

Hobsbawn, E J *The Age of Empire, 1875–1914* (London, 1987)

Hodson, H V *Slump and Recovery 1929–1937* (New York, 1983 [1938])

Hohenberg, P *Chemicals in Western Europe, 1850–1914* (Chicago, 1967)

Holtfrerich, C L *Die deutsche Inflation, 1914–1923: Ursachen und Folgen in internationaler Perspektive* (Berlin, 1980)

Howe, Charles W *Natural Resource Economics* (New York, 1979)

Hunter, John M and Foley, James W *Economic Problems of Latin America* (Boston, 1975)

James, H *The German Slump. Politics and Economics 1924–1936* (Oxford, 1986)

Joseph, Philip (ed) *Adaptability to New Technologies in the USSR and East European Countries* (Brussels, 1985)

Kahn, Herman *The Coming Boom* (New York, 1982)

Kaser, M C *The Economic History of Eastern Europe, 1919–1975, vol 3* (Oxford, 1986)

Kelley, Donald R, Stunkel, Kenneth R and Wescott, Richard R *The Economic Superpowers and the Environment. The United States, the Soviet Union and Japan* (San Francisco, 1976)

Kemp, T *Economic Forces in French History* (London, 1971)

Kenwood, A G and Lougheed, A L *The Growth of the International Economy* (London, 1971)

Keohane, Robert O *After Hegemony: Cooperation and Discord in the World Political Economy* (Princeton, N J, 1984)

Killick, Tony *Development Economics in Action. A Study of Economic Policies in Ghana* (London, 1978)

Kindleberger, C P *Economic Growth in France and Britain 1851–1950* (Cambridge, Mass., 1964)

Kindleberger, C P *Europe's Post-War Growth. The Role of Labour Supply* (Cambridge, Mass., 1967)

Kindleberger, C P *The World in Depression 1929–1939* (London, 1987)

Komarov, Boris *The Destruction of Nature in the Soviet Union* (White Plains, New York, 1980)

Kunio, Yoshihara *Japanese Economic Development* (Tokyo, 1979)

Landes, D S *The Unbound Prometheus* (Cambridge, 1969)

Lane, David *Soviet Economy and Society* (Oxford, 1985)

Latham, A J H *The Depression and the Developing World, 1914–1939* (London, 1981)

Lewin, M *The Making of the Soviet System: Essays in the Social History of Interwar Russia* (London, 1985)

Lewis, C M *British Railways in Argentina, 1857–1914: a case study of foreign investment* (London, 1983)

Lewis, W A *Economic Survey 1919–1939* (London, 1969 [1949])

Lieberman, S *The Growth of European Mixed Economies, 1945–1970* (New York, 1977)

Lyashchenko, P *A History of the National Economy of Russia* (New York, 1949)

Maddison, Angus *Economic Growth in Japan and the USSR* (London, 1969)

Maddison, Angus *The World Economy in the 20th Century* (Paris, 1989)

Maddison, Angus *Two Crises: Latin America and Asia 1929–38 and 1973–83* (Paris, 1985)

Maier, C S *Recasting Bourgeois Europe. Stabilization in France, Germany and Italy in the decade after World War I* (Princeton, M J 1975)

Maltby, Richard (ed) *Dreams for Sale: Popular Culture in the 20th Century* (London, 1989)

Mathias, Peter and Postan, M M (eds) *Cambridge Economic History of Europe, vol 7* (Cambridge, 1978)

Mathias, Peter and Pollard S (eds) *Cambridge Economic History of Europe, vol 8* (Cambridge, 1989)

Meadows, Donella H et al *The Limits to Growth* (New York, 1972)

Milward, A S *War, Economy and Society 1939–1945* (London, 1977)

Milward, Alan S *The Reconstruction of Western Europe 1945–56* (London, 1984)

Minford, Patrick *Unemployment: Causes and cures* (Oxford, 1983)

Morawetz, David *Twenty-Five Years of Economic Development 1950 to 1975* (Washington D C, 1977)

Munting, Roger *The Economic Development of the USSR* (London, 1982)

Murdoch, William W *The Poverty of Nations. The Political Economy of Hunger and Population* (Baltimore, 1980)

Myers, Ramon H *The Chinese Economy, Past and Present* (Belmont, 1980)

Myres, Robert L *Banking on the Poor. The World Bank and World Poverty* (Cambridge, Mass., 1984)

Nicholls, C S (ed) *Power: A Political History of the 20th Century* (London and New York, 1990)

Nove, Alec, Hohmann, H H and Seidenstecker, Gertrud *The East European Economies in the 1970's* (London, 1982)

Ohkawa, Kazushi and Shinohara Miyohei *Patterns of Japanese Development. A Quantitative Appraisal* (New Haven, 1979)

Perkins, Dwight H (ed) *China's Modern Economy in Historical Perspective* (Stanford, 1975)

ACKNOWLEDGEMENTS

Pollard, S *Peaceful Conquest. The Industrialization of Europe, 1760–1970* (London, 1981)

Pollard, S *Britain's Prime and Britain's Decline: the British Economy 1870–1914* (London, 1988)

Postan, M M *An Economic History of Western Europe 1945–1964* (London, 1967)

Prebisch, Raúl *Change and Development – Latin America's Great Task.* (New York, 1971)

Ratner, S, Soltow J H and Sylla R *The Evolution of the American Economy* (New York, 1979)

Ravenhill, John (ed) *Africa in Economic Crisis* (Basingstoke, 1986)

Reynolds, Lloyd G *Economic Growth in the Third World 1850–1980* (New Haven, Connecticut, 1985)

Riedel, James *The Industrialization of Hong Kong* (Tübingen, 1974)

Robbins, L *The Great Depression* (London, 1934)

Robertson, R M *History of the American Economy* (New York, 1973)

Rostow, W W *Why the Poor Get Richer and the Rich Slow Down* (Austin, 1980)

Rubinstein, W D (ed) *Wealth and the Wealthy in the Modern World* (London 1980)

Saint-Etienne, C *The Great Depression 1929–1938. Lessons for the 1980's* (Stanford, 1984)

Schneider, Hartmut *Meeting Food Needs in a Context of Change* (Paris, 1984)

Schuker, S A *The End of French Predominance in Europe. The Financial Crisis of 1924 and the Adoption of the Dawes Plan* (Chapel Hill, N C, 1976)

Silverman D P *Reconstructing Europe after the Great War* (Cambridge, Mass., 1982)

Singh, Tarlok *India's Development Experience* (London, 1974)

Svennilson, I *Growth and Stagnation in the European Economy* (Geneva, 1954)

Swamy, Subramanian *Economic Growth in China and India 1952–1970* (Chicago, 1973)

Temin, P *Did Monetary Factors Cause the Great Depression?* (New York, 1976)

Tew, Brian *The Evolution of the International Monetary System 1945–1977* (New York, 1977)

Thorp, R (ed) *Latin America in the 1930's. The Role of the Periphery in the World Crisis* (London 1984)

Thorp, R and Whitehead, Laurence *Latin American Debt and the Adjustment Crisis* (Basingstoke, 1987)

Tilly, C et al *The Rebellious Century 1830–1920* (Cambridge, Mass., 1975)

Timoshenko, V P *World Agriculture and the Depression* (Ann Arbor, 1953)

Veit, Lawrence A *India's Second Revolution* (New York, 1976)

Vries, de J *The Netherlands Economy in the Twentieth Century* (Assen, 1979)

Vries, de Margaret Garrison *The IMF in a Changing World 1945–85* (Washington D C, 1986)

Weber, E *France. Fin de Siècle* (Cambridge, Mass., 1986)

Wee, van der H (ed) *The Great Depression revisited. Essays on the Economics of the Thirties* (The Hague, 1972)

Wee, van der H *Prosperity and Upheaval. The World Economy 1945–1980* (Harmondsworth, 1986)

Weinstein, B *The Amazon Rubber Boom, 1850–1920* (Stanford, 1983)

Wood, Neil and Young, Stephen *The Economics of Multinational Enterprise* (London, 1979)

Woodruff, W *Impact of Western Man.* (London, 1966)

Picture Credits

1 A Komsomol at the wheel, Balakhna 1931: Arkady Shaikher
2–3 Constructing the Empire State Building: International Museum of Photography at George Eastman House
4 Beach at Ostende: HDC
6 Woman living in a drainpipe, Calcutta: ME/SP
20–21 Workers leave the Belfast shipyards after a shift constructing SS Titanic, 1911: Ulster Museum
56–57 German weapons captured in 1918: IWM
92–93 Civilians fleeing from the Allied advance, March 1945: M/Robert Capa
128–129 Advertising the latest model, 1959: M/H Cartier Bresson.
164–165 Technical education in China, 1958: M/Cornell Capa
200–201 Hong Kong financial district, 1989: Financial Times Photography

9 CPI **10–11** LC **12** CPI **15** PF **16** ME/SP **18–19** M/Hiroji Kubota **25** International Museum of Photography at George Eastman House **26, 27t** HDC/Bettman Archives **27b** TPS **28–29** AEG Aktiengesellschaft **29** TPS **30** UB **31t** HDC **31bl** Siemens Institut, München **31br** MEPL **32t** Joseph Byron **32b** HDC **33l** Unilever Information Services **33r** MEPL **34** Staatliche Landesbildstelle, Hamburg **35** Ulster Museum **36t** Chicago Historical Society **36–37** City of Toronto Archives **37t** PF **38t, 38–89, 38c** Henry Ford Museum **39tl** PF **39tr** Minnesota Historical Society **39br** M/René Burri **40–41** PF **42** RV **43t** HDC **43b** Mausell Collection **44t** De Beers Consolidated Mines **44b** Angela Murphy **45** PF **46t** MEPL **46b** Foreign and Commonwealth Office Library **46–47** TPS **47tr** RV **47** HDC **48–49** Foreign and Commonwealth Office Library **50** PF **51t** Fotomas Index **51c** MEPL **51b** Foreign and Commonwealth Office Library **52t** Zefra/Orion Press **52b** City of Toronto Archives **54l, 54r** Bell Canada Telephone Historical Collection **55** AEG Aktiengesellschaft **61** HDC **62–63, 62b** IWM **63bl** E.T. Archive **63br** British Petroleum **64t** E.T. Archive **64b** RV **65t** Illustrated London News **65b, 66t, 66b, 66–67** IWM **68t, 68b** HDC **69** National Archives, Washington DC **70t** Alexander Meledin **70b** David King Collection **71t** MEPL **71b** New York Public Library **72t** MEPL **72b** PF **73** TPS **74t** SI **74b** PF **75** RHL **76t, 76c** PF **76b** Deutsche Afrika-Linien **77t** TPS **77c** Peter Inglis **77b** CP **79** UB **80t** E.T. Archive/IWM **80b** RV **81b** HDC **82t** TPS **82b** RV **83** MEPL **84b, 84–85** RV **85** UB **86t** TPS **86b** PF **87** International Museum of Photography at George Eastman House **88l** MEPL **88r** PF **89t** Arkady Siskir **89b** Max Alpert **90–91** PF **90t** Harry Ransom Humanities Research Center, University of Texas **90c** CP **90b** ME/SP **91t** BPL **91b** N/Laurie Sparham **97** Fotomas Index **98–99** TPS **99t** HDC **99b** PF **100t** Mainichi Newspapers **100b** Newspaper Library **101, 102t** HDC **102b** TPS **103t** UB **103b** HDC **104–105** Arthur Rothstein/Dover Pictorial Archive Series **105t** LC **105b** Glenbow Archives **107** Brown Brothers **108t** PF **108b** HDC **109** Canadian High Commission **110tl** MEPL **110–111** HDC **111** CPI **112** PF **113** Aramco **114–115** RHL **114** MEPL **115t** PF **115c** SPL/US Department of Defense **115b** CP **116–117** HDC **118t** PF **118b** UB **119** IWM **120, 121t, 121b** HDC **122t** Deutsches Museum, Munich **122–123** AP **123** UB **124** IWM **125t, 125b** HDC **126t** Arkady Sajaket **126b** JH/Marc Riboud **126–127** Fotomas Index **127tl** Ivan Sajin **127bl** PF **127r** Bettman Newsphotos **133, 134t, 134b** PF **135t, 135b** HDC **136t, 136b** PF **1 37t, 137b** Jean Mohr **138** HDC **138–139** PF **139** TPS **140–141, 141b** PF **141t** TPS **142l, 142tr** Radio Corporation of America **142br, 143t, 143c** PF **143bl, 143bc, 143br** Novosti Press Agency **144–145** PF **146t** TPS **147t** HDC **146–147, 147b, 148, 149** PF **150** M/Cornell Capa **151** M/Henri Cartier-Bresson **152t** PF **152b** CP **152–153** J. Allan Cash **153tl, 153tr** FSP **153bar** Eurotunnel **155, 156, 156–157, 157t, 157b, 158t, 158tr, 159** HDC **160, 161t** PF **161b** MEPL **162t** HDC **162b** Colorific **163t, 163b** PF **169, 170t** HDC **170b, 171t** BPL **171b** HDC **172** CP **173** TPS **174** CP **175** BPL **176t, 176b** PF

176–177 HL **177tr, 177bl** CP **177br** ME/SP **179** BPL **180t, 180–181** Japan Information Centre, London **180b** HL/M MacIntyre **181** Japan Information Centre, London **182t, 182b** CP **183t** Korea National Tourism Office **183b** HDC **185** N/Barry Lewis **186, 187, 188, 189** Society for Cultural Relations with the USSR **190b** PF **190t, 191t, 191b** HL **192b** M/Steve McCurry **192–193** FSP **193tl** M/Erich Hartmann **193bl, 193br** N/Mike Goldwater **193tr** Art Direction/Craig Aurness **195** HL **196** ME/SP **197** United Nations **198–199** RF **198** F/Maggie Murray **199** BPL **204–205** RF **206** PF **207** Woodfin Camp Associates/Dan Budwik **208–209** Shell Photo Service **208t, 209t, 210–211, 211** PF **212t, 212b** FSP **213t** N/Steve Benbow **213b** FSP **214, 215t** BPL **215b** N/Barry Lewis **216** M/S Perkins **217t** M/Gilles Peress **217b** M/S Frank in **218t** TPS **218b** M/E Hartmann **218–219** F/Maggie Murray **219t** SPL/Gerry Mason **219c** M/E Hartmann **219b** SPL/Paul Shambroom **221** H/Hiroji Kubota **222** HL/D Brinicombe **223** N/Mike Goldwater **224b** HL/JG Fuller **224t, 224–225** FSP **226t** N/Peter Bialobrzeski **226b** HL/P Edward Parker **227** FSP **229** Telegraph Colour Library **230** ME/SP **231t** F/Joanne O'Brien **231b** M/Thomas Höpker **232t** N/Mike Goldwater **232b** ME/SP **233t, 233b** FSP/Rafael Wollmann **234t** CP **234b** N/Mike Goldwater **235t** FSP/Lochon **235c** ME/SP **235b, 235binset** CP **236l** Interfoto **236c** United Press International **236r** HDC **237l** HDC/Bettmann Archive **237c** SI **237r** PF **238l** SI **238c** HDC **238r, 239l, 239c, 239r, 240l** PF **240c, 240r** HDC **241l** Mirrorpic **241c** PF **241r** HDC **242c, 242r, 243l** PF **243c** SI **234r, 244l, 244c, 244r, 245l, 245c, 245r, 246l, 246b, 246r, 247c, 247r** PF **247l** SI

Abbreviations

AP	Associated Press, London
BPL	Barnaby's Picture Library, London
CP	Camera Press, London
CPI	Culver Pictures Inc, New York
F	Format, London
FSP	Frank Spooner Pictures, London
HDC	Hulton Deutsch Collection, London
HL	Hutchinson Library, London
IWM	Imperial War Museum, London
JH	John Hillelson, London
LC	Library of Congress, Washington DC
M	Magnum, London
ME/SP	Mark Edwards/Still Pictures, London
MEPL	Mary Evans Picture Library, London
N	Network, London
PF	Popperfoto, London
RF	Rex Features, London
RHL	Robert Hunt Library, London
RV	Roger-Viollet, Paris
SI	Syndication International, London
SPL	Science Photo Library, London
TPS	Topham Picture Source, Kent, UK.
UB	Ullstein Bilderdienst, Berlin (West)

Abbreviations

t = top, tl = top left, tr = top right, c = center, b = bottom etc.

Editorial and research assistance

Steve Chapman, Jane Higgins, Louise Jones, Nick Law, Andy Overs, Maria Quantrill, Graham Speake, Michelle Von Ahn, Elaine Welsh

Artists

Alan Hollingbery, Ayala Kingsley, Colin Salmon, Dave Smith, Del Tolton

Photographs

Shirley Jamieson, David Pratt

Cartography

Maps drafted by Euromap, Pangbourne; Alan Mais (Hornchurch); Sarah Rhodes

Typesetting

Brian Blackmore, Catherine Boyd; OPUS Ltd

Production

Stephen Elliott, Clive Sparling

Color Origination

J Film Process, Bangkok

Index

Ann Barrett

INDEX

Page numbers in *italics* refer to
illustrations or their captions. **Bold** page
numbers refer to the subjects of special
or ancillary text features.

256